The
Complete
Fish
Cookbook

The Complete Fish Cookbook

by Dan and Inez Morris

The Bobbs-Merrill Company, Inc.

Indianapolis · New York

Library of Congress Cataloging in Publication Data

Morris, Dan.
   The complete fish cookbook.

   (Stoeger sportsman's library)
   Includes index.
   1. Cookery (Fish)   I. Morris, Inez, joint author.
   II. Title.
   TX747.M797   1978   641.6'92   77-90757
   ISBN 0-88317-078-7

Published by Stoeger Publishing Company
55 Ruta Court
South Hackensack, New Jersey 07606

This Stoeger Sportsman's Library Edition is published by
arrangement with The Bobbs-Merrill Company, Inc.
Fourth Printing, June 1986

Distributed to the book trade and to the sporting goods trade
by Stoeger Industries, 55 Ruta Court, South Hackensack,
New Jersey 07606

In Canada, distributed to the book trade and to the sporting
goods trade by Stoeger Canada, Ltd., 169 Idema Road,
Markham, Ontario L3R 1A9

Printed in the United States of America

Cover photograph by William Pell

This book is dedicated to Mrs. Fred Johnston
of Hannibal, Missouri, and to the many, many
· others the country over who told us that
there is only one way to cook fish: "Dip it
in milk, roll it in flour, and fry it."

They were all so nice but, oh, so wrong.

Contents

ACKNOWLEDGMENT

These many people helped to bring this book into being and to them all we say "thank you":

Gale Steves, home economist with the U.S. National Marine Fisheries Service; Margaret Myer, Chief, Consumer Branch, Department of Fisheries, Canada; Velma Seat, the Cooperative Extension Service's Food Marketing Specialist at Oregon State University; John Von Glahn of the Fishery Council of New York's Fulton Fish Market; Georgia R. Rothrock, home economist with the National Fisheries Institute in Chicago; cookbook authors Arthur Lem and Don Bevona (and their wives, Rose and Donna); Vinnie, Charlie and Ralph Fiore who, with their father, Antonio, have been selling fish for about 150 years; Betty Inlow, cook at the Mark Twain Hotel in Hannibal, Missouri; fellow author Norman Strung and his wife, Priscilla, who without a doubt are Montana's lobster-cooking champs; Buddy and Doreen Kreidell, whose fish cookery is out of sight; and Harold LeVander, who, while governor of Minnesota, quite unwittingly first pointed up the need for this book.

PART ONE

All About Fish

1

Why This Book Is for You

A True Story

Inez tried and tested a new recipe for this book; we ate some for supper and put the leftovers in the refrigerator. That night our collegiate son, a buddy in tow, made one of his unannounced flying visits home. The first thing they did was open the front door and shout, "Hello!" The second thing they did was open the refrigerator door and shout, "Oh boy! Whipped cream cake."

Then they bit in, reared back in shocked surprise—and went on eating in delight.

We did not have a name for the recipe up to that moment. But now we do. We call it Fish Cake. You'll find it on page 323. It took no more than 40 minutes to prepare, bake and serve. The ingredients, all of them combined—and they include slivered almonds and sour cream—are available in every supermarket in the country and cost less than $1.40 to buy; price per serving, less than 35 cents.

If anyone were to ask us, writers with six cookbooks prior to this one under our belts, what we like to cook and eat most, we in all honesty could and would answer, "Fish." So long as it wears fins and wiggles its tail we like it. Just as we do their relatives that wear shells. Sweet water or saltwater, fish taken from their native habitat or fish bred on a farm, it makes no matter. We like them all.

This book will tell you why. And how. Starting right here with this swift summation:

- Fish tastes good.
- Fish offers great variety.
- Fish is quick and easy to cook.

3

· Fish, ounce for ounce, pound for pound, is generally cheaper than most good meat that you can buy, be it beef, lamb, pork or whatever.

· Fish is the most convenient of convenience foods ever marketed.

· Fish is a diet food.

· Fish is good for you and your children.

· Fish is excellent for entertaining.

Let's take a quick look at all those reasons we have for liking fish.

FISH TASTES GOOD

That is a simple declarative sentence. Three words, noun, verb, adjective: Fish tastes good.

But already we see some of you sneering and smirking and hear some of you using even simpler language to vent your disagreement. You've eaten fish. It tasted terrible. You wouldn't feed it to a cat.

Well, we've eaten that kind of fish, too. It tasted terrible. We didn't feed it to a cat.

However, that was not the fault of the fish. It was the fault of the cook. If she, or he, louses up a steak or an omelet, you don't forevermore say that steaks and eggs don't taste good. You keep an open mind; you maybe tell the cook to go read a cookbook. You give the cook a second chance. Apply that same open-mindedness to fish, and if you don't already know that fish tastes good, just pay heed to this cookbook's basic premises about fish cookery and you'll soon find out that fish *does* taste good.

There is a chapter further along in this book whose title is another simple declarative sentence: "How to Cook Fish Properly." The instructions are as simple as the title. Read them, heed them.

FISH OFFERS GREAT VARIETY

Nutritionists say we should eat a variety of food in order to be sure of getting the more than 50 nutrients nature scatters in a baffling pattern throughout our different foods.

Well, fish then is just what the nutritionists ordered. At last count— and this is no exaggeration—there were something like 250 forms in which fish was being marketed. This fact alone should tell you that, once you let yourself go and get involved with fish cookery, variety in your meals can grow by leaps and bounds.

There is no food more versatile and adaptable to different ways of cooking than fish, no food more easily combined with other foods, be they vegetables, cereal grains, legumes, dairy products, meat or poultry.

That is why we dedicated this book to Mrs. Fred Johnston and all the other good people we've met, including Minnesota's former Governor

Harold LeVander, who have told us that the only way to cook fish is to dip them in milk, roll them in flour and fry them.

Inez met Mrs. Johnston while we were on a 6,000-mile, 19-state motor camping trip in which we combined business with pleasure. The business: collecting recipes for this book. The pleasures: meeting new people, seeing new places, making new friends, catching fish, cooking them and eating them. And not once did we dip them, roll them and fry them.

It was in a camera shop in Hannibal, Missouri, that Inez met her. Inez had gone in to buy some film but stayed to chat when Mrs. Johnston turned out to be a nice, affable lady and civic booster. They talked about Mark Twain, Tom Sawyer, Huckleberry Finn, Becky Thatcher and all the other people, both factual and fictional, who made Hannibal, perched there on the west bank of the Mississippi River, famous. Eventually the conversation got around to what we were doing there other than sightseeing, and when Inez told Mrs. Johnston we were collecting recipes for a fish cookbook, she was amazed.

"Why," Mrs. Johnston said, "there is only one way to cook fish. Dip it in milk, roll it in flour and fry it!"

Then it was Inez's turn to be amazed. She always, naïve girl, had taken it for granted that everyone knew that fish could be cooked a thousand different ways. But, for Dan, Mrs. Johnston's words only rang a bell.

Every year at the start of the fishing season the State of Minnesota has what it calls a Governor's Fishing Party and outdoor writers gather from all corners of the country on one of the state's marvelous lakes to have at it with the walleye pike.

One year after one such party at Leech Lake, Dan was returning to Minneapolis in the governor's plane and Mr. LeVander was taking home with him a package of fresh-caught fish fillets.

"Governor," Dan asked him, "how are you going to cook your fish?" To which Governor LeVander replied with words very much like those Inez heard two years later from Mrs. Johnston: "Dip them, roll them, fry them."

That's when Dan was shocked. In a governor's mansion, he thought, they should know how to cook thick, succulent fillets better than that. But he recovered and gave Governor LeVander a quick method to try. We don't know if he ever did. But you can and you should. We call it "water-broiling." You'll find the instructions on page 240, along with several recipes.

Those water-broiling recipes are only a small part of the 500 fin-fish and shellfish recipes that you will find in this book, augmented by about 100 sauce and garnish recipes. Add those 500 recipes to the 250 or so market forms, bear in mind that many if not most of those 500 recipes are interchangeable, envision what you can do when you switch one of the 100 sauce and garnish recipes for another. Spike the total with your own imagination, your own culinary creativity.

Now you'll begin to get an idea of how much variety there can be in the cooking of fish.

Nor do we overlook dip-roll-and-fry fish cookery, because if there are so many people like Mrs. Johnston and Governor LeVander who swear by it, there obviously must be something good about it. So we include in this book several such recipes, among them Catfish Hannibal (page 273) just as we got it from the Mark Twain Hotel in Hannibal. Try it.

But if catfish isn't available to you, use any other fish that is. If you don't like the batter the recipe calls for, substitute any of the other batter recipes you'll also find between these covers. If you don't like one of those, use one of your own. If you don't have one, create one. By then the finished dish will be quite a bit removed from the catfish fry that Tom and Huck grew up on. Be that as it may, you'll like it so long as you cook it right.

In fish cookery the variations, the adaptations, the substitutions of this for that are as many as your imagination is rich. There is virtually nothing that you can do to spoil the taste of fish so long as you stick by the cooking rules and don't go completely off your rocker.

If you're in a cooking rut, fish offers you a chance to get out of it and let variety add spice to your eating life.

FISH IS QUICK AND EASY TO COOK

Those fish cooking rules that we just mentioned are spelled out in the "How to Cook Fish Properly" chapter. There you'll learn that the most important rule is not to overcook fish, which is another way of saying that fish is quick to cook.

How quick?

So quick that, even though we give you cooking times in each recipe, we also tell you to start testing with a fork at half that time. (You'll learn why in the how-to chapter.) Just probe the flesh gently with the tines and the moment it flakes easily the fish is done and ready to be eaten. Then it's at its fine-flavor best. One second more and the fish is beginning to overcook, the fine flavor is beginning to fade. The more it cooks, the worse it will taste.

And that's a fact, a fact that boils down to this: no matter how you choose to cook fish, generally speaking, it should be at its eating-best within 10 to 15 minutes, rarely over 30 minutes and often no more than 5 minutes. Your fork, not your clock, will tell you when.

So we go now from the quick to the easy. To give you an idea of just how easy it is to cook fish, we'll remind you (1) that in quite a few highly civilized places in the world they prefer to eat their fish raw, and (2) that oysters and clams also are fish, albeit shellfish, and that, when you go into a fine restaurant and see them on the menu under the title "on the half shell," what you are reading is a euphemism for the word "raw" because most Americans find that word crude and the idea unpalatable.

It follows, then, that anything that can be eaten raw can be easily cooked. It is the very versatility of fish that makes it so simple; it can be cooked by so many different methods; it can be cooked just as it comes from the water or from the market; it can be cooked in combination with so many other foods; it can be cooked simply by soaking it in a marinade and never exposing it to any heat.

Beyond that, let the recipes in this book speak for themselves.

FISH IS ECONOMICAL

The best way we could think of for backing up this statement is to do what Dan did on the day, December 8, 1970, that this section was written. He visited the local outlet of a nationwide supermarket chain and did some price checking. This is how fish compared with meats per pound:

Shoulder lamb chops, $1.39.
Chuck fillets, 95 cents.
Chuck, bone in, 88 cents.
Ground chuck, 79 cents.
Fresh flounder with head, tail, fins and innards removed, 69 cents.
Frozen codfish fillets, 65 cents.

Add to those price comparisons the shrinkage-in-cooking factor in red meats—which is virtually nonexistent in fish—and you can readily see how much less expensive it is to serve fish to your family than it is to feed them red meat.

We could make similar comparisons with pork and poultry, but all we want to do is make a point and not prove a case. Far better that you do your own price comparing while shopping for your family larder. At that time you'll be able to effect additional economies by practicing what we preach in Part One, Chapter 2, in which we tell you what, where and when to buy seafood.

As you know, pennies add up to dollars—and so an important additional pennysaver factor in fish cookery is the many and varied ways in which leftovers can be put to delicious, health-giving use.

Unlike most leftover cooked foods, which usually are eaten cold or not at all, leftover cooked fish provides the perfect base for countless other fish dishes that make grand second-day dishes that are completely different from your first-day fare. You'll find recipe after recipe in this book that will bear this out, particularly in the Soups, Salads, Casseroles, Pies, Loaves, Simmering, Poaching, Steaming, Flaking and Baking sections.

Additionally, and also better than most foods, fish lends itself ideally to stretch recipes. Combine just the minimum amount of the fish of your choice—just enough for flavor and needed protein—with almost any other foodstuff that your pocketbook can afford and you can place on your family table epicurean creations that will figure out to only pennies per portion. You'll find many such recipes in this book.

FISH IS A CONVENIENCE FOOD

At the start of this chapter we were even more emphatic than that. We said flatly that fish is the most convenient of convenience foods ever marketed. We meant it then, we mean it now. Canned tuna fish was on the grocery shelves before television was ever invented, much less TV dinners. Ditto for sardines and salmon. If you think it takes too long to open a clam or an oyster, you can buy them already shucked of their shells, fresh and ready to be eaten. Shucked, individually frozen shrimp can be rinsed, boiled and ready to eat in from 10 to 15 minutes of the time you take them from the freezer.

But let's not dwell upon such simple things. Let's talk, instead, about things you may not already know. Like, for instance, how convenient it is, how quick it is, how easy it is to whip up a grand-tasting seafood dish with a still solidly frozen block of fish (for example, that cod fillet that sells for 65 cents a pound).

There is no need to defrost fish in order to cook it and there's a whole section of frozen-fish recipes in this book to prove it. One of them is the Fish Cake that we mentioned in the story at the opening of this chapter. The cake that our son and his friend liked so much was baked with a still solidly frozen block of fish as its main ingredient.

And today, what with all the modern food processing and packaging advances that have been made in the past few years, frozen fish is as easy to buy as any of the so-called convenience foods. No matter where you live, West Coast, East Coast, Gulf Coast or far inland. We know because we found out for ourselves on that trip we took. In state after state and town after town far removed from the sea we dropped into supermarkets and headed straight for their frozen-foods department. Towns like Idaho Springs, Colorado, in the Rocky Mountains; Belleville, Illinois, in the heart of the Great Plains; Corinth, Mississippi, just about four miles south of the Tennessee border; and Santa Fe in New Mexico's beautiful high desert country. In all of them we discovered that the stores stock just as great a variety of frozen fish as do the stores in the town where we live, Long Beach, New York, on the Atlantic Coast. Perhaps more so, because we have fresh-caught fish more readily available to us.

Nor is it just fish from the sea that these inland supermarkets stock. On the contrary, they have an amazing variety of freshwater fish, for example, catfish and trout that have been bred on fish farms, of which there is an ever-increasing number in our hinterland states. And a good thing, too, because the water in which the fish are raised is as pure, perhaps purer, than the water that comes from your kitchen tap.

Which means this: a working gal or guy, whether unmarried or with a passel of kids howling for their supper the second you walk in the door, can stop in any supermarket in the land on the way home from work, choose from an ever-growing assortment of frozen fish, prepare any frozen-fish recipe in this book, slip it into the oven and go about doing not all of the things, just some of the things, working folk have to do upon coming home from work. Like, for instance, mixing and having a drink. The fish will be done before those things will be done. And, we guarantee you, much tastier than any "just heat and serve" packaged dinner that you can buy. Simply follow the basic instructions for cooking frozen fish and you won't go wrong.

As for canned fish, if you've been brought up to think that all a can of tuna fish is good for is to make sandwiches or a salad, this is the time to change your thinking. Canned fish—tuna, salmon, mackerel or whatever—can be used as the base for many fine dishes and you'll find many such recipes in this book.

Okay, you say, but how about fresh, nonfrozen, noncanned fish? Just turn to the recipes in this book in which fish is combined with vegetables. Some also include a starch. In other words, a complete, well-balanced, one-dish meal. Check the estimated cooking time, bearing in mind that you start testing with a fork at half that time. Add a few minutes for preliminary preparations.

Now compare the total with the cooking-time directions on any package of the so-called convenience foods that you can buy in the store. You'll have your answer.

Many of the recipes in this book can be prepared in less than 10 minutes and cooked and ready for the whole family to eat in 12 to 15 minutes. A store-bought packaged dinner for one will take from 25 to 35 minutes to be ready to serve. Longer if you heat more than one such dinner at a time.

FISH IS A DIET FOOD

This is not a diet cookbook, because the prescribing of diets is the province of doctors, not cookbook writers. But we know that if, for any reason whatsoever, your doctor has placed you on a restrictive diet, there's a good chance he made fish part of that diet. And so we've planned this book in a way we hope will help you carry out your doctor's orders.

The National Fisheries Institute says there is a seafood for just about everyone on a restricted diet. Or suppose there's nothing wrong with you, but you are growing old? The Institute says this in one of its booklets: "Fish are also useful in the diets of the elderly; soft boneless fish fillets and steaks may even be enjoyed by those without dentures." Or suppose you have a baby in your house? The handbook goes on: "Babies, too, after they are six months old, may enjoy boneless white-meated fish if it is poached and carefully flaked to be certain all bones are removed."

Earlier we talked about the great versatility of fish. Well, that versatility is of special importance to anyone who must count calories in order to lose weight. You needn't take our word for it, though. Rather, just feast your eyes on this one sentence in another National Fisheries Institute pamphlet: "Pound for pound fish has only half to two-thirds the number of calories of beef or pork."

Fish, of course, like all animals, contains fat (but of a polyunsaturated variety that is beneficial to man, of which we'll say more in a few minutes); fish also contains any degree of fat content the dieter might desire. Nutritionists have analyzed the fat-content differences, so that we now know how much each species of fish contains.

You, too, now can know merely by turning to page 100. There you'll find a listing of 121 of the most commonly available fish. Two important facts are alongside each name: the number of calories in 100 grams (about 3½ ounces) of raw edible fish meat, and whether it's a fat, lean or intermediate fish.

A fat fish contains 6 to 20 percent fat; an intermediate fish, 2 to 6 percent; a lean fish, less than 2 percent.

Any fish below 5 percent is ideally suited for weight reduction, which means that all of the intermediate fish on the list are excellent for cutting down on the pounds, while the lean fish (and there are 46 on the list) are just about perfect.

Dr. Seymour H. Rinzler is director of New York's Anti-Coronary Club, which for many years has studied the relationship of food to heart disease and has devised a food plan that has come to be known as the Prudent Diet. And Dr. Rinzler says this: "Do not be limited to the leaner fish but include fat fish as well as they are good sources of polyunsaturated fatty acids."

As for those who must watch their salt intake, all fin fish are naturally low in sodium content, so much so that it is virtually nonexistent. The same is true for oysters and soft clams.

Which means this: what you add to the fish, oysters or soft clams you cook will determine how well they fit into a salt-free diet. If you combine a number of foods into one recipe, a very interesting and satisfying flavor is produced without the addition of any salt whatsoever.

That is one of the benefits hidden in this book's combination recipes.

Choose any one of them that calls for foods, other than the fish, that your doctor says you can eat, cross "salt" off the list of ingredients and you'll probably never miss it. Some of those recipes combine a small amount of one or more shellfish with a larger percentage of delicately flavored fin fish, some combine several vegetables with the fish, others fruits and/or nuts. Result: you not only get an interesting flavor, you also add variety and nutrients to your diet.

While we're on the subject, let's not overlook the convalescent. Many kinds of fish, fin or shell, provide the nutrients needed for tissue repair and recovery of strength in a form that is readily digestible.

FISH IS GOOD FOR YOU AND YOUR CHILDREN

How good? We eat 21 meals a week. Some experts say 4 of those meals should have fish as the main course; others say 7, and some recommend a middle-of-the-road 5 or 6.

When it comes to top-quality protein, nutritionists rate fish right up there with meat, milk and eggs. The National Fisheries Institute says it this way:

> In addition to their valuable protein content, fish and shellfish provide a treasure chest of minerals and vitamins. In general, they are all good sources of niacin, thiamine and riboflavin. Seafoods also contain an impressive array of minerals, the most common of which are iodine, calcium, phosphorus, iron, potassium and copper.
>
> The contribution that a food makes to the body depends largely on the body's ability to utilize its constituent parts. One of the unique and valuable properties of the proteins in fish is the ease with which the body digests and absorbs them. Because the flesh of fish contains none of the coarse fibrous membranes found in so many animal meats, it is therefore more easily broken down by body processes. In addition, because the protein in fish is not bound up with large quantities of firm fat, the body uses it more readily.

That seems to be enough for just one type of food to contribute to our physical well-being. Yet that is only part of the story, because the Institute also says this:

> Within the last decade, nutritionists and physicians have tackled the problem of a mounting heart disease rate, not only to help those with heart diseases but to find a preventive program. Studies of diet have figured importantly in this work, and, in many of the reports on results, one of the recommendations is unequivocal—eat more seafood!

We needn't take up much time telling you what that means to every adult in your family, other than this: more than half a million Americans die every year from heart attacks, a staggering percentage of them while still in the prime of life.

Some members of the medical profession urge that children be introduced to fish very early in their lives, not only because of the possibility it may help avoid heart attack in their later years but, more immediately, to help strengthen their growing bones and to guard against the so-called baby fat, or puppy fat, that once upon a time was considered so cute.

In fact, says the National Fisheries Institute in a pamphlet entitled *Good Eating, Good Health, Long Life,* a major reason why pediatricians watch the weight of babies so carefully is this:

A fat baby is no longer considered a healthy baby. Puppy fat in pre-adolescents is not shrugged off as normal nowadays. Life-long weight control is recommended.

Seafoods—low in calories and high in appetite satisfaction—fit perfectly into a diet plan that makes weight control easy and natural.

That's why we earmark so many recipes with the letter "I," for "introductory," in the upper right-hand corner. They're dishes aimed at introducing youngsters to the taste of fish, mainly by the inclusion of other ingredients that children like. Peanut butter, for instance. You'll find one such recipe on page 244.

And, especially if you are an adult who always has thought fish wasn't your dish, some of these recipes will be just right for introducing you, too, to a culinary pleasure you've been missing.

Let's now talk about cholesterol. *Collier's Encyclopedia* tells us that it is present in all animal tissues and that "it is deposited in abnormal amounts in certain diseases," such as gallstones and arteriosclerosis, which science also calls "atherosclerosis" but which is more commonly called "hardening of the arteries."

The National Fisheries Institute tells us this:

Fish contain as much as three times more polyunsaturated fatty acids than vegetable oils, as much as seven times more than beef.

The relationship of polyunsaturated fats and cholesterol levels to health is being studied now as one of the possible factors in heart disease.

Cholesterol is a waxy substance, normally present in the body and absolutely essential to body functions. It becomes a problem when excessive amounts are released into the bloodstream and minute particles begin to cling to the walls of the blood vessels. Time goes on, the deposits become thicker. Gradually there is less space for the blood to flow through. Passageways are blocked and the tissues are not nourished.

The effects may be shortness of breath, loss of energy and vigor, nervousness and irritability. Mental alertness can be seriously impaired. In the acute stage, a blood vessel feeding the heart is blocked and the result is coronary thrombosis—heart attack!

Then, on the relationship of fats to cholesterol, the Institute says:

The problem of how fats in the diet affect health is more complicated than simply controlling the intake of excess calories. Fats are essential to body functions. Because of their chemical structure, fats are classified as (1) saturated, usually found in foods of animal origin; (2) monosaturated; (3) polyunsaturated, found in foods like fin fish, liquid vegetable oils and poultry. Based on what is now known, it is believed that saturated fats tend to raise the blood cholesterol level; polyunsaturated fats lower blood cholesterol; monosaturated fats have little effect.

The direct link between saturated fats, cholesterol and heart disease has not been finally established. However, so much research has turned up statistically significant incidence of high cholesterol level in people suffering from heart disease, that many nutritionists and physicians recommend that everyone —young and old—restrict the amount of saturated fat eaten as a preventive measure which may be beneficial.

And Dr. Laurence W. Kinsell and Barbara Gunning, of the Institute for Metabolic Research in California's Highland Alameda County Hospital, say this in their report "Fish Fats, Blood Fats and Atherosclerosis":

It has been known for many years that fish contain fats which are very much more polyunsaturated than those present in vegetable oils. Actually many of the fish oil fatty acids may be as much as three times more polyunsaturated than the average fatty acids of vegetable fat. Since men are more prone to development of the complications associated with atherosclerosis, such as heart disease and strokes, it behooves the good housewife who wishes to help keep her husband's arteries in good condition, to plan new and intriguing ways of preparing fish and to serve seafoods frequently in the weekly diet.

There, in those unhedging words, is a summing up of what this book is all about: to help you "plan new and intriguing ways of preparing fish" so that you, too, can "serve seafoods frequently in the weekly diet," not only to the man of the house, but to every member of the family.

And to help you keep up that resolve, we add just one very vital statistic:

In Japan, where fish is the main fat-providing food in people's diets and their intake of saturated fats is only three percent, a controlled study over a ten-year period showed that only 20 out of every 10,000 male deaths are due to heart disease.

In the United States, where red meat is the main fat-providing food in the people's diet and intake of saturated fat is 17 percent, the same controlled study showed that 185 out of every 10,000 male deaths are due to heart disease.

Nine times greater in meat-eating America than in fish-eating Japan!

FISH IS EXCELLENT FOR ENTERTAINING

You've read by now, we hope, all that's gone before. You know that fish tastes good, that it is inexpensive, that it is quick and easy to prepare and cook, that it is a safe food to serve to just about anyone who has to watch his diet, that it is not fattening, that it is a healthy food.

But there are a couple of other things that we still have not told you. To wit:

- Fish can be made into highly decorative table pieces.
- Fish is ideal for making into mighty attractive molds.
- Fish is fun to cook, to serve, to eat.

So you put it all together and what do you get? Excellent company fare, that's what. Excellent for children, especially if you let them help you shape and decorate the finished dish; excellent for women who watch their weight; excellent for men who think of themselves as meat-and-potato guys; excellent for luncheons, excellent for bridge clubs and afternoon teas; excellent for dinner with all the trimmings.

But, most of all, excellent for full-scale party company, whether that company is nighttime company or all-day Sunday company or summer-outing company. There are many recipes between these covers for you to try for whatever the occasion, but for real fun and festivity we highly recommend two of them in particular, the Kitchen Clambake on page 341 and the Dar Bin Loo on page 330. What is a Dar Bin Loo? You'll find out when you read the recipe.

Another True Fish Story

Our children are full-grown now, but we'll always remember when they were not yet ten and we were trying to cultivate in them a taste for fish. With our son it was not so difficult because he somehow acquired a yen for lobster at a very early age. But with our daughter it was a constant battle.

Only until the day, however, when Dan cooked a fish dish that we'd never tried before. We had it for supper and our daughter, as usual, rebelled. For a brief moment there was a conflict of wills, but as usual parental power prevailed. Sue condescended to take at least a bite. She took a tentative taste and then—oh, then!—a surprised smile lit up her face.

"Oh boy," she said, "it tastes just like candy!" And she gobbled down every bit and asked for more.

You'll find the recipe on page 241. We call it Cod Candy. It takes about one minute to prepare and about five to cook. What it cost then doesn't matter; the ingredients today would cost less than a dollar; price per serving, less than 35 cents.

2

What Seafood to Buy and
Where and When to Buy It

A Matter of Semantics

The word "seafood" can be quite confusing. Strictly speaking, it means anything edible that comes from the ocean, any ocean. By that definition, then, what is salmon, which lives part of its life in the sea and part inland? Or striped bass, which though a saltwater fish, more and more is being successfully introduced to rivers and lakes so that freshwater sports fishermen can have a try at them?

This book is about edible creatures of both worlds, saltwater and freshwater. So when we use the word "seafood," let it be known here and now and forevermore that we are referring to anything edible that comes from any water whatsoever, salt or sweet.

Additionally, when we use the word "fish" in a general sense, we mean both fin fish and shellfish, whether the latter be mollusks or crustaceans. If there is need to be more specific, we will say either "fin fish" or "shellfish." Rarely, if ever, will we use the words "crustacean" and "mollusk," because, if we did, we would be getting into the nuances of the ichthyological sciences and it would be more difficult to comprehend this book, which is meant to be an easy-to-follow discussion of fish cookery.

For those of you, however, who may want to add to your fount of scientific knowledge, strictly speaking, mollusks are shellfish with no visible means of propulsion; some, such as abalone and conch, have only one shell; some have two shells—clams, oysters, mussels and scallops.

Crustaceans have one shell and claws, which also serve as legs for

15

walking around, aided by finlike, shell-enclosed tails—lobster, shrimp, crab, prawns and crayfish (also called "crawfish" and, in some places, "crawdads").

Then there is the squid, which, for reasons beyond our comprehension, is also classified as a mollusk, yet it wears its shell more inside than out, and besides, what there is of it is more cartilage than shell.

To sum up and to close this semantic digression: in this book they are all simply shellfish. And all of them, together with their fin-fish cousins, are seafood, no matter if they come from the sea or from a freshwater mountain stream, meadow lake, farm pond or inland river. And all of them, collectively, we will mainly from now on simply call—fish.

FRESH FIN FISH

Since all fish not only taste good but also have much the same health-giving qualities, although perhaps in varying degrees, the main considerations when buying fish should be freshness and price. They go together. The cheapest fish in the local market should also be the freshest; conversely the most expensive would also be the one that is longest removed from the water and therefore the least palatable.

That's because, of all foods known to man, fish is the only one that delivers itself most of the way to market. Like man, they follow the seasons; like man, some prefer warm surroundings, others prefer cold. So, depending on their individual natures, if they prefer warm water, they go north in the summer, south in the winter; if they prefer cold water, they go south not at all. At least, not very far south.

Commercial fishermen follow the fish, catch the fish, deliver the fish to the closest possible port of call, where the wholesale fishmongers then deliver them to the local retail outlets either still alive and swimming in tanks or just killed and packed in ice.

Those fish will be both the tastiest and the cheapest for obvious reasons: the more quickly the commercial fisherman unloads them from his boat, the more quickly he can go out and catch some more; unlike the stockman or poultryman, the commercial fisherman's breeding and feeding costs are nil; the commercial fisherman never has too far to go to unload his catch; the wholesaler or jobber does not have far to go to make delivery.

So all you need know to purchase fish is which fish are being caught at what time in waters closest to your home.

How to find out requires no magic. Ask any sports fisherman. They're not hard to find; in fact, chances are you have one living in your house. It's a sure bet that he'll be fishing for the same fish as the commercial fisherman, unless, of course, he is some far-out nut who fishes only for the fish that are hard to find.

But suppose you don't know any fishermen? Just flip through your local newspaper to the fishing column, or turn on your local radio or television station and listen to its fishing report. If for some reason you don't have access to such, call up the sporting-goods store in your town. If it sells supplies to sports fishermen, it will know what fish are being caught.

If you live inland where commercial fishermen do not go, the same sources of information still hold true. Just ask any sports fisherman. You'll recognize him by the odd-ball look in his eye and the fish hooks in his hat.

Until fairly recently it was only the person who lived close to salt water who had access to the freshest commercial-catch fish at the lowest price. But now inland residents have a great big plus going for them: fish farms.

It is only in the past 10 or 15 years that they started coming into being. Now more and more are opening up in more and more states of the union. And so more and more fresh fish, tasty and inexpensive, is more and more available in inland markets.

No longer is there any logistic reason for a person not to eat fish. Not anywhere in the United States.

SHELLFISH

The farther away from any saltwater coast that you live, the more expensive it will be to buy shellfish. However, thanks to today's efficient transportation and refrigeration methods, more fresh shellfish than ever are finding their way to inland markets.

How fast they become available where you live is up to you; the law of supply and demand is the prevailing factor, just as it is with all other consumer commodities. If you want it, and if you are willing to pay the price, your fish dealer or your butcher can get it for you. The more people in your town who want it, the lower the price will be.

Additionally, there are shellfishermen around the country, especially in Maine, who ship lobsters and clams and all the other makings for a Down East clambake almost anywhere in any of the 50 states and Canada packed in ice in metal containers, all ready to steam and serve. You'll find their ads in the larger, nationally circulated newspapers (*The New York Times,* for instance) and in magazines. The clambake is wonderful eating, by the way, and wonderful fun and you can have one far from the sea in your own backyard. Or, for that matter, even in your kitchen without paying the price that the prepackaged variety will cost. The recipe is on page 341.

While fresh shellfish may not be easily purchased everywhere, some varieties are to be found wherever frozen foods are sold. For example: shrimp, lobster tail and Alaskan king crab meat.

Shellfish, too, is now also packed in cans and stocked by supermarkets everywhere. Mind you, still in their shells. For example: clams. Shucked and out of their shells, you'll also find canned lobster, abalone, shrimp, conch, mussels, crabs, clams and oysters. You'll find recipes for all of them inside these covers.

FROZEN, CANNED AND CURED FIN FISH

Frozen: The price of frozen fish never varies to any appreciable extent, and when it does, it's usually because of national economics of the moment and other such factors. Seasons mean little; the cost should be roughly the same in winter as in summer.

You should remember, though, that proximity to marketplace from processing plant is decidedly one of those other factors. Frozen farm-bred catfish will cost less, let's say, in Oklahoma than in Massachusetts and vice versa when it comes to frozen commercially caught cod.

So, too, with domestically bred trout as against, let's say, its Norwegian cousin.

As to where to buy frozen fish, as though you did not know: any supermarket in the country, plus most groceries, delicatessens and butcher shops that have frozen-food departments.

Canned: Need we take the time and space to tell you where to buy canned fish? Decidedly not. So all we'll say is what we said before: you'll find many recipes in this book that call either for fish left over from a previous meal or for fish that comes from a grocer's canned-goods shelves. Look the assortment over. You'll find tuna, salmon, bonito, mackerel, sardines, herring and probably more. One or two cans and you have the main ingredient for a delicious fish dish that will feed a family of four for no more than 50 cents a serving, probably closer to 25 cents.

Cured: Fish is cured in a variety of ways, and all or at least some of them should be found in virtually every larger-than-crossroads town in the country. The place to look, depending somewhat on the manner in which the fish has been cured, are delicatessens, supermarkets, butcher shops, specialty-food stores and grocery stores, particularly those which cater to ethnic groups. For example: smoked fish in Jewish stores, salt fish in Oriental and Scandinavian shops, kippered in Scottish-English-Irish neighborhoods.

The various methods are these:

· Pickled in vinegar, onion and spices and eaten as they come from the store.

· Hot-smoked, meaning they've undergone a siege in a smokehouse where the fire may be fed by hickory, cherry or any number of aromatic woods. Fish so smoked are ready to be eaten.

· Cold-smoked fish need additional cooking.

· Dry-salted fish have been packed inside and out in salt and allowed to age. Most of the salt must be removed by soaking in water and they must be cooked before eating.

· Wet-salted fish have been soaked in a brine. They may be eaten as is after the salt has been rinsed away.

Cured fish are marketed in many ways: in cans, jars, wooden or cardboard boxes or wooden kegs, and by the pound.

Some cured fish will keep for a long time; others for only a few days, and then only under refrigeration. It's best to handle lightly cured fish in the same manner as fresh fish. Buy all cured fish from reputable markets and ask the fish dealer's advice about how to care for and store it.

The most-fun way we know of to purchase the freshest-caught fish of all is to do what we do:

If you live within driving distance of any body of water, salt or fresh, large enough to support a commercial fishing operation, just hop into your car and head for the waterfront. Cruise around and look for the fishing boats. Look for their hallmark; you'll be able to see their nets hanging out to dry even if you can't see the boats themselves.

Get out of your car, walk over and take a close-up look. You'll be fascinated by the lines of the rugged little fishing boats, by the booted commercial men doing what needs be done upon coming back into port. Many of them will sell what they catch right from the boat, others will have small retail outlets right by their dock. Some will clean and dress the fish for you, others will not (but that's okay because we'll tell you how in this book). Do this and you can be sure you'll be buying the freshest possible fish and at the lowest possible price. Just as important, you'll have had a wonderfully different day. Especially if you get to talk to and to know the commercial fisherman and what it is about him that instills in him the urge to go out and catch food for your table, no matter what the weather.

3

Things You Should Know About Buying, Cleaning and Caring For Fin Fish

First of all, let us tell you this: the best fish to eat is the fish that you catch yourself. The best time to eat it is as soon as possible after you take it from the water. (However, this is not a book about how to catch fish. For that we commend to you two books written by Dan, *A Family Guide to Saltwater Fishing* and *The Fisherman's Almanac.*)

This chapter is highly important to the family that eats fish, no matter whether the fish is caught or bought. When to market you go to buy fish, you will have to know what choices are open to you. So let's begin there.

THE MARKET FORMS IN WHICH FRESH FISH MAY BE PURCHASED

1. Whole or round: a fish just as it comes from the water.
2. Drawn: only the innards, and nothing else, have been removed.
3. Dressed or pan-dressed: all that can be removed has been removed, entrails, scales, fins, and usually head and tail.
4. Split: a dressed fish that has been split down the middle, lengthwise, and its backbone removed and therefore virtually boneless.
5. Chunked: a fish, usually dressed, that has been cut into wide cross sections.

Whole or Round

Drawn

Dressed or Pan-Dressed

Steaks

Single Fillet

Butterfly Fillet

Sticks

6. Steaks: a fish, usually dressed, cut crosswise into three-quarter to one-inch steaks.

7. Fillets: the sides of a fish cut lengthwise away from the spine; practically boneless; the skin may be left on or removed—it's a matter of personal preference.

8. Butterfly fillets: the two filleted sides of a fish, held together by the uncut flesh, and sometimes the skin, of the belly. This is more of a carriage-trade cut, not usually found in fish markets. However, any fishmonger worthy of his calling can so fillet any fish of your choice for you.

9. Sticks: fillets that have been sliced either crosswise or lengthwise into strips about 3 inches long and 1 inch wide.

How to Be Sure the Fish You Buy Is Fresh and Wholesome

For this, you must put three of your senses to work: sight, touch and smell. Let them look for these signs:

· The flesh of whole, drawn and dressed fish should have a bounce to it, an elasticity; after you press it, it should come back to its natural shape. The eyes should be full, clear and bright; the skin should be shiny, its color unfaded; the gills should be red and free of slime; the odor should be fresh and mild; if it's what people call "fishy" don't buy that fish. If the tail of a fish presented as "fresh" is brittle, broken, and jagged, it may have been frozen and defrosted.

· Chunks, steaks, splits and fillets should be fresh-cut and the flesh should look it—still moist and bright, not dry and dull; no traces of brown around the edges; firm in texture, not beginning to look as if it's coming apart. The odor should be fresh and mild, again not "fishy." If they're wrapped, the wrapping should be a material that is both moisture-proof and vaporproof; there should be little or no air space between the fish and the wrapping.

The Most Economical Form to Buy

The best and easiest way to determine which form of fish to buy and when to buy it in order to effect the greatest economy is to turn to the "buys of the week" box that most newspapers carry in their food sections, go to market and buy that best buy, and then choose any recipe in this book that fits that form.

If your newspaper does not carry such best-buy information, you can figure it out for yourself by applying this basic slide-rule data:

· Whole or round fish is about 45 percent edible.
· Drawn fish is about 48 percent edible.
· Dressed fish is about 67 percent edible.

· Steaks and chunks are about 86 percent edible.

· Fillets are 100 percent edible; splits should be, too.

Therefore, if the price per pound of fillets is no more than about 55 percent higher than the price of whole fish, it's more economical to buy the fillets.

· If fillets are no more than 50 percent higher than the price of drawn fish, fillets again are the better buy.

· Ditto if fillets are no more than 33 percent higher than the cost of dressed fish.

· Ditto if the fillets are no more than 15 percent higher than the cost of steaks or chunks.

How Much of Each Form Constitutes One Serving

No one but you knows best how much each member of your family can and/or does eat at each meal. Therefore, no one can tell you how much of anything constitutes one serving in your house. Nor can anyone know—sometimes not even you—how many times someone will go back for extra servings.

Which all leads up to this: the figures that we are about to give you are not gospel; rather, they are educated guesses, based upon the recommendations of nutritionists as to how much the average adult should eat, and upon the findings of home economists who specialize in fish cookery.

To that, you'll have to apply your own yardstick as to how much fish you'll need to feed your family a satisfying meal.

The experts say that the average serving should consist of 3½ ounces of completely edible cooked, boneless fish, which means that, uncooked, you'll have to buy this:

· Whole fish: one pound per person.

· Dressed or chunked: one-half pound per person.

· Fillets, sticks or steaks: one-third pound per person.

But again we caution: let that slide-rule table be only your guide. Only you know how large or small is the appetite of each member of your household.

We've planned the recipes in this book to minimize the amount of slide-rule arithmetic you'll have to do. Since the above figures are based upon what's-best-for-everyone calculations and since only you know what your family appetites are and since realistically we believe that the average person eats more than the experts say he should, we've allowed a bit more in each of our recipes than the experts recommend.

Therefore, when we say a recipe will serve 4–6 we mean:

· Six servings close to the amount nutritionists recommend to maintain a healthy body.

· Four servings of a size that is a bit more generous.

Another reason for our so doing is this: the nutritionists usually base their size-per-serving recommendations as being part of a soup-to-dessert meal although the fact is that more and more families every day are sitting down to one- or two-dish meals.

With all this, if we've still underestimated the appetites in your house, all you need do is double, triple or quadruple the quantities any recipe in this book calls for.

Or, if we've overestimated, vice versa.

The finished result will still taste good, and be good, if you've abided by the rules of basic fish cookery.

A Word About Lean and Fat

On page 100 there begins a rundown on the various fish that you'll find in the consumer marketplace. Part of that rundown includes the oil content of each fish, the entire fish, just as it comes from the water. Actually the oil content of any fish varies within that fish. Generally there is more oil near the head than near the tail. Or, another way of putting it, there is more oil in the thick parts of a fish than in the thin parts.

So you should do this:

· Serve to those in your family who should eat lean fish a portion taken from near the tail; for those who should eat fat fish or to whom it makes no difference, a portion nearer the head.

· Or, if you have no need for an entire fish, when marketing, purchase chunks that come from the appropriate end.

From Hook to Home

If you never go fishing, not now, not forevermore, you can skip this. But if you catch the fish that you put on your table, or if ever you hope to do so, please read on.

Fish flesh begins to deteriorate the moment the fish is dead, its fine flavor begins to fade, its tastiness begins to wane; the more so as time passes. That is why the fish should be eaten as soon as possible after being taken from the water. Therefore, it behooves you, the fisherman or fisherwoman, to keep your catch alive for as long as possible.

So, if you fish from a boat or from a stay-put place on shore, be it bridge, pier, bulkhead, lakefront or riverbank:

· Attach a stringer (of the type that is fitted with a series of clasps that work like safety pins) to a boat cleat, oarlock, low-hanging tree limb, ground stake or whatever.

· As you catch each fish, pin it through both lips and dangle it in the water, allowing enough slack line for the fish to swim deeper than the sun's rays can penetrate.

· Never use the no-pin type of stringer that must be threaded through the fish's mouth and gills, because that will only force the fish to keep its mouth open and thus drown.

· If the fish you catch are small, you can substitute a burlap bag or gunny sack for the stringer. Weave a long length of line around the open end so that it works like a drawstring and secure one end to the boat cleat or whatever. Then, as you catch each fish, slip him headfirst into the sack, lower it into the water and let the whole kit and kaboodle frisk around in the shadows below.

· If you are a surf fisherman or jetty jockey who walks the beaches, casting as you go in quest of quarry, attach the clasp stringer to your web belt; then at each place that you tarry awhile refasten it to something secure that will permit your catch to frisk in the water.

· If you are a freshwater angler who wades the streams, line your shoulder-strap creel with swamp grass, hay or twigs—preferably willow— so that they make a bed for the fish you catch, dampen every now and then to keep it moist. If you stay put anywhere long enough to warrant, slip the creel from your shoulder and attach the strap to anything that will permit the creel to lie in the water.

Practice whichever of the above alternatives suits your situation best and your catch will stay alive until it's time to go home. If you live no more than, let's say, 30 minutes away, the fish should remain among the living until you get there. If not, you should give them a preliminary cleaning before starting the homeward trek. Like this:

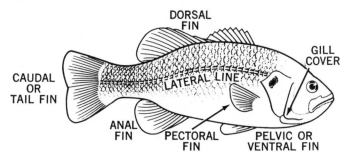

The outer anatomy of a fish.

· Clobber the fish on the noggin with a cudgel.

· Using a sharp knife, slit the stomach open, starting back at the anus and slicing forward to the head.

· Remove the innards by hand, using your knife to help if need be.

· Scrape away the blood alongside the spine with the blunt side of the knife tip and/or the back of your fingernail.

· That's all. Do no more in the way of cleaning: apply no water, because at this stage water can only hasten the breakup of tissues.

For the journey home, wrap the fish loosely in burlap, leaves, seaweed, newspaper or some such moisture-holding material, place them in an open ice chest, galvanized can or wooden box, pick up some ice, place it in the center of your fish carrier and continue merrily on your way dreaming sweet dreams of how you're going to cook them. And enjoy eating them.

Scaling fish with the back of a knife.

The two simple steps in the removal of all of a fish's fins.

The scaling, finning and more complete cleaning of the innards are chores best done at home:

· Place newspaper over a butcher's block or other heavy board.

· Lay the fish on its side on the newspaper.

· Holding the fish down by its tail, remove scales by scraping the dull edge of a knife or a scaler (which you can buy anywhere that fishing tackle is sold) along the skin from tail to head. If the tail is too small or too slippery to hold, stick an ice pick through the tail flesh and hold the handle. Turn fish over and repeat.

· Discard the top couple of newspaper sheets, along with the scales that have accumulated.

· To remove the fins, place the fish on one side again, insert the tip of a sharp, pointed knife at one end of a fin to the depth of about one-quarter to one-half inch, depending upon the size of the fish, and run the blade up one side of the fin; then repeat on the other side of the fin with the blade leaning in toward the first cut so that the two form a rough **V**. Now you need only lift out the fin, perhaps giving a slight tug if the cuts did not meet. Remove the remaining fins in the same way.

· Discard another sheet or two of newspaper.

Now is the time to clean more thoroughly the insides of the fish:

· Remove the roe carefully—they're mighty good eating. You'll find them in two triangular-shaped compartments, one on each side of the cavity. The roe ranges in orange-tinge colors from near white to rich orange. The male roe are soft and somewhat mushy; the female are firmly elastic.

· Completely scrape away all the blood that you missed during the water-side cleaning.

· Cut away any bits and pieces of entrails that may have remained.

· Hold the fish you're going to eat immediately under the cold-water faucet and let hydraulic power help the cleaning chore. Not only inside, but outside, too.

· Pat it dry, inside and out, with an absorbent, lintfree cloth or paper towel.

· Wipe the fish you're going to eat another day thoroughly, inside and out, with a damp lintfree towel until completely clean.

· Now wipe until thoroughly dry.

· Place the fish that you're going to refrigerate in a covered icebox dish or wrap in freezer paper. (We'll tell you how to freeze your catch later in this chapter.)

· Go pour yourself a drink—after cleaning up the mess you've made, of course.

Heads and Tails, Splits, Steaks and Chunks

We've said nothing up to now about removing the head and tail of a fish. We did not for a very good reason: if you're going to cook an entire fish, you should cook it all, not just its body. That's because the head and tail perform an extremely useful service, particularly if the fish is going to be baked, to wit: they help keep the flesh on either end of the body flaky and juicy. You might say they are heat insulators that help prevent the body flesh—the part of the fish you're going to eat—from becoming tough and dry.

What's more, if it's a large fish, there is lots of good eating in the head. People in foreign lands know this, as do their relatives here in the

United States. Besides, a fish that's been baked and is still intact makes a mighty pretty platter, and, as you know, sight has a lot to do with appetite.

Speaking of sight, for that very same reason some of you may want to remove the head from a fish before anyone ever sees it, because some people are mighty squeamish about having a pair of fish eyes staring at them. If the cook is not one of those persons, the time to remove the head is after the fish comes from the oven and before it goes on the table.

If the cook is allergic to the sight of fish heads, still no harm done. The flesh will not dry enough to notice if she or he observes the basic fish cookery rule given in Part One, Chapter 5, the fork test.

So now we'll tell you how to remove the head while cleaning a fish. Not only for the squeamish cook but also because (1) in many recipes there is no reason for leaving it in place, (2) there are prize morsels in every fish head, particularly the large ones, which we'll tell you about in a moment, and (3) many recipes call for the use of the head, particularly in the making of sauces (see Poached Big Fish with Conch Sauce, pages 333–334, and Fish Broth, page 118, for detailed instructions) and soup. A soup recipe that we recommend to you very highly is Buddy Kreidell's Slumgullion, which you'll find on page 187. Buddy is one of Dan's fishing partners, but more than that, he and his wife, Doreen, are proprietor-chefs of the Old Harbour Inn in Island Park on Long Island, just across Reynold's Channel from where we live, and what they can do with fish is out of sight. Several of their recipes are in this book; be sure to try them all. You'll be glad you did.

If the fish is small enough, just slice through the flesh and spine to remove head; if large, snap spine on edge of table after slicing through the meat.

Back to the head. Here's how to remove:

· Following the gill cover's **V** shape, slice through the flesh just behind the gills.

· If the fish is small and your knife is good, you'll be able to slice through the spine.

· If the fish is large, slice through the flesh all around the spine.

• Now cut through the spine with a cleaver or butcher's saw.

• Or, if you have neither, just place the head over the edge of your table and snap.

Did you know that fish have tongues and cheeks? Well, those are the prize morsels we mentioned. Cod tongues and cheeks are the most famous of all. They're delicious, no matter how you choose to cook them, yet very few fish dealers bother to remove them and sell them. Too time-consuming, they say, and besides there is no demand for them. Others remove them—and then sell the cheeks as scallops. That's how good they are. Not ethical but profitable.

And if anything is done for profit lately why that's okay. As witness the way our environment is being polluted and all of our foodstuffs are being contaminated. All done in the name of profit, as if that were the only way to make money. There need be no pollution, no contamination, and still there can be profit if only all of us start thinking that way and insisting that things be done properly or not at all.

But we're talking about fish tongues and cheeks. And where to find them. And how to find them.

If a fish had ears, the cheeks would be just behind them. Gently and carefully probe away the skin and gill covering with a knife, and you'll come close to them. A nice bite-size morsel somewhat resembling the so-called oyster that you'll find in fowl.

Look inside the mouth of a large fish and you'll see the tongue. Just cut it out.

Both tongues and cheeks are delicious buttered and broiled, breaded and fried, or however you choose to cook them. Or you can cook the cheeks as you would scallops.

As for the person who cooks fish head and all, you can remove the cheeks after the fish is cooked and eat them just as you would that poultry oyster.

Splitting a dressed fish is simple. Just place it on its side, the cleaned, open cavity toward you, and slice all the way through lengthwise, taking care not to cut through any spinal bones. When done you'll have two nice long pieces with the backbone in one of them. Using your knife tip, you now can remove it without much trouble.

Steaking and chunking are even easier. Decide what width you want your steaks or chunks to be, then slice accordingly just as you did to remove the head. You'll need either a good heavy-duty knife with steel tough enough to cut through the spine, a small butcher's saw or a cleaver. The knife and the saw you can buy in any good cutlery shop, or your butcher (if you ask him politely) will buy them for you. So, too, with the cleaver. But if there is an Oriental grocery store anywhere near you, we suggest that you buy it there.

Dan learned while writing *The Hong Kong Cookbook* with Arthur

Lem, who incidentally is the finest Chinese cook we've ever met, that the Chinese use three different kinds of cleavers: one for cutting bone, another for meats and the third for vegetables. You'll want the first one. Just ask the friendly Chinese clerk for a *quat dao* (day-oh) and tell him Arthur sent you.

How to Fillet a Fish

Filleting requires a bit of skill that you can acquire only by experience. But it's worth learning because (1) to fillet fish you also will bone a fish, (2) if you fillet a fish, you don't have to clean it, and most important of all, (3) fillets are necessary to so many fine recipes.

To fillet, lay knife parallel to spine after slicing through outer edge, then work it gently between flesh and backbone.

To skin a fillet: pull on skin while running sharp knife in opposite direction.

You'll need one good instrument if ever you're going to become an expert filleting artist, and that is a good filleting knife. The blade should be thin, narrow, flexible, sharp and made of good steel. But not stainless because it will not hold an edge.

Basically speaking, but only basically, there is nothing at all to the art. Just lay a fish on its side and slice a long slab of flesh away from the spine. That's all there is to it. Or so it seems until you try.

Where, for example, do you begin? In front of the tail? Behind the gills at the head end? Well, if you're interested in ending up with a fillet that has every possible bit of meat included in it, you'll start at the hind end and work your way forward. But if you're interested in top quality, you'll want to exclude the less tasty belly meat and so you'll begin up forward. It's for you to make the determination.

At whichever end you begin, here's the play by play:

· Lay the fish on its side on a cutting board.

· Slice gently through the flesh at your starting point, which will be either just in front of the tail or just behind the gill covers. But slice only until the knife blade just touches the backbone. Do not cut through it or into it.

· Turn the blade gently so that it lies parallel to the spine, the cutting edge facing the direction in which you want to go.

· Slowly, smoothly, steadily, firmly, work the blade along the spine, thus separating the meat from the bone.

· Turn the fish on its other side and repeat the process.

What you'll have is two long sections of fish, completely boneless if you've achieved perfection. If you started your slice at the tail, the belly meat will be included; if at the head, you'll have eliminated it.

If you prefer your fillets with the skin remaining on them, you should have scaled the fish before beginning the filleting. But if you want skinless fillets, scaling is unnecessary. Once the fillets are cut, to remove the skin do this:

· Place the fillet skin side down on your cutting board.

· Using your knife, work just enough flesh away from the skin so that you can get a grip on the latter.

· Turn the knife blade flat against the skin.

· Get a tight grip on the skin and run the blade forward, pulling on the skin as you do. Put a bit more emphasis on the pulling than you do on the cutting and the skin will come away nicely.

Now all that's left to do is throw out all the leavings, a simple, no-mess chore because the fish remains—head, tail, backbone, fins, everything except the skin—will still be intact. But if you're smart, you'll save the head for a broth or a sauce or, as we said a moment ago, for Buddy Kreidell's Slumgullion.

HOW TO REFRIGERATE, GLAZE AND FREEZE FIN FISH PROPERLY

So now, whether you've bought it or caught it, your fish is properly dissected. But for reasons best known to yourself you are not yet ready to cook it and eat it. It follows then that you must store it properly until you will be ready. If not, no matter how perfectly you've cleaned it, all sorts of chemical reactions will set in; bacteria will start running all over the place, enzymes will start breaking up like crazy, all sorts of things will start happening.

Suffice it to say that once they begin, the longer they continue, the more your fish will lose in the way of quality and flavor. What's even worse, eventually they will become contaminated.

It is incumbent upon you, therefore, to see to it that your fish is properly stored from the moment it enters your home until the moment you cook it. There are only two ways to do this: (1) refrigerate it properly, or (2) glaze and freeze it properly.

Make the most of a large dressed fish by cutting it into a chunk near the head, then several steaks, finally two single fillets near the tail. (National Fisheries Institute)

Here's the right way to refrigerate:
· Place your fish, if it or its pieces are small enough, in a covered icebox dish.
· If too large for that, place it on a platter or in a glass baking dish and cover with a length of freezer paper. Wrap the paper around the dish so that it will be as nearly airtight as possible. Do not wrap the fish itself.

· Put the package into the refrigerator and keep it there until ready to cook, at temperatures no higher than 40 degrees Fahrenheit and preferably from 32 to 35 degrees. The lower the temperature, the longer the fish will keep.

If you've purchased the fish, cook it within one day of the time you brought it home from market; at the most two days, but only if you know and have absolute confidence in your fishmonger and are sure that he purchases only fresh-caught fish and does not waste any time in transferring them to his own refrigerator or ice beds.

· If you've caught the fish, cook it within 2 days; if you must keep it longer, absolutely no longer than 3 days.

Some people, and some cookbooks, may say that fish can be refrigerated longer. But we do not. We recommend the briefest possible storage time and we repeat now what we've said several times before: a fish tastes best the moment it comes from the water; every minute longer than that the quality and the taste deteriorate that much more.

There is only one safe way to store a fish for any length of time beyond a couple of days and that is to freeze it. We'll tell you how now but we must warn you right at the outset: **never freeze fish that you have not caught yourself unless it has been just caught by a fisherman friend whom you know and whom you trust to have handled it properly from the moment he caught it until the moment he gave it to you. Never freeze fish that you bought in a store, no matter how fine, no matter how reputable, that store might be.**

There are several ways that fin fish can be frozen, but the method that we practice at home and recommend now to you is a method devised and tested by Gale Steves, the government home economist in charge of the New York division of the U.S. Commerce Department's National Marine Fisheries Service and a girl who knows her business.

Before you start to freeze fish you should have on hand the proper materials in which to package it for storage: a good moistureproof and vaporproof freezer paper, a roll of tape, and labels. Aluminum foil and plastic bags make easy-to-use, effective wrappings. However, they add to the volume of ecologically nondisposable material that is beginning to clog our world. If you use them anyway, please buy the heavy-duty kinds that can be washed, dried and reused.

Do not freeze a whole, uncleaned fish. Any other market form into which you might dissect your catch will do: drawn, dressed, split, chunked, steaked or filleted. Let the size of your freezer and the forms that will best suit your future cooking plans be the determining factors.

The fish should be glazed before it is frozen, and since some fish are lean and some fish are fat, two different solutions will be needed.

First, the lean:

· Set in the freezer as much water as you'll need and leave it until almost frozen, then remove and transfer to a pot or pan large enough to immerse the fish.

· Dissolve ½ cup of salt in every quart of almost-frozen water you have.

· Immerse the fish in the solution for 1 minute, then remove and place on lintfree or absorbent paper towels for 2 minutes.

· Now dip once again for about 30 seconds, remove and wrap immediately.

For fat fish, substitute 2 tablespoonsful of ascorbic acid powder per quart of almost-frozen water for the salt and follow the same step-by-step procedure. The powder can be bought in any drugstore.

In wrapping the fish, make sure that no openings remain and that there is no air space between the fish and the wrapping material. Tape securely and label with (1) the date, (2) the species of fish, (3) the market form, and (4) whether it's fat or lean.

Now into the freezer it goes—but first you've made sure that it is down to minus 10 degrees Fahrenheit or less because that's the temperature required to freeze fish properly. Once it's frozen, the temperature can go up to zero.

There you have it. So glazed and frozen, a lean fish will keep safely for 6 months, a fat fish for 3 months. Unless you open the freezer door too often or let it stay open longer than is absolutely necessary to remove a package. Thank you, Gale Steves.

Freezing Cooked Fin Fish

Follow instructions for freezing cooked shellfish, page 87.

Frozen Fish in the Marketplace

For all of you for whom fresh fish is difficult to come by, these few paragraphs are specially important. And, too, for working men and women who have to whip up a good meal in a hurry when the day's work is done.

Fish is available in supermarket frozen-fish departments. Freshwater fish, saltwater fish, native-bred fish, farm-bred fish—you'll find all of them there in whatever form you want them: whole, dressed, filleted, steaked. If not the exact species you want, a similar species so you'll never notice the difference.

The handiest form to purchase, the form that is our favorite, is the fillet. Usually 2 or more fillets to a 12- or 16-ounce package. They are frozen into a solid block 1 to 1¼ inches thick, but there is no need ever to separate them or even to thaw them.

The recipe section will tell you how to prepare them and cook them, just as they come from the freezer, in any number of epicurean ways. Follow the instructions closely, particularly as to timing and testing, and be prepared for compliments—and taste treats that normally you would expect only from properly prepared fresh-caught fish. Depending upon the recipe and what else, if anything, you plan to have at the same meal, one 16-ounce package will make 2 to 4 normal servings.

While shopping you'll also notice frozen fish already breaded or otherwise doctored and made oven-ready. About them, we have a few things to say:

1. They'll cost more.

2. They won't taste as good.

3. They'll take at least as much time to "just heat and serve" as if you'd started from scratch to rustle up a fish dinner.

Two other commodities that we suggest you steer clear of are frozen sticks and something that the packers call "portions." Government food inspectors have found too many of them to be not solid chunks of fish as they should be but, rather, fish that has been ground in with, for example, cornmeal. If you want sticks or portions, buy a package of frozen fillets, defrost them and cut your own. To size.

We mentioned that frozen fillets usually come in 12- to 16-ounce packages; as for other market forms, the cartons vary in weight from 8 ounces to several pounds.

Some tips about the purchase and care of frozen fish:

· Check carefully to make sure the package is not torn, bent or otherwise damaged.

· Market freezers have, hopefully clearly visible to the customer's eye, what may be called either a "frost line" or a "load line." Buy only packages that are stacked well below that line; better still, shun the top layer altogether.

· Take only packages that are solidly frozen.

· Don't buy packages that have been thawed and refrozen. You'll be able to tell by looking for ice or evidences of drip on the outside.

· If it's a see-through package, check for discoloration or other signs of freezer burn.

· If any package has an odor, don't buy it. Frozen fish should be virtually odorless.

· Make frozen fish the last item you add to your cart before hitting the checkout line.

· Don't dally to chat or have a cup of coffee on the way home.

· When you get there, either cook it right away or place it in your freezer immediately.

· Don't keep store-bought frozen fish longer than a month.

· If you want to defrost it, buy tomorrow's supper today and store it in the refrigerator. It will take that long to thaw properly.

ROE

Earlier, we told you where to find roe in fish that you catch. Now we'll tell you that you'll also find it in fish markets the country over and if you're smart, you'll buy some and whip up for yourself a delicacy such as you've never had before.

Everyone, we think, has heard of shad roe and bacon. A great delight, any meal of the day, and if you don't believe us, go down to Sloppy Louie's in New York's Fulton Fish Market and watch the fisherfolk eat it for breakfast, Wall Street brokers for lunch and the slumming carriage trade for dinner. But only when the shad are running.

However, you can have it, too. No matter where in the world you live, no matter what fish are running, because all fish have roe and all roe is good.

They range in size from a few ounces to more than a pound, depending upon the size of the fish from which they come, and that is how they are sold. They come, as we said earlier, in varying shades of orange; they should look fresh and smell fresh.

Roe consists of many tiny eggs, the same eggs that, when salted, are called caviar and command fantastically outrageous prices because they are then considered one of the world's greatest delicacies. The eggs are enclosed in a membrane and the roe requires frying on medium heat (or poaching for 30 seconds, if you prefer) to firm it up and thus keep the eggs from scattering hither and yon when further cooked. Fried Roe (page 259) is a basic recipe that applies to any and all roe no matter what the fish from which they came, saltwater or fresh.

Although roe can be served by itself as a main course, it is very rich and therefore is most often served in combination with other foods; or, after the quick frying, cut into bite-size pieces and added to an hors d'oeuvre table. Eight to 10 ounces in combination with other foods will serve 6 people.

You'll find a number of roe recipes in this book. Try them all. Enjoy them all. But remember these things:

Roe is very perishable so store it at 32 to 35 degrees Fahrenheit in a covered dish and use it within 24 hours of the time you buy it. Slice into a piece of roe to be sure it's cooked all the way through before serving. If the center is raw, it will look moist and be a different color from the cooked outer area.

EELS

Americans don't think of them as fin fish but they are, complete even to tiny scales and flesh that separates into flakes. These snakelike creatures graced the banquet tables of the ancient Greeks and Romans and still are an increasingly eaten treat throughout most of the world, including the United States, except, perhaps, along the West Coast, which for some reason unknown to man eels shun like the plague. Salmon-stream fishermen may dispute this, but the fact is that the critters they run into there are lampreys, not eels.

Eels live part of their lives in salt water, most of their lives in freshwater lakes, rivers and ponds. The females grow to about 3 feet in length, the males only about half that size. Baked eels are an Italian Christmas Eve delicacy, smoked and pickled eels a favorite of Germans and Scandinavians, fried eels a breakfast that's different for game-fish anglers who hook one by mistake.

Additionally, eels also are good poached, broiled, or included in a fish stew or salad, and if you want a dish that's different, try the Smoked Eel Omelet recipe on page 265. In short, eels lend themselves to just about any form of cookery. But don't eat them as weight-loss food because a raw 3½-ounce chunk packs a bit more than 230 calories.

THE MARKET FORMS OF EELS

· *Live:* Fishmongers who sell them this way, which, incidentally, is the best way to buy them, will have them swimming around in clean-water tanks. They're graded large (2 pounds and over), medium (1 to 2 pounds) and small (under 1 pound). Pick the one you want, pay for it by grade or pound and have the clerk kill it, skin it and eviscerate it for you.

· *Whole but dead:* Thus they're graded and sold the same as live. Make sure they're free of slime and have a pleasant odor. If he hasn't already done so, the fishman will dress them for you. All you need do is ask. Politely.

· *Smoked:* So processed, they're usually then cut into about 3-inch pieces and sold by the pound in delicatessens and delicacy shops, whole in fish markets.

· *Pickled:* Cut into 2- or 3-inch pieces and sold in jars that range from 8 ounces to a gallon and sometimes more.

· *Canned:* Usually they've been poached and packed in their own broth or jelly; a great gourmet-shop item.

PROPER CARE AND STORAGE OF EELS

· *Live at time of purchase:* If you don't dally in getting home from market, they'll keep raw one or two days if stored in a covered dish in a 32-degree refrigerator; 3 or 4 days if you first cook them.

· *Whole:* It's best that you cook them soon after purchase, then store them as above but only for a day or two.

· *Smoked and pickled:* Check with the market where purchased.

• *Canned:* Unopened, they'll keep a year; opened, 3 or 4 days if re-packaged and refrigerated.

HOW MUCH TO BUY FOR SIX PEOPLE

Three pounds of eel should suffice for 6 people.

TO SKIN AND CLEAN EEL YOU'VE CAUGHT

If you've caught your own, remember this: Eel should be skinned *before* cooking. So do this:

Kill it with a sharp knock on the noggin with a club of some sort; a heavy knife handle will do. Cut through the skin completely around the neck. Peel a bit of the skin back enough with a knife to hold it firmly with your fingers or, better still, a pair of pliers. Grasp the head tightly between the first three fingers of your other hand, middle finger on top, the other two below, so your knuckles work something like a vise. Now pull your hands in opposite directions. Zip! Off will come the skin. If it didn't, you need practice, so try again.

Once the skin is removed, cut away the head and eviscerate the eel as you would any fish. Cut into three-inch lengths, discarding the tail, and the eel is ready for cooking.

4

Things You Should Know About Buying, Cleaning, Caring for and Cooking Shellfish

LIQUIDS HAVE THE FIRST WORD

It holds true for all shellfish, just as it does with all vegetables and many other foodstuffs that contain high amounts of health-giving, body-building vitamins, proteins, minerals and such: don't throw out the liquids in which they have in any way been precooked.

Instead, with shellfish, strain the liquid through several layers of cheesecloth or anything else that will serve the purpose, to remove any foreign matter it might contain, chill immediately after cooking and save in the refrigerator for use in soups, sauces, chowders or whatever fancy strikes you. For example, try a spoonful in your next omelet. The next time you may make it 2 or 3. Use within 2 days.

To freeze extra shellfish broth: see page 118 in the sauce section and follow the instructions given there for freezing fish fumet. Use within 10 days.

NOTE: When steaming or simmering shellfish (fin fish too) you may sometimes find it necessary to use a can not originally intended for cooking. Since you probably will not know the metallic content of the can, it's best that you avoid adding any acid ingredients to the liquid.

It's well-nigh impossible to lump together all you should know about the various shellfish for which there are recipes in this book. So instead let's discuss them one at a time.

CLAMS

Of the hundreds of species of clams found in North American waters, we eat only a few, mainly because they're the most easily gathered and therefore the most easily marketed. People on the East Coast have certain species available to them, folks on the West Coast have others, and clam-lovers closest to Gulf waters have some of each. Some names are the same here as they are there, and vice versa, yet the clams that bear those monickers are not necessarily the same at all.

So, dear readers, please stay with us as we try to tell you which clam to buy where. Of course, always remember this: no matter what the name, all clams cook the same and, if you cook them right, they all taste good.

The most commonly marketed hard-shell clam in New England is called the "quahog," an Indian word. A bit of Long Island, which is in New York State, also knows the hard-shell mainly by that Indian name, no doubt somewhat influenced by Walt Whitman, who roved the island's beaches and tidal flats gathering and eating the quahog just as they came from the water, raw on the half shell.

But from there and on south, all the way round to Texas, the hard-shell clam is known by a simple four-letter word: clam.

Fishmongers call the hard-shell by three names, each name designating the size of the clam. Littleneck and cherrystone clams are small and are delicious eaten raw, made into a stew or dipped in a batter and fried. Chowder clams are large and are made to order for soups and, you guessed it, chowders. Also a very popular Atlantic Coast delicacy is the soft-shell clam, which is more commonly known as the steamer clam. Just try them steamed in a bit of water, then dipped first into the hot broth in which they were cooked, then into melted butter, and accompanied by a glass of beer. They're as American as apple pie and therefore not regarded as gourmet fare.

THE MEANING OF "GOURMET"

Since we've mentioned the word "gourmet," and we promise not to do it too often, let's digress for a moment and tell you that we think it's become one of the most horribly overused and misused words in the English language—pardon, French language, today—so much so that we shudder every time we hear it.

To us, "gourmet food" has come to mean any food that has been overelaborately prepared (as apart from properly prepared), saturated in quality-concealing sauce and called by a foreign, usually French, name.

As for the meaning of the noun "gourmet" by itself, the dictionary definition is this: "a connoisseur in eating and drinking, an epicure."

Well, perhaps once upon a time. But to us today and again because of overuse and misuse, a "gourmet" has come to mean nothing more than a person who orders such dishes by foreign title, usually mispronounced, and at prices ten times higher than they should be. He would probably be quite surprised to know that many French recipe names translate into a description of a very folksy nature. Shad, or any fish, "à la meunière," for instance, means "in the manner a miller's wife" would prepare it. (See page 252 for the simple fried recipe.)

To us, true, honest-to-goodness gourmet food is nothing more than any good food that has been properly grown, properly harvested, properly prepared and properly served.

Try going into a field and picking a vine-ripened tomato or green pea that's been allowed to grow without aid of insecticides and chemical stimulants. Eat it raw right then and there.

To us, that's gourmet eating.

Let's get back to that four-letter American word, "clam."

A third East Coast resident is the surf clam which also is known by such other names as skimmer, beach, giant, sea, hen and bar clam. You can gather them yourself, but they're sold in stores principally in cans.

On the West Coast, the clams that most often find their way to the dining table are the pismo, the razor, the littleneck and the butter. The pismo, one of the world's most famous eating clams, is a very unselfish fellow who gave his name to Pismo Beach, California, where he lives and thrives. The delicious razor clam is found mainly around Long Beach, Washington. As for the littleneck, which also is mighty good eating, he bears absolutely no kinship whatsoever to his East Coast namesake.

Other Pacific species, not generally marketed but highly prized by folks who dig their own, are the cockle and horse—also called "gaper"—clams.

Clams are marketed in three forms:

• In shell, often also called "shell clams," meaning just as they came from the water and therefore still very much alive. You can tell very easily: the shells should be tightly closed. If there is a separation between the two shells, tap one of them gently. With hard clams, the shells should immediately clamp together; with soft clams and other varieties, the siphon or neck should immediately constrict. If freshly dug and refrigerated at about 35 degrees Fahrenheit, shell clams will remain alive and fit to eat for several days. They are sold by the dozen or by the pound.

• Shucked, meaning the shells have been removed and chucked away. Shucked clams should be plump and smoothly free of air holes, the liquid should be clear or opalescent and free of shell particles. The smell should be sweet. Fresh shucked clams are available in either waxed or metal containers that usually have see-through covers. Properly refrigerated or packed in ice, they should remain fresh enough to eat for a maximum of 5 days.

· Canned. Not only surf clams, but also pismo, hard, soft and razor clams are available on grocers' shelves either still in their shells or shucked and then minced. Can sizes range from 3½ ounces to 4 pounds. Clam broth, juice and nectar come both bottled and canned.

HOW MUCH TO BUY FOR SIX PEOPLE

As we've said before, you know best what your family appetites are, so only you know how many clams you'll need to feed them. Additionally, only you know how you're going to prepare the clams. So take these recommendations and add or subtract as best suits your needs.

Shell clams: 3 dozen.

Shucked: 1 quart.

Canned: 2 7-ounce cans.

HOW TO CLEAN CLAMS

Even though you've purchased them in a reputable store and they look as though the job has been done for you, shell clams should be thoroughly cleaned both inside and out once you get them home. That goes double if you've dug your own. And while we're on the subject, a word about gathering your own clams or, for that matter, any species of shellfish.

With all the contamination that man is adding to our waters, people no longer can do in safety what Walt Whitman did—dig up and eat a clam from whatever beach or tidal flat fancy chanced to take him. So confine your shellfish-hunting expeditions to waters that have been certified safe for swimming by local health authorities. Their stamp of approval for swimming and bathing is your assurance for harvesting and eating because they will not certify polluted waters.

Back to the cleaning. Starting on the outside, scrub each hard-shell clam vigorously with a stiff brush while holding it under cold, running water. Scrub each soft clam gently but well with a soft brush, sponge or dishcloth. This will rid the shells of the sand and/or mud that the clams gather in a lifetime of living in same. Oh yes, throw out any clams whose shells are broken or, if open, didn't close while all that scrubbing was going on. They're dead.

As for the shiny-clean live ones, place them in a pot and let them clean their insides for you. For a clam, this is an exceedingly natural process.

A clam lives a very sedentary life, never going anywhere in search of food. He lets it come to him. Merely by pumping vast quantities of sea water into one side of its shells and out the other side, he feeds himself like crazy, for sea water is alive with plankton. And plankton, you know, are tiny organic matter upon which all fish thrive. Even whales.

Anyhow, all that sea water passing through a clam's shells is bound to carry some sand and mud with it. And, of course, some of it is bound to remain in the clams in your sink.

So fill the pot in which you've placed your clams with sea water and the clam will keep right on pumping, clean water in one side, water spiked with sand or mud out the other. If you don't have any sea water, add a third of a cup of salt to a gallon of tap water.

Change the water once and the sand-purging operation should be done in about 30 minutes. That's all there is to it.

But if you want to do a well-nigh perfect purging job, not only of sand and mud but also of man-made pollutants that the clam might have ingested, do this: in a large pot combine 1 cup of cornmeal and 1 cup of salt to every gallon of tap water that you'll need to cover your clams, set in a cool place and let the clams do their pumping for at least 8 hours, changing the water solution several times so that it always contains enough oxygen for the clams to stay alive and to get rid of the sand and mud that will start collecting on the bottom. Thus, in will come the highly edible cornmeal on one side, out will go the foreign matter on the other side.

If you're in a hurry, give the clams a hotfoot simply by adding pepper to the pot. The clams will pump like mad and the job will be done in 3 hours.

What you will have is corn-fed clams. Already seasoned, if you've used the pepper.

HOW TO OPEN CLAMS

After the cleaning and purging are done, and if you intend to serve the clams raw or use them raw in a recipe in which shells have no place, there comes the matter of separating the succulent meat from its housing.

The job is simple with soft-shell clams since they practically break apart with a squeeze of the fingers. With hard clams, however, the chore is somewhat more difficult. First of all, you should have a clam knife. It's short and stubby and costs very little. But if you don't have one, any strong, thin knife with a blunted round tip will do. It should be sharp, but not very.

So armed, this is what to do:

· Lay the clam flat in the palm of one hand, the hinge against your thumb cushion.

· Insert the knife blade between the two shells, which will be clamped tightly shut, and twist slightly to force open.

· Run the blade, which should be parallel to the shells, around the

Insert knife between clam's two shells and twist.

The rim muscle is next to feel the steel.

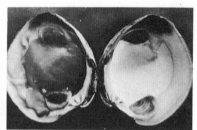

Now for separation of adductor muscle from shell.

Result: clam on the half shell.

clam until the 2 halves come apart and stay apart but with the hinge still linking them together.

· You'll see then a comparatively thin membrane around the clam's outer perimeter but still very much attached to one of the shells. Insert the knife blade between the membrane and the shell and work it around the perimeter until they separate.

· Now there still will be a fleshlike link holding the clam to its two shells, near the hinge. About ½ inch in diameter, it's called the "adductor muscle." Run your knife between it and the shells and the meat will then be free.

· Your clam is now ready to serve on one of its shells or whatever. Look over the recipes that call for clams and make your choice. But, whichever, don't waste the liquid. It is tasty sipped from the shell, made into a sauce, cooked into a broth or added to a stew, a bisque or a chowder.

If those shucking procedures sound complicated, take our word for it, they are not. But some skill is necessary. And practice, even to do nothing more than force the knife between the two shells at the very outset. But keep trying. You'll make it. Or find a gimmick-gourmet shop and buy a gadget that's made especially for the epicure who has everything. Except patience.

And who knows? Between the time this is being written and the day that this is published, they may be electrically operated. Simpler than that technology cannot make it for you.

Or, better still, try a trick that a Long Island clam connoisseur passed on to us: Store your unopened clams in the freezer for about an hour, and then immediately open them as directed above. You'll have rendered all of the clams' moving parts hors de combat, including the muscles that hold the shells closed tight, and so you'll encounter no resistance. Very simple (even though the meat must then thaw for a few minutes), and thank you Mr. Long Island Clam Connoisseur for the tip.

To open clams for chowders, soups and such not even a clam knife is necessary. Just put them into a pot, add a bit of water, cover and steam or simmer just until the shells pop apart. Be sure to save the liquid, because it can be used in so many ways and in so many recipes.

Some people also will tell you to drop clams in boiling water for a few seconds to open and then to eat them on the half shell just as if they were raw. But they will not be raw and so will not taste the same. Nor will all clams open in a few seconds. Some may take 10 minutes. However, they do taste good, although not raw and perhaps somewhat rubbery.

REMEMBER THIS WHEN COOKING CLAMS

Clams are naturally plump, tasty creatures. Since, more than any other way, they are eaten raw, it is obvious that they need very little cooking when you do decide to cook them. All heat will do, not *for* them, but rather *to* them, is make them tough and rubbery.

Generally, just a minute or so—the time it might take until their edges start curling—is all the heat to which they ever should be subjected. Actually, the only reasons there are for cooking them at all are (1) because coatings in which they have been blanketed must be cooked, or (2) to lend their flavor to other ingredients with which they are being combined.

The specifics about when to add them to the cooking pot are spelled out in each clam recipe in this book. Follow them closely.

CLAM DIGGING, CLAM SHELLS AND CHILDREN

Earlier we told you how important seafood is for the healthy growth and physical development of children, and therefore how important it is that you instill in them a taste for seafood at a very early age.

Now we'll tell you how to fit that objective—healthy, happy children —into a family outing that will have the additional dividend of putting free food on the table.

Head for the nearest salt water and spend the day bathing, swimming, frolicking on the beach and digging clams. Anyone can do it who has reached the age of two or three. Clams are free for the taking almost everywhere in the United States where salt water flows, be that salt water an ocean beach, a wetlands estuary, an inshore bay or a brackish river mouth where the salt water mingles with the fresh. If the water is clean enough for swimming, the clams generally will be good enough to eat.

Some dedicated clam diggers arm themselves with all sorts of paraphernalia, shovels, rakes, long-handled tongs. But really all you need are your toes, plus a basket and an old tire tube to fit it in so that it will float no matter how full you load it with clams. Or, for children, a sand pail. Low tide is the best time.

Then all you do is this: wade around in from 6 inches to 3 feet of water. Every time you step on anything round and hard, keep your foot on it, bend down and pick it up. Usually it will be a clam. If the water is too deep for bending, dive down and retrieve the clam, but be quick about it because they are quick, too.

Kids love sport like that. Just keep your eye on them and they'll have a ball. If they're toddlers, take them by the hand and stay in water that's no more than 1 foot deep.

Make a chowder out of the clams that they've helped dig and we guarantee you, they'll love it, especially if you make it right there on the water's edge. See the Easy Beach Clam Chowder recipe on page 368.

As for the shells, they make grand baking and/or serving dishes for any number of recipes. So don't discard them. Instead, when you get home, scour them to make sure you've removed any bit of clam flesh that may be clinging to them. Then they'll be ready to use anytime you want them. Again we guarantee you: kids will eat what's served to them in those shells.

But, we warn you, you'll have to guard them because kids will take them and paint them and make them into any number of things that only children's imaginations can conjure up. Or, better still, share the cleaned shells with them so that you both will have some when you want them.

HOW TO CLEAN CLAM, OYSTER
AND SCALLOP SHELLS

· Scrub shells from which meat has been removed inside and out, with a stiff brush or soapless metal pot cleaner.

· Place in a large pot, cover with water, add a tablespoonful of baking soda and boil for about 10 minutes.

HOW TO FREEZE CLAMS

We frown on the idea of freezing clams for future use, perhaps because for us, living on a salt island as we do, they're so easy to come by that we can always have them fresh.

Still, however, clams can be frozen and kept from 3 to 4 weeks. But, please, freeze only clams that you've harvested yourself and provided that you've begun the simple process at almost the moment you've taken them from the water. Never freeze clams that you've purchased, because you cannot possibly know their life history and you should take no fish dealer's word for it.

So, with those admonitions out of the way, here's how:

· Keep the clams you've dug alive in the tire-encased bushel basket floating in the water where you've dug them until you're ready to start for home.

· Now transfer them to a large pot that you've brought with you for the purpose.

· Cover them with sea water.

· Add cornmeal to the water as described earlier in this chapter so that the clams can be purging themselves of sand, mud and other possible foreign matter while enroute home.

· Change the water when you get home, adding salt and cornmeal to tap water as described earlier, and let the purging process continue for at least 8 hours from the moment it began at the beach.

· Now scrub the shells and shuck the clams as described earlier, being sure to save the clam liquid inside the shells.

· Dip the clam meat in a solution of 1 tablespoonful of salt to 3 cups of water.

· Remove the clams from the solution and place them in metal containers with snap-on lids or glass jars made for freezing or canning. We prefer the latter.

· Add the shucking liquid (strain it first) and, if necessary, just enough tap water to cover completely. Be sure to allow ½ to 1 inch of expansion space between the contents and the top of the container.

· Seal according to instructions that come with the containers.

· Paste or tie on containers labels that include dates clams were taken from water and placed in freezer, and the waters from which you took them.

· Place containers in freezer at temperatures at least 10 degrees below zero Fahrenheit, if possible, until frozen, and no higher than zero afterward. Use in 1 month.

OYSTERS

Perhaps more than any other food, the oyster has been in the limelight down through the history of man. Just as they did for spices, men and ships ranged far and wide in search of the oyster. Lands were invaded and lands were conquered, all for the oyster. The same oyster that ancient Greeks and Romans ate in their bacchanal feasts, that cavemen ate before dragging their women off by the hair, that Indians presented to Pilgrims in gestures of friendship, that today are more popular than ever.

More than 100 million pounds of them are sent to market every year in the United States alone, millions of pounds more in Canada, Europe and the cultural capitals of the other continents.

As for how many oysters are consumed every year by peoples of all lands, including ours, who gather their own we have no idea. But we are sure the figure is astronomical.

And the oyster industry continues to grow. So much so that today oyster farms are springing into being the world over and the oysters that they cultivate and harvest are more succulent than ever.

There are many benefits that go with the eating of oysters. Not only do they have a fine, truly epicurean natural flavor, they also are easy to prepare, and, most important, of all the edible shellfish known to man, the oyster contains the greatest health-giving qualities. An average serving of 6 medium-sized oysters contains (1) more than the human body's daily need of iron and copper; (2) half of the required amount of iodine; (3) one-tenth of the body's need for protein, calcium, magnesium, phosphorus, thiamine, riboflavin, niacin and vitamin A.

Nutritionally speaking, few foods are better balanced than oysters. And, like clams, they are 100 percent edible. And again also like clams, they can be prepared by at least a dozen different methods and used in as many different recipes as your creative senses are sharp: raw on the half shell, in a cocktail or in salads; cooked into stews, bisques and chowders; baked, broiled, pan-fried and oven-fried, creamed, scalloped, poached or steamed; all of them alone or in combination with such other goodies as rice—wild, brown or white; cheese, sharp or mild; bacon, celery, spinach, cauliflower or any other vegetable that you grow in your garden or buy in a store. If that is not enough, try a poultry stuffing made with oysters.

Cultivated on all three of our coasts, oysters are available to everyone in 3 market forms. In any of them, you need have no fear of pollution because both the federal government and coastal-state governments have stringent regulations that the oyster industry must, and gladly does, abide by. Those regulations are embodied in what is known as the Shellfish Sanitation Program. Under them, once an oyster is harvested in open waters, which may or may not be polluted, it must be transferred to so-called fattening grounds, where the water must be as pure as the purest drinking water. And there they must remain until they have purged themselves of any contaminants they may have picked up while growing on the oyster farm.

How do they purge themselves? By the same natural process we told you about in describing how to purge clams of sand and mud and possible pollutants: by ingesting clean water on one side and expelling whatever is in their systems on the other.

When the oysters have remained in the purifying tanks long enough for the purging process to have done its work, they are then packed for shipment to market, double tagged. The wholesaler keeps one part of the tag, the retailer gets the other part. Thus, if an oyster is found to be bad, it can readily be traced to the oyster beds from which it came. No more oysters from those beds will be permitted to be shipped to market until whatever caused the condition is corrected.

"OYSTERS R IN SEASON"

You no doubt, somewhere, have seen a sign bearing those words. All they are meant to tell you is that oysters are plentiful in months that include the letter R, September through April, the cold-water months.

But somehow, down through the years, those words also have come to mean that oysters are not good to eat, are perhaps even poisonous to eat, in the months of May, June, July and August. Well, let's lay that myth to rest right here and now. Oysters are not poisonous, not in any month of the year. Nevertheless, there is justification for the "Oysters R in Season" sign. It is this: the non-R months are the warm months and the warm months are the months in which oysters spawn, i.e., deposit their eggs and give birth to a new generation. While spawning, they are too busy to eat. So they grow thin and less tasty. By the time September rolls around they are becoming fat and flavorsome once again.

So, you see, the oyster industry has two good reasons for marketing their product only in the R months: (1) you wouldn't like them and therefore wouldn't buy them, and (2) most important, it's good conservation not to disturb them while spawning. If other industries were to take a page from the oysterman's book, this would be a better world in which to live.

SPECIES AVAILABLE IN THE
AMERICAN MARKETPLACE

Three important species are harvested and marketed in the United States. From Maine down the Atlantic Coast and around the Gulf Coast to Texas, there is the species known as the Eastern oyster; on the Pacific Coast, there is the small Olympia oyster and the larger Pacific, or Japanese, oyster. All of them are known by any number of regional names, among them blue point, Yaquina, Kumamoto, pearl, petit point.

THE MARKET FORMS

1. Shell oysters, meaning just as they came from the water. They must be alive, the shells must be tightly closed or, if open, they must clamp

tightly shut when tapped or handled. Refrigerated at temperatures of about 35 degrees Fahrenheit, they will keep several days. The tap test will tell you exactly how long. Shell oysters usually are sold by the dozen.

2. Shucked, meaning they've been removed from their shells by professional hands. They should be plump with a natural creamy color and smoothly free of air holes, the liquid should be clear or slightly opalescent and free of shell particles. They should have not even a smidgeon of offensive odor or sour smell. Shucked oysters are fresh-packed in jars, metal containers or waxed cartons with see-through lids. Properly refrigerated, they will remain edible for a maximum of 5 days. They are sold by the pint and quart.

3. Canned, meaning oysters that have been shucked and packed under highly sanitary conditions. Gulf and Atlantic Coast canners pack theirs in 7½-ounce drained-weight containers. Drained weight of Pacific Coast cans is either 5 or 8 ounces.

4. Frozen oysters are among the latest additions to the seafood marketplace. First they're shucked, then they're culled so that the pack includes only the best, then they're quick-frozen in their own juices. At this writing, the pack sizes are measured in ounces. Store in the frozen food compartment of your refrigerator for a maximum of 1 week; in the freezer for 1 month.

Canned and frozen oysters R always in season, so you need not be bothered by any old witches' tale when it comes to eating them and enjoying them every month of the year.

HOW MUCH TO BUY FOR SIX SERVINGS

Shell oysters: 3 dozen.
Shucked oysters: 1 quart.
Canned oysters: 2 7½- or 8-ounce cans.
Frozen oysters: 16 ounces.

HOW TO CLEAN OYSTERS

Unlike the clam, the oyster already has been given a stringently enforced interior cleaning before going to market and it has had no opportunity to pick up any dirt or contamination before being sold to you. Not, at least, if the market where you bought it is as spotlessly sanitary as health laws say it must be; if not, you'd better get out of there in a hurry and shop somewhere else.

So all the cleaning you need give most shell oysters that you buy is to hold them under cold running water and rub-rinse the shell with a cloth.

HOW TO SHUCK OYSTERS

It's more difficult to open an oyster than it is a clam, although the principle is the same. So, in addition to the clam knife, you'll need a hammer. Yes, a hammer. Thus armed do this:

Use a hammer to chip an oyster's bill if you have to.

Insert knife in opening left by hammer.

Cut the rim muscle that holds oyster to shells.

Finally, cut the adductor muscle free of shell.

- Place the oyster on a hard, flat surface, flat shell up.
- Take the hammer in one hand, hold the oyster down with the other and chip off the thin end of the shells, called the "bill."
- Now insert the knife between the shells and run it around the perimeter, twisting as you do to separate them.
- Now cut the large adductor muscle that holds the oyster to the flat upper shell and thus remove the shell.
- Cut the lower end of the same muscle that holds it to the deeper bottom shell.
- If the oyster is to be served on the half shell, leave it in place in the

deep shell. If to be used otherwise, slide the oyster from the shell to a container along with the liquid.

Two footnotes:

The guy or gal who thinks he's good enough has our permission to do without the hammer. Just try inserting the knife between the shells without first chipping off the bill. The professionals don't need hammers; maybe you won't either.

The guy or gal who can't open an oyster even with the help of a hammer could try one of those commercial openers that are allegedly supposed to make the job easy for you. Or you might place the oysters on a rack over a bit of water and heat just until the steam opens the shells wide enough for you to apply the knife. But not a moment longer. Or try quick-freezing them as we told you to do with clams in order to easily open.

A WORD ABOUT COOKING OYSTERS

Oysters have a naturally fine flavor that is lessened by cooking. The longer you cook them, the tougher they will become, the less tasty they will be.

Never cook them longer than just enough to heat them through. Cooking until the edges start to curl is a good way to tell when an oyster should be cooked no more.

Many oyster recipes call for cooking oysters in their liquor, which is rather thick and viscous. You may find it easier to follow these instructions if you first thin the liquor with an equal amount of water. This will also make it easier to incorporate the liquor into any sauce you may be making, and it will reduce its acid content.

CRABS

Thanks to modern marketing and processing methods, crabs are available everywhere in the United States. And a good thing it is, too, because this sometimes overlooked delicacy is rich in proteins, vitamins and minerals. What's more, crab meat need not be expensive to use. A can of it, yes, will cost more than a can of tuna fish or salmon. But the per-serving cost brings the price way down, especially when you consider the epicurean possibilities that crab meat offers. On that score we recommend to you very highly the Chinese recipes that appear in this book, just as they first appeared in *The Hong Kong Cookbook,* which Dan wrote with Arthur Lem, particularly one called Hai Yook Par Sun Goo, which, translated into words that you can pronounce, broadly means "Crab Meat White Cloud with Mushrooms." It's on page 256. And Hai Yook Par Choy Far, which means "King Crab Meat over Cauliflower," on page 213.

Four species of crab are to be found in the American marketplace:

• Rock crabs, in stores closest to the California and New England coasts.

• Dungeness crabs, in all of the West from Mexico to Alaska.

• Blue (also called "hard") crabs in retail outlets handiest to the Atlantic and Gulf Coasts.

• Last, but by no means least, the famous Alaskan king crab, which is available frozen and canned everywhere but fresh only adjacent to its home waters.

• Additionally there are some purely regional crabs, for example, Florida's so-called stone species and New England's Jonah crab.

• Then, too, there are soft-shell crabs. All crabs have life cycles that, for the purposes of this cookbook, can be differentiated by whether their shells are hard or soft. They all have both at different times in their lives. Laws in states where dungeness crabs are harvested prohibit them from being caught or sold when in their soft-shell state. Rock crabs, because of their smaller size, are not too profitable for mass marketing purposes when in their soft-shell cycle.

Therefore the main soft-shell crab to be found in the legal American marketplace is the "blue crab," at a stage in its life when it has shed its hard shell and has not yet developed its replacement armor.

Hard crabs are sold live mainly within fairly short distances of their feeding grounds, but soft crabs are packed and iced with special care and shipped hundreds of miles inland.

THE MARKET FORMS

• Live. No matter what the species, all crabs should show definite leg movement when purchased alive. But don't expect to buy a live Alaska king crab because their leg span may be anywhere from 6 to 11 feet. Imagine trying to carry one of those critters home, live, from the market.

• Cooked whole. This is a crab that's been cooked whole and still in the shell. The shell should be bright red and there should be no disagreeable odor. You can give them the sniff test by lifting the lid of the underbody section. If the smell is strong, not only don't buy it, but don't buy any at that market.

Cooked crab meat comes in a variety of forms, depending upon the species of crab from which the meat is taken.

BLUE CRABS

• Lump meat, meaning solid lumps of white meat from the body of the crab. Lump meat is excellent for recipes where visual appeal is important, for example, cocktails and salads. It is usually sold either canned or frozen; however, some specialty fish markets cook their own and sell it by the ounce or pound.

· Flake meat, meaning small pieces of white meat that were missed when the lump was removed. Canned is the main market form in which it is sold. When using, be sure to remove any bits of shell or cartilage that may have sneaked into the pack.

· Lump and flake meat. A combination of the above.

· Claw meat is meat that's been picked from the claws of the cooked crab. It has a brownish hue and therefore is lower priced and is most used in recipes where appearance is secondary, or with sauces.

DUNGENESS CRABS

There is no distinction with this westerner as to where or in what form the cooked meat comes. It is equally delicious whether it comes from claw or body, it all has a pinkish tinge and it is all packed as one grade. Markets sell the meat either in cans, frozen or fresh-cooked.

KING CRABS

The prime meat of the king crab comes from its legs, claws and shoulders and that is therefore the meat that is most popular in the retail marketplace. There you'll find it fresh-frozen in various lengths of still-in-shell cooked claw or leg pieces. It also is canned in 5-, 6½- and 13-ounce containers.

ROCK CRABS

All of it brownish in color, the meat is picked from both the body and the claws and is marketed as one grade.

HOW MUCH TO BUY FOR SIX SERVINGS

Blue crabs:
  Live: 18 to 36 crabs.
  Cooked and still in shell: 18 to 36 crabs.
  Cooked meat: 1 pound.
Dungeness crabs:
  Live: 3 to 6 crabs.
  Cooked and still in shell: 3 to 6 crabs.
  Cooked meat: 1 pound.
King crabs:
  Cooked meat: 1 pound.
  Frozen claw or leg section: enough more than a pound to allow for shell-weight loss.

Rock crabs:

Live: 24 to 48 crabs.
Cooked and still in shell: 24 to 48 crabs.
Cooked meat: 1 pound.

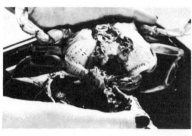

Remove the top shell after cooking hard-shell crab like this.

Scrape away the gills with a paring knife.

These are digestive organs, this is how to remove them. Be sure you do.

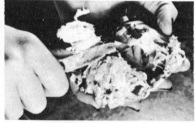

Slice off top of right side to get at meat in pockets.

HOW TO CLEAN HARD-SHELL BLUE CRABS

All such crabs should be cooked before they're cleaned, a simple procedure: fill a pot with water, add salt and bring to a fast boil; slide the crabs into the water headfirst, cover, bring back to a boil for 5 minutes; simmer for another 15 minutes; remove crabs from pot, douse in cold water to halt the cooking process and so that they're cool enough to handle, and get on with the cleaning chore:

· Snap off the tail.
· Hold the crab body with your left hand, keeping the large claws to the right, and snap them off. That's if you're right-handed; if you're a southpaw, hold with your right, snap with your left.
· Place your thumb under the top shell midpoint in the back edge, yank up and thus remove it. Save the shell for use as a dish.
· Break off the legs. If you can't break them off, cut them off.

• Using a paring knife, scrape away the gills and either cut away or wash away the digestive and other organs located in the center of the body.

• Starting near the front, slice away the top of the right side of the inner skeleton and remove all meat from the slice.

• Starting at the right back fin pocket, cut away the meat from the lower part with a **U**-shaped motion of the knife.

• Remove the meat from the remaining pockets by inserting the knife blade underneath and prying upward.

• Slice the top from the left side of the inner skeleton and remove the meat in the same way you did the right.

• Be sure to discard all material that clings to the upper shell, and to yank out the orange waxy matter and spongy white substance between the halves of the body at each side.

Now the claws:

• Crack each claw either with a nutcracker or by placing it on a hard surface and smacking the shell smartly with the knife handle. If that doesn't do it, try a hammer.

• The meat now will be exposed. Grip it with the fingers of one hand and pull out the tendon with your other hand. If that doesn't do it, try prying the meat out with the knife tip or a nut pick.

HOW TO CLEAN SOFT-SHELL CRABS

Use scissors to cut away the face of a soft-shell crab.

Use fingers to remove the apron, gills, stomach and intestines.

If you've purchased your soft-shell crabs, you can skip this, because markets clean them and prepare them for cooking. But if you've caught your own, read on.

• First kill by stabbing between the eyes with a sharp knife.

• Snipping at a point just back of the eyes, cut away the face.

• With a pair of scissors, cut away the apronlike segment that folds under the body at its hind end.

· Lift each point at the sides with your fingers.

· Remove the spongy parts—meaning the gills, stomach and intestines—located under the points of the body covering. You need not remove the new outer shell because it will be paper thin.

· Wash thoroughly in cold salted water.

· Pat dry on absorbent paper or lintfree towels.

HOW TO CLEAN DUNGENESS CRABS

In the Pacific Northwest, where they know good seafood when they taste it, there are two dungeness-crab cleaning schools. Folks who buy their crabs mainly insist that they be cleaned and then cooked.

The Cooperative Extension Service at Oregon State University at Corvallis, which deals primarily with consumer affairs, gives these instructions for cleaning crab cooked in the shell:

Crab cooked in the shell is more economical to buy . . . and should not be overlooked by the purchaser because of lack of know-how in handling it. The butcher or fish dealer may clean and crack the crab as a customer service. If not, it can be done easily by the buyer.

Hold the underside of the crab with one hand, place the thumb under the shell at midpoint of the back edge and pull off the back. Let water run over the crab as you clean all excess waste away. Run the thumb around the body, removing the leaflike gills. Leave only the body meat enclosed in the shell and the legs. Break the body lengthwise into two pieces and separate the legs, keeping a segment of the body attached to the legs.

With a small hammer or mallet, crack the legs and the back so that the meat can be readily removed. The sharp point of the walking legs is a perfect tool for removing the crab meat, or you can use nut picks to remove the meat from the shell.

You may want to save the crab shells to use as baking and serving dishes for various crab recipes. To prepare crab shells, select large, perfect ones, scrub with a brush or soapless metal-sponge pot scrubber until clean. Place in a large kettle with enough water to cover, and add one teaspoon of baking soda. Cover kettle closely and boil for about 10 minutes. Drain, wash and dry the shells.

The Department of Fisheries and Wildlife, also at Oregon State University, which is concerned, among other things, with recreational affairs, has this advice for folks who catch their own (or buy) live crab:

Freshly caught crabs are most easily and quickly cleaned if this is done before they are cooked. The cleaning procedure takes less than thirty seconds per crab.

Cleaning prior to cooking eliminates visceral taste, facilitates salt penetration in the body meat and increases the keeping qualities of the crab meat. The procedure is as follows:

1. Remove the carapace or back of the crab by forcing edge of the shell against any solid object [authors' note: such as the edge of a table].

2. Break crab in two by folding it back like a book—first up and then down.

3. Shake out viscera [authors' note: internal organs] from each half.

4. Shake off gill filaments. Nothing remains but shell and edible meat.

Crabs should be cooked as soon as practical after cleaning. Add about three to five ounces of salt per gallon of fresh water, or two ounces of salt per gallon of salt water. Bring the salty water to a boil, drop crabs in and time for twelve to fifteen minutes after the water again starts boiling. Remove crabs from water and immediately immerse them or spray them with cold water until cool. This stops the cooking process, prevents drying and shrinkage of the meat and tends to prevent meat from adhering to the shell.

CRAB CARE AND STORAGE

No matter what the species may be, these recommendations apply:

· If you purchase live crabs, cook them the moment you get home.

· If you net your own crabs, you should keep them for no more than a day in the refrigerator. Some people may argue that live crabs you've caught yourself can be kept much longer. But we obviously disagree, if for no other reason than that it's better to be safe than sorry.

· Store-bought cooked crab meat, properly packaged, should be kept in a 32-degree Fahrenheit refrigerator no longer than 2 or 3 days.

· Home-cooked crab meat can be kept for several days if stored in covered containers at 32 degrees.

· If you purchase frozen crab meat, keep it no longer than a month in a freezer, no longer than a week in a refrigerator's freezer compartment —in either case, still in its original package.

CRAB COOKING VERSATILITY

All crab meat must be cooked before it is eaten, a pleasant chore since the ways in which it can be prepared are seemingly endless: canapés, cocktails, cakes, soups, bisques, chowders, oven-fried, pan-fried and deep-fried, broiled, scrambled with eggs, stuffed into tomatoes, avocados, squash and such, barbecued, burgers, boiled, steamed, in soufflés and salads, baked, and with many sauces.

As with all seafood, the trick is not to overcook.

Since Alaskan king crab legs have been precooked, all they need is reheating:

· Defrost each piece completely if time permits but at least until shell can be cut easily.

· Split shell lengthwise.

· Brush exposed meat generously with butter or margarine.

· Place on cookie sheet or in baking pan.

· Heat in 350- to 400-degree Fahrenheit oven for 5 to 10 minutes or until heated through.

· Serve with melted lemon butter for dipping. And enjoy a delicacy that rates on a par with lobster.

LOBSTERS

We don't know which, of all the fish in the sea, ought to be called "king." But this we do know, of all the shellfish the lobster has to reign supreme.

We could tell you why, in a few thousand well-chosen words, but suffice it to say that, though it may be prepared in every conceivably possible way and though it lends itself beautifully to scores of gastronomical combinations, lobster is so naturally delicious that our favorite way of cooking and eating it is simply to steam it and dip each juicy morsel in nothing more than melted butter spiked with a bit of lemon juice.

So, with the preliminaries thus out of the way, let's proceed to the nitty gritty of lobster lore.

Two species are native to American waters, northern lobsters and rock lobsters, the latter a species that may be known either as spiny lobster or crayfish where you live.

The northern has two large, heavy claws in front of his head and, in comparison with the rock lobster, a narrow tail. Its choicest meat comes from the claws.

The rock, in place of the claws, has two long, slender appendages that the trade calls "antennae," its body and legs are pocked with lumps that give it its "spiny" nickname and its choicest meat comes from its broad tail. Those wonderful frozen lobster tails that you'll find in your supermarket's frozen-food section come from the rock lobster.

The northern is caught from Labrador to North Carolina, with the bulk of the harvest coming from Maine and Massachusetts waters. Modern methods of handling, packing and transportation make it easily accessible, still very much alive, in every state of the union. When taken from the water, its shell is a dark bluish green.

The rock lobster ranges through most of the world's tropical, subtropical and temperate waters. In the United States it is found most in Florida and Southern California waters and therefore, together with those that come from the Caribbean and the west coast of Mexico, is the species most likely to be available live in fish markets in our Southern states. The tails of Florida and Caribbean lobsters have a smooth shell and large yellow or white spots on the first segment, and the color generally is brownish green. Pacific lobster tails have smooth shells, lack spots and stripes, and vary in color from dark red to orange and brown.

Frozen rock-lobster tails marketed in the United States come from several widely separated countries, chief among them, Australia, Brazil,

Denmark, New Zealand and South Africa. They have a wide variety of markings and colors and the thickness of their under shells may vary, but they all taste delicious. Ask the man who's had one.

When any lobster, no matter what the species or the waters from which it comes, is purchased alive, its legs should be moving and its tail should curl under the body when it is picked up. Make sure it has those traits right up to cooking time.

A tasty relative of the lobster is the freshwater crawfish (alias craw-dad, crayfish, freshwater crab and freshwater lobster), which can be found the country over in lakes, streams, farm ponds and even drainage ditches. The place to look for them is in water from a few inches to a foot or two deep. Or you can fish for them, much as you would for crabs, at greater depths. They're usually grayish green, from 3 to 6 or 7 inches long and they're mostly all tail.

THE MARKET FORMS

Live lobsters. They're sold in four sizes, each with an identifying name:
- Chicken: ¾ of a pound to a pound.
- Quarters: 1¼ pounds.
- Large: 1½ to 2¼ pounds.
- Jumbo: over 2½ pounds.

The less they weigh, the younger they are and the more tender the meat will be. Therefore stick to the chickens and the quarters if you're going to bake, broil, boil or steam them and eat them with nothing more than melted butter and lemon juice as an additional flavoring agent. Use the large and jumbo sizes for salads and when cooking with sauces and such. However, there are some people who insist that large lobsters are just as tender as the small and, in fact, prefer them. So, if only large lobster is available, don't hesitate to buy it for whatever purpose.

Cooked in shell. Many markets sell them this way. The shell should be a bright "lobster" red, they should have a seaside smell and the tail should spring back to a curl when straightened out; the last is your evidence that the lobster was alive right up to the time of cooking.

Cooked meat. Picked from the shell immediately after cooking, this choice eating is available either fresh, by the ounce or pound, fresh-canned and frozen-canned. Can sizes are about 3 ounces, 6, 14 and 16 ounces. Cooked meat should be reddish-white or pinkish-white and, in either case, firm.

Frozen lobster tails. Cut from the rest of the lobster, usually after it has had a chance to mature and has spawned at least once, they're quickly frozen and packaged while still raw in their shell and shipped to the United

States for marketing. There are no U.S. government standards to regulate their size, packaging and labeling and so the consumer is flying blind when shopping for them.

Some facts that will confuse the buyer:

· Market weights of each frozen tail should vary from ¼ pound to 1 pound or more since a lobster to have spawned at least once should have a tail that weighs at least 4 ounces.

· Packers with scruples pack 2 of the smaller tails together, or 1 of the larger tails split in half, and so the package should weigh from 8 ounces to about 2 pounds.

· Most packers, whether with or without scruples, use cartons which cannot be seen through. Nor do the labels say how many tails are enclosed.

Unscrupulous packagers take advantage of these factors to victimize the trusting American consumer who walks into a supermarket, buys a box of tails thinking it contains dinner for 2 people, gets home, opens the box and discovers that it does not contain 2 serving-size tails. Instead, it contains 3 small tails which cannot be divided into 2 satisfying servings. Even worse, so small that the 3 lobsters from which they came hadn't had a chance to give birth even once in their lives, thus signaling a situation that, if permitted to continue, eventually could result in extinction of a species.

On a recent shopping trip, we visited 3 markets in our town and found that all of them carried only these deceptively packaged, undersized tails. And this we are ashamed to say, all of them were packed in South Africa by two well-known American frozen-seafood companies.

However, on the bright side of the coin, we visited Fiore Brothers, in Freeport, Long Island, the finest fish market we've ever seen, and the only tails in stock there were frozen in individual see-through wrappers. And they came from Brazil, not South Africa. Packaged so that Ralph, Charlie and Vinnie Fiore's customers can see what they're buying.

If you do not have a Fiore Brothers-type market near you, then you'd better pay heed to that meaningful bromide: Let the buyer beware.

HOW MUCH TO BUY FOR SIX NORMAL SERVINGS

Live: 1 chicken or one quarter lobster per person if to be served whole; 3 either large or jumbo lobsters if to be served halved; 4 to 6 pounds total weight of any size lobsters if to be shelled and the meat used in other ways.

Cooked in shell: The same as above. To have ½ pound of cooked meat, you'll need 2 1-pound lobsters.

Cooked meat: 12 to 16 ounces, depending upon how it is to be prepared; 8 ounces will skimp you through canapés.

Frozen tails: 5 to 8 ounces each including shell weight, per person.

PROPER CARE AND STORAGE

Live: Although they'll stay alive and keep 2 or 3 days if stored in a refrigerator vegetable crisper on a bed of seaweed, it's best to cook them the moment you get home.

Cooked in shell at point of purchase: 2 or 3 days in refrigerator at 32 degrees.

Cooked meat: about 4 days in covered refrigerator container and, of course, in refrigerator.

Frozen: 1 month in freezer, 1 week in freezer compartment.

Canned: 1 year.

HOW TO TRANSPORT LIVE LOBSTERS

As we told you earlier, lobstermen now ship their catch, alive and kicking, just about everywhere in the country, including to your house. All you need do is order them and pay the price.

Or, if you have an air-traveling man in your family and if his travels take him to coastal areas where live lobsters are sold, let him do what a Bozeman, Montana, friend of ours does. He is Norman Strung, a hunting and fishing guide and an outdoor writer with whom Dan wrote two books (*The Fisherman's Almanac* and *Family Fun On and Around the Water*).

The parents of both Norman and his wife, Priscilla, live on Long Island and every time they come East for a visit Norman and Sil take live lobsters back to Montana with them for feasts that by now must have half of Bozeman counting the days until the next time. We asked Norman how he does it and this is the letter we received in reply:

Lobsters must be packed in a crush-proof box marked "right side up." The boxes must have airholes. Pack them on top of other heavy stuff, if anything else is to be packed with them. Clams, for instance. And ersatz ice that goes directly below them. Never use real ice because fresh water kills most sea creatures. We use that frozen jelly stuff. The lobsters must be packed in fresh seaweed, both for moisture and for cushioning.

Be sure to buy as fresh a lobster as you can find. We always fly home on Tuesday because they arrive in Long Island markets on Monday evening.

If we don't want to dine right away and even though we know that the live ones will keep for several days, it's always best to boil them or steam them as quick as we can. Cooked meat keeps longer than uncooked.

Sorry for the hurry in this letter, but I just got back from a hundred-mile, seven-day float down the Middle Fork of the Salmon River. Quite a trip. Quite a wilderness area.

We threw that last paragraph in just to make you drool a bit. And we don't mean for lobster. If you ever want to go float-fishing with Norman, just write to him in care of High Country, Bozeman, Montana 59715.

This is how to administer coup de grace to an uncooked lobster.

To split, cut lengthwise and slice through soft undershell.

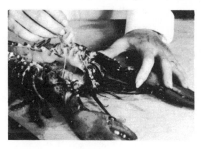

Now lift out innards like this. But save that tasty tomalley!

Next step is to crack claw shells with a nutcracker or hammer.

The uncooked lobster is now ready for oven garnishment.

HOW TO CLEAN AND SERVE LOBSTERS

The cleaning method pretty much depends upon on how you intend to serve them. If you plan to bake, stuff or broil your lobsters, you must clean them before you cook them. If you plan to steam or boil them, the cleaning comes after the cooking, with two choices open to you: the conventional way and the Maine way.

Before cooking:

· Kill the lobster by laying it on its hard-shell back, inserting a knife tip between the head and the body and slicing through the spinal cord.

· Split lengthwise by slicing through the soft bottom shell but taking care not to cut through the hard upper shell unless you plan to serve the 2 halves separately.

· Fold the body out and remove the stomach and intestinal vein, which then will be visible. The stomach (the small sac between the eyes and just back of the head) will lift out easily. If the vein doesn't come out with the tummy, lift it out with a fork, nut pick or toothpick. (Be sure not to discard the green liver and red roe, no matter how unappetizing they may look to you. Called the "tomalley," they're considered possibly the greatest lobster delicacy of all when cooked; what's more, that's where most of the lobster's many health-giving assets are stored.)

· Crack the large claws with a nutcracker or hammer.

· The lobster is now ready for baking, stuffing, broiling.

· When cooked, serve immediately just as it comes from the stove.

The conventional way:

· Boil or steam your lobster (instructions on pages 66–67).

· Lay it on its back and split the body in half lengthwise by slicing through the soft bottom shell. Do not sever the hard upper shell if you do not plan to serve the 2 halves separately. If too hot to handle, use something to protect your hands; do not let the lobster cool.

· Remove the stomach and whatever is left of the vein. And, remember, be sure to save the tomalley and the roe.

· Your lobster is now ready to serve.

The Maine way:

· Steam your lobster (see page 66). Dedicated Down East lobstermen seldom, if ever, boil theirs and we agree with them that lobster tastes so much better cooked above the water than in the water. When cooked, hold them vertically above the pot until water that accumulated inside shell drains out.

· Using something to protect your hands from the heat, twist off the large claws at the point where they join the body.

· Crack each claw with nutcracker or hammer.

· Take the tail in one hand, the body in the other and bend them in toward each other until they separate.

· Snap the flippers free from the tail.

· Hold the tail flat, poke fork tines into the hole left by the flippers and push. The meat will slide out in one chunk.

· Take the body in one hand, insert the thumb of your other hand between the meat and the hind end of the shell and lift up. This step will leave the eating part of the lobster in one hand, the shell, head and stomach in the other. But don't discard the shell just yet because still in it

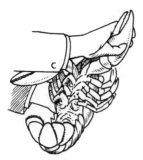

1. Twist off the claws.

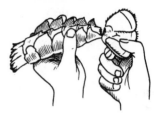

2. Crack each claw with a nutcracker, pliers, knife, hammer, rock, or what-have-you.

3. Separate the tail-piece from the body by arching the back until it cracks.

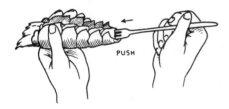

4. Bend back and break the flippers off the tail-piece.

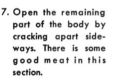

PUSH

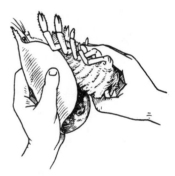

5. Insert a fork where the flippers broke off and push.

6. Unhinge the back from the body. Don't forget that this contains the "tomalley," or liver, of the lobster, which turns green when it is cooked and which many persons consider the best eating of all.

7. Open the remaining part of the body by cracking apart sideways. There is some good meat in this section.

8. The small claws are excellent eating and may be placed in the mouth and the meat sucked out like sipping cider with a straw.

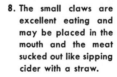

The 8 Easy Steps for Cleaning a Cooked Lobster the Maine Way. (The Maine Department of Sea and Shore Fisheries)

will be the creamy tomalley. Spoon it out; then do what you will with the shell. (One good thing to do with the shell, after removing the head and stomach, is to use it for making sauces.)

· Hold the body meat lengthwise in your two hands and fold it back like a book and, lo, open to view will be many choice morsels that you might otherwise miss. Most of them will be too small for eating with a table fork, but cocktail forks, nut picks and fingers are ideal for separating them from their cartilage-encased nooks.

· Additional morsels are tucked away inside the small claws. The best way to enjoy them is to suck on one end of the claw as though it were a straw.

Lobster tails:

· Transfer from freezer to refrigerator, removing package as soon as able, and let stand until thawed, or for at least 4 hours for a 6-ounce tail.

· Either split or remove the softer under shell; sometimes it is a matter of preference, sometimes it may be too hard to split but not to remove. To split, insert a knife blade between under shell and thawed meat and slice backward toward the tail. To remove, use knife in same manner but instead of slicing down the center, slice around the edges where the under and upper shells meet; the former is soft enough to cut at that point.

· Tail is now ready to cook according to recipe instructions.

THE BASICS OF LOBSTER COOKERY

To steam live lobster: This, as we said at the start of this section, we think is the tastiest possible way to cook lobster, unadorned by any garnishments whatever, yet to us truly fine epicurean eating. Here's how to do it:

· Put no more than 1 inch of water in a deep pot, one that has a tight-fitting lid, a steamer, or, if you have neither, a pretzel can with a tight-fitting lid in which you've poked some vent holes with an ice pick.

· Add a pinch of salt.

Place a wire rack, one with V-shaped legs that will keep it above the water, in the pot, steamer or can. If you don't have a rack with legs, 4 spring-type wooden clothespins make very good limbs.

· Place the lobster, or lobsters, on the rack. You can do this without being nipped by picking them up by the back of the head, just behind the large claws. Or you can kill them (see page 64).

· Cover tightly, turn on the heat and have yourself a beer, meantime watching so that you'll know when steam starts to come through the vents.

· When the steam starts gushing heavily, steadily, check the clock and start timing for 20 minutes—no more, no less for lobsters weighing 1 to 1½ pounds. Add an additional 5 minutes for each additional pound of lobster.

· Uncover the container and your lobster will be a bright lobster red. If by some chance it isn't, replace the lid and steam until it is.

· Take the lobster out of the container, holding it on end so that any steam that has condensed inside the shell will drain back into the broth.

· Dissect the Maine way and serve with melted butter or margarine to which lemon juice has been added—or if you prefer, with lemon wedges on the side.

· Offer broth to those who want it, and those who don't should have their heads examined.

To boil (simmer) a live lobster:

· Add enough water to pot to cover your lobster, or lobsters, along with a tablespoon of salt for each quart.

· When water comes to a rapid boil, plunge each lobster into it head-first, picking them up by the back of the head, just behind the large claws. Or kill them first (see page 64).

· Cover pot, return to a boil and then simmer 12 minutes for the first pound and 1 minute for each additional ¼ pound.

· The shell then should be a bright lobster red. Immediately remove the lobster from the cooking pot, drain, clean and serve either the conventional way or the Maine way.

About the broiling of whole lobster and lobster tail: As we've said, the best possible way to cook a lobster is to steam it.

Still, there is something good to say about broiling. If done properly, it does give lobster a different touch: a nice glaze, a nice surface, a highly attractive browning, shell edges a bit of a crunch.

What is proper? We refer you to these 4 recipes: Lobster au Jus (page 232), Priscilla Strung's Broiled Lobster (page 232), Lobster Tail Kreidell (page 233) and Lobster Tail Fiore (page 233).

Now with all of those cautionary preliminaries behind us, and because so many Americans think that broiled lobster is a way of life, here's how to broil one if broil you must:

· Kill, split and clean as described on page 64.

· Lay lobster on broiler rack, shell side down, and spread as flat open as possible.

· Brush with oil, melted butter or melted margarine. Sprinkle with pepper, paprika and/or garlic powder if you desire. Let the person who is going to eat it add salt if he is silly enough to want to.

· Set rack in place so that lobster is about 4 inches from source of broiler heat and broil until meat becomes a light opaque brown and the shell a bright red. This should take from 8 to 12 minutes, but don't hesitate to open the broiler door and keep looking.

We will have a lot more to say on the "broiling" of lobster in the recipe section.

Mussels

We live, as we all know, in the most advanced nation on the face of the earth. So much so that we don't deign to do many things that people of other lands have done for centuries, including eating mussels.

In the United States about the only people who enjoy their delicate flavor and reap the benefits of their health-giving qualities are those who forage their own among the seaside rocks and piers and jetties and such to which the mussels cling. Only those Americans know the wonder of mussel-eating, they and a comparative handful of their fellow citizens whose roots are still close to their Old World origins. Americans, for instance, whose families came from Italy, where mussel cooking and eating is so much a way of life that mussels are cultivated strictly for sale in the consumer marketplaces of just about every village and town.

It was our good friend Don Bevona, food writer and author of *The Love Apple Cookbook* (a love apple is a tomato), who first introduced us to the taste of mussels. Before that, Dan had gathered them but used them strictly as bait. But once Don had given us our first taste and told us that mussels could be purchased just about everywhere that the clientele is mainly foreign, we became mussel aficionados and have remained such ever since.

At Don's suggestion, we did some basic research and this is what we found in a U.S. Department of the Interior booklet entitled *Food from the Sea,* which, incidentally, was written by Rachel Carson, who, in her book *Silent Spring,* tried to warn us of what we were doing to our environment but we wouldn't listen:

Another virtually untapped shellfish resource is the common sea mussel which lines hundreds of miles of the Atlantic coast with its small black shells. Except for the few gathered locally by people who appreciate its delicate flavor, the mussel beds are almost wholly neglected. In Europe, by contrast, the demand for mussels is so great that for many years propagation has been practiced extensively to augment the natural supply.

Like most other shellfish, sea mussels are rich in minerals, vitamins and proteins. They are among the most digestible of foods, for the human body is able to use practically all of the nutriment contained in their meats and liquor. Because their shells are thinner, a bushel of mussels contains considerably more food than a bushel of oysters.

That should convince you. If it doesn't, come around and we'll introduce you to Don, and his wife, Donna, who can cook like crazy, and their daughters Catharine and Caroline, who was born on Christmas Day 1970.

Food from the Sea did not say so, since it concerned itself only with New England fin fish and shellfish, but mussels are to be found in their wild state on just about all of our seacoasts.

Don't, however, after reading what we've said about the goodness of mussels, rush right out to gather your own. In some areas—along the Pacific coast, for instance—they sometimes contain a highly toxic matter and at those times should not be eaten by humans. First check with local people—fish dealers, conservation officials, bay constables, fish and game wardens and such—to learn if mussels in their waters are safe to eat. Additionally, a permit to harvest shellfish is sometimes required.

Mussels that reach the marketplace generally are gathered by shell fishermen who know their business, as well as their gathering grounds. Therefore, we suggest that you buy your mussels rather than gather your own, at least until you learn a great deal about them.

As for folks who live far inland, all we can suggest is to head for the sea for the next vacation, find a nice Italian or Greek or Spanish or sometimes even a French restaurant for a taste treat. Or, better still, rent a cottage with kitchen and try one of the recipes in this book. If you don't find a mussel recipe that strikes your fancy, pick one for oysters or clams and use mussels instead. The taste of all three is somewhat similar. They all cook very quickly and none has more than a 6-percent fat content.

While the outer shell of the mussel is drab, its rainbow-hued inner lining is almost as lovely as that of the abalone. Although more fragile, it can sometimes be used as a serving dish in the same manner as the clam or scallop shell. See page 46 for cleaning directions.

We find that mussels make an exceptionally good spaghetti sauce and highly recommend Don Bevona's Mussels Neapolitan Style, which you'll find on page 305, just as we found it in *The Love Apple Cookbook*.

THE MARKET FORMS

· Alive and in the shell: you can tell if they're still with us the same way as you do clams and oysters—if there is a gap between the shells, it should close tightly the moment you touch the mussel. They are sold by the pound.

· Canned: either smoked or in a hot barbecue sauce, the can weight is about 5 ounces.

Mussels are very perishable and we recommend that you cook and eat them on the day of purchase.

HOW MUCH TO BUY FOR SIX NORMAL SERVINGS

· Live: 5 pounds; if they're the choicest jumbo size, this will mean about 6 mussels per serving.

· Canned: 1 can will do as an appetizer or if added to a recipe.

HOW TO CLEAN AND OPEN MUSSELS

· Scrub them well with a stiff brush while holding them under cold running water to remove both any mud on the outer shell and most if not all of the beardlike appendages that stem from the meat inside.

· Place in pot, cover with cold tap water and let stand for 2 hours. The live mussels will head for the bottom. The dead ones will float to the surface. Discard them.

There are two ways of opening mussels, with a knife or with steam.

With a knife:

· Place pan on table to catch liquid, which you'll want to save for a sauce.

· Hold scrubbed mussel over pan, insert knife tip between shells in the bearded area and run the blade around the edge, working first toward the broad end. No skill is necessary because the shells are so thin.

· Remove meat from shells, trim away any whiskers that may remain and place meat in separate dish from liquid.

· Strain liquid through double thickness of cheesecloth or through a clean piece of linen to remove any sand or shell particles that may remain.

To steam open: actually, it is not steam but simmering water that does the job.

· Add just enough water to a pot to cover mussels, add salt and bring to a boil.

· Slide cleaned mussels gently into water, cover pot and let water simmer for 3 minutes, or less if mussels open sooner.

· Remove opened mussels carefully from pot so as not to lose any liquid inside shells. Let stand just until shells are cool enough to handle.

· Pour liquid from shells through double thickness of cheesecloth or piece of linen to strain out sand and possible shell particles and save for sauce.

· Remove mussels from shells; trim away remaining whiskers, if any. Pop one in your mouth while it's nice and warm. If it's not done enough for your liking, return to strained, reheated broth and simmer for 1 to 3 minutes, depending on size.

SCALLOPS

One of the most beautiful seashells known to man also houses one of his tastiest and healthiest seafoods, a true delicacy in every possible respect—the scallop. The shell, a work of art. The meat, a gastronomical delight.

Botticelli and Titian painted Venus with a scallop shell. The buildings of ancient Pompeii had scallop-shell adornments in their design. During the Crusades scallop shells were the symbol of holy pilgrimages. In fact, one European variety to this day is known as either "the pilgrim" or "St. James" shell. And thus came the name "Coquilles Saint-Jacques," Mollusks of St. James, for a saucy French creation that unfortunately has become a symbol of social snobbishness.

The shape of the scallop shell brought the phrase "scalloped edges" into the needleworkers' trade. That tasty dish, scalloped potatoes, is nothing more than sauced-up spuds baked today in a casserole but in years gone by in scallop shells. So, too, scalloped oysters.

As for Coquilles St. Jacques, that truly epicurean dish if prepared properly: in today's usage, those words mean simply scallops in the shell. You'll find the recipe on page 237.

The scallop is a delicacy that lends itself ideally to many fine cooking methods. Yet far too many restaurants, eager for the quickest and easiest possible buck, have brainwashed too many Americans into thinking that the only way to cook them is to fry them.

As for the frozen-food industry, of late it's been flooding the nation with heat-and-serve breaded scallops, and other spiced-up concoctions. We hate to knock industry, because it's done so much for America, but we do think that some segments of it should be taken to task, to put it mildly, for what they are doing to the nation's health and, in this instance, eating habits.

Speaking of health, scallops contain high levels of well-balanced protein and many of the essential minerals and vitamins. Sodium content is low, thus making scallops ideal in salt-free diets.

Like clams, oysters and mussels, scallops are two-shelled creatures of the sea. But, unlike them, scallops are not sedentary. In fact, they go scooting around the ocean floor by a peculiar means of locomotion that is easiest described by that post–1950 term: jet-propelled.

Between the two shells are sandwiched meat, roe and a muscle somewhat akin to the clam's and oyster's adductor muscle, which is also called the "eye." In Europe the meat and the roe are highly regarded, but, for some peculiar reason that is beyond our comprehension, in the United States only the eye is eaten.

Four species are native to American waters:

· Atlantic sea scallop: they're dredged in deep waters of the Middle and North Atlantic coasts, with the bulk of the harvest being reaped by boats out of the old whaling port of New Bedford, Massachusetts. The shells may grow to as much as 8 inches in diameter, with the meat inside in proportion, but only the 1- to 2-inch adductor muscle will go to market. As for the oh-so-good meat, it ends up as cat and dog food and bait and fertilizer, probably not bringing as much revenue as the shells, which are sold the country over for use as ramekins, baking dishes, candy dishes, ashtrays, wall ornaments and such.

· Pacific sea scallop: it's a different mollusk from the Atlantic variety, but it will hold its own on anyone's table. Deep water from Oregon to Alaska is its habitat.

· Bay scallop: this fellow, whose eye is no more than about ½ inch in diameter, is the tastiest of all scallops. Its home grounds are the bays and salt estuaries from the east coast of Canada to the Gulf of Mexico.

· Calico scallop: this morsel, which gets its name from its mottled shell, is a close relative of the bay scallop but slightly larger. Its nesting grounds are the waters off Florida and the Gulf of Mexico.

All scallop meat is lean, light, firm. The color is light cream, varying to a delicate pink. The shape is like a marshmallow. The flavor is sweet.

THE MARKET FORMS

Scallops are sold only as dressed meat, never in the shells, because there is no way that they can be kept alive for any meaningful length of time after being taken from the water. The reason: they cannot close their shells tightly as do clams, oysters and mussels.

Because of their perishability, scallops are shucked aboard ship as soon as they are caught and the meats are packed in ice.

Sea scallops harvested close to port may find their way to market while still fresh. But the bulk of the catch is fast-frozen. Until recently they were always packed raw, unadorned by crumbs, spices or any other quality-concealing ingredients. But now, as we told you earlier, they also are being sold as a quick and easy so-called convenience food. Our advice to you: don't buy them if they are not packaged in their natural state.

Bay scallops are sold only fresh, by the pound.

Fresh scallops and frozen scallops, when thawed, should have a sweetish odor. When purchased in packages, they should be almost totally free of liquids.

HOW MUCH TO BUY FOR SIX NORMAL SERVINGS

A pound and a half to 2 pounds, depending upon how you plan to serve them. Less for appetizers, more for entrées.

CLEANING

Fresh or frozen, scallops should be rinsed well under cold running water in order to wash away any particles of sand and shell that may still be with them. But do this only when you are about to cook them, never earlier.

STORAGE

Refrigerate fresh raw scallops, loosely covered, at 32 to 35 degrees Fahrenheit for no more than 1 or 2 days. Store frozen scallops for a maximum of 1 week in refrigerator frozen-food compartment, 1 month in freezer.

SOME SCALLOP COOKERY BASICS

· Although they are not, scallops can be eaten raw. So the big rule to remember is the one we harp on all through this book: don't overcook. If you do, you will ruin their natural tenderness, succulence, flavor.

· Follow recipe times exactly. There is no fork test for scallops.

· Scallops are ideal for every conceivable style of cooking, family cooking or company cooking, appetizers, cocktails, salads, soups, bisques, chowders, poached, steamed, simmered, baked, broiled, pan-fried, deep-fried, oven-fried. Try them in poultry stuffings, too. Or bake a scallop pie, just as you would a clam pie (page 311).

· Bay scallops are bite size. But sea scallops usually are not, so do not hesitate to cut them in half and even in quarters before cooking. (A word of warning: some fishmongers will cut up sea scallops in hope of passing them off as more-expensive bay scallops. You'll be able to tell, though, because they won't be round like a marshmallow; rather more like a square or a triangle but with one curving edge.)

· Never precook scallops. All you will do is destroy the fine flavor if you cook them now, eat them later.

SHRIMP

When Henry V was crowned king of England, 79 years before Columbus allegedly discovered America, shrimp was on the menu at the coronation supper. Centuries before that, shrimp was one of the glories that was Rome. In Greece Aristotle ate shrimp too, as did his learned compatriots. In the Orient shrimp made Confucius say words of praise.

In America today we're trying to catch up. We eat more shrimp than we do any other seafood. In New Orleans, the shrimp capital of the nation, shrimp are eaten at breakfast, dinner and supper; pushcart vendors have been known to sell them on street corners much as hot dogs are sold on the sidewalks of New York; some of the finest French Quarter restaurants were made famous by their shrimp creations, and globe-trotting epicureans know the chefs by their first names.

Obviously shrimp have something. What they have is outstanding flavor, ease of preparation, health-giving goodness, low calorie count, eye appeal, the ability to combine with many other fine ingredients and, most of all, availability and versatility.

Every one of us, no matter where we live in any one of the 50 states, can purchase some form of shrimp—fresh, frozen, canned—any day of the year. And any one of them is ideal for any cooking method, ideal for any meal, plain or fancy, family or company. For starters see the omelet and jambalaya recipes on pages 267 and 205 or Arthur Lem's Gai Lun Hai Kow on page 260.

We have in our waters three major species of shrimp:

· Northern shrimp are found in the offshore waters of Maine, Massachusetts, Alaska and British Columbia. Their size ranges from about 3 to about 6 inches.

· Southern shrimp, which grow to about the same size as the northern, are harvested in the waters off our Gulf and South Atlantic states.

· North Pacific shrimp, which come from California, Oregon, Washington and Alaska waters, are tiny but every bit as tasty as their northern and southern relatives.

Besides those three species, there is a long, slender cousin of the shrimp, called the "prawn." Their market size is 6½ inches, but don't trouble yourself looking for them, since not all stores handle them, and besides, their flavor and nutritional qualities are the same.

Shrimp shells are a variety of colors, but their qualities are alike. The most common gray shrimp is called "white" shrimp in the marketplace; pink is called "pink-gold," the deep red is called a "royal red." Fish dealers call all of them, when raw, "green" shrimp. But whatever the shell color, the meat inside turns to an opaque white with varying shades of pink, light brown or red and, to quote a government pamphlet, is "tender, delicate and delicious."

THE MANY FORMS IN WHICH SHRIMP ARE SOLD

Frozen:

· Raw and still in their shells but with their heads removed.

· Raw but shucked and deveined.

· Cooked and packed in solid blocks in packages that range from 1 to 5 pounds.

· Cooked, individually glazed and packaged in from 5-ounce to 2-pound pasteboard cartons or polyester bags. Our personal preference in buying shrimp is the 2-pound carton because (1) we can remove from the freezer only as many shrimp as we intend to use at the moment, (2) a pasteboard box is disposable while a polyester bag is not, and (3) it is economical.

And then there are more frozen forms for so-called quick and easy cooking than you can shake a garbage can at. And that is where we think many of them belong.

Canned: they're fresh-cooked in their natural juices and come to you ultra-clean and fresh-tasting in 4- to 5-ounce cans from both South and North Pacific catches, some of them packed in brine, some of them dry.

Fresh:

· Whole: they're raw, still in their shells and still with their heads on. Mainly they are sold this way only close to the shrimp trawlers' ports of call.

· Uncooked tails in shell: a shrimp just as it came from the water, but with its head removed. The industry calls them "tails" but you and I would refer to them simply as "headless."

· Peeled uncooked tails: a shrimp that's been shelled, deveined, beheaded but is still raw.

· Peeled cooked tails: same as above but, of course, cooked. The color will be a reddish pink and white, the texture firm.

All fresh shrimp should have a pleasant, mild odor when purchased, the shells should have a fresh, somewhat shiny appearance and be free of slime, the meat should be firm. They are graded according to size and sold by the pound:

- Jumbo: 15 and under per pound.
- Large: 16 to 20 per pound.
- Medium: 21 to 25 per pound.
- Small: 26 to 30 per pound.

Beyond that, there are the still smaller shrimp that run up to 42 to the pound, and beyond even that, the tiny ones that may range up to 100 or more per pound.

The larger grades will cost more, but will take less time to peel and devein; the smaller shrimp will cost less but take much longer to make ready for the table. Since all of the market forms are available to all of us and are equally good, the determining factors when shopping should be (1) how much your time is worth, and (2) the use to which you intend to put them. You'd have difficulty stuffing a tiny North Pacific shrimp, and jumbo shrimp would be wasted if diced.

HOW MUCH TO BUY FOR SIX NORMAL SERVINGS

- Frozen raw, either with or without shell: a pound and a half.
- Cooked: 1 pound.
- Canned: 3 5-ounce cans.
- Fresh whole: 3 pounds.
- Fresh in shell, cooked or uncooked: a pound and a half.
- Fresh peeled and deveined, cooked or uncooked: 1 pound.

When purchasing, make slight adjustments either upward or downward in those approximations depending upon the grade, size, how you intend to serve them and the appetites of your diners.

PROPER CARE AND STORAGE

- Frozen, raw or cooked: still packed as they were when you bought them, frozen shrimp can be kept 1 month in freezer, 1 week in frozen-food compartment of refrigerator. If you open container to remove only some of the shrimp, reseal tightly if you can; if not, repackage all that remain in heavy, reusable plastic bag and tie tightly shut.
- Cooked: stored in covered refrigerator container, they should keep well 3 or 4 days if the temperature remains at 32 degrees. The higher the temperature goes beyond that, the less time the shrimp should be stored.
- Canned: unopened, the can will keep about a year but it's best not to keep any canned food that long. If can is open and contents not used entirely, transfer to covered dish and store in refrigerator no more than two or three days.

· Fresh raw, still in shell, whole or headless: wrapped in foil or butcher paper, they'll keep in 32-degree refrigerator for a day or two but it's best not to store them that way. You'll have to clean them sometime anyhow, so you might just as well do it soon after returning from market.

· Fresh, peeled and deveined but uncooked: two days in refrigerator container at 32 degrees should be the limit.

HOW TO PEEL AND CLEAN SHRIMP

We know 4 good ways of performing this chore, so let's discuss them by the numbers. But first, in case any preservatives have been used, rinse off the shell under running water.

Peel uncooked shrimp thusly.

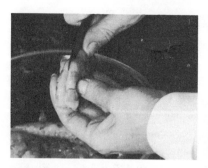

Slit and remove vein thusly.

Rinse in cold water, then add to cooking pot. Thusly.

Method number one:

· Grip shrimp so that its tentacle-like feelers are against palm of one hand.

· Lift off segments of the shell, one at a time if necessary, with your other hand. With practice, you'll become dexterous enough to remove them all at once. For some recipes it might be best to leave the fins intact and in place so that they can be used as a sort of handle when eating, butterfly shrimp for instance; for other recipes they're best removed along with the shell, shrimp cocktail for instance.

· If any feeler bits still cling to the meat, pull them free with your fingers or, if necessary, with a paring knife.

· Still gripping the shrimp, now make a shallow cut lengthwise along the back to expose the sand vein, a black threadlike part.

· Remove it with your fingers, a knife tip or a toothpick.

· Place shrimp in colander and rinse under cold water.

Method number two: This and the method that follows were recommended to us by John Von Glahn, of the Fishery Council at New York's famous wholesale Fulton Fish Market.

· Place one pound of shrimp, still in their shells, in colander and rinse well under cold water.

· Add enough water to pot to cover shrimp, along with 1 teaspoon of salt and a half stalk of celery, cut up.

· Bring to a boil, reduce to a simmer and so cook for 5 minutes.

· Add shrimp, return to simmer and so cook for another five minutes.

· Transfer shrimp immediately to colander and rinse under cold water to halt cooking process.

· Peel and devein as in method number one, but with far less difficulty.

Method number three:

· Remove shells as described in method number one.

· Prepare stock as described in method number two and simmer 5 minutes.

· Add peeled shrimp and return to simmer.

· Continue simmering until they are cooked, but do not try to determine this by the clock because simmering time of shelled shrimp differs according to size and type.

· So, instead, keep your eye on them and as soon as they begin to lose their translucent texture, remove one with a fork, pinch and take a nibble if you like. The shrimp will be done when the flesh is opaque, springs back from the pinch and there is a slight resistance to your bite. This should take no more than 4 or 5 minutes, perhaps only a minute or less for the tiny ones. Don't hesitate to repeat the test as often as necessary.

· Immediately transfer shrimp to colander and place under cold running water to halt the cooking process.

· Slit back of shrimp lengthwise as described in method number one and remove vein with a simple pinch-pull.

Method number four: This is the method we most prefer. We give it to you just as we learned it from Buddy and Doreen Kreidell at Island

Park's Olde Harbour Inn, who learned it from an old Greek chef who learned it from his father who learned it from his father and so on back for we don't know how many generations.

· Peel shrimp as in method number one, leaving fins in place.

· Slit back of shrimp as also described there. Do not bother to remove vein because this will be done for you.

· Add enough water to pot to cover, add celery top in any reasonable amount and 2 or 3 tablespoons of vinegar. Do not add salt.

· Bring water to a boil, reduce to simmer, add shrimp, return to simmer and so cook until they become opaque pink or red and white, which should be no more than 5 minutes depending upon size and amount of shrimp. Test as often as you like as described in method number three.

· Transfer shrimp immediately to colander and rinse in cold water (1) to stop cooking process, and (2) to wash away veins which will have come loose in the simmering.

SHRIMP COOKERY BASICS

Like all seafood, shrimp should never be overcooked. No matter how you intend to cook them, the maximum time they should be exposed to heat is only a very few minutes, about 2–5 depending on size. Raw, the flesh will have a grayish translucence. Cooked, the flesh will become an opaque white, with varying shades of pink that may range from a soft brown to a deep red, depending upon the species of shrimp and the waters from which they came.

A very important point to remember: shrimp must *never* be boiled. Never, no matter what you've been told or read. Boiling will turn shrimp to rubber. Nothing more. There are only two ways of cooking shrimp in water properly: **simmer** or **poach** them.

SQUID

Frankly, like most Americans, we had never thought of this strange-looking creature of the sea as a food that was fit for human consumption. In fact, Inez, ranch-raised as she was, had never in her life seen a squid until once she went fishing with Dan. As for him, his only acquaintanceship with them was the same as millions of other saltwater fishermen the country over. He used squid for bait.

Then, after our first cookbook, *The Savor of the Sea*, was published in 1966, we got the surprise of our lives. Many readers wanted to know why it did not contain a single squid recipe! So we vowed that, whenever again we wrote a fish cookbook, we would find out all that we could about the eating qualities of squid, put all that we learned to the test, and pass it on to our readers.

Our sources of information were many: encyclopedias, government and private-foundation literature, Gale Steves, John Von Glahn, Don Bevona, Arthur Lem and Vinnie Fiore. This is what we learned:

· Millions of Americans with roots in Mediterranean and Oriental countries include squid as a regular part of their diets.

· Commercial squid fishing is big business on the Pacific coast, a growing business on the Gulf and Atlantic coasts.

· Though you'd never know it by looking at one, a squid is a mollusk, related to clams, oysters and scallops.

· Squid is inexpensive. A dollar's worth is a main course for a family of 4.

· The Italian word for squid is *calamari,* which we'd eaten once or twice before. And, we might add, liked.

· Squid is extremely easy to prepare and cook.

· Nutritionally, squid is high in protein and phosphorus, and contains traces of calcium, thiamine and riboflavin; a good watch-your-weight food.

Squid is one of the most delicious fish foods we've ever tasted.

To prove to you the accuracy of that last statement, we recommend to you the squid recipes in this book, some of them created by Inez, some of them given us by master chefs such as Arthur Lem, and fine cooks such as Don and Donna Bevona, and all of them home-tested to the ohs and ahs of friends whom we invited for the most-important test of all, the taste test.

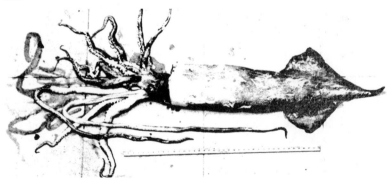

This is a squid.

The squid has a long, circular, well-nigh hollow body, with arms and tentacles extending out the rear that are even longer; two skatelike fins are located just aft of the forward tip of the body. Fully extended, a squid has been known to measure 75 feet from tip to tip. But you needn't fret about that, because the only sizes to reach the market are from about 5 to 14 inches long. Their weight runs not much over half a pound, if that.

They have very little waste; we'd say they are about 98 percent edible. Their tubular bodies are ideally shaped for stuffing and baking; almost every bit of a squid, from tip to tip, can be cut up and sautéed or mixed into a sauce in any number of ways. Their meat is lean, firm, sweet. Try dicing a small squid and mixing it in with your favorite spaghetti sauce. You'll be glad you did. Or try Donna Bevona's Squid Sauce Neapolitan (page 205). We think you'll be glad then, too.

THE MARKET FORMS

· Fresh whole: packed on ice, they are shipped daily to retail outlets all along our three saltwater coastlines and up to about 100 miles inland; they are sold by the pound. The purplish speckled skin should be clear, free of slime; the odor should be sweet, pleasant.

· Frozen: first cleaned, they are soaked in a brine solution for about 4 hours to glaze, then freeze-packed in 1- to 10-pound cartons for shipment to markets throughout all 50 states where there are concentrations of Oriental, Italian, Spanish or Greek Americans. And also to specialty food stores.

· Canned: a good part of the American catch is canned and shipped to foreign lands, with Greece and the Philippines receiving about 90 percent of the export. Some, we are told, are available in our specialty food stores, but we have been unable to find any.

· Dried: cleaned squid also are processed in this manner but here again the bulk is shipped overseas. If you find any specialty stores that stock it, you're luckier than we are.

HOW MUCH TO BUY FOR SIX NORMAL SERVINGS

· Frozen: you'll have to take it in whatever size carton your market carries. Then, however, you can remove 1 small squid per person if to be baked and/or stuffed; 3 or 4 small squid if to be cut up for sautéeing or saucing. Repack the remainder in a tie-top, heavy-duty reusable plastic bag and keep in freezer.

· Fresh whole: if to be stuffed and/or baked, 6 squid of from ¼ pound to ½ pound each.

· If to be cut up for sautéeing, a pound and a half.

· If to be cut for use in a sauce, from ½ to 1 pound.

HOW TO CLEAN SQUID

We can't imagine a fish market anywhere in the country not cleaning them for you. However, if you don't have such cooperation in your store, or if by chance you should catch your own, you'll soon find that squid are the quickest and easiest of all seafood to clean. There are two ways, depending upon how the squid is to be used:

If to be cut into pieces:

· Insert knife inside large opening at end of body and slice lengthwise toward the forward tip.

· Grasp everything inside of body and give a slight yank. It all should come free, including the clear plastic-like cartilage that you'll see there. The innards still will be attached to the head and tentacles. Set it all aside.

· With your fingers, pick out any bits of innards that might remain.

· Rub one small edge of the purplish tissue-paper-thin skin with a finger until you can get a grip, then peel it away almost as easily as you would peel a banana.

· Now turn to the innards, head and tentacles. Stretch them out flat; with a knife, cut through the "neck" about ¾ inch behind the eyes on the tentacle side of the head. Discard the innards, to which the head and eyes will still be attached.

· Squeeze the broad end of the tentacles between two fingers and out will come a whitish-yellowish piece of meat that somewhat resembles a scallop. Discard it.

· Rinse body and tentacles in cold water and rub away any unwanted matter that may remain.

· It sounds like a lot, but it's not. All you need do now is cut up the body and tentacles into any size pieces the recipe calls for. When cutting up, check heavy end of tentacles to be sure no bits of the plastic-like cartilage remains.

If to be stuffed or cut into rings:

· Poke fingers into opening at end of body, grab innards and yank. Almost all of it will come out very easily.

· Put your fingers back into opening and remove the cartilage.

· Probe around inside with your fingers for anything you may have missed. Remove whatever it is, if anything.

· Rub away skin of body as described above.

· Cut tentacles free of head, eyes and innards as described above.

· Squeeze out "scallop" as described above.

· Rinse body and tentacles in cold water and rub away remaining alien matter, if any, on outside.

· Turn body inside out and do the same there.

· Turn body right side out again and the task is done.

Now, if you plan a recipe such as Arthur Lem's Soo Jow Yaw Yu (page 278), cut the body into ¼-inch circles. If not, leave intact and stuff in accordance with instructions in any recipe you plan to use.

During the cleaning, you'll suddenly notice what looks like ink on both the squid and your hands. It's a harmless liquid that the squid discharges to hide himself from sea predators. Don't be alarmed, because it washes away easily. As for the sac from which it comes, you'll have removed that with the cleaning.

PROPER CARE AND STORAGE

· Fresh, cleaned, raw: stored in tight-covered container or wrapped in moisture-proof paper, it will keep well for 2 days if refrigerated at 32 degrees Fahrenheit.
· Frozen: 1 month in freezer; 1 week in freezer compartment of refrigerator.
· Canned: 1 year.
· Dried: 2 to 3 months in refrigerator.

THE BASICS OF SQUID COOKERY

Because squid is so thin (yet tasty), its body meat is hardly more than a casing, much as the skin of a chicken neck sometimes is used for stuffing. Therefore it needs very little cooking.

If frying or sautéeing, it should be ready to eat in about 1 minute of cooking over medium flame.

If cooked in a liquid sauce, either on top of the stove at medium heat or in the oven at 350 to 400 degrees Fahrenheit, it should be done in 20–50 minutes, depending on size and recipe. The thing to do is look and feel with a fork. Generally if it looks as though it is done, it is done; if the tines enter easily, it is done.

When cooked properly, you'll be able to cut it with a fork. If overcooked, it will be rubbery.

ABALONE

One of the great delicacies of the shellfish kingdom is the abalone. Unfortunately, however, it is one that few of us have an opportunity to sample in its fresh and therefore tastiest state. That's because, in the United States, it is found only along the California coast, and that state, in order to save the abalone from extinction, prohibits its shipment to other parts of the country.

We can, however, purchase canned or dried abalone from Mexico and Australia and so we're in luck because it has all the low-calorie, food-giving values of other shellfish, and when we serve it to guests we can be reasonably sure they've never tasted it before. Therefore for them it's quite a treat.

THE MARKET FORMS

As we said, outside of California, dried or canned are the only ways you can buy abalone. We recommend that you don't bother with the former because where you can buy it dried you can also buy it canned and the latter requires little cooking preliminaries.

There are two can sizes: 8 ounces, and 1 pound. You'll find them in Oriental and Spanish groceries and specialty food shops. Californians can buy abalone fresh in fish markets, by the pound. As with scallops, the adductor muscle is the portion sold in United States stores.

HOW MUCH TO BUY FOR SIX NORMAL SERVINGS

Either canned or fresh, 1½ pounds will do fine. There is no waste.

PROPER CARE AND STORAGE

Fresh abalone is very perishable and should be kept under refrigeration at 32 degrees and cooked and eaten as soon as possible after it has been removed from its rocky abode at the edge of the ocean.

So Californians take note: do not keep it longer than a day, even under the most perfect of refrigerator conditions.

Canned abalone, even though the can is unopened, should not be kept on your pantry shelf for more than a couple of weeks. It well might be that it could be stored for a year, but the fact is that you have no way of knowing the conditions under which it was canned.

Once the can is opened, any abalone that is not used immediately will keep well in covered refrigerator container, at 32 degrees Fahrenheit, for 2 or 3 days.

ABALONE COOKERY BASICS

The abalone shell being quite a bit on the large side, the muscle that it contains therefore is a bit on the large side. So you'll have to slice it into thin, round circles or strips before adding it to most recipes. About ⅛ inch thick is perfect. To cut the rounds, place the abalone flat on a cutting board, hold it down with the heel of one hand and slice parallel to the table with the other.

After the abalone is cut into either rounds or strips, it should be pounded a bit with a rolling pin or bottle to tenderize. If to be cooked whole, the edges should be pounded.

Whole, abalone can be baked or pot-roasted; sliced, it makes a chowder that is different; sliced, it also lends itself beautifully to breading and frying. Be very careful not to overcook—about a half minute to a side or until lightly browned. It is the main ingredient in Arthur Lem's Ho Yu Bow Pan (recipe on page 221).

SNAILS

In France, toilers in the vineyards take home with them every night this epicurean favorite that they call *escargot*. On the Greek islands, peasants while foraging in the hills for herbs and wild vegetables carry with them sacks into which they drop the snails they come upon. In Italy, children gather them for their mothers in the seaside surf, making sure to reclaim the shells for themselves when their mothers are done with them. And so, in so many foreign lands, is easily harvested the main ingredient for a meal that would command top prices in America's most plush restaurants.

Snails have never caught on to any appreciable degree, however, in the United States, and so, although they abide just about everywhere both on land and in the sea, they are sold fresh only in scattered areas around the country. But—and this is all to the good—they are becoming increasingly available in cans. Look for them in specialty food stores if your supermarket doesn't have them. Look there, too, for frozen snails which will soon be available.

We don't recommend that you try gathering your own but leave that to the experts, who know what it's all about.

THE MARKET FORMS AND HOW MUCH TO BUY

· Fresh snails are no more than 2 inches in diameter and are sold by the pound. You'll need from 6 to 12 snails per person, depending upon how you intend to prepare them. Have the fish dealer put the snails in a bit of tap water. A live snail will pop his head out of his amber-transparent trapdoor to see what's going on.

· Can sizes have not yet been standardized, at least not that we know of at this writing, but the snails come either still in their shells or removed from them, and the label should tell how many the can contains. So again figure on 6 to 12 per person.

CLEANING, CARE, STORAGE, AND COOKING

Live snails should be cleaned as soon as possible after purchase, a step that requires a cooking process. Here we give you a simple, basic way, and in the recipe section we tell you how to bake them in a delicious butter sauce (page 306).

· Cover snails with water. Discard any that do not poke their heads out of their trapdoors.

· Scrub and rinse outer shells.

· Place in cooking pot, cover with water or court bouillon, bring to a boil and simmer for a minute or two to open the trapdoor for keeps.

· Drain, and remove meat from shells with olive fork, nut pick or toothpick.

· Slice away and discard tip of snail's head and black portion at his opposite extremity.

· Rinse under cold water.

· If not to be used immediately, place in covered dish and store in refrigerator at 32 degrees. But keep them no longer than 1 day; or, much better, use them the same day.

To clean canned snails, follow package directions.

Unopened canned snails will keep a year. If can is open, transfer un-used portion to container and refrigerate at 32 degrees. But for no longer than a day.

This is a conch, also a whelk, also a periwinkle.

CONCH, WHELK, PERIWINKLE

We'll talk about them as though they are really one and the same since just about their only difference is the size of their spiral-shaped conical shells. In fact, they're often called one for the other and in some sections of the country are known as "snails" (the true snail's shell is not conical), in others they are known as "winkle" and on canned goods shelves as "scungilli," that being the Italian name for "conch."

While we're on the subject of semantics, let's just add one more word about pronunciation: when you order conch, make it sound like a knock on the head: conk.

So, too, are called some peoples of the Bahamas and the Florida Keys—Conks, because the meat of this single-shell mollusk is so much a part of their diets.

Conch, the name we'll use for all of them, are to be found on all of our coasts. If you don't find them, your children will, not only because their graceful shapes can be made into so many things but also because, when held to the ear, a child can hear the sound of the sea. Adults, too, if only they (we) would listen.

But this is a cookbook.

THE MARKET FORMS

· Fresh, meaning alive in their shells. They are available the year round in fish markets within easy shipping distance of southern fishing boats' ports of call, in northern areas whenever the boats can get them back to port without freezing. They are sold by the pound in some markets, by the piece and according to size in others. The smaller the shell, the more tender the meat. Tap the shells and watch the plastic-like trap-door. If the conch is alive, you'll see him move, closing his fortress door tightly behind him.

· Frozen, either fully cooked, uncooked or partially cooked but always with the meat shucked from the shells. Package weights range from 8 ounces to 1 pound.

· Canned, usually after cooking. The label will tell. Can sizes vary but generally are about 8 ounces.

HOW MUCH TO BUY FOR SIX NORMAL SERVINGS

· Fresh: 12 conch if to be the main ingredient in a recipe; as few as 4 if to be combined with other foods.

· Frozen: 1 pound if the main ingredient for, say, a chowder; less if to be combined in, say, a seafood cocktail.

· Canned: here again the use will be the determining factor, but probably not more than 2 8-ounce cans.

CLEANING, CARE AND STORAGE

Before the meat of a conch can be cleaned, it must be removed from its nursery-rhyme shell house. We know of 2 ways of doing this. Don Bevona, who has two very young daughters and knows how dearly youngsters love conch shells, adds about 1 inch of water to a pot, places a rack in the pot, places the conch (which he has thoroughly scrubbed) on the rack, covers the pot and steams them open in 10 minutes or so.

Arthur Lem, whose three sons are full-grown and for whom speed is a factor in his professional cooking chores, simply wraps the shells in an old towel and cracks them with a hammer. But, confesses Arthur, when his sons were small, he too opened them with steam no matter how many diners were waiting to be fed in his restaurant.

But, no matter how you shuck a conch, then do this:

· Cut away and discard the stomach, which you'll find in its mid-section.

· Cut away and discard the dark, tapering tail.

· Peel away the leathery skin on the meat that remains. The meat is a yellowish white and very tasty, but also rather tough, so it needs tenderizing. Some people simply grind the meat, but this limits the ways you can use it. Don has two ways of tenderizing conch, Arthur only the traditional Chinese way. Both, however, start by slicing the meat as thinly as possible.

Then Don either pounds the slices with the edge of a heavy plate, an old Italian method that he learned from his grandfather, or parboils them until tender in a solution of about 1 teaspoon of baking soda to 1 pint of water.

Arthur places the slices in a bowl, sprinkles a teaspoon of baking soda over them and lets stand for at least 1 hour, stirring them often so that each slice gets equal treatment.

When done, the tenderized slices are rinsed well and patted dry with a lintfree towel or absorbent paper. Thus the conch is ready for use in a salad, stew, sauce, chowder, cocktail or omelet.

Or in Arthur Lem's Dow Jai Chow Heung Lor (page 255).

Or, if you can't wait, eat them right then and there the way Don's grandfather, Damiano Bevona, and his Sicilian and Gloucester fishermen friends did: simply by squeezing lemon juice over the steamed meat.

Or, if you must wait, put the meat in a covered container and store in refrigerator at 32 degrees. It will keep a day or two, perhaps three, but it's best not to wait more than 24 hours before using fresh conch. We recommend that you use frozen conch, too, as quickly as possible, keeping it for a maximum of one week in the freezer.

WHEN TO FREEZE SHELLFISH

Anything, of course, can be frozen. The question is: what is wise to freeze, what is practical to freeze?

That is why, of all the shellfish in this chapter, clams are the only one for which we included home freezing instructions. It is wise to freeze them if you've dug your own and so know exactly when and where they were taken from the water. It is practical to freeze them because anyone who has gone to the trouble of donning bathing clothes and wading around in the water for them realistically is going to take home with him more than he needs for just an immediate meal.

Neither such yardstick applies to other shellfish. For example, in most states it is illegal to dig oysters, just as it would be to go into a farmer's field and pick his corn; very few people will ever catch a lobster; crabs can be had simply by dropping a net into the water, so there is no reason to take any more than you'll immediately need.

As for freezing shellfish that you buy, that is something we think you should never do, for the pure and simple reason that, except for farm-bred oysters, you know nothing at all about their life history.

FREEZING COOKED SHELLFISH

There is a time when it is feasible to freeze shellfish (fin fish, too) and that is when you've cooked more than you can eat and you're sure that what you're freezing is the very best. It makes sense to freeze such leftover shellfish, just as it's both wise and practical to freeze any other top-quality food that you cook but can't consume.

Here's how to freeze if no breading or other coating has been used:

· Chill both the shellfish and its broth, if any, quickly by setting the cooking utensil in a pan, or sinkful, of ice water. Stir the shellfish frequently to make sure that every bit of it cools equally.

· Remove meat from shell and clean if you hadn't done so before cooking.

· Place shucked, cleaned meat in 1- or 2-cup freezer containers (2 cups equal 1 pint).

· Cover with broth, if you have any; if not, with either homemade or canned chicken broth. Be sure to leave enough room at top for expansion; i.e., about ½ inch for a 2-cup container. More or less depending on the percentage of solids in the container since it's the liquid that expands when frozen. If you are not sure how much expansion space is necessary, leave an inch, freeze loosely covered, when solidly frozen add enough water to fill, freeze and cover tightly.

· Cover container tightly to seal out air and seal in moisture and label, either with marking pencil or tie-on tag, as to date, content and cooking method. For example: "1/1/72 steamed lobster."

· Place in freezer and freeze solid at minus 10 degrees Fahrenheit.

· Store at no higher than zero degrees until used, which should be within 10 days.

Keep a thermometer in your freezer at all times so that you can keep tabs on temperature.

Except for the broth bit, all of the above-mentioned steps also apply in the freezing of cooked shellfish that has been breaded or otherwise coated and that then you obviously would not want to cover with a liquid. So, instead, do this:

· Wrap just enough such pieces (for example, floured and fried scallops or breaded shrimp) to make a serving-size portion together in a single airtight package, using a good pliant freezer paper. Press the wrapper tightly to eliminate all possible air pockets and fasten with freezer tape.

Place several such packages in a see-through heavy-duty plastic bag, press all air possible out of it and tie tightly with a wire twist. (*We urge use of heavy-duty plastic bags because they can be washed and reused many times and thus you can help cut down on the waste that is polluting our land.*)

Then follow all of the other freezing procedures given above and you'll be able to remove speedily only as many individual packages as you'll need at the moment, retie the bag and allow what's left to wait another day. **Never refreeze any fish, shell or fin, after it's begun to thaw, and never open your freezer door for longer than is necessary to remove a container of food. Changes in temperature can cause deterioration of frozen foods.**

5

How to Cook Fish Properly

We include in this all-important chapter the general information that applies to the cooking of all fin fish, and some that also applies to shellfish. Specific instructions that apply only to one method of cookery will be found in the introduction to each particular recipe section. Much of the shellfish cooking process is also part of the cleaning and shelling process. Therefore, most of the shellfish cooking instructions will be found in the individual shellfish sections of the preceding chapter.

If ever we were to open a cooking school, fish would be the food to which we devoted the least amount of time for teaching the basics, because fish is the easiest and quickest of all foods to cook. There are only a few cooking basics that you need know and you're ready to go. Here they are, one by one:

WASHING

The place to start cooking fish properly is at the kitchen sink. Whether you caught and gave it a preliminary cleaning (page 25) or whether you bought it and the fishmonger cleaned it for you, fish should be washed more thoroughly, as the first step preparatory to cooking. That's because, as we told you earlier, little or no water should be used at the time you catch a fish or buy a fish. The reason: water speeds the breakdown of fish flesh, thus enabling deterioration to set in, thus causing the flesh to be less delicate and less tasty.

But now you're ready to cook it, so do this: run cold tap water into a pot and stir in a couple of tablespoonsful of salt or, if you'd prefer, the juice of half a lemon. Dip your fish completely in the water. Dunk it well two or three times and quickly dry it as much as possible by patting it inside and out with a lintfree towel, cloth or absorbent paper. If the fish is filleted, steaked or chunked, simply lay it on absorbent paper. Turn it once or twice and that's all there is to it. Any shellfish not thoroughly cleansed in the shelling process should be handled in the same way.

Defrosting

If you have frozen fish and you want to defrost it before cooking, remember this cardinal rule: fish should be thawed just until it is pliable, but still icy cold and, unless you are going to fry it, with some of the frost crystals still in it. The longer you let fish stand beyond that point before starting to cook it, the less tasty it will become.

There are several ways of defrosting fish, but, before telling you what they are, let's tell you what you should not do. And that is this: never thaw a whole, drawn or dressed frozen fish by setting it out of the refrigerator at room temperature. True, it is a time saver, but it also is a spoiler, because a fish will not defrost equally. Thick sections will take longer than thin ones. Thus, by the time the upper end is ready for the pan, the hind one may be ready for the garbage can.

Instead, therefore, defrost in one of the following ways:

· To us, the best possible method of defrosting frozen fish in any form is to transfer it from your freezer to your refrigerator and let it sit, all the time in its wrappings, until it's pliable enough to handle. A 1-pound package of frozen fillets will take from about 10 hours to be barely pliable to 18 hours to almost completely thaw.

· The quickest safe way to thaw a dressed or drawn frozen fish is to set it, still wrapped, in a pot under the cold faucet and let the water run. How long it will take to defrost depends upon the shape and the size of the fish.

· It's messy, slow and inconvenient, but dressed and drawn fish also can be thawed by burying them completely in crushed ice.

· Fillets and steaks, still wrapped tight, will thaw in about a half hour when immersed in cold running water. Chunks will take longer, how much longer depending upon shape and size. If you resort to this quickie method, don't try to hasten the process still more by removing the wrappings. Let them remain until the fish is pliable.

Shellfish can be defrosted in the same ways as fin fish.

Timing Fresh or Defrosted Fish While Cooking

As we've told you many times before because we want to impress this fact upon you, fish is the easiest and the quickest of all foods to cook. That's because fish is the most tender of all flesh foods. Many meats, for example, have to be cooked for a long time in order to make them chewable. However, the longer fish is cooked, the tougher it becomes.

Fish is cooked for only two reasons: to enhance its naturally fine flavor and to firm up the flesh. The flesh of raw fish is translucent. The protein must coagulate before it can become the way most people like it best. Heat is the coagulating force—but just so much heat and no more. The moment the color loses its translucency and becomes opaque, the moment the flesh flakes easily, the fish is done. Then the flavor is at its height. Every second it is cooked beyond that moment, the drier and tougher the fish becomes, the worse it will taste.

Which all adds up to this one basic rule for fine fish cookery:

Forget your clock and test a cooking fish for doneness with a fork.

Just probe the fish where the flesh is thickest gently with the tines. When the flesh flakes easily at the touch of the tines, the fish is done.

Remember that one simple rule, practice it, and you can't go wrong.

As for the cooking times that you'll find with the recipes in this book, use them only as a rough guide and no more. If a recipe calls for a 4-pound fish, we have no way of knowing if the fish you cook will be a long, thin 4-pounder or a short, fat 4-pounder. The thickness of fillets and steaks varies greatly. The temperature of a fish or any of the ingredients you combine with it; the dish you put it in; the depth and temperature of a sauce you pour around it—all these things (and others, too) have a bearing on how long it will take fish to cook.

So another rule to remember:

· Always start testing with a fork at half the time given in a recipe, no matter whose recipe, in this book or any other. Don't worry about how often you open the oven door. A fish is not a cake. It will not fall.

If you're not following a recipe, here's what to do:

· Use 10 minutes per inch of thickness as a rough timing guide—unless the fish is baked in a moderate, 350-degree to 375-degree oven, then figure about 15 minutes per inch of thickness. But, whichever of the two guides you use, start testing with a fork at half that time.

Just one last word on the subject of timing by way of emphasis: over-cooking is a fish cook's worst enemy. Cook a fish too long and all you'll have to show for it is dry fish, tough fish and a houseful of people who swear that never again will they eat fish.

But, once you learn to trust a fork and not a clock, that same house-ful of people will rave about what a great cook you are. Better praise than that you cannot get, especially if you're a mother and it is your children who are doing the raving.

TIMING STILL-FROZEN FISH WHILE COOKING

There are only four ways of cooking frozen fish that has not been de-frosted, four good ways, that is. We know. We researched, we innovated, we tried, we tested, we tasted.

And this is our report: still-frozen fish should be either cooked in the oven, simmered, poached or steamed if it is to taste as delicious as fish should taste. Never should it be fried or broiled.

IN THE OVEN

This is where Inez cooked that "cake" we told you about at the start of this book, the one, you'll recall, that fooled our son. That will give you an idea of how tasty still-frozen fish baked in the oven can be.

We season and/or sauce solidly frozen rectangles of fish just as they come from the 12- to 16-ounce box. Then we cook them 20–24 minutes per inch of thickness at 450 to 500 degrees. Since frozen fillet rectangles are evenly cut, this timing method works well *as a guide* but only as a guide. It's about right for most frozen fish you buy at the supermarket on the way home because it will have started to defrost by the time it goes in the oven. However, fish that is moved directly from a 0-degree freezer to the oven will require longer cooking.

Which means this: **just as with fresh or defrosted fish, you still must test it with a fork for doneness.**

Start testing at 15 minutes for rectangles that are 1 inch thick, at 20 minutes if 1¼ inches thick.

Evenly cut fish steaks can be timed this way, too.

As for a whole fish, it also can be baked while frozen, but we think you'll be happier with the results if you thaw it until pliable before introducing it to the oven. However, if you don't thaw it, start testing it for doneness on the basis of 15 minutes per inch, measuring for thickness halfway between the thick and the thin parts.

We've said it before and now we'll say it again: don't buy commercially breaded frozen sticks and portions.

However, if some unkind soul gave you a package as a gift and you can't bear the thought of throwing it out (don't bother feeding this junk to the cat, she won't eat it), follow the instructions we've given for frozen fillets or those given on the package. Use the same measurement guide as above for timing.

Then, when done, smother it in a sauce, any sauce, that you'll find in this book starting on page 117.

SIMMERING, POACHING, STEAMING

Still-frozen blocks of fillets or steaks or small dressed fish can be simmered, poached or steamed in the same manner as fresh fish and with the same excellent results.

When simmering and poaching, apply the fork test after 15 minutes and as often thereafter as necessary to assure that the cooking process will not continue for a second beyond the moment the flesh flakes easily.

But remember that precious steam will escape every time you remove the lid. When steaming, keep the liquid at a low boil and cook frozen fish 10 minutes for the first ½ inch of thickness and 6 additional minutes for each additional ½ inch.

CARE OF LEFTOVERS

Throughout the book we recommend tasty and economical ways of using leftovers, but please remember that all forms of fish as well as the sauces used with them are very perishable. Don't let them stand around in a warm kitchen before quickly chilling and storing in the refrigerator. Use the next day, or, if you can't eat them that soon, freeze and use within 10 days. (See Freezing Cooked Shellfish, page 87, for freezing instructions.) Only freeze leftover fish, or soup or sauces made from fish that you know was very fresh (and not frozen) when you cooked it. We don't recommend freezing leftovers containing such perishables as fish roe or lobster "tomalley," and we throw out leftover Hollandaise and other egg type sauces. Be sure to reheat leftovers (especially cream-type sauces) to a minimum of 140 degree F. before serving.

FATS AND OILS

Since all fish are oily, some more than others, it is not necessary to use fats when cooking except to prevent the fish from sticking to the cooking surface and, sometimes, from drying out on top. So, if you're counting calories, the less fat you use, the better. Although not conclusively proven, it is generally believed that the best lubricants to use for reasons of good health are the vegetable oils. Safflower, corn, soybean and cottonseed (or any combination of them) are the best of the best, in that order, because they have a high degree of polyunsaturation.

Therefore, no matter what you have on the fire, be it fish or meat or eggs or whatever, they are the oils in which you should do your cooking if your prime consideration is dietary.

After that, if you prefer a slightly different flavor, and if health poses lesser problems for you, feel free to use peanut oil, which is polyunsaturated too, but to a lesser degree. Olive oil, again if health is the main consideration, is on the bottom of the permissible list because it contains almost no polyunsaturated qualities at all. As for the few of you out there who do your cooking with coconut oil, know now that it is a saturated fat.

Slim, trim, rosy-cheeked folk to whom weight is no problem and who have never had a health care in their lives can probably use the most flavorsome lubricant of all: good old-fashioned butter. There is nothing that will bring out the best in fish so well.

As for those of you who would like the flavor of butter but with a polyunsaturated touch, do this: mix 1 part of melted butter with from 2 to 4 parts of vegetable oil. Lo, you have the flavor of butter! You also have an added bonus if you're frying with the mixture, because vegetable oil does not burn so easily as does butter.

As for those of you who are hung up on the taste of olive oil: put five black olives in a pint of vegetable oil and let them marinate for a few hours. Or add a few drops of olive oil to a pint of vegetable oil, mix well and use as needed. Lo, you have the flavor of olive oil!

A few drops of sesame oil, which has a fair degree of polyunsaturation but which has too strong a flavor for use by itself, can be added to a more delicately flavored vegetable oil with interesting results.

Some margarines that have been vitamin-fortified also make a good butter substitute. When shopping, compare the labels for dietary qualities and remember when so doing that the ingredient at the top of the list is the ingredient that there is most of.

So now that you know what fats and oils to use in fish cookery, let's talk about how much and when.

Throughout this book we'll use the adjective "well-greased." When we do, we will mean properly greased, not heavily greased or excessively greased. We'll mean just enough to do the job that is to be done and no more.

Since most fish recipes are interchangeable and since some fish are fat and some fish are lean, the amount of oil it will take to "grease well" will vary accordingly. Add oil when substituting a lean fish for a fat fish, subtract oil when substituting a fat fish for a lean fish. But only if any oil at all is necessary. Bearing these factors in mind, this is how much you'll need for the various cooking methods that require any fats or oils at all:

Pan-frying: No more than 1/16 to ¼ inch of oil or melted fat, which includes butter or margarine, in a heavy skillet. The thickness of the fish and whether or not it's coated with flour, crumbs or meal will have a lot to do with just how much lubricant you use.

The utensil has some bearing, too. You can cook almost fatfree in some of the good-quality porcelain-lined heavy metal skillets. Ditto for Teflon-coated frying pans, a coating that you will not find in our kitchen.

Deep-frying: The deep pot should contain enough oil to cover the fish pieces so they do not touch. But in no case should it ever more than half-fill the pot. The oil should be heated to 365 degrees to 375 degrees, then, after food is added and temperature drops, maintained at 355 degrees to 365 degrees.

Broiling: The broiling pan should be preheated and then lightly greased. (If cooking on a rack, grate or grill, that's where you put the grease.) The fish should be brushed with oil, melted butter, melted margarine, a marinade or a barbecue sauce.

Baking: The baking pan should be greased just enough to prevent sticking and no more. The fish should be brushed with oil, melted margarine or melted butter.

Planked fish: If you use a hardwood plank, grease it well and place it in a cold oven to heat thoroughly as the oven preheats. If you use a metal or glass oven platter, grease it lightly before putting it into the oven. Brush the fish with oil, butter or margarine.

Oven-frying: This is the best possible way for weight-conscious folks to "fry" their fish because, actually, it is not frying at all. What it really is, is baking at a very high temperature. We'll tell you exactly how on page 249. Right now we're talking about the amount of fat or oil to use for this method of cookery: 2 tablespoons to each pound of fish.

No matter how or in what form you use them, oils should never be allowed to overheat and smoke.

Those are the basics for the application of fats and oils in the cooking of fish. But before we get off the subject, we'd like to pass on a labor-saving tip for dotting with butter or margarine:

Keep a stick of whichever you prefer in the freezer at all times. Then, whenever a recipe calls for dotting, use a coarse grater and grate just the amount needed directly onto the fish that's to be oven-fried, broiled, cooked in casserole or whatever. When done, return the stick to the freezer and you're all set for the next time.

Cooking with Liquids

When steaming, poaching, simmering or water-broiling, or in making soups, sauces and chowders, the only liquid you'll ever need to bring out the fine flavor of fish is water—plain water just as it comes from the tap.

However, you can change the flavor to almost anything that you like simply by changing the liquid, or adding to the water. Substitute beer, wine, milk, cream, even lemonade or chicken broth, the latter preferably homemade. And/or add some mixed pickling spices or a packaged combination called sometimes "Shrimp Spice" and sometimes "Crab Boil." You'll be duly amazed and delighted by these new taste treats.

Nor should you ever overlook the broths from canned and frozen fin fish and shellfish, nor the liquids that you've saved from a previous fish-cooking session. Always find a use for them, especially in soups, chowders and sauces, because they'll add to the flavor.

A cautionary note about liquids from store-bought cans or packages: read the label; it may contain a warning that the liquid must be discarded. If so, don't use it.

Marinating Fish

Fin fish may be marinated in almost any liquid or mixture of liquids you like. It can be a court bouillon (page 197); one of the spicy sauces or marinades (starting on page 144), lime juice, lemon juice or wine, full strength or diluted. White wines such as Sauterne, Chablis or the Moselle or Rhine varieties are traditionally used to flavor (or drink with) fish. However, the stronger-flavored red wines can be nice too, especially with fat fish. And, like the red wine, vinegar, lime or lemon juice will break down the oils in a fat fish, thus making them less odorous and more palatable to those who object to strong flavors.

The best marinades for shellfish are those which are delicately flavored, because shellfish themselves are so delicately flavored. However, if your taste buds call for something strong, there is nothing to prevent you from marinating shellfish in the same liquids suggested for fin fish.

The strength of the marinade and the length of time the fish remains in it will determine the effect on the flavor of the fish, be it shell or fin. On the texture, too. If the marinade is a concentrated acid such as full-strength lemon or lime juice, it will change the texture of fish, giving it a cooked appearance and taste.

All or part of the marinade can be used in cooking the fish as well as in making a sauce to pour over it when done.

Marinate only in a glass (or nonporous ceramic bowl)—never metal of any kind.

Seasonings

Go easy, think twice, before adding any spices or seasonings of any kind to a fish. We are not opposed to them. In fact, we urge their use. Recipe after recipe in this book calls for them. But only where we have found through testing, tasting and experimentation that the finished dish will benefit from them, because, remember, fish is a naturally flavored food.

Bearing that warning in mind, now go ahead and experiment with seasonings to your heart's content, but add them a bit at a time, tasting, tasting, tasting as you do so. And bear these other pointers in mind, too:

· Before adding any at all, consider the other ingredients that a recipe may call for. Will heavily seasoned broths, canned vegetables or whatever be among them? The labels should tell you. If so, perhaps you should wait before sprinkling in any salt, pepper, or anything else.

· Don't restrict your seasonings to the two or three that spice charts may list as being best suited for fish. Try anything that you like. But go easy and add with a light touch until you know what the results will be.

· Try wines for a pleasant seasoning surprise, not just sherry wine, or a white wine, but any wine.

· Check the spice rack periodically in your supermarket to see what new additions might add flavor to a fish dish. Different seasonings are to be found in different sections of the country. Try any that tickles your imagination. But taste as you do so, lightly, lightly. Use the instructions on the container as a guide.

· When it won't interfere in any way with the preparation and taste of the fish, add salt and pepper after it is cooked. You will discover that the blending of the other ingredient flavors in a recipe will make little or no salt (and pepper) necessary—a boon to those on restricted diets!

· Seasonings such as curry and dry mustard will blend more easily into a sauce if you mash them into a bit of butter, then stir the butter into the hot sauce.

If you like to use fresh garlic but hate to peel it, especially when you're in a hurry and don't want the odor on your hands, try this:

· *Peel several cloves at one time, thereby getting the unpleasant job over with for some time to come.*

· *Chop the peeled cloves.*

· *Put into a small jar.*

· *Cover with vegetable oil.*

· *Replace lid and use garlic from it as needed.*

· *When the garlic is all gone, use the beautifully flavored oil.*

Not only is this a time-saver and a garlic-odor minimizer, it also is a garlic preserver.

HOW TO AVOID FISH ODORS

If anyone in your house ever squawks that the fish you're cooking smells terrible, be warned: they're not smelling fish at all. They're smelling the fat or the oil in which you're cooking. Fresh fish have a naturally sweet smell. There is nothing unpleasant about it.

What to do about it in order to make sure that nobody in your house starts squawking? Simple. Always use clean oil and don't ever let it reach the smoking stage. Not only will this prevent cooking odors, it also will prevent the flavor of the fish you are cooking from lessening.

TEMPERATURES

It's always best to follow the temperature given in a recipe. If it is not given or if you are not following a recipe, the following guides should help:

Slow oven	250 degrees to 325 degrees (Fahrenheit).
Moderate oven	350 degrees to 375 degrees.
Quick or hot oven	400 degrees to 450 degrees.
Very hot oven	450 degrees to 500 degrees.
Pan-frying	350 degrees.
Deep-frying	350 degrees to 375 degrees.
Oven-frying	500 degrees.
Baking	350 degrees to 375 degrees.
Broiling	550 degrees to "Broil" as marked on stove.
Planked (baked)	400 degrees.
Water-broiling	500 degrees to 550 degrees.

The type of sauce or other coating on a piece of fish has some bearing on its reaction to temperature. A sauce containing sugar or breadcrumbs dotted liberally with butter may brown very quickly. The thing to do is check your fish frequently and if it's browning too quickly, turn the heat down or, if it's in the broiler, move a little farther from the source of heat.

INTERCHANGEABLE RECIPES

Much of what we have to say under this heading, you might think, might better have been said under the "Fats and Oils" heading earlier in this chapter. However, here we talk about a different kind of fat and oil. There we talked mainly about lubricants that you add; here we talk mainly about the fat and oil content of fish, a key factor in the interchanging of recipes.

No matter what recipe you're using, whether you found it in this or any other cookbook, in a newspaper or in a magazine, or got it from your next-door neighbor or (Heaven forbid!) the Galloping Gourmet, there is one important thing to remember: virtually all fish recipes are interchangeable. No matter what fish, saltwater or sweetwater, a recipe may call for, you can almost always substitute any fish you like, fresh or salt, for it—provided, however, that you keep these things in mind:

1. Some fish are fat and some are lean and the degree of fatness and leanness varies greatly, from almost zero to more than 20 percent. So check the list starting on page 100 that shows whether your fish is oily, moderately so, or lean, then adapt the fat ingredient in your recipe accordingly. If you're a beginner in fish cookery and that seems confusing, limit your substitutions to fish within each of the three categories; i.e., fat fish for fat fish, moderate for moderate, lean for lean. Stick to that principle until you become more sure of yourself and you'll never go wrong.

2. If perchance you suddenly find yourself in possession of a fish that's not included in the list, it's a pretty safe assumption that, if the flesh is white, it's a lean fish; if the flesh is dark, it's a fat fish; if the flesh is an in-between tannish-brown color, it's a moderately fat fish.

3. In the interchange of recipes, the fork test becomes more important than ever. Probe with those tines as often as you like, remove from the heat the moment the flesh flakes easily, and your finished dish will always be one of which you can be proud. That's because stopping the cooking process at just the right moment has a lot more to do with the moistness or dryness of the finished product than does the oil content.

4. The oil content of a fat fish makes it well suited to broiling, which is a drying process, with just a light touch of a lubricating fat or oil on the surface. But a lean fish can taste very good broiled, too, if you baste 2 or 3 times with a lubricant while cooking, or use one of the water-broiling recipes you'll find starting on page 240.

5. If you don't care for the oily taste of a fat fish, and a fat fish is all that you have to cook, choose a recipe that calls for wine, vinegar, lime or lemon juice. They're all great oil-taste reducers and/or eliminators, depending upon the fish.

6. The list, in addition to fat content, also will tell you the approximate number of calories you would consume if you cooked and ate a normal serving (100 grams or about 3½ ounces) of raw fish. The amount of fat a fish contains will vary as the result of a number of things. The list is therefore based on averages, which, though not 100 percent accurate for every fish, still serve as an extremely helpful guide.

7. The majority of both fin fish and shellfish have a delicate or mild flavor. Thus, taking into consideration the other factors we mention in this section, they can all be used interchangeably. Even shellfish, if chopped, can be used instead of a flaked fin fish. There are a few fish, however, that have a strong or distinctive flavor of their own with which you should become familiar before using them as substitutes. With the exception of mudfish such as carp and catfish (unless the catfish is farm raised, in which case it's sweet-flavored), these fish are pretty much confined to the oily category. They include bonito, mackerel, mullet, salmon and dark-fleshed tuna. Once you've tried these fish, you'll find that they also can be substitutes in many recipes.

8. Even with the above-mentioned oily fish, there may come a time when you'll find that the fat content of one of them is quite low. Why? For example, it may have been netted at the end of a long, hard migration during which its body consumed a great deal of stored-up fat. So, if you're broiling, let's say, a mackerel and it looks dry, don't feel guilty about basting it with a little fat, two or three times if need be.

9. Small fish will show less oil variation than will the large ones, and meat cut from the head end of a big fish will be much fatter than meat cut from the tail end.

10. You could do it, but not without a great deal of forethought, improvisation and imagination, so think twice before substituting a whole fish for a fillet. Or vice versa. Or some such thing. But, if you still want to try it, remember that all-important fork test. Here you'll probably need it more than ever.

There you have them. Ten basic facts to always bear in mind when interchanging recipes. If you think that is overly much, cheer up simply by remembering this: we have just as many variables, perhaps more, to contend with when cooking meat from the four-legged kingdom (and poultry, from the two-legged kingdom).

But we know about them and so we adapt our cooking accordingly.

Becoming as well acquainted with fish cookery as you are with meat and poultry cookery is well worth the effort. Give it a chance to prove its versatility and you'll be repaid many times over in the pleasure you receive from both the preparation and the eating. And the praise of your family and friends.

MOST COMMON FIN FISH AND SHELLFISH

The list that follows should mean much to everyone who cooks and/or eats fish, but particularly to weight watchers and others who count their calories either through choice or necessity. The calorie content of each fish is based upon government-nutritionist estimates of how many calories there are in a 100-gram (about 3½ ounces) serving of raw, edible fish.

To carry that over, however, into how many servings there are in each recipe in this book would drive us and you out of our and your minds because of the fractions that we would have to deal with continually. So we'll stick to the closest realistic whole number: i.e., a 1-pound fillet will serve 4, not 4½.

Also we will take into consideration individual appetites (some people might call them "human frailties") and the fact that some people eat more than others. So when we say that a recipe will serve 4–6, we will mean 6 nutritionist-recommended servings and 4 hearty-appetite servings.

Additionally, as a particular courtesy (how good we are!) to weight watchers, we include at the end of this list another list giving the calorie content of common foods most often used in combination with fish.

LIST OF MOST COMMON FIN FISH AND SHELLFISH

Calories:* food energy contained in 100 grams (about 3½ ounces) raw
    edible food.
Fat fish:* 6 to 20 percent or more fat.
Intermediate fish:* 2 to 6 percent.
Lean fish:* less than 2 percent fat.
(*A*) Atlantic Ocean fish, (*P*) Pacific Ocean fish, (*F*) Freshwater fish

Common Name of Fish	Regional Names**	Calo-ries	Fat	Inter-mediate	Lean
Abalone (*P*)		98			X
Albacore (*A, P*)	Long-finned tuna	177	X		
Alewife (*A, F*)		127		X	

* Number of calories and percentage of fat from *Composition of Foods,* Agriculture Handbook No. 8, Agricultural Research Service, United States Department of Agriculture.

** Regional names of fish from *The Fisherman's Almanac,* by Dan Morris and Norman Strung (Macmillan).

Common Name of Fish	Regional Names**	Calo-ries	Fat	Inter-mediate	Lean
Barracuda (P)		113		X	
Bass, sea (A)	Common sea bass, rock bass, blue-fish, blackwill, hannabil	93			X
Bass, smallmouth (F)	Bronzeback, black bass	104		X	
Bass, largemouth (F)	Bigmouth bass, Oswego bass, green trout, green bass, black bass	104		X	
Bass, striped (A, F, P)	Striper, rockfish, greenhead, squid-hound, rock bass	105		X	
Bass, white (F)	Silver bass	98		X	
Bluefish (A)	Tailor, skipjack, fatback, snap-ping mackerel	117		X	
Bonito (A, P)	Atlantic bonito, skipjack, bone-jack, horse mackerel	168	X		
Buffalo fish (F)		113		X	
Bullhead, black (F)	Horned pout	84			X
Burbot (F)		82			X
Butterfish (A) from northern waters		169	X		
from Gulf waters		95		X	
Carp (F)		115		X	
Catfish (F)	Fiddler, willow cat, spotted cat, Southern chan-nel cat	103		X	
Chub (F)		145	X		

Common Name of Fish	Regional Names**	Calories	Fat	Intermediate	Lean
Clam, soft (A, P)		82			X
hard or round (A, P)		80			X
Cod (A, P)	Atlantic: group, black snapper Pacific: gray cod, sea bass	78			X
Crab, blue, dungeness, rock and king (A, P)		93 (Cooked)			X
Crappie, white (F)	Papermouth, bachelor perch, speckled perch (NOT a perch)	79			X
Crayfish (F) and spiny lobster (A, P)		72			X
Croaker, Atlantic (A)	Texas croaker, chut, hardhead, golden croaker	96		X	
Croaker, white (P)		84			X
Croaker, yellow-fin (P)	Surf fish, roncador, yellowtail, golden croaker	89			X
Cusk (A)		75			X
Dogfish, spiny (A, P)	Grayfish	156	X		
Drum, fresh-water (F)	Sheepshead, croaker, white perch, thunder pumper	121		X	
Drum, red (A)	Channel bass, red-fish, spottail, puppy drum	80			X
Eel, American (A, F)		233	X		

Common Name of Fish	Regional Names**	Calo- ries	Fat	Inter- mediate	Lean
Eulachon (smelt) (*P, F*)	surf smelt, silver smelt, whitebait, Columbia River smelt	118	X		
Finnan haddie (smoked had- dock) (*A*)		103			X
Flatfish (*A, P*)		79			X
Winter flounder: Flatfish, sand dab, blackback					
Fluke: Summer flounder, plaice, northern flounder, doormat					
Sole: Petrale, rex, sand sole, brill, English and California sole, sand dab, flounder, turbot					
Grouper (including red, black and speckled hind) (*A*)		87			X
Speckled hind: Rock hind—hind Red hind: Calico, coney, polka dot					
Hake (including Pacific hake, squirrel hake and silver hake or whiting) (*A, P*)		74			X
Haddock		79			X
Halibut, Atlantic and Pacific (*A, P*)	Alabato, northern halibut	100			X
Halibut, Cali- fornia (*P*)	Chicken halibut, albato, southern halibut	97			X
Halibut, Green- land (*A*)		146	X		
Herring, Atlantic (*A*)		176	X		
Herring, kippered (smoked)		211	X		

Common Name of Fish	Regional Names**	Calories	Fat	Intermediate	Lean
Herring, Pacific (*P*)		98		X	
Jack mackerel (*P*)		143		X	
Kingfish, southern, Gulf and northern (whiting) (*A*)		105		X	
Lake herring or cisco (*F*)		96		X	
Lingcod (*P*)	Cultus, bocalao, skilfish, leopard cod, greenling	84			X
Lobster, northern (*A*)		91			X
Lobster, spiny: *see* Crayfish					
Mackerel, Atlantic (*A*)	Boston mackerel, common mackerel, spike, tinker	191	X		
Mackerel, Pacific (*P*)		159	X		
Mackerel, Spanish (*A*)	Cero, sierra, spotted mackerel	177	X		
Mullet, striped (*A, F, P*)	Lisa	146	X		
Muskellunge (*F*)	Muskie, great pike, lunge, tiger pike	109		X	
Mussels (*A, P*)		95		X	
Ocean perch, Atlantic (*A*)	redfish	88			X
Ocean perch, Pacific (*P*)		95			X
Octopus (*P*)		73			X
Oysters, eastern		66			X

Common Name of Fish	Regional Names**	Calo-ries	Fat	Inter-mediate	Lean
Oysters, Pacific and western	Olympia	91		X	
Pickerel (F)	Chainsides	84			X
Pike, blue (F)		90			X
Pike, northern (F)	Common pike, snake, Great Lakes pike	88			X
Pike, walleye		93			X
Pollack (A)	Silver cod, harbor pollock, green cod, Boston bluefish, queddy salmon, saithe, sea salmon	95			X
Pompano (A)	Permit, golden pompano, Carolina permit	166	X		
Porgy (A)	Fair maid, scup, northern porgy	112		X	
Rockfish (P)		97			X

There are 49 species of rockfish in the Pacific. Here are a few:

Black rockfish: Black sea bass, black snapper

Bocaccio: Salmon grouper

Yellowtail rockfish: Gialota, green snapper

Orange rockfish: Canary rockfish, codalarga, bosco, filione

Tambor rockfish: Cowfish, turkey rock, red snapper

Roe, from carp, cod, haddock, herring, pike and shad		130		X	
Roe, from salmon, sturgeon and turbot		207	X		

Common Name of Fish	Regional Names**	Calo-ries	Fat	Inter-mediate	Lean
Sablefish (P)	Black cod, butterfish	190	X		
Salmon, Atlantic (A, F)	New England or Maine salmon, Kennebec salmon, silver salmon	217	X		
Salmon, chinook (P, F)	Tyee, king salmon, tule, quinnat, spring salmon	222	X		
Salmon, chum (P, F)	No figures available for raw salmon	139		X	
		Canned solids and liquids			
Salmon, coho (A, F, P)	Silver salmon, silverside, sko-witz, hooknose	153	X		
		Canned solids and liquids			
Salmon, pink (A, F, P)	Humpback	119		X	
Salmon, red (P, F)	Sockeye No figures for raw salmon	171	X		
		Canned solids and liquids			
Salmon, smoked		176	X		
Sanddab: see Flatfish					
Sardines, Atlantic (A) (canned)		203	X		
		Drained solids			
Sardines, Pacific (P)		160	X		
Sardines, Pacific (P) (canned)		196	X		
		In brine or mustard solids and liquids			
		197	X		
		In tomato sauce, solids and liquids			
Sauger (F)	Sand pike, pike, jack salmon	84			X
Scallop, bay and sea (A)		81			X

Common Name of Fish	Regional Names**	Calo-ries	Fat	Inter-mediate	Lean
Sea bass, white (P)	Sea trout, weak-fish, king croaker, white croaker	96			X
Shad, American (A, F, P)	White shad	170	X		
Shad, gizzard (A, F)		200	X		
Sheepshead, Atlantic (A)	Sargo, prison fish, convict fish, sea bream	113		X	
Shrimp (A, P)		91			X
Skate	Raja fish	98			X
Smelt, Atlantic, jack and bay (A, F, P)	Winter fish, frostfish	98		X	
Smelt, eulachon: see Eulachon					
Snail		90			X
Snapper, red and gray (A)	Mangrove snap-per, lawyer, pargo, Pensacola	93			X
Sole: see Flatfish					
Spot (A)		219	X		
Squid (A, P)		84			X
Sturgeon (A, F)		94			X
Sucker, including white and mullet (F)		104			X
Sucker, carp (F)		111		X	
Swordfish (A, P)	Broadbill, espada, albacora	118		X	
Tautog (A)	Blackfish, white chin, chub, oysterfish, black porgy, moll	89			X
Tilefish (A)		79			X

Common Name of Fish	Regional Names**	Calo-ries	Fat	Inter-mediate	Lean
Tomcod (A)		77			X
Trout, brook (A, F)	Brookie, square-tail, speckled trout, native trout, coaster, salter	101		X	
Trout, lake (F)	Laker, mackinaw, mack togue, gray trout	168	X		
Trout, rainbow or steelhead (A, F, P)	Hardhead, silver-sides, redsides, summer salmon, salmon trout, bow	195	X		
Tuna, bluefin (A, P)	Giant tuna, school tuna, horse mackerel, horse tuna, thon, albacore	145		X	
Tuna, yellowfin (A, P)	Long-fin, yellow-tail, tunny, atun	133		X	
Tuna, canned in oil		288 Solids and liquids	X		
		197 Drained solids	X		
Tuna, canned in water		127 Solids and liquids			X
Weakfish (A)	Shad trout, sea trout, common weakfish, gray weakfish, tide runner, gator trout, sque-teague, squit, summer trout, sun trout	121		X	
Whitefish (A, F)	Ostego bass, hump-backed whitefish	155	X		

Common Name of Fish	Regional Names**	Calo-ries	Fat	Inter-mediate	Lean
Whiting: *see* Kingfish					
Wreckfish (*A*)		114		X	
Yellowtail (*P*)		138		X	

Calorie Values in Common Foods That Might Be Used in Combination with Fish in Preparing a Recipe*

	Amount	Number of Calories
Milk and Cheese:		
Fluid milk:		
Whole	1 cup or glass	165
Skim (fresh or nonfat dry reconstituted)	1 cup or glass	90
Buttermilk	1 cup or glass	90
Evaporated (undiluted)	½ cup	170
Condensed sweetened (undiluted)	½ cup	490
Half-and-half (milk and cream)	1 cup	330
	1 tablespoon	20
Cream, light	1 tablespoon	35
Cream, heavy whipping	1 tablespoon	55
Yogurt (made from partially skimmed milk)	1 cup	120
Cheese:		
American, Cheddar type	1 ounce	115
	1-inch cube (⅗ ounce)	70
	½ cup, grated (2 ounces)	225
Process American, Cheddar type	1 ounce	105
Blue-mold (or Roquefort type)	1 ounce	105

* From United States Department of Agriculture Home and Gardens Bulletin No. 74.

	Amount	*Number of Calories*
Cottage, not creamed	2 tablespoons (1 ounce)	25
Cottage, creamed	2 tablespoons (1 ounce)	30
Cream	2 tablespoons (1 ounce)	105
Parmesan, dry, grated	2 tablespoons (⅓ ounce)	40
Swiss	1 ounce	105
Bacon, broiled or fried	2 very thin slices	95
Eggs:		
Hard- or soft-cooked, "boiled"	1 large egg	80
Scrambled or omelet (including milk and fat for cooking)	1 large egg	110
Poached	1 large egg	80
Nuts:		
Almonds, shelled	2 tablespoons (about 13 to 15 almonds)	105
Peanuts, roasted, shelled	2 tablespoons	105
Peanut butter	1 tablespoon	90
English or Persian, halves	2 tablespoons (about 7 to 12 halves)	80
Coconut:		
Dried, shredded, sweetened	2 tablespoons	45
Vegetables:		
Cabbage, raw	½ cup, shredded	10
Cauliflower, cooked	½ cup flower buds	15
Celery, raw	2 large stalks, 8 inches long, or 3 small stalks, 5 inches long	10
Corn, kernels, cooked or canned	½ cup	85
Cucumbers, raw, pared	6 slices, ⅛ inch thick, center section	5
Lettuce, raw	2 large or 4 small leaves	5
Mushrooms, canned	½ cup	15

	Amount	*Number of Calories*
Mustard greens, cooked	½ cup	15
Okra, cooked	4 pods, 3 inches long, ⅝ inch in diameter	15
Onions:		
Young, green, raw	6 small without tops	25
Mature, raw	1 onion, 2½ inches in diameter	50
Peppers, green, raw or cooked	1 medium	15
Potatoes:		
Baked or boiled	1 medium, 2½ inches in diameter (5 ounces raw)	90
Chips (including fat for frying)	10 medium, 2 inches in diameter	110
Mashed:		
Milk added	½ cup	70
Milk and fat added	½ cup	115
Radishes, raw	4 small	10
Spinach, cooked or canned	½ cup	20
Tomatoes:		
Raw	1 medium, 2 by 2½ inches (about ⅓ pound)	30
Cooked or canned	½ cup	25
Tomato juice, canned	½ cup	25
Fruits:		
Apples, raw	1 medium, 2½ inches in diameter (about ⅓ pound)	70
Apricots, canned, heavy sirup pack	½ cup, halves and sirup	110
Avocados, California varieties	½ of a 10-ounce avocado (3⅓ by 4¼ inches)	185
Florida varieties	½ of a 13-ounce avocado (4 by 3 inches)	160
Cranberry sauce, cooked or canned, sweetened	1 tablespoon	30

	Amount	*Number of Calories*
Grapefruit: raw, white	½ medium (4¼ inches in diameter, No. 64's)	50
Grapes, raw:		
European type (including Malaga, Muscat, Thompson seedless, and Flame Tokay), adherent skin	½ cup	50
Lemon juice, raw or canned	½ cup	30
Oranges, raw	1 orange, 3 inches in diameter	70
Orange juice:		
Raw	½ cup	60
Frozen concentrate, diluted, ready to serve	½ cup	55
Peaches, heavy sirup pack	½ cup	100
Pineapple, sliced	2 small or 1 large slice and 2 tablespoons juice	95
Pineapple juice, canned	½ cup	60
Bread and Cereals:		
Bread:		
White	1 slice, ½ inch thick	60
Whole wheat	1 slice, ½ inch thick	55
Cereals:		
Cornflakes	1 ounce (about 1⅓ cups)	110
Macaroni, cooked	¾ cup	115
Macaroni and cheese	½ cup	240
Noodles, cooked	¾ cup	150
Rice, cooked	¾ cup	150
Spaghetti, cooked	¾ cup	115
Wheat flours:		
All-purpose (or family)	¾ cup sifted	300
Whole wheat	¾ cup, stirred	300
Fats, Oils, and Related Products:		
Butter or margarine	1 tablespoon	100
Cooking fats, vegetable	1 tablespoon	110

	Amount	*Number of Calories*
Salad Dressings:		
Low-calorie	1 tablespoon	15
Mayonnaise	1 tablespoon	110
Soups:		
Bouillon, broth, and consommé	1 cup	10
Chicken	1 cup	75
Cream soup (asparagus, celery, or mushroom)	1 cup	200
Tomato	1 cup	90
Beverages:		
Beer, 4 percent alcohol	8-ounce glass	115
Wines:		
Table wines (such as Chablis, claret, Rhine and Sauterne)	1 wine glass (about 3 ounces)	70–90
Sweet or dessert wines (such as muscatel, port, sherry, and Tokay)	1 wine glass (about 3 ounces)	120–160
Miscellaneous:		
Bouillon cubes	2 cubes, small	5
Pickles, sweet	1 pickle, ¾ inch in diameter by 2¾ inches long	20
Relishes and sauces:		
Chili sauce	1 tablespoon	15
Tomato catsup	1 tablespoon	15
White sauce, medium (1 cup milk, 2 tablespoons fat, and 2 tablespoons flour)	½ cup	215
Cheese sauce (medium white sauce with 2 tablespoons cheese per cup)	½ cup	250
Sugar: white, granulated or brown	1 teaspoon	15

How to Carve a Fish

Removing the flesh from the bones of a whole cooked fish is really no different from filleting it as shown in the pictures on page 30. The big difference is that the cooked flesh needs only to be lifted from the bones forming the main structure of the carcass, but it must be cut away when the fish is raw. With a little practice, you'll soon learn how to get rid of the small bones while removing the flesh. The best place to practice is in the kitchen, not at a dinner party. At first, it will help you learn where the smaller bones are if you pull the tender meat away from the carcass with your fingers. If it falls apart, don't worry; you can pour sauce over the pieces and no one will know the difference.

Although cooking a whole fish and then removing the flesh may be more work than just buying fillets, there are advantages. One is that you'll never have more moist, better tasting meat than when you cook a fish whole—nothing removed but the innards and scales. Another is economy; most people who fillet their own fish leave a lot of choice flesh on the carcass, much more than is needed to make a good bouillon. It's a lot easier to get that flesh away from the bones after the fish is cooked than when it's raw. And if the man at the fish market fillets the fish for you, well, all you have to do is compare the cost of the same fish whole to what it costs for fillets to see whether you win or lose by having him do it.

Cleaning Dishes and Utensils

Never apply soap to a dish or a utensil that you've used for fish cooking, eating or otherwise handling until you've first rubbed them with slightly moistened salt and then rinsed them with hot water. Only then should you wash them with soap.

We warn you: Ignore this rule and slowly but surely your dishes and utensils will acquire a built-in taste and smell of fish.

And please: never use detergents. All they do is pollute. Stick to soap.

PART TWO

Recipes

~~~~~~

Now you've come to the nitty-gritty of this book, the Recipe Section. To get the most from it, you should first have read Part One. We'd like just very briefly to remind you of one thing we spelled out there and that is that the recipes are highly interchangeable.

The "O" and "I" of It

You'll note that some recipes have the letter "O" in the upper right hand corner and some have the letter "I."

The "O" stands for "Outdoors," meaning that the recipe can be just as well prepared out of doors as anywhere else.

But the "I" does *not* stand for "Indoors."

Rather, it stands for "Introductory," thereby indicating a recipe that is made to order for introducing people of all ages, from babes in arms to oldsters in wheelchairs, to the fine taste of properly cooked fish.

And all the ages in between.

1

Sauces

It is the sauce that gives a fish dish its individuality, in many cases its name. It is the sauce that provides the area of fish cookery that allows for the greatest flexibility. It is the sauce that enables the cook to cater to individual likes and dislikes.

Therefore, it is the sauce that allows the greatest, the grandest display of your creative cookery talents. It is the sauce that will win you the loudest praise from family and friends.

That is why we choose sauces to lead off the recipe section of this book. They're that important. Read, heed, practice. Become perfect. And when the plaudits start pouring in, lean back and bask, bask, bask in your moment of glory.

Fish Broth and Fumet

If there is a secret to making an outstanding sauce, it's not to be found by understanding French or by knowing how or when to add cream or butter. Rather, it is knowing how to make good use of your fish scraps, the head, the tail, the bones and such, to make fish broths:

· If you're counting calories, savory broths that can be used just as they are, unthickened.

· Or thickened as is done in many sauce and soup recipes that you'll find between this book's covers.

· Or reduced as a flavor essence for sauces and soups. (The French word for this is *fumet*, and since it has no simple English translation, it will be one of the few French words that we'll use in this book.)

If you're buying fillets from a market that carries the whole fish, don't just buy fillets if you plan on serving a sauce with them. Instead, buy the whole fish, have the clerk fillet it for you and wrap all but the innards to take home with you. Thus you'll have both the fillets for cooking and the scraps for saucing.

If you're planning on using frozen fillets or steaks or you're rushed for time and you have no frozen fish broth in reserve to fall back on, use canned clam broth or chicken broth, preferably your own.

If you do have fish scraps or a small drawn fish, the making of a broth is simplicity itself. A basic recipe follows in a moment, but even more fundamental are the steps that it takes to make:

· Clean and wash thoroughly (see page 89).

· Put in pot with water and seasonings and simmer until you have a good broth.

To transfer into a fumet, continue simmering until the quantity has been reduced to about one-fourth. A small amount added to a sauce or soup will enrich the flavor enormously, or it can quickly be reconstituted to its original substance by the addition of water.

We like to store the concentrated fumet in the freezer in 2-tablespoon cubes that are easily available for use anytime, in any way. Here's how:

· Strain by pouring through several layers of cheesecloth into a bowl. Set the bowl in a pan filled with ice water and stir occasionally to hasten cooling.

· When cool, pour into an ice-cube tray, cover and freeze.

· When cubes of fish fumet are frozen solid, remove from tray, place in a heavy-duty freezer bag, squeeze out all the air possible, fasten securely so air can't get in, tie on a dated label and return to freezer. Use within 10 days.

When you need fish broth seasoning for a sauce, presto, remove one or more cubes from the bag, reseal and you're set. If you feel like having some refreshing hot broth, dilute a cube in a cup of hot water and enjoy.

Before you freeze any broth, be sure of one thing: it must have been made from fresh-caught fish that were given the best of care from the time they were caught to the time the broth you made from them went into the freezer.

If broth contains an acid, instead of pouring into metal cube tray, use a glass or plastic container, leaving some head space for expansion. Empty plastic butter tubs are fine for this purpose.

FISH BROTH

(When fish broth is one of the ingredients in a sauce recipe and you cooked the fish you are going to use with it in a liquid, then that liquid becomes the broth you will usually use in making the sauce. If your fish was not cooked in a liquid, if the liquid wasn't suitable for your sauce or if you want to complete the sauce by the time the fish is cooked, this is a good recipe to follow. You can add to or change the ingredients in this basic recipe to suit your taste. Add more wine, or use none at all. Add more spices, or use none at all. You can even strengthen it if you like with a little chicken or veal broth.)

> 1–2 *pounds of fish trimmings (carcass, including head and tail) or whole dressed fish, head and tail on*
> 4–6 *cups of water*
> ½ *cup white wine or 2 tablespoons vinegar*
> 1–2 *carrots, sliced*
> 1–2 *onions, sliced*
> 1 *large stalk of celery, chopped*
> *Mushroom stems and peelings (optional)*
> 1–2 *bay leaves*
> 1–2 *sprigs of parsley (add last 5 minutes only for delicate flavor)*
> 1–2 *sprigs of fresh thyme or dried thyme to taste*
> 2–4 *peppercorns*
> 1–2 *pinches garlic powder or 1 clove garlic for more garlic flavor*
> *Salt and pepper to taste (go easy on these seasonings until after broth is reduced)*

Simmer, covered, for at least ½ hour, taste, adjust seasonings and strain.
NOTE: For a slightly stronger, different flavor, leave skin on carrot. For a delicate flavor, use a delicately flavored fish; removing the skin also results in a less strong flavor.

FISH FUMET

Boil broth down to ½ to ¼ normal strength. Traditionally fumet is a strong broth.

THE BASIC SAUCES

Quite a number of sauces (and some things we may not think of as sauces) can be served just as is with fish, or as the base for many other sauces. These are:
· White Sauce, in which the liquid used is milk ("gourmets" call it by its French name, Béchamel Sauce).
· Thickened Fish Broth Sauce (Velouté Sauce to an alleged gourmet).
· The egg sauces such as mayonnaise and Hollandaise.
· Sour cream or yogurt.
· Canned or frozen soups such as cream of cheese, cream of mushroom, cream of celery, cream of tomato, cream of shrimp, lobster, crab or oyster.

· Chicken or veal broth.

· Lemon juice, vinegar or wine.

Some canned and frozen soups are the consistency of a medium sauce, so all you have to do is heat them and serve. Others, such as condensed cream of mushroom, can be turned into a medium thick sauce for fish simply by adding ¼ to ½ cup of water, fish broth, milk or cream.

WHITE SAUCES

Both the White (Béchamel) and Fish Broth (Velouté) Sauce are considered to be the basic white sauces. And no longer from now on will we, if we can possibly avoid it, use the French names. Henceforth it's only White Sauce and Fish Broth Sauce.

The liquid used, as we said a moment ago, is milk in the making of White Sauce, but for the Fish Broth Sauce it can also be chicken or veal broth.

The fat in both these sauces can be butter, margarine or a vegetable cooking oil. It's easier to keep a combination of half butter and half vegetable oil from burning than if butter alone is used—unless you first clarify the butter. To do this, place butter in a heavy saucepan, turn heat on low and let butter melt slowly without stirring. Pour off the clear, golden liquid that forms on top (the clarified butter), discarding the milky substance that sinks to the bottom of the saucepan.

Although the thickening agent can be arrowroot, cornstarch or flour, we are limiting our specific instructions to flour in this section, since it is the most commonly used. Cornstarch will be found further along in the book in individual sauces for which we consider it best suited. If possible, the flour in a sauce should be cooked for 10 minutes; it takes about that long for it to lose its starchy taste and to become easy to digest. (Cornstarch needs to cook until the sauce becomes clear. Arrowroot cooks more quickly than does flour, needing only a total of 5 or 6 minutes. Use amount given in recipe or follow package instructions when thickening with cornstarch or arrowroot.) Since milk contains solids, White Sauce requires a little less starch to thicken than does the water-based Fish Broth Sauce. Here are the proportions of liquid, flour and fat you should use in making a thin, medium or thick sauce:

For Approximately 1 Cup of Thin Sauce

WHITE SAUCE	FISH BROTH SAUCE
1¼ *cups milk*	1¼ *cups broth*
⅞ *tablespoon flour*	1 *tablespoon flour*
⅞ *tablespoon fat*	1 *tablespoon fat*

For Approximately 1 Cup of Medium Sauce

WHITE SAUCE	FISH BROTH SAUCE
1¼ cups milk	1¼ cups broth
1¾ tablespoons flour	2 tablespoons flour
1¾ tablespoons fat	2 tablespoons fat

For Approximately 1 Cup of Thick Sauce

WHITE SAUCE	FISH BROTH SAUCE
1¼ cups milk	1¼ cups broth
2½ tablespoons flour	3 tablespoons flour
2½ tablespoons fat	3 tablespoons fat

Low-Calorie (and Low-Animal-Fat) White Sauce

1. Reduce the number of calories in White Sauce by more than 50 per cup by substituting skim for whole milk.

2. To replace some of the taste of cream without the calories of cream, add 1 teaspoon of nondairy creamer, which may be a soybean product (about 12 calories per teaspoon), to your cup of skim milk.

3. A liquid vegetable oil or a margarine that is of the unsaturated fat variety can be combined with the flour in making this sauce.

4. Use thin instead of medium or thick sauce, and use a small amount of it.

Low-Calorie (and Low-Animal-Fat) Fish Broth Sauce

If you make Fish Broth Sauce with chicken broth or veal broth, chill it and lift off the solidified fat before using.

Follow 3 and 4 in recipe for Low-Calorie and Low-Animal-Fat White Sauce.

Making the Sauce: There are three ways in which the ingredients in White Sauce and Fish Broth Sauce can be put together and cooked. But, before we go into them, let us impress upon you that the utensils you use for so doing are highly important.

• While they are thickening, always stir your sauces with a wire whisk or, lacking this, an old-fashioned hand eggbeater.

• Cook only in a heavy pot or skillet that the sauces won't stick to; however, some recipes call for a double boiler instead.

Now for the combining and cooking. We'll give you first the easiest way for a beginner to mate flour, fat and liquid without creating lumps, the best way of so doing last.

1. Melt fat in a heavy skillet or saucepan, turn off heat and let the utensil lose most of its heat. Put liquid to be used (milk, broth, water or whatever) in a mixing bowl and drizzle flour slowly into it, stirring constantly. When well blended and smooth, stir mixture into fat (which

should still be melted) in pan. Turn heat on medium and cook, stirring constantly, until the sauce starts to boil. Adjust heat so sauce remains at simmer and continue cooking for about 10 minutes, stirring frequently, or until sauce reaches desired thickness.

2. Another fairly simple easy method is to combine the fat and flour and roll into small balls. The French call them *beurre manié* (kneaded butter). Heat the liquid, drop the balls into it and stir until liquid boils. Turn down and simmer about 10 minutes, stirring frequently or until sauce reaches desired thickness.

3. The disadvantage with methods 1 and 2 is that the liquid must simmer for the full amount of time the flour is cooking. But this most commonly used method sidesteps this problem. That's why it's considered the best way:

Combine flour and fat in heavy skillet or saucepan, turn on medium heat and stir until the mixture begins to froth. Continue cooking for 3 or 4 minutes, stirring constantly and keeping heat very low so that the mixture doesn't bubble and does not burn. Turn off heat and stir as you add liquid all at once.

Turn heat back on to medium and continue stirring until sauce is evenly thickened and simmering, observing these cooking times:

· If the sauce is to be poured over fish and baked in the oven, cook and stir only for 2 or 3 minutes and then add to the baking dish.

· If the sauce is to be served over an already cooked fish, no matter what the cooking method, turn the heat down so that the sauce remains at a simmer and cook long enough to make a total cooking time of 10 minutes from the time you first added flour to the pan or until sauce reaches the desired consistency.

Smooth-sauce insurance: It's generally easier to combine ingredients and avoid the sauce maker's bugaboo of lumps forming if the temperature of those ingredients does not differ radically. This is more important with milk and eggs than water or a water-base broth. Here's what you can do to give yourself a little smooth-sauce insurance:

· Heat milk until it's warm before adding to hot flour-and-butter mixture. Try to cook the flour for at least 3 minutes before adding, to cut down on length of time milk must be cooked. (There are different opinions among cooks about this: some find they can avoid lumps regardless of temperature of liquid if they keep the whisk going constantly until mixture thickens.)

· Stir a little hot sauce into egg yolks to warm them before adding them to a hot sauce.

· Don't cook a sauce any longer than necessary after adding heavy cream.

· Remove hot sauce containing egg from fire before stirring in an acid such as lemon juice, tomato juice, vinegar or wine and serve at once or sauce may become thin.

· A lot of acid or heavy seasonings will sometimes curdle a milk sauce. Add them at the last minute whenever possible and serve at once.

· You cut down on the risks if you simmer sauces instead of cooking them at a rolling boil.

· Cook difficult sauces in a double boiler over boiling water instead of directly over the flame. This is a must when making egg-yolk sauces.

See also "To Avoid Curdling Milk-Based Soups," page 179.

SAUCES MADE BY SIMPLE ADDITIONS TO THE BASICS

(Pour some over fish before baking it; serve some with poached, steamed, boiled or fried fish and use some as creamy cocktail sauces, salad dressings or dips. Sauces containing shellfish, such as Oyster Sauce [page 130], can be poured, hot, over toast, rice or noodles.)

Here we give you some of the sauces you can make by combining a few ingredients with the basics: White Sauce, Fish Broth Sauce, mayonnaise, Hollandaise, sour cream or yogurt, canned or frozen soups and broths. You take it from there and enjoy the pleasure of easy, creative fish cookery. Using the simple methods we've outlined and which we demonstrate in the following combinations, it's almost impossible to prepare a sauce that won't result in a delicious fish dish—as long as you don't overcook the fish. (Most people prefer a basic sauce to be medium thick.)

Heating Sour Cream, Mayonnaise and Yogurt: Sour cream, mayonnaise and yogurt are usually served cold, but they can be warmed slightly in the top of a double boiler, just enough so they won't chill any hot fish with which they may be served, yet not so much that sour cream or yogurt will lose all its body, because the longer you warm these two the thinner they become. Also because mayonnaise, sour cream and yogurt will all curdle and separate if heated too much.

A Message for Calorie Counters: Wherever the first line of a sauce in this section is marked with a dot (·), you can reduce the calorie count of a serving if, instead of choosing one of the ingredients listed, you substitute the most appropriate of the following:

Low-Calorie Fish Broth Sauce, page 121.

Low-Calorie White Sauce, page 121.

Almost Mayonnaise, page 135.

You can reduce calories still further by eliminating cream from a sauce recipe wherever it is marked "optional." And you can sometimes substitute yogurt for sour cream, but it has an unusual flavor that you may not find compatible with all ingredients. So experiment with it, tasting as you test. See Yogurt Sauce, page 133.

ANCHOVY SAUCE

> · 1 *recipe White Sauce, page 120, or 1 cup mayonnaise or sour cream if serving cold*
> 1 *teaspoon anchovy paste or to taste or 4 anchovy fillets, mashed*
> ½ *teaspoon garlic powder or to taste*

Mix all ingredients well, tasting as you add anchovy paste.
Makes 1 cup.

ALMOND SAUCE

(Amandine Sauce)

Add ½ cup or more of slivered or chopped almonds, with or without skin, to White Sauce or any other sauce to which they will add interesting flavor.

BÉCHAMEL SAUCE

See White Sauce, page 120.

CHEESE SAUCE I

Add 2 tablespoons or more, to taste, of grated cheddar or other cheese to White Sauce or any other sauce to which it will add interesting flavor.

CHEESE SAUCE II

(Mornay Sauce)

> · 1 *recipe White Sauce, page 120*
> ¼ *cup heavy cream (optional)*
> 2 *tablespoons grated Parmesan cheese*
> 2 *tablespoons grated Gruyère cheese*

Remove White Sauce from heat, stir in other ingredients and serve.
Makes about 1¼ cups.

CRAB SAUCE

> · 1 *recipe White Sauce, page 120, or 1 cup sour cream if serving cold*
> 1 *cup flaked crab meat*
> 1 *teaspoon prepared mustard or to taste (optional)*
> ¼ *cup heavy cream (optional)*

Combine all ingredients and serve.
Makes about 2 cups.

CREAM SAUCE

Add ¼ to ½ cup heavy cream to White Sauce, page 120.

DIET CREAM SAUCE

Instead of cream, add 1 teaspoon of nondairy, vegetable sauce creamer, which contains about 12 calories per teaspoonful.

CUCUMBER SAUCE

- *1 recipe White Sauce, page 120 (or 1 cup sour or whipped cream if to be served cold)*
- *½ cup minced and drained cucumber*
- *1 tablespoon minced chives*
- *¼ teaspoon crumbled dry dillweed*
- *1 tablespoon vingear*
- *¼ cup sour cream (optional); omit if sour cream is used as base*

Combine and serve. If made of sour or whipped cream, chill before using.
Makes 1½–1¾ cups.

CURRY CREAM SAUCE

- *1 recipe White or Fish Broth Sauce, page 120, or 1 can condensed mushroom soup diluted with ¼ to ½ cup milk or cream*
- *½ teaspoon onion powder*
- *1–2 teaspoons curry powder blended into 1–2 teaspoons butter or margarine*
- *¼–½ cup heavy cream*

Stir onion powder into hot sauce or soup, remove from fire and stir in curry butter mixture and cream.
Makes 1¼–2 cups.

DILL SAUCE

Add 1 tablespoon minced fresh dill or 1 teaspoon or to taste dried dill to any suitable sauce.

DRAWN BUTTER SAUCE

- 1 *recipe Fish Broth Sauce, page 120*

4 *tablespoons butter or margarine*

1 *teaspoon lemon juice or to taste*

Add butter or margarine bit by bit to hot Fish Broth Sauce, stirring each piece to combine before adding the next. Remove from heat, stir in lemon juice and serve.

Makes about 1¼ cups.

EGG SAUCE

- 1 *recipe White Sauce, page 120, or 1 can condensed mushroom soup diluted with ¼–½ cup milk or cream*

2 *hard-boiled eggs, chopped*

1 *teaspoon very finely chopped green pepper*

½ *teaspoon onion powder*

½ *teaspoon celery salt*

Add eggs, green pepper and seasonings to hot sauce or soup, stir and serve.

Makes 1½–2 cups.

FISH BROTH SAUCE

(Velouté)

See page 120.

FISH GLAZE SAUCE

(Chaud-Froid Sauce)

- 1 *cup Fish Broth Sauce, page 120*

1 *envelope (1 tablespoon) unflavored gelatin*

¼ *cup cold fish broth*

¼ *cup heavy cream*

Prepare Fish Broth Sauce. In top of a double boiler, dissolve gelatin in cold fish broth, place over boiling water and stir until gelatin completely dissolves. Stir into hot Fish Broth Sauce, remove from flame and stir in heavy cream. Let sauce cool but not set and use to glaze fish (traditionally salmon) that is to be served on buffet.

Makes about 1½ cups.

GINGER SAUCE

½ cup mayonnaise
½ cup sour cream
¼ cup slivered candied ginger
1 tablespoon lime juice
¼ cup slivered, toasted and blanched almonds (optional)

Combine all ingredients except almonds, blend well and chill. Stir in slivered almonds just before serving.
Makes about 1½ cups.

GREEN SAUCE

(Sauce Verte)

* *1 cup mayonnaise or sour cream*
1 cup watercress, spinach and parsley leaves

Boil green leaves for 3 or 4 minutes, drain and cool. Press out all water, grate, stir into mayonnaise or sour cream and chill before serving.
Makes about 1¼ cups.

GREEN GRAPE SAUCE

(Sauce Véronique)

* *1 recipe White Sauce, page 120*
1 cup green or white seedless grapes, whole and preferably small in size
¼ cup heavy cream (optional); dieters use 1 teaspoon nondairy creamer
Salt and pepper to taste

Add grapes to White Sauce last minute or two of cooking. Remove from heat and stir in cream and salt and pepper.
Makes about 2 cups.

HERBED WINE SAUCE

(Ravigote Sauce)

* *1 recipe White Sauce, page 120*
3 tablespoons white wine
1 tablespoon vinegar
¼ teaspoon dried tarragon

1 *tablespoon minced shallots or onion*
1 *tablespoon minced chervil (optional)*
Salt and pepper to taste

Simmer wine, vinegar and seasonings until reduced to half and strain. Stir into White Sauce and serve.
Makes about 1¼ cups.
VARIATION: *Add 2 teaspoons finely minced parsley to finished sauce.*

HOT SAUCE

Stir Louisiana Hot Sauce (which is also called Tabasco Sauce and Hot Pepper Sauce) or chopped canned green chili peppers to taste into any suitable sauce. Add Hot Sauce a drop at a time and chilis ½ teaspoon at a time, stirring and tasting as you add.

CREAMY HORSERADISH SAUCE

1 *cup sour cream*
1 *tablespoon freshly grated horseradish or to taste or prepared horse-*
   radish from which liquid has been squeezed
Salt to taste
¼ *cup finely diced red apple, skin on (optional)*

Combine all ingredients, stir and serve at once.
Makes about 1¼ cups.

LEMON SAUCE

· 1 *recipe White Sauce or Fish Broth Sauce, page 120*
2 *teaspoons finely chopped shallots, scallion or onion*
2 *or 3 tablespoons lemon juice*

Combine all ingredients.
Makes a little more than 1 cup.

LOBSTER SAUCE I

· 1 *recipe White Sauce or Fish Broth Sauce (page 120) or 1 can*
   condensed mushroom soup diluted with ¼–½ cup milk
½ *cup chopped cooked lobster meat*
¼ *cup heavy cream (optional)*
1 *tablespoon wine*

Stir lobster meat into sauce or soup 1 or 2 minutes before it is done. Remove from heat, stir in cream and wine and serve.

Makes 1½ to 2 cups.

NOTE: See page 131 for Lobster Sauce II.

LOUIS SAUCE

- • 1 *cup mayonnaise or ½ cup each mayonnaise and sour cream, combined*
- 5 *tablespoons chili sauce or catsup, or to taste*
- 1 *hard-cooked egg, chopped (optional)*
- 1 *teaspoon prepared horseradish (optional)*
- 1 *tablespoon finely chopped green pepper (optional)*
- ¼ *teaspoon Worcestershire sauce (optional)*
- 1 *teaspoon lemon juice or to taste (optional)*
- 2 *tablespoons chopped scallions (optional)*

Combine all ingredients and mix well. Include any or all of the optionals.

Makes about 1½ cups.

REMOULADE SAUCE

Eliminate chili sauce or catsup from preceding sauce. Use any or all of the other ingredients, and add:

- 1 *tablespoon prepared mustard*
- 1 *teaspoon anchovy paste*
- 1 *tablespoon chopped gherkins*

LOW-CALORIE HOT FISH SAUCE

Pour hot Fish Broth (page 118) or Fish Fumet (page 119) over baked, broiled, steamed or poached fish. If you go easy on the wine it contains, this is one way a calorie counter can make lots of sauce and eat it, too.

LOW-CALORIE COLD FISH SAUCE

Dissolve ½–1 teaspoon unflavored gelatin in 1 cup of Fish Broth (page 118) or Fish Fumet (page 119), and chill to give it a little body. If you made your broth with plenty of bones and skin, the addition of gelatin is not necessary. Just chill the broth and that's it.

MUSHROOM SAUCE

> · 1 *recipe White Sauce or Fish Broth Sauce, page 120, or* 1 *can con-*
> *densed mushroom soup diluted with* ¼–½ *cup milk*
> 1 *cup sliced, sautéed mushrooms or* 1 4-*ounce can sliced mushrooms*
> 2 *tablespoons chopped onion, lightly sautéed*
> ¼ *cup heavy cream or sour cream (optional)*
> *Salt and pepper to taste*

Add sautéed mushrooms and onion to White or Fish Broth Sauce or soup and heat to boiling. Remove from fire, stir in cream and seasonings and serve.

Makes about 2 cups.

ONION SAUCE

> · 1 *recipe White Sauce, page 120*
> 1 *medium onion, sliced and lightly sautéed*

Add sautéd onion to White Sauce last 2 or 3 minutes of cooking.

Makes about 1¼ cups.

OYSTER SAUCE

> · 1 recipe thick Fish Broth Sauce, page 121
> 1 *cup oysters and their liquor*
> ½ *cup sliced, sautéed mushrooms*

Heat oysters in their own liquor until edges curl. Set oysters aside and stir liquor into Fish Broth Sauce. When smooth, stir in oysters and mushrooms; heat, but do not boil, and serve.

Makes about 2½ cups.

RUSSIAN DRESSING

> · 1 *cup mayonnaise*
> 2 *tablespoons tomato paste or to taste*
> 1 *teaspoon chopped pickle (optional)*
> 1 *tablespoon red caviar (optional)*
> 1 *tablespoon minced onion (optional)*

Combine and mix well.

Makes about 1¼ cups.

SALMON SAUCE WITH WINE AND MUSHROOMS
(Geneva Sauce)

· 1 *recipe Fish Broth Sauce, page 120*
Head, bones and skin of small salmon or ½ to 1 pound scraps from a large one
1 *cup dry red wine*
1 *cup water*
Salt and pepper to taste
½ cup sliced, sautéed mushrooms (optional)

Combine salmon scraps, red wine and water in a heavy saucepan and boil for 30 minutes or until reduced so there will be about ½ cup of liquid. Strain, season with salt and pepper, add to hot Fish Broth Sauce, stir in mushrooms and serve.

Makes about 2 cups.

NOTE: If you don't have the carcass of another fish more delicately flavored than salmon for the Fish Broth Sauce, make it with chicken broth.

SHRIMP SAUCE I

· 1 *recipe White Sauce, page 120, or if to be served cold, ½ cup mayonnaise and sour cream, combined*
¼ *cup cooked and deveined shrimp, chopped*
1 *tablespoon chopped scallion (green onion)*
½ *teaspoon celery salt*

Combine last 3 ingredients with White Sauce just before removing it from heat. If to be served cold, add to mayonnaise and sour cream, mix well and chill before serving.

Makes 1¼ cups.

SHRIMP OR LOBSTER SAUCE II
(Sauce Nantua)

· 1 *recipe White Sauce, page 120*
1 *recipe Shrimp or Lobster Butter, page 143*
2 *tablespoons white wine*
¼ *cup heavy cream (optional)*

Add shrimp or lobster butter, 1 teaspoon at a time, to White Sauce just before it is finished cooking. Stir until well blended, remove from heat, stir in wine and cream and serve.

Makes about 1½ cups.

TARTAR SAUCE

> · 1 *cup mayonnaise or ½ cup each of mayonnaise and sour cream combined*
> 1 *teaspoon prepared mustard or to taste*
> 2 *tablespoons chopped pickle, sour or sweet according to taste*
> 2 *tablespoons finely chopped scallions, including some of the green*
> 1 *tablespoon finely chopped parsley*
> 1 *tablespoon chopped capers (optional)*
> ¼ *teaspoon dried tarragon (optional)*
> ¼–½ *teaspoon garlic powder*

Combine all ingredients, mix well, chill and serve.

Makes 1¼–1½ cups.

THOUSAND ISLAND DRESSING

> 1 *cup mayonnaise*
> ¼ *cup heavy cream (optional)*
> ¼–½ *cup chili sauce or tomato paste (optional)*
> *Minced green pepper to taste*
> 2 *tablespoons finely chopped ripe olives*
> 2 *teaspoons chopped chives*
> *Bits of leftover food that will add to the flavor and increase the* "*islands,*" *chopped (optional)*

Combine all ingredients, mix well, chill and serve.

Makes 1¾–2 cups.

TOMATO SAUCE

(Sauce Aurore)

> · 1 *recipe White Sauce, page 120*
> ¼ *cup tomato puree or tomato paste or to taste*
> ¼ *teaspoon paprika or to taste (optional)*

Stir tomato puree or paste and paprika into hot White Sauce. Stir until well blended and hot and serve.

Makes about 1¼ cups.

VELOUTÉ SAUCE

See Fish Broth Sauce, page 120.

RICH WINE SAUCE

1 *recipe thick Fish Broth Sauce, page 121*
½ *cup dry white wine*
¼ *cup cream*
1 *egg yolk, beaten*
Salt and pepper to taste

Stir wine into Fish Broth Sauce while cooking. Add cream to beaten egg yolk and stir until smooth. Remove sauce from heat. Stir 1 tablespoon of the hot sauce into egg-yolk mixture, then add the yolk mixture to the hot sauce in saucepan, stirring constantly until well blended. Add seasonings and serve at once.

Makes about 2 cups.

RICH WINE SAUCE WITH MUSHROOMS

Add ½ cup sliced mushrooms, lightly sautéed, and 1 teaspoon lemon juice to Rich Wine Sauce, above, and serve.

RICH WINE SAUCE WITH MUSSELS OR OYSTERS

(Sauce Normande)

Cook 1 pint shucked mussels or oysters or half pint of each in their own liquor (add ½ cup water) until edges curl. Strain liquor and substitute for all or part of liquid used in making Fish Broth Sauce in recipe for Rich Wine Sauce. Add shellfish to cooked sauce.

YOGURT SAUCE

A cup of plain yogurt made from partially skimmed milk contains only 120 calories compared to more than 400 in the same amount of commercial sour cream. But yogurt shouldn't be thought of simply as a substitute for people whose dietary restrictions won't permit them to eat sour cream. It's good in its own right. If, as is the case with many people, you must try yogurt a few times to acquire a taste for it, it's well worth the effort. You can substitute plain yogurt for another basic sauce ingredient in many of the preceding recipes. It can even be warmed slightly in the top of a double boiler, and although it will thin out a little, it will still be the consistency of a thin white sauce and very nice when poured over hot fish.

Try any of the following combinations that appeal to you. If this is your first experience with yogurt, let us suggest that you select the lemon and honey mixture as your introduction:

1 *cup of plain yogurt or* 1 *cup of plain yogurt mixed with* 1 *to* 2 *tablespoons lemon juice*

Combine either of above with one or more of the following:

1–2 *tablespoons honey (only* 60 *calories per tablespoon but still it makes a delicious dip or salad dressing)*
1 *tablespoon or to taste dry mustard powder*
1 *tablespoon or to taste ginger powder*
1 *tablespoon or to taste garlic powder*
1 *teaspoon grated lemon or orange peel*
Hot chopped green chili pepper or Louisiana Hot Sauce (Tabasco Sauce) to taste.

EGG YOLK SAUCES

MAYONNAISE

(A commercial mayonnaise may be substituted)

1 *large egg yolk, room temperature*
⅛ *teaspoon dry mustard or to taste*
½ *teaspoon salt or to taste*
1 *tablespoon vinegar or lemon juice*
1 *cup cooking oil, room temperature*

Put yolk in a room-temperature mixing bowl. Stir in dry mustard and salt, and mix well. Beat with electric beater at medium speed, slowly adding ¾ tablespoon of the vinegar. Add oil a drop at a time, beating constantly until sauce begins to thicken. Continue to beat, increasing flow of oil to a thin stream. If mayonnaise becomes too thick, add remaining vinegar, a drop at a time, until it reaches the desired consistency.

Makes about 1¼ cups.

MAYONNAISE AND CREAM SAUCE

Add ¼ cup whipped, sour or heavy cream and 1 teaspoon sugar to ¾ cup of mayonnaise. Mix well and serve.

ALMOST MAYONNAISE

(For Calorie Counters)

(This recipe came to us from the Department of Fisheries of Canada.)

2 *tablespoons flour*
1 *teaspoon celery seed*
1 *teaspoon dry mustard*
1 *teaspoon salt*
1 *cup skim milk*
1 *clove garlic (optional)*
2 *egg yolks, beaten*
¼ *cup vinegar*
4 *drops noncaloric liquid sweetener (optional)*
Few grains monosodium glutamate (optional)

Combine flour, celery seed, mustard and salt in top of double boiler. Add milk slowly. Cook and stir until sauce begins to thicken. Add garlic if desired. Cook about 10 minutes. Add egg yolks and cook 3 minutes. Remove garlic and stir in vinegar, liquid sweetener and monosodium glutamate. Chill.

Makes about 1¼ cups—approximately 15 calories per tablespoon.

HOLLANDAISE SAUCE

½ *cup butter*
2 *egg yolks*
2 *teaspoons lemon juice*
1 *teaspoon water*
Salt to taste
Small pinch cayenne pepper

Whip egg yolks with lemon juice and water until light and foamy. Place in a double boiler over water that is steaming but not boiling hard. Using a wire whisk or electric mixer, beat in butter, 1 small piece at a time. Each piece should be completely incorporated before adding the next one. Continue to beat and cook just until thick. Add salt and cayenne pepper and serve at once or, if necessary, keep warm over tepid, not hot, water until time to serve.

Makes about ¾ cup.

MOUSSELINE SAUCE: Just before serving, stir ¼ cup stiffly beaten cream into warm Hollandaise Sauce.

Makes about 1 cup.

BÉARNAISE SAUCE

1 *teaspoon dried tarragon*
½ *teaspoon dried chervil*
1 *small scallion chopped*
1 *teaspoon wine vinegar*
3 *tablespoons dry white wine*
1 *small sprig fresh tarragon, leaves removed and finely minced (optional)*
1 *small sprig fresh chervil, leaves removed and minced (optional)*
1 *recipe Hollandaise Sauce, page 135*

Simmer all ingredients except last 3 until reduced to about 1 tablespoon. Strain, cool to room temperature, add chopped tarragon and chervil leaves, stir into tepid Hollandaise and serve at once.

Makes about 1 cup.

CHORON SAUCE: Fold ¾ tablespoon tomato puree into Béarnaise Sauce.

Makes about 1 cup.

THE EASY BUTTER (OR MARGARINE) SAUCES*

Although the butter sauces are probably the easiest of all to make, this fact in no way reflects on their goodness. Most of those included here can be made with soft butter, served while creamy or stored in the refrigerator until time to use (then just the amount needed cut off), or they can be made with hot melted butter and used immediately.

Either way, not a speck of these sauces need be wasted, because even small amounts of leftover melted butter sauces can be refrigerated for later use. And, since these sauces are good on other foods as well as on fish, there's no need to keep them overlong in the refrigerator before using them.

An economy feature of the butter sauces is that you can use up delicious little dibs and dabs of things that might otherwise have no place to go: a bit of caviar, one lone anchovy fillet, some lobster coral, etc. Here are a few suggestions for using these sauces:

1. Spread (if cold) or pour (if hot) on a sizzling hot fish steak, fillet or whole fish that's just come from the frying pan, broiler or oven. Use less on a fat fish than on a lean one.

2. If you're trying to pare down your calories, a teaspoon of one of

---

* Margarine may be used instead of butter in any of the sauces. If you're on a diet that calls for replacing saturated fats with polyunsaturated ones, check margarine label to be sure the one you're buying supplies this quality.

the zestier butters can work a little magic and transform boring diet fare into exciting eating.

3. Melt a teaspoonful of cold, flavored butter in a fish broth or fish milk soup.

4. Use the melted butter sauces (you can melt the cold butters and use them this way too) to pour over a baking fish.

5. Brush them on fish fillets or steaks or split fish that's being broiled indoors or out.

Please note that we didn't say *pour* it on the broiling fish; we said *brush* it on. There's no need to waste good sauce on coals, because you aren't going to eat the coals. Nor is an indoor broiling pan very palatable. The more sauce you burn onto it, the harder it is to clean. Additionally, when you pour a sauce rather than brush it on, there are usually bare spots left on the fish. So any way you look at it, brushing is better.

It's much harder to combine liquids such as lemon juice or wine with cold butters, even though they may be soft, than it is pastes or dry powders. But these liquids (up to about 20 percent of total volume) *can* be blended in. If you have difficulty doing it with a spoon or fork, try an electric mixer.

Hot butter sauces will be a little nicer if made with clarified butter (see page 120).

A Word About Butter Sauce Recipes for Marinades: Any of the butter sauce recipes make very good marinades, but since fish and shellfish should be marinated in the refrigerator and since butter or margarine will solidify very quickly in the refrigerator, it's best to substitute a cooking oil for this ingredient.

If sauce has an acid content, marinate in glass or nonporous ceramic dish.

HOT OR COLD BUTTER SAUCES

Once you try a few of these combinations, you'll want to experiment with your own ideas.

ALMOND BUTTER

(Amandine Sauce)

¼ cup butter or margarine
2 tablespoons blanched and roasted almonds, ground

Let butter or margarine stand out of refrigerator until pliant. Blend in almonds and use at once or refrigerate for future use.

(OR)

Melt butter or margarine, stir in ground almonds and use at once.

ANCHOVY BUTTER

¼ cup butter or margarine
1 teaspoon anchovy paste or 1 to 2 anchovy fillets, mashed

Let butter or margarine stand out of refrigerator until pliant. Blend in anchovy paste and use at once or refrigerate for future use.

(OR)

Melt butter or margarine, stir in anchovy paste and use at once.

BASIL BUTTER

¼ cup butter or margarine
1 tablespoon dried basil or 1 to 2 tablespoons finely chopped fresh basil
1 tablespoon lemon juice or to taste
Salt and pepper to taste

Let butter or margarine stand out of refrigerator until pliant. Blend in remaining ingredients and use at once or refrigerate for future use.

(OR)

Melt butter or margarine, stir in remaining ingredients and use at once.

BLACK BUTTER

Slowly heat butter until deep brown and frothy but not smoking. Use as is or in lemon or other butter sauce.

HOT CHILI BUTTER

¼ cup butter or margarine
1 teaspoon or to taste of grated canned green chili peppers (taste as you add)
1 tablespoon red chili sauce (optional)

Let butter or margarine stand out of refrigerator until pliant. Blend in grated chili peppers and red chili sauce and use at once or refrigerate for future use.

(OR)

Melt butter or margarine, stir in grated chilies and red chili sauce and use at once.

CUCUMBER-DILL BUTTER

¼ cup butter or margarine
¼–½ cup finely diced cucumber, drained

1–2 *teaspoons finely chopped fresh dill*
Salt and pepper to taste

Let butter or margarine stay out of refrigerator until pliant. Stir in remaining ingredients and use at once or refrigerate for future use.
(OR)
Melt butter or margarine, stir in remaining ingredients and use at once.

CURRY-MUSHROOM BUTTER

¼ *cup butter or margarine*
¼–½ *teaspoon curry powder*
1 *teaspoon dried mushroom powder*

Let butter or margarine stay out of refrigerator until pliant. Blend in remaining ingredients and serve at once or refrigerate for future use.
(OR)
Melt butter, add remaining ingredients, mix well and serve at once.

DILL BUTTER

¼ *cup butter or margarine*
2 *teaspoons minced fresh dill or* 1 *teaspoon crumbled dry dillweed*

Let butter or margarine stay out of refrigerator until pliant. Mix in minced dill and serve at once or refrigerate for future use.
(OR)
Melt butter, stir in minced dill and serve at once.

GARLIC BUTTER

¼ *cup butter or margarine*
½–1 *teaspoon garlic powder or mashed garlic to taste*

Let butter or margarine stay out of refrigerator until pliant. Blend in garlic powder or mashed garlic and serve at once or refrigerate for future use.
(OR)
Melt butter, stir in garlic powder, mix well and serve at once.

HERB AND WINE BUTTER
(Fines Herbes Butter)

¼ *cup butter or margarine*
1–2 *tablespoons minced chives*

1 *teaspoon minced fresh parsley*
1 *teaspoon minced fresh tarragon and/or rosemary and dill*
1 *tablespoon white wine (optional)*

Let butter or margarine stay out of refrigerator until pliant. Blend in other ingredients and serve at once or refrigerate for future use.
(OR)
Melt butter or margarine, stir in remaining ingredients, mix well and serve at once.

VARIATION: Use any combination of dried and fresh herbs of your choice.

HONEY-WINE SAUCE

¼ *cup butter*
1 *teaspoon honey or to taste*
1 *tablespoon white wine*
1 *teaspoon lemon juice or to taste*
Salt to taste
Paprika to taste

Melt butter, stir in remaining ingredients and serve at once.

LEMON BUTTER

½ *cup butter or margarine*
3 *tablespoons lemon juice*
½ *teaspoon grated lemon rind*
½ *teaspoon grated orange rind*
Salt and pepper to taste

Melt butter, stir in remaining ingredients, mix well and serve at once.

LEMON-ONION BUTTER

¼ *cup butter or margarine*
2 *tablespoons finely chopped onion*
¼ *teaspoon garlic powder*
1 *tablespoon lemon juice*
Salt and pepper to taste

Cook onion in butter or margarine until lightly browned. Add remaining ingredients, mix well and serve at once.

LEMON-PARSLEY BUTTER
(Maître d'Hotel Butter)

¼ *cup butter or margarine*
2 *teaspoons lemon juice*
1 *tablespoon finely chopped parsley*

Let butter or margarine stay out of refrigerator until pliant. Blend in lemon juice, mix in chopped parsley and serve or refrigerate for future use.
(OR)
Melt butter or margarine, add remaining ingredients, mix well and serve at once.

LOBSTER CORAL BUTTER

½ *cup butter or margarine*
1 *tablespoon lobster coral (red roe)*

Let butter or margarine stay out of refrigerator until pliant. Blend in lobster coral and serve at once or refrigerate for later use the same day.
(OR)
Melt butter or margarine, add lobster coral, mix thoroughly and serve at once.

MEDITERRANEAN OIL, WINE AND BUTTER SAUCE

1–2 *tablespoons olive oil*
1 *tablespoon cooking oil*
1 *tablespoon butter or margarine*
1 *clove garlic, minced*
1 *shallot, minced (substitute ½ small onion)*
½ *cup dry white wine*
1 *tablespoon finely minced fresh parsley*
Salt and pepper to taste

Heat olive oil, cooking oil and butter or margarine in large heavy skillet. Add garlic and shallot and lightly sauté. Pour in white wine, stir and simmer for about 5 minutes. Add parsley and simmer for an additional 5 minutes. Serve at once over cooked fish or use to marinate or baste baking, broiling or barbecuing fish.
   Makes about ¾ cup.

MUSTARD BUTTER

¼ cup butter or margarine
1 teaspoon powdered mustard or to taste

Let butter or margarine stay out of refrigerator until pliant. Blend in powdered mustard and serve at once or refrigerate for future use.

(OR)

Stir powdered mustard into butter or margarine in saucepan. Heat, mix well, and serve when butter is melted and hot.

PAPRIKA-BUTTER SAUCE

(Coral Sauce)

¼ cup butter or margarine
1–2 teaspoons paprika
2 tablespoons lemon juice
1 tablespoon orange-drink concentrate
Onion powder to taste
Salt and pepper to taste

Melt butter or margarine, add remaining ingredients, mix well and serve at once.

SARDINE BUTTER

¼ cup butter or margarine
1 tablespoon sardine paste or to taste or 1 or 2 tablespoons mashed boneless sardines

Let butter or margarine stay out of refrigerator until pliant. Blend in sardine paste and serve at once or refrigerate for future use.

(OR)

Melt butter or margarine, stir in sardine paste, mix well and serve at once.

SHRIMP BUTTER

¼ cup butter or margarine
¼ cup finely minced or ground cooked shrimp
1 teaspoon lemon juice
½ teaspoon horseradish (optional)
2 or 3 drops Louisiana (Tabasco) Hot Sauce or to taste (optional)
Salt to taste

Let butter or margarine stand out of refrigerator until pliant. Blend in remaining ingredients and use at once or refrigerate for use in a day or two.

SHRIMP OR LOBSTER BUTTER

¼ cup butter or margarine
*Shells from about 1 pound of cooked shrimp or 1 or 2 cooked lob-
sters, meat removed*
1 cup water

Spread shells out on a cookie sheet or shallow baking pan and heat in
250-degree oven for 15 minutes. Place in a mortar or wooden bowl along
with butter or margarine and crush and blend. Transfer the mashed shell
and butter mixture to a saucepan, add water and simmer, covered, for
about 15 minutes. Strain, discarding the shells. Chill the liquid, lift off the
shrimp or lobster butter that solidifies on top and use it to season White
Sauce, to brush over hot cooked fish or an omelet or as the base for an
appetizer spread.

SNAIL BUTTER

¼ cup butter or margarine
1 clove garlic thoroughly mashed and pulverized
1 teaspoon finely minced shallots or green onion tops
2 teaspoons finely minced fresh parsley
1 small pinch ground nutmeg
Salt and pepper to taste

Work all ingredients together with a spoon until thoroughly blended.
Traditionally used in the preparation of snails but also good brushed over
fish while baking, broiling or barbecuing.
Makes a little more than ¼ cup.

SOY BUTTER

¼ cup butter or margarine
1–2 tablespoons soy sauce
1 tablespoon lemon juice
Pepper to taste

Melt butter or margarine, stir in other ingredients, simmer for 2 or 3
minutes and serve at once.

TARRAGON BUTTER

¼ cup butter or margarine
1 teaspoon dried, crumbled tarragon

Let butter or margarine stay out of refrigerator until pliant. Blend in crumbled tarragon and serve at once or refrigerate for future use.

(OR)

Melt butter or margarine, stir in crumbled tarragon, mix well and serve at once.

SPICY, WINE AND VINEGAR SAUCES

(For marinating, barbecuing, basting, cocktails, salads and dips indoors or out.)

The red sauces included here are sometimes referred to as "barbecue sauces" but their use shouldn't be limited to outdoor cooking. They're just as good brushed over a steak or fillet or split fish that's broiling in the indoor stove or baking in the oven. No matter what the use, use them sparingly. They can add color and flavor to fish, or drown it so you don't know the fish is there. Some also make good cocktail sauces and dips.

For broiling very lean fish, add 1 to 2 tablespoons olive oil or cooking oil to following recipes (but not if you're on a very low-calorie diet).

Spicy sauces based on the tomato condiments that contain no (or very little) sugar, honey or fats are generally lower in calories than are the creamy "white" sauces or the butter sauces. A little of them usually can go further in adding flavor, too, than will the sauces containing a greater concentration of calories.

Use only glass or nonporous ceramic dishes when marinating in sauce containing an acid.

Danger, Fire!

Many, if not most, of the spicy sauce recipes that follow call for the use of Louisiana Hot Sauce, which is also known as hot pepper sauce and Tabasco Sauce, and/or chili peppers. Well, be warned. All of them are hot, so be careful how you use them.

For example, 1/4 teaspoon (16 drops) of Louisiana Hot Sauce in 3 cups of sauce is fiery enough to leave a burning sensation in your mouth.

Chili peppers also are burning hot for some palates. So nibble-taste the ones you intend to use in order to make sure that the amount you add to a recipe won't set folks afire.

BASIC RED SAUCE

1/2 *cup catsup, chili sauce or tomato sauce*
1/2 *medium onion, grated, or onion powder to taste*
1/2 *clove garlic, finely minced or to taste*
1/4 *cup water*
From 2 drops to 1/4 teaspoon Louisiana Hot Sauce, according to taste

Combine all ingredients in a heavy saucepan and simmer slowly, stirring frequently for 5 to 10 minutes or until well blended and the desired consistency. Use either hot or cold.

Makes ½ to ¾ cup.

NOTE: Add strong seasonings a little at a time, tasting as you add.

VARIATIONS: Add one or more of the following to the preceding recipe:

1 *tablespoon prepared mustard*
1 *to 2 tablespoons wine vinegar or ¼ cup red wine*
1 *tablespoon lemon juice or to taste*
1 *teaspoon honey or brown sugar or to taste*
½ *teaspoon or to taste prepared horseradish*
¼ *teaspoon or to taste Worcestershire sauce*
2 *red chili peppers, cooked and mashed*
1 *sprig thyme, minced*
1 *pinch sage*
1 *teaspoon or to taste chopped canned green chili peppers and their very hot liquid*

BARBECUE SAUCE AND MARINADE

¼ *cup catsup*
2 *tablespoons honey*
1 *tablespoon wine vinegar*
2 *tablespoons frozen concentrated orange juice*
8 *drops Worcestershire sauce*
⅛ *teaspoon Tabasco Sauce (Louisiana Hot Sauce)*
½ *teaspoon prepared horseradish*
¼ *teaspoon garlic powder*
1 *tablespoon lemon juice*

Combine all ingredients, mix well and use for marinating and/or basting any fish for either indoor or outdoor cooking. If fish is delicately flavored, use just a touch of this sauce, perhaps brush lightly with it once or twice. If fish is oily or has a strong flavor, marinate it for several hours in the sauce. Makes about ⅔ cup.

MUSTARD DIP: Add ¼ cup prepared Dijon mustard to preceding. Cut down on catsup to increase mustard flavor.

TARRAGON-FLAVORED WINE MARINADE

¼ *cup sherry*
½ *teaspoon dry tarragon, finely crumbled*
¼ *teaspoon garlic powder*
2 *pinches powdered ginger*

Combine (use very sparingly on delicately flavored fish).
Makes about ¼ cup.

TAWNY PORT MARINADE

> ½ *cup tawny port wine*
> 1 *teaspoon garlic powder*
> 1 *teaspoon finely ground rosemary*
> 1 *pinch cayenne pepper (optional)*

Combine all ingredients and use as a marinade for fish to be broiled either outside or inside.
Makes ½ cup.

SOUTHWEST BARBECUE SAUCE

> ½ *of 9-ounce jar tomato paste*
> 1 *large clove garlic, crushed*
> 2 *tablespoons water*
> 1 *tablespoon strong mustard*
> 1 *teaspoon Worcestershire sauce*
> ½ *teaspoon red chili powder*
> ¼ *cup red wine or 2 tablespoons wine vinegar mixed with 2 table-spoons water*

Combine in heavy pot over medium heat, stirring frequently, until it starts to boil. Turn down to a low simmer and continue cooking for 5 minutes, continuing to stir frequently.

This sauce is excellent on fish with a distinctive flavor. Just a light touch will add interesting zest to those with a delicate flavor.
Makes ¾–1 cup.

VINEGAR (OR VINAIGRETTE) SAUCES

A few drops of vinegar all by itself can be very nice on a fat fish. Try it on canned salmon or mackerel served just as they come from the can, either hot or cold.

Or you can mix vinegar with olive oil or any vegetable oil in any proportions (most people prefer it with equal parts of oil or more, but calorie counters should settle for a greater proportion of vinegar), then season and use. The seasonings should be added gradually as you taste and can be one of the following: basil, cayenne, garlic powder or chopped or slashed garlic cloves, honey, mustard, onion powder or chopped onion, paprika, pepper or hot pepper sauce, rosemary, salt, sugar, tarragon, thyme—just about anything you'd like them to be.

If possible, prepare vinegar sauces several hours before serving. Unless you add perishable ingredients, do not store in the refrigerator, except when you keep them for more than a day or two, in which case remove from refrigerator at least ½ hour before using.

Lemon or lime juice can be substituted for some of the vinegar.

These acid sauces should be mixed and stored in a glass or nonporous ceramic dish or container.

Following is a recipe for French Dressing, perhaps the best known of the vinegar dressings, with common variations. Use them, or combinations you create yourself, sparingly to marinate or baste fish or stir into a fish and vegetable salad.

FRENCH DRESSING

¼ cup vinegar
¼ cup olive oil
¼ cup other vegetable oil
1 teaspoon salt or to taste
1 pinch cayenne
⅛ teaspoon pepper or to taste
¼ teaspoon powdered mustard (optional)

Mix together several hours before you need it. Shake well before serving.
Makes about ¾ cup.

VARIATION: Add ½ teaspoon sugar or to taste.

GARLIC FRENCH DRESSING: Add 2 cloves finely minced garlic or 1 teaspoon garlic powder.

FINES HERBES DRESSING: Add 2 tablespoons chopped fresh herbs such as tarragon, basil, parsley and rosemary to French Dressing. Mix well and serve at once.

ROQUEFORT FRENCH DRESSING: Mash 1 teaspoon or more Roquefort cheese and blend into the oils before combining French Dressing ingredients.

MISCELLANEOUS SAUCES

(Sauces containing acid should be stored—or used as a marinade—only in glass or nonporous ceramic dishes.)

CURRIED SALAD DRESSING

¼ cup vegetable oil
¼ cup orange juice
2 tablespoons pineapple juice (optional)
1 tablespoon lemon juice

1/8 *teaspoon onion powder*
1 *teaspoon sugar or to taste*
1 *pinch salt or to taste*
1 *pinch white pepper or to taste*
1/4 *teaspoon curry powder or to taste*

Combine all ingredients, mix well and let stand for about an hour; shake and serve over salad or as a marinade or to baste cooking fish.

Makes about 3/4 cup.

LOBSTER SHELL SAUCE
(Made from Leftover Shell)

1 *large lobster shell, most of meat removed*
2 *cups water*
1/4 *cup cocktail sherry*
1 *carrot, scraped*
1 *small onion*
2 *celery stalks*
2 *sprigs parsley*
1/4 *cup butter or margarine*
3 *tablespoons flour*
Salt and white pepper to taste
1/2 *cup coffee cream*

Break up lobster shell and put in saucepan with water, sherry, carrot, onion, celery and parsley, and boil rapidly for 30 minutes. Strain off liquid and measure. You should have 1 cup; if less, add water; if more, boil it down. Melt butter or margarine in top of double boiler, add flour and stir until smooth. Gradually stir in strained stock and cook for about 10 minutes on low heat, stirring frequently. If it gets too thick, add water. Season with salt and white pepper, and blend in cream. Reheat if necessary, but don't boil after cream has been added.

Makes about 1 1/2 cups.

NOTE: Refrigerate lobster shell as soon as meat has been removed.

LOBSTER SAUCE WITH ROE AND GREEN LIVER: Mash up the red roe and green liver, which are very tasty, and blend into the sauce after adding cream.

NEWBURG SAUCE: Add 1/2 cup of milk. Stir 1 egg yolk into cream, stir a little of the hot sauce into the mixture, then add to sauce in double boiler. Do not boil. Season to taste with nutmeg, paprika and cayenne.

MINT SAUCE

¼ cup mint jelly
¼ cup apple or currant jelly
1 tablespoon lemon juice
1 tablespoon grated orange peel
1 teaspoon grated lemon peel
Sprigs of mint

Mix all ingredients together and spread over sizzling-hot fish or heat and pour over. Slightly crush sprigs of mint between finger and thumb to release aroma and use to garnish each serving.

OKRA-TOMATO SAUCE

(Creole Sauce)

1 tablespoon olive oil
1 tablespoon cooking oil
1 medium onion, chopped
½ medium green pepper, chopped
1 clove garlic, finely minced
1 cup okra, sliced raw, or 1 10-ounce package, frozen
2 cups chopped ripe tomatoes or canned
¼ cup fish or chicken broth
1 teaspoon celery seed
1 bay leaf
1 to 2 teaspoons sugar
1 tablespoon parsley, finely chopped
4 whole cloves (optional)
¼–½ teaspoon chili powder (optional)
Salt and pepper to taste

Heat oils in heavy saucepan and sauté onion, green pepper and garlic in it. Add remaining ingredients and simmer 30 minutes or until nice consistency. Steam fish or bake fish on top of this sauce, pour it over baking fish, or pour it, hot, over already cooked fish.

Makes 2½ to 3 cups.

VARIATION: Add ½ cup sliced mushrooms and include them with sautéed vegetables.

MIXED VEGETABLE SAUCE: Substitute chopped celery for the okra and eliminate cloves and chili powder in preceding recipe. Mixture can be pureed or blended in an electric mixer or blender for smooth consistency.

NOTE: For the ultimate in eating pleasure in the two preceding sauces, use the very best and freshest vegetables available. If they follow that recommendation, those on a low-sodium diet can leave out the salt and still find the flavor delicious.

HAWAIIAN-STYLE SWEET AND SOUR SAUCE

1 *cup fish or chicken broth, strained*
⅓ *cup brown sugar*
⅛ *teaspoon ground ginger*
2 *tablespoons butter or margarine*
⅓ *cup pineapple juice*
4 *tablespoons red wine*
4 *tablespoons lemon juice*
2 *tablespoons soy sauce or to taste*
2 *tablespoons cornstarch or 2 tablespoons arrowroot*
3 *tablespoons water*
¼ *cup slivered almonds, toasted*
Salt to taste

Combine fish or chicken broth, brown sugar, ginger, butter or margarine, pineapple juice, red wine, lemon juice and soy sauce in heavy saucepan and stir. Mix cornstarch or arrowroot with water and drizzle into mixture in saucepan, stirring constantly. Bring to a boil, turn down to a simmer and cook, stirring constantly, until sauce thickens. Continue cooking, stirring as needed, until sauce is nice and clear: 4 to 5 minutes for cornstarch, half that time for arrowroot. Add almonds and salt and serve.

Makes about 2 cups.

HONG KONG–STYLE SWEET AND SOUR SAUCE

See Sweet and Sour Sea Bass, page 276.

POLONAISE SWEET AND SOUR SAUCE

With Gingersnaps, Almonds and Raisins

1½ *cups fish broth, strained*
½ *cup crushed gingersnaps or to taste*
⅓ *cup corn syrup*
⅓ *cup raisins*
⅓ *cup blanched, slivered almonds*
Juice of ½ lemon or to taste
Salt to taste

Combine all ingredients, bring to a boil, turn down to low simmer and cook 5–10 minutes or until ingredients are well blended. Adjust to taste by adding more salt and/or lemon juice. Serve over any cooked fish; especially good with boiled, poached or steamed recipes and traditional with carp.

Makes about 2 cups.

TEMPURA SAUCE

¾ *cup fish broth boiled down to rich but not heavy flavor*
¼ *cup soy sauce or to taste*
¼ *cup rice wine or any dry white wine or to taste*
1 *teaspoon sugar or to taste (optional)*
¼ *teaspoon ground ginger or to taste (optional)*

Combine all ingredients, mix well, divide into individual small sauce bowls and serve. (We once borrowed tiny bowls and cups from our daughter's tea set because we had nothing suitable that was pretty enough for this purpose.) Serve with tempura or other fried fish or shellfish.

TUNA AND ANCHOVY SAUCE

1 *7-ounce can tuna fish*
1 *2-ounce can anchovy fillets*
2 *tablespoons olive oil*
2 *tablespoons wine vinegar, or to taste*
2 *tablespoons prepared mustard (optional)*
Pepper to taste
2 *hard-cooked eggs, riced*

Combine all ingredients, including the liquid from the 2 cans, but not including the eggs. Blend or sieve into a smooth sauce. Sprinkle the sauce with riced egg and spread over hot or cold fish.

Makes approximately 1¼ cups.

TUNA AND ANCHOVY DIP: Use preceding recipe as a dip for sliced cucumbers, chips or crackers.

TUNA-ANCHOVY SALAD DRESSING: Do not mash tuna and anchovies. Break into small pieces instead and mix into vegetable salad. Slice eggs and use as garnish.

WHITE SAUCE CROQUETTE BASE

(Panada)

Here is a recipe for a very thick white sauce that, when combined with flaked or pureed raw or leftover fin fish and shellfish and other ingredients, can help transform them into fish balls or croquettes and fish dumplings (quenelle) that will be an epicurean delight.

1 *tablespoon butter or margarine*
2 *tablespoons flour*
⅝ *cup milk*

Melt butter or margarine in a small heavy saucepan over low heat or in top of a double boiler over lightly boiling water. Add flour and thoroughly mix. Be sure ingredients don't brown. Add milk and cook, stirring constantly with a wire whisk for 4 or 5 minutes until sauce is smooth and very thick. It should cook long enough for at least 2 tablespoons of the milk to steam away, making approximately ½ cup of sauce, and the flour to lose most of its starchy flavor. If using a saucepan, you may find it easier to achieve the desired result by holding it above, rather than directly on, the fire as you stir. Cover and let cool before using. Combine with 2 cups of well-drained, flaked or pureed fish mixture to make croquettes, etc. See pages 268–269 for detailed instructions.

RICH WHITE SAUCE CROQUETTE BASE: For a richer sauce, substitute 1–2 tablespoons cream for same amount of the milk.

LEFTOVER SAUCE CROQUETTE BASE: It's smart to save ½ cup of a nice leftover cream sauce (other than egg types such as Hollandaise) in the refrigerator for a day or two, then mix with leftover fish in some type of fish cake or ball. If it's not thick enough (remember that it will thicken quite a bit in refrigerator), reduce it by cooking in the top of a double boiler over slowly boiling water. If you don't expect to serve fish within 2 days, freeze the leftover sauce and keep it for a week or so. Don't let it stand around in the warm kitchen first, though. Chill immediately, pour into a freezer container (leaving a bit of head room for expansion), cover tightly and freeze. For safety, reheat to at least 140 degrees before or when using.

2

Appetizers

(Including Hors d'Oeuvres and Cocktails)

The line dividing appetizers, hors d'oeuvres and cocktails is uneven and ever-shifting. Therefore, rather than try to separate one from the other, we are grouping all three together in this section, which, you'll note, is quite thin. No more than perhaps 25 recipes and/or appetizer-making procedures are included in it.

The reason? Not because there are no more, but precisely because there are so many more. In fact, you'll find scores of tidbit recipes and procedures within these book covers, so many that it would be space-wasting to repeat them under this all-encompassing appetizer heading, and time-wasting to have you read them a second time.

What makes a fish appetizer, hors d'oeuvre, cocktail, tidbit, canapé or whatever you want to call them? They can be prepared from scratch, of course, but, more than anything else, the best such treats come from leftovers.

There is nothing so delicious as a cold tidbit that, in fact, is nothing more than the leftover of a hot fish dish you cooked and ate yesterday. In our house we have them all the time, not just when company comes. We'll eat, for example, from a Poached Big Fish with Conch Sauce (pages 333–334) recipe as a main course tonight and have the refrigerated, jellied leftovers as the first course in a meat dinner tomorrow night. Or as a cocktail-hour canapé, or a TV-watching tidbit, or as a sleep-time snack.

As we said, this book is replete with such leftover ideas. If we don't point all of them out specifically, no harm done. You and your culinary imagination will spot the ones we missed, besides creating leftover ideas of your own virtually every time you cook fish. In fact, you'll find yourself cooking and planning so that you'll have leftovers for appetizer use the next day. And planning too, we hope, to give your highly perishable tidbits the care they deserve. (See "Care of Leftovers," page 93.)

Fish salad and baked, broiled and deep-fried shellfish are great for company or for family treats. So, too—and here we'll name some specific recipes—are Cold Fish in Jelly, Shrimp Curry, Charcoal-Broiled Alaska King Crab, Fried Flounder Roe, Barbecued Oysters, Cheeky Tongues Oriental, Tongue 'n' Cheeks, Scallop-Stuffed Mushroom Caps and—well, we could go on and on. But you get the idea.

You'll also find appetizer recipes tucked away in other places: for example, Smoked Mollusks in Onion Boats in the section that we devote to Company Menus.

You'll also find that many of this book's recipes are definitely two-way affairs. Prepare them either to be served by themselves, perhaps as a main-course dish, or to take their place among a host of other goodies on an appetizer table. What it all adds up to is this: there are, as we said, scores of appetizer recipes in this book, although there are only a couple of dozen in this section because, more than our giving you do-it-this-way formulae, we want to whet your appetite for creating appetizers of your own. Not only because they are quick and easy, almost ever-ready and good to the taste, but also because appetizers are an excellent means of adding nutrients to a nonfish meal.

Keep Them Cold!

Throughout this book we stress that fish, especially shellfish, must be kept very cold in order to prevent the growth of harmful bacteria. At no time is this more important to keep in mind than when setting up the appetizer table. The treats that go on it must never be set out and allowed to stand at room temperature.

Which means you'll need ice. So, since the use of ice must therefore be a part of your appetizer, you might just as well make the most of it by seeing to it that the ice becomes a part of the decorative scheme. Therefore, color your ice. Using only edible food dyes, of course. Or fruit juices.

This can often be a grand project for children. Here are just a few ideas:

· Make a trayful of pink ice cubes. Crush them and set shrimp cocktails, or any other appetizer, in the crushed ice.

· Freeze tomato or pineapple juice. Crush the ice, place it in stemmed goblets and ring the rims with shrimp or whatever.

· Freeze edibly colored blue or green water in a solid cake (it will last longer than crushed ice or solid cubes) in the bottom of a large Corning Ware baking pan. Set the wire racks that come with the pan atop the ice, and set your appetizer dishes on the racks.

· If you don't have such a pan, use any large, shallow baking pan. If it needs a bit of camouflage, arrange foil around it.

You and your children can take it from there. Let them have free rein, and be prepared to be amazed by the ice formations and colors that they'll come up with.

KEEP THEM HOT!

Temperatures between 45 and 140 degrees are considered hazardous for certain perishable foods such as fish and the cream-type sauces often served with it. (Disease-producing bacteria grow most rapidly at the middle of that temperature range.) So, if it's a hot appetizer you're serving, keep it good and hot. This will mean special serving equipment or leg work. By that last we mean carrying from stove to appetizer table only as many hot goodies as will be gobbled up within seconds.

CANNED FISH-TOMATO APPETIZERS

½ *cup mashed canned fish, skin and bones removed (sardines, salmon, tuna)*
12 *firm cherry tomatoes, sliced in half and left that way or pulp removed*
3–4 *tablespoons fish or chicken broth*
1 *3-ounce package cream cheese*
2 *cooked egg yolks, coarsely crumbed*
1 *tablespoon pulverized freeze-dried shallots (optional)*
¼ *cup grated cheese of your choice*

Blend enough broth into cream cheese to make it spreadable, stir in mashed fish, crumbled yolks and pulverized shallots and pile in mounds on top of tomato halves, or fill cavity if pulp was removed. Sprinkle with cheese, arrange on platter and serve.

Makes 24 appetizers.

CLAM-STUFFED RAW MUSHROOM CAPS

1 *7½-ounce can mixed clams, drained, liquid reserved and strained*
24 *small raw mushroom caps, from ¾ to 1½ inches in diameter*
1 *teaspoon sesame oil*
1 *3-ounce package cream cheese*
1 *tablespoon lemon juice*
1–2 *tablespoons liquid from canned clams*
Garlic powder to taste
Paprika

Thoroughly wash and drain-dry the mushroom caps. Dip the tip of a clean cloth into sesame oil and wipe the outside of each cap with it.

Mash cream cheese together with minced clams, lemon juice and enough of the clam liquid to make a spreadable paste. When thoroughly blended, fill each mushroom cap with the mixture, sprinkle with garlic powder and a dash of paprika for color and serve.

Makes 24 appetizers.

CLAM-AND-ROE-STUFFED RAW MUSHROOM CAPS: Add 2 or more tablespoons cooked fish roe, membrane removed and mashed, to preceding recipe.

CLAM SPREAD: Serve cream cheese–clam mixture as a spread instead of using it to fill mushroom caps.

COCKTAIL KEBABS

String a colorful assortment of tiny fish and vegetable tidbits on an hors d'oeuvre pick and serve as an appetizer. What you have in your refrigerator and on your pantry shelves can determine the lineup. Besides being attractive, these picks full of goodies can easily be geared to calorie-counter appetites. For some satisfying, nonfattening protein start with bits of canned or home-cooked or smoked fish (small cooked shrimp, mussels and oysters can sometimes be used whole) and alternate with some of the following components:

> *Raw cauliflower (or leftover cooked that has been marinated in vinegar)*
> *Celery (sliced)*
> *Cucumber (cut in chunks instead of sliced)*
> *Green pepper (small chunks)*
> *Green chili peppers (cooked or canned and cut in pieces for those who like it hot)*
> *Olives*
> *Onions (either pearl or pieces of raw onion)*
> *Pickle (sliced or tiny whole)*
> *Pimento (cut in small pieces)*
> *Pineapple (canned or raw chunks)*
> *Radishes (sliced or in chunks)*

COOKED SHRIMP, SCALLOP, CRAB OR LOBSTER APPETIZERS

> 24 *medium cooked shrimp, bay scallops, or chunks of cooked crab or lobster meat*
> 1 *recipe of one of the spicier of the creamy sauces made with sour cream or mayonnaise such as Creamy Horseradish Sauce, Louis Sauce, Remoulade Sauce, Tartar Sauce or Yogurt Sauce. Or one of the Basic Red Sauces*

Chill cooked shellfish. If canned shrimp are used, soak them for 3 minutes in ice water, drain and dry on absorbent paper towels. Arrange on a serving dish around bowl of sauce, garnish with lemon wedges and parsley, and serve with picks. (Place dish over ice to keep very cold.)

Makes 24 appetizers.

COOKED SHRIMP, SCALLOP, CRAB OR LOBSTER COCKTAIL: Combine shellfish and any of sauces listed in preceding recipe, thoroughly mix, and divide into 4 cocktail glasses or salad plates lined with crisp lettuce leaves. Serve with lemon wedges. If serving nicely shaped shrimp with tails on, arrange them around edge of bowl, with sauce in center. Serve while very cold with cocktail forks.

Serves 4.

DECORATED FISH DAINTIES

Any variety of picturesque and delicious little hors d'oeuvres can be made by decorating and adding fish or shellfish in many different ways to good-quality bread that has been cut into rounds, hearts, stars, diamonds and squares, then toasted. Pick your cookie-cutter pattern, prepare the dainty little pieces of toast or buy toast rounds or crackers and biscuits cut in many shapes, then do one of these things:

• Spread with one or more of the cold butters (pages 137 to 144) or cream cheese and top with one or more bits of cold fish or small whole sardines or shrimp or caviar.

• At this point you can serve as is or decorate further with bits of greenery: tiny parsley leaves, chopped fresh basil, chopped fresh mint, chopped fresh spinach or—for a very zesty touch—chopped fresh nasturtium leaves or scallion tops. Lacking fresh greens, you can make do with the dried or freeze-dried varieties that come in jars.

• Again, you can stop there and serve your pretties to what is sure to be an appreciative audience, or you can go the ultimate in releasing your pent-up creative desire and pipe a white border around the outside edge. The decision to pipe or not to pipe should be based at least partially on whether or not the addition of mayonnaise, sour cream or cream cheese softened with milk (the most suitable piping materials) will add to the flavor of your hors d'oeuvres. Piped decorations look elaborate and difficult, but they are not, and gadgets with an assortment of tips creating different designs can be purchased for very little.

CLAM AND CHEESE BALLS

1   *cup chopped and drained cooked clams (or any chopped shellfish or flaked fin fish)*
1   *3-ounce package cream cheese*
1   *tablespoon chopped pimento*

¼ cup chopped toasted almonds
1–2 tablespoons cream or mayonnaise
*½ cup chopped fresh basil, chopped parsley, chopped nuts or
    crushed cornflakes*

Mash first 4 ingredients together, add cream or mayonnaise to make
workable consistency and shape into small balls. Roll in whichever one
of the fifth ingredient you prefer, chill and serve with picks.

Makes about 18.

VARIATION: Add chopped gherkins and/or chopped, drained pineapple or substitute for pimento.

CLAM AND CHEESE SHAPED LIKE A FISH: Place clam and cheese mixture on small serving dish and mold into a fish shape. Add an olive-slice
eye, pimento-outlined lips and celery- or lettuce-leaf fins.

GUACAMOLE FISH DIP

½ cup cooked or canned fish, mashed
1 ripe avocado, peeled, seeded and mashed
1 tablespoon lemon juice
2 tablespoons mayonnaise, or as needed
Onion salt to taste
Garlic powder to taste
Salt and pepper to taste
Louisiana Hot Sauce (Tabasco Sauce) to taste
Corn chips, crackers or toast rounds

Sprinkle mashed avocado with lemon juice. Add fish and next 5 ingredients and thoroughly mix together. Serve at once as a dip and/or spread.

Yield: 1¼–1½ cups.

GUACAMOLE FISH SALAD: Mound Guacamole Fish Dip on lettuce
leaves and serve at once as a salad.

GUACAMOLE-AND-FISH-FILLED CHERRY TOMATOES: Remove centers
from tiny cherry tomatoes and fill with gaucamole-fish mixture. Garnish
top with tiny wedge cut from top of tomato.

PICKLED EELS KREIDELL

5 medium eels, 1½ to 2 feet long
1⅔ cups distilled white vinegar
2⅔ cups hot water, or enough to cover eels
⅓ cup white wine
1 medium onion, quartered
1 whole clove

4 *whole cloves garlic*
6 *whole black peppercorns*
1 *tablespoon pickling spice*
5 *teaspoons salt*
1 *bay leaf, broken in half*
1/6 *cup sugar*
1 *small pinch marjoram*
1 *whole allspice*
3 *onions, thinly sliced*

Have your market man skin and clean eels and cut into 3-inch lengths. Combine all ingredients except sliced onion in a large, heavy pot (do not use metal unless coated with nonporous ceramic finish). Bring to slow boil and immediately turn off heat. Stir sliced onion into pot. Let pot stand in a cool place (about 35 degrees) until marinade and eels are cool, then divide into jars. Let the jars stand (covered with 3 or 4 layers of cheesecloth) in a cool place for 24 hours. Refrigerate (covered tightly) and let stand for another 72 hours or until liquid forms a soft jelly around the eels. Keeps at least 2 months in refrigerator if properly prepared and stored.

Makes about 24–36 appetizers.

NOTE: In storing, be sure that the marinade liquid always completely covers the eels.

PICKLED RAW FISH

2 *pounds raw fish cut in small chunks*
½ *cup water*
⅓ *cup brown sugar or to taste*
1 *tablespoon pickling spices or shrimp spice*
2 *large onions, thinly sliced*
2 *lemons, thinly sliced*
1½ *cups white vinegar*

Simmer water, brown sugar and spices for 5 to 6 minutes. Arrange fish, onions and lemons in alternate layers in a glass or nonporous ceramic dish. Add spiced water mixture (do not strain) to vinegar and pour over fish. Cover and refrigerate overnight. Keep refrigerated and use within a few days either plain or with sour cream as an appetizer.

As an appetizer, serves 30 to 36.

NOTE: Although commercial jars of pickled fish are most often herring, try other, more delicately flavored fish when preparing your own and you may be in for a delightful surprise.

VARIATION: Substitute white wine for half of vinegar.

RAW CLAMS, OYSTER OR MUSSELS ON THE HALF SHELL

> 24–36 *raw clams, oysters or mussels* (24 *if large*, 36 *if medium size*)
> *Crushed ice*
> *Basic Red Sauce, 2 or 3 recipes of variation of your choice, page 144*
> *Parsley*
> *Lemon wedges*

Clean and open clams, oysters or mussels according to directions given for individual shellfish in Chapter 4, Part One. Wash by dipping in lightly salted water and remove any bits of broken shell. Return shellfish to deeper half of shell, discarding the second half. Fill 6 bowls with crushed ice. Arrange 4–6 shellfish over ice in each bowl, place a small container of sauce in center and garnish with sprigs of parsley and a lemon wedge.

Serves 6.

COOKED CLAMS OR MUSSELS ON THE HALF SHELL: Clean outer shell, then steam shellfish just until shells open (page 45 or 70), remove from shells, chill and serve in the same manner as preceding recipe.

COOKED OYSTERS ON THE HALF SHELL: Clean shell, place oysters on a baking sheet and roast in oven preheated to 450 degrees for 10 to 15 minutes or until shell starts to open. Remove from oven, finish opening and serve on the half shell as in two preceding recipes. You can also open oysters by steaming in the same manner as clams and mussels, but they will take longer to open than do the other shellfish.

COOKED CLAMS, OYSTERS OR MUSSELS SERVED HOT ON THE HALF SHELL

> 24–36 *clams, oysters, or mussels*
> ½ *pound melted butter*
> *Lemon wedges*
> *Salt and pepper*

Cook shellfish either by steaming or roasting as directed in preceding recipe. While still hot, arrange on half shell on heated platter along with 6 individual containers of melted butter. Garnish platter with lemon wedges and place on appetizer table where people can help themselves to salt and pepper.

Serves 6 or more as an appetizer.

HOT SHELLFISH COCKTAIL: Arrange 6 hot shellfish on half shell on each of 6 plates, place container of melted butter in center and garnish with lemon wedge.

ROE DIP

½ *pound fish roe*
1 *tablespoon butter or margarine*
1 *teaspoon garlic powder*
⅛ *teaspoon dried tarragon, crumbled*
1 *tablespoon soy sauce*
½ *pint commercial sour cream*

Fry roe in butter or margarine until all raw look disappears from center, breaking it up as it cooks. Mash, and combine with remaining ingredients. Serve as a dip.

Makes about 2 cups.

SALMON ROLLS (I)

1 *cup canned salmon, mashed*
2 *tablespoons mayonnaise*
1 *teaspoon lemon juice*
1 *tablespoon freeze-dried shallots, mashed, or grated onion*
1 *tablespoon grated cheese*
1 *10-ounce package pie-crust mix*

Mix first 5 ingredients together and mash into a paste. Divide into 3 parts and place in refrigerator. Prepare pie crust according to package instructions. Divide into 3 parts and roll into balls. Roll each dough ball between 2 sheets of freezer paper until it is a thin circle. Put in freezer for about 15 minutes or until frozen almost hard. Then peel away paper. Using a small spatula or a butter knife, spread each circle with ⅓ of salmon mixture and cut each into 16 small wedges. Let dough defrost until it is pliant. Then start with wide end of wedges and roll each one up jelly-roll fashion. Arrange on cookie sheet and bake in 450-degree oven for 5 minutes. Reduce heat to 350 degrees and continue baking about 15 minutes or until the rolls are cooked and lightly browned. Check frequently.

Makes 48 appetizers.

SALMON LUNCHEON ROLLS: Serve rolls to children for luncheon. Heat and dilute a can of celery soup to pour over them as a sauce.

SARDINE–CREAM CHEESE DIP OR SPREAD

2 *3¾-ounce cans boneless sardines (use just 1 can if you like a delicate sardine flavor)*
1 *8-ounce package cream cheese*
1 *teaspoon horseradish (optional)*

Salt and pepper to taste
Approximately ¼ cup mayonnaise
Paprika

Mash sardines, cream cheese, horseradish and salt and pepper together. Stir in mayonnaise to make it the consistency you want for dip or spread, mix well, put into a small bowl, sprinkle with paprika and serve.

Makes about 2 cups.

SARDINE–CREAM CHEESE SANDWICH: Any leftover spread can be served for lunch the next day as a delicious sandwich filling. Add lettuce.

SMOKED FISH, THE PERFECT APPETIZER

Smoked fish is so good and it generally needs nothing at all done to it to make it the perfect appetizer. Just place it on a dish along with a knife, some crackers or sliced cucumbers if you like, but they really aren't necessary. Then listen to the raves, especially from people who have never eaten smoked fish before.

NOTE: The fact that fish is smoked doesn't mean that it is preserved, so it should be given the same care as any other fish.

3

Garnishes

Garnishes serve many useful purposes when added to a fish dish, so many in fact that it seems a shame that so many people garnish their culinary creations only when company comes. That's because, we suppose, they think of a garnish only as something that looks pretty but not as something that also is to be eaten.

Well, with some fish dishes nothing can make them look prettier than they are. Cooked lobster, for instance, on a plain white plate. They're that colorful and attractive. But a lemon wedge and the juice therefrom adds precious vitamin C. A sprig of parsley also is loaded with good nutrition. Garnishes both of them, but important garnishes. Provided, of course, that you consume rather than just look at them.

The garnish suggestions that follow, therefore, were chosen with double-duty purpose: to add eye appeal to the dish, while also adding a touch of nutrition. The spray of parsley, for instance: it will make a nice contribution toward your daily intake of vitamin A and C, calcium, iron and other things. Tomato wedges and slices will give you vitamin C.

Lovely white or delicately hued fish lend themselves so beautifully to being touched up with a bit of yellow (lemon), green (parsley) and red (tomato) that it would be a shame to miss any opportunity of giving your family the pleasure of seeing so nicely garnished a dish—and you the nefarious pleasure of sneaking a bit of additional nutrition into their diets. Remember: what pleases the eye is apt to also please the palate.

ANCHOVIES	
BEETS	cooked whole, sliced or pickled. Use the juice to flavor and color mayonnaise.
CARROTS	sticks, curls, shredded, grated and cross-cut circles.

CELERY	tops, hearts, sticks, curls, beautifully shaped inside stalks.
CRANBERRY	and other fruit jelly that can be chilled and sliced or cut into shapes with knife or cookie cutter. Cranberries cooked whole.
CUCUMBERS	sliced or sticks. Leave skin on for more color and nutrition. Score sides before slicing for variety.
DILL	powdered, chopped, part of sprig (use sparingly).
FRUIT, CANNED	sliced, whole or diced, fresh or spiced.
GELATIN	made very stiff, poured in thin sheets and cut into decorative shapes.
GRAPEFRUIT	peeled sections.
GREEN PEPPERS	strips or rings or cut in other shapes.
HARD-BOILED EGGS	sliced, wedged, riced, chopped. Mix crushed yolk with mayonnaise for golden color.
LEMONS	sliced, wedged, grated peel, lemon shell halves filled with dressing or garnish.
LETTUCE	crisp leaves, torn (with fingers), shredded.
LOBSTER CLAWS	cooked.
MARASCHINO CHERRIES	
MAYONNAISE	serve as sauce or pipe over fish.
MUSHROOM	caps and filled caps.
MUSSELS	steamed open but left in the shell.
OLIVES	black or slices of stuffed green.
ONIONS	sliced, rings or pickled pearls.
ORANGE	sliced, peeled sections, grated peel or stuffed shell.
PAPRIKA	sprinkle sparingly.
PARSLEY	fresh sprigs, chopped and dried flakes.
PICKLES	whole, sliced, relish.
RADISHES	sliced, whole, flowers.
RELISHES	
SARDINES	canned.
SEASHELLS	
SHRIMP	

SOUR CREAM

SPINACH   pureed for borders. Juice can be used to flavor and color mayonnaise.

TOMATOES   sliced, wedges, and tiny cherry tomatoes whole or filled.

WATERCRESS   sprigs or chopped.

4

Sandwiches

Want a sandwich that's distinctively different? Then try fish, any fish, fin or shell, cooked in any number of ways, on any kind of bread, man-sized, kid-sized, tea party-sized, bite-sized.

Want some specific ideas?

· Fish fried in a batter and eaten piping hot in a roll that's been lightly toasted is delicious.

· So is fish inside a hollowed-out individual French loaf (see Oyster Loaves on page 316).

· How about a Hot Peanut Butter and Fish Sandwich (page 244)?

· Or maybe you'd prefer flaked fish mixed with a bit of a creamy sauce and tucked between two slices of a nice white or whole-grain bread.

There are any number of such sandwich possibilities throughout this book. Some we've pointed out in the recipes, some we haven't because we're sure you'll recognize them when you see them. So we'll give you only a few more suggestions and then leave any further selections to you:

· Any fillet, baked or broiled, hot or cold.

· A leftover Devil or Angel on Horseback (pages 235 and 236) cut into small pieces.

· A fishburger made with a croquette stuffing (page 269).

· Shrimp Pizza Muffins (page 239).

· Slices from the Molded Fish Pudding (page 318).

That should put you on the proper sandwich-seeking track. Browse through the book and you'll find lots more.

5

Salads and Molds

Pick a fish, any fish, fin or shell, and combine it with vitamin-rich salad vegetables or fruit. Don't restrict yourself to the pale green iceberg types of lettuce for your greens. Branch out to the dark-green, loose leaf varieties such as romaine. Add slivers of raw cauliflower and cabbage. Add bits of very fresh raw broccoli, chard and spinach. Add dressing from the sauce section. If you're a calorie counter, you *can* have your salad and a dressing, too, if you follow some of the suggestions you'll find there.

If you choose your vegetable and fruit components wisely, a fish salad can be a cornucopia providing your body with many of the things it needs and add all-important variety, too.

Something more that's important to all of us: it also can be inexpensive. Salads are one of the best ways there is to use up fish left over from dinner the night before. Don't let fish leftovers stand around; chill them quickly and rush them into the refrigerator. Flake them for a salad the next day and serve for either lunch or dinner.

Cook a fish you caught or bought because it was in season and therefore inexpensive. Poach it, cool, then flake every scrap of its meat away from the bones for a salad. Combine some of that flaked meat with one of the creamy sauces, pages 124 to 136, and stuff tomato or avocado cavities with the mixture. Mmmmm . . . Good!

If your salad's going to be put on the appetizer table, see that it stays good and cold—for safety's sake as well as appetite appeal. (See suggestions for taking the proper care of fish while away from the refrigerator's protection on pages 154–155 of the Appetizer section.)

Besides the salads we give you here, also see Cooked Shrimp, Scallop, Crab or Lobster Appetizers and Cooked Shrimp, Scallop, Crab or Lobster Cocktail, pages 156–157.

167

FISH WITH VEGETABLE SALADS

BOUILLABAISSE SALAD

(Just as with bouillabaisse soup, bouillabaisse salad can be made of any combination of shellfish and fin fish you choose. Here's one assortment.)

> 1–1½ *pounds lobster or crab, cooked, flesh removed from everything but claws, and flaked*
> ¼ *pound cooked, shelled and deveined small shrimp*
> ¼ *pound cooked bay scallops (or sea scallops cut in ½-inch cubes)*
> 1 *pound delicately flavored, skinned and boned cooked fish, cut into bite-size pieces*
> 1 *head lettuce (preferably romaine) or mixed salad greens torn into pieces*
> 1 *recipe Louis Sauce, page 129*

Combine fish and shellfish. Arrange atop lettuce or mixed greens on a small serving platter or in a shallow bowl. Garnish with 2 claws and serve. Pass the Louis dressing.

Serves 10–12.

CONCH SALAD

> 8 *live conchs, 5 or 6 inches long, cleaned and sliced (see page 86) or 1 8-ounce can sliced conch*
> ¼ *cup olive oil*
> ½ *cup chopped parsley*
> 1 *large clove garlic, finely minced*
> 1 *lemon*
> *Salt and pepper to taste*

Rinse conch in hot water, drain and, while still hot, arrange on 4 salad plates. Divide olive oil, chopped parsley and minced garlic over the conch. Squeeze entire lemon over the contents of the 4 plates. Then cut the squeezed lemon peel into bits and sprinkle them over the salads. Season with salt and pepper to taste and serve.

Serves 4.

LOUIS SALAD   (I)

> 1 *pound cooked and flaked or chunked crab, shrimp, lobster or delicately flavored white-meated fish such as any of the flounders or cod, all bones removed*

1 *small head of lettuce, washed, drained and cut into 6 wedges*
1 *recipe Louis Sauce, page 129*
3 *hard-cooked eggs, sliced*

Cut each wedge of lettuce crosswise into several pieces and place in 6 bowls. Divide crab meat into bowls on top of lettuce, top with Louis Sauce, garnish with sliced eggs and serve.

Serves 6.

AVOCADOES STUFFED WITH LOUIS SALAD: Cut ripe avocados in half lengthwise, remove seed and stuff cavities of two halves with any of the preceding Louis salads. Eliminate egg and lettuce from ingredients. Serve one stuffed avocado half to each person.

NORWEGIAN FISH SALAD

2 *cups cooked flaked fish*
2 *red apples, cored and diced, skin on*
2 *boiled potatoes, peeled and diced*
2 *tablespoons cucumber pickle, chopped (sweet, dill or sour according to taste)*
1 *tablespoon minced onion*
1 *cup cultured sour cream*
2 *tablespoons wine vinegar*
1 *tablespoon sugar*
Lettuce leaves
¼ *cup pickled red beets, chopped*
2 *hard-cooked eggs, sliced*

Combine all except last 3 ingredients, mix well and pile in salad bowl on top of lettuce leaves. Make circle of chopped beets in center of salad and arrange row of egg slices around outer edge, or use beets and egg slices to decorate top of salad in any way that suits your fancy; just remember that the beets will leave a red mark wherever you place them. Refrigerate for 1 hour.

Serves 6–8.

HERRING SALAD: Substitute pickled herring whole or in chunks for fish flakes, soaking it in water to cover until it is the desired taste, drain and dice.

SALMON CAESAR SALAD   (I)

Add 1 1-pound can drained salmon broken into large pieces to Caesar Salad in Company Menus section, page 338 (remove skin and bones or not as you prefer).

SARDINE CAESAR SALAD

Add 3 3¾- or 4-ounce cans drained sardines (whole or broken into pieces) to Caesar Salad in Company Menus section, page 338.

SARDINE SLAW

    2 4-ounce cans boned sardines
    ½ cup commercial sour cream
    ½ teaspoon sugar or to taste
    ¼ head of cabbage, shredded
    ½ small onion, finely chopped

Combine sour cream and sugar. Add cabbage and onion and thoroughly mix. Stir in sardines (either broken up or all in a piece) and serve. Serves 4–6.

NOTE: If you have access to very heavy sweet cream, substitute it and about 1 teaspoon vinegar (to taste) for the sour cream in above.

SARDINE SLAW WITH RAISINS, CARROTS AND APPLES: Add ¼ cup of raisins, ¼ cup of grated raw carrot and ½ to 1 cup of chopped apple to Sardine Slaw.

SMOKED OYSTER OR MUSSEL SLAW: Substitute 2 4-ounce cans drained smoked oysters or mussels for the sardines in Sardine Slaw or Sardine Slaw with Raisins, Carrots and Apples.

SMOKED OYSTERS WITH HOT GREENS

    1 3⅔-ounce can smoked oysters in oil
    Cooked greens for 4 (mustard, chard, spinach, young dandelion, collard greens, etc.)

Drain hot cooked greens and arrange on salad plates. Divide smoked oysters and oil from the can over the greens and serve. Serves 4.

SPICED FISH SALAD   (I)

    1–2 cups cold Spiced Fish, page 210, removed from bones
    ¼ to ½ head of dark green lettuce
    1 medium cucumber
    1 cooked carrot, sliced crosswise (optional)
    1 medium avocado, peeled and chopped (optional)
    ¼–½ medium onion, thinly sliced
    2–4 cooked artichoke hearts, sliced (optional)
    1 to 2 tomatoes, cut in small wedges

2 *tablespoons tiny snips of fresh dill or other fresh herb*
½–1 *recipe French Dressing, page 147, or other dressing of your*
   choice

Mix together, toss and serve.
   Serves 4–6.
   SPICED MUSSEL SALAD: Substitute 2 4½-ounce cans mussels in hot
sauce for spiced fish in preceding recipe.
   FISH IN MIXED VEGETABLE SALAD: Substitute any cooked flaked fish
or shellfish for spiced fried fish in Spiced Fish Salad.

VEGETABLE SALAD WITH TUNA
AND ANCHOVY DRESSING
(Our Version of Salade Niçoise)

1 *recipe Tuna and Anchovy Sauce, page 151*
½ *pound fresh green beans or 1 10-ounce package frozen, cooked in*
   minimum amount of water and chilled
1 *medium tomato, cut in small wedges*
½ *cup pitted, sliced black olives*
½ *sweet red onion, thinly sliced*
Lettuce leaves (optional)

Combine all ingredients except sliced egg called for in dressing and toss
until ingredients are coated with oily dressing. Line salad bowl with lettuce
leaves, fill with salad, garnish with sliced eggs and serve.
   Serves 4–6.

FISH AND FRUIT SALADS

ANY-FISH, THREE-FRUIT SALAD   (I)

1 *pound fin fish or shellfish cooked, chilled and in bite-size pieces*
1 *large ripe pineapple*
2 *large oranges*
½ *cup green seedless grapes*
½ *cup large purple grapes*
½ *cup blanched, toasted and slivered almonds (optional)*
1 *tablespoon lemon juice*
1 *recipe Ginger Sauce, page 127, or Mayonnaise and Cream Sauce,*
   page 134

Cut pineapple in half lengthwise; discard core and cube meat. Peel and
section oranges. Combine sections with pineapple cubes, grapes, almonds

and lemon juice. Stir well and heap pineapple shell cavities with the mixture. Top with chilled fish or shellfish and serve with bowl of sauce.
Serves 6–8.

FISH OR SHELLFISH CANTALOUPE SALAD: Substitute large, ripe cantaloupe cut in half and cantaloupe balls cut from the flesh for the pineapple shell and cubes.

FROSTY FISH SALAD   (I)

With Grapefruit, Cottage Cheese and Avocado

¼ *pound any cooked or canned delicately flavored white-meat fin fish or shellfish in small pieces*
1 *1-pound can grapefruit sections*
1 *large ripe avocado*
Lettuce leaves
1 *8-ounce package cottage cheese*
¼ *cup mayonnaise, sour cream or plain yogurt*

Spread grapefruit sections and juices from can over bottom of pie plate and put in the freezer 2 or 3 hours before making salad. Peel and slice avocado lengthwise into 12 slices. Stir partially frozen grapefruit sections to break them apart and arrange in a circle on each of 4 lettuce-covered plates. Stir fish and cottage cheese together and spoon into mounds in center of the 4 grapefruit circles. Arrange 3 slices of avocado on each mound and top with a heaping tablespoon of mayonnaise or sour cream.
Serves 4.

CALORIE COUNTERS: Use cottage cheese without cream in making salad and top it with yogurt.

SHRIMP WALDORF SALAD   (I)

1 *cup small cooked shrimp or 1 8-ounce can drained*
½ *cup yellow raisins*
½ *cup apple juice*
1 *tablespoon brandy or rum (optional)*
1 *tablespoon lemon juice*
1 *large unpeeled red apple, core removed and cut into small pieces*
1 *cup crisp celery, chopped*
¼ *cup crushed walnuts (substitute any other nut)*
¼ *cup mayonnaise*
¼ *cup sour cream*

Soak raisins overnight in a mixture of the apple juice and rum. Sprinkle lemon juice over diced apple, mixing as you sprinkle so that each piece is coated—otherwise they may turn brown. Drain the raisins (the juice in which they were marinated makes quite a drink), combine with shrimp, diced apples, celery and crushed walnuts. Mix mayonnaise and sour cream together, stir into salad and spoon onto lettuce leaves, on individual salad plates or on a small serving platter if salad is to be used on a buffet.

Serves 4–6.

VARIATION: Omit raisins, apple juice and rum.

CRAB OR LOBSTER WALDORF SALAD: Substitute crab or lobster meat for shrimp.

RAW FISH SALAD

(Japanese Sashimi)

In this popular dish, the Japanese enjoy eating their fish completely raw, cut in slivers about ¼ inch thick, and dipped into a mixture of fresh chopped gingerroot, grated horseradish and mustard. We add dishes of very fresh greens, turning the Sashimi into a salad.

If your fish is very, very fresh, your dishes colorful and attractively arranged, and if you accompany your first bite of raw fish with a generous mouthful of crisp greens, you will probably be able to overcome your prejudices and discover what the Japanese have known for centuries: fish doesn't have to be cooked to taste good.

1 *pound slivers of raw bass or tuna or other fish of your choice, fresh-water or salt, bones and skin removed*
½ *cup fresh chopped gingerroot or ¼ cup powdered ginger*
½ *cup grated horseradish*
½ *cup mustard sauce or ¼ cup mustard powder*
Water for mixing sauce ingredients
Bowl of very fresh salad greens, broken or cut into small pieces

Set out the slivered fish, 3 dishes of seasonings and salad greens and let everyone mix his own sauce, tasting and testing as he does, and help himself to greens.

Serves 6–12.

RAW FISH APPETIZER: Omit salad greens from preceding recipe.

MARINATED RAW FISH SALAD

(Seviche)

(Marinated raw fish is a little more to the American taste than Sashimi because the acids in the marinade act upon the fish protein so that it both appears and tastes cooked.)

½ pound very fresh fish fillets
1 medium red onion, sliced
1 green pepper, sliced in rings
½ cup lime juice
Salad greens

Cut fillets in 1-inch strips, cut each strip at an angle into inch-long pieces. Place in a glass or nonporous ceramic dish (do not use metal) along with sliced onion and green pepper, pour the juice over and stir to be sure each piece is thoroughly covered with juice. Marinate for 3 to 6 hours. Rinse off lime juice and arrange fish with onion and green pepper atop salad greens and serve.

Serves 4–6.

MARINATED RAW FISH APPETIZER: Serve preceding recipe on a platter instead of dividing onto salad plates.

MARINATED RAW FISH, FRUIT AND NUTS SALAD

1½ pounds any fresh-caught, white-meat fish fillets
1 cup lemon juice
1 banana
1 apple
1 orange
1 peach
2 or 3 plums
1 cup shelled nuts of your choice
Lettuce

Cut fish fillets lengthwise into 1-inch strips; then, slicing at an angle, cut the strips into 1-inch pieces. Place in glass or nonporous ceramic bowl, add lemon juice, stir to make sure fish is thoroughly saturated and let stand 3 to 6 hours in refrigerator, the longer the better, stirring and turning about once an hour.

Cut the fruits into bite-sized pieces into a large mixing bowl, letting their juices drip into the bowl as you do. Add nuts and toss gently until well mixed.

When fish is done marinating, transfer to colander, rinse well in cold water, add to fruits and nuts and stir in gently. Place beds of lettuce on 6 salad plates, heap the mixture onto lettuce and serve.

Serves 6.

NOTE: You don't have to use these fruits or these quantities. Any fruit in season, in any amount, will do.

Seafood Molds

There are very few if any foods that can outdo a gelatin mold for beauty. Seafood, with its delicate colors and flavors, adds not only to this beauty but to the taste as well. Don't save these delightful dishes for company, even though they always look dressed up. Serve them often as a salad with everyday family meals. They're really easy to make.

Use about 2 tablespoons less liquid than a 3-ounce package of gelatin calls for if you want it to unmold easily. If you are adding anything that will increase the amount of liquid—fruit or vegetable juice, for instance—deduct whatever you think that amount will be from the amount of liquid you use in making your gelatin. It's better to have it a little bit stiff than too runny. If you want to control your solid materials, get them to stay in place in a design, pour a thin layer of gelatin and let it almost set. Place your pieces of solid food in place, then pour some more gelatin that is beginning to get stiff over them. Practice will make perfect. After you master those basics, the possibilities are endless.

Prepare a 3-ounce package of gelatin (lime or lemon combines well with fish), replace some of the water with a little fresh lemon juice and perhaps add a little sugar, a little fish or chicken broth if you have it. Then add any mixture of fish you like combined with some congenial vegetables or fruit, 1 or 2 cups altogether. The combinations of foods in this salad section may suggest ideas. Leftover fish soups can be used to make beautiful and delicious molds. Substitute the liquid in them for part of the liquid called for on the package or envelope of gelatin you use.

You can lightly grease a mold or rinse it with cold water before adding the gelatin. Then dip it, for just a few seconds, in hot water before inverting to unmold. This may or may not result in perfection. Or you can buy a Tupperware mold, grease it lightly, invert when ready to unmold, release the vacuum seal and the chances are just about 100 percent (if you didn't make your gelatin too thin) that your mold will look just like gelatins pictured in homemaking magazines.

EASY FISH AND VEGETABLE GELATIN SALAD   (I)

1   *cup flaked delicately flavored fin fish or shellfish (leave small shell-fish whole)*
1   *3-ounce package lime-flavored gelatin*
¼   *teaspoon salt or to taste*
1   *cup boiling water*
1   *tablespoon lemon juice*
1   *tablespoon sherry wine*
¾   *cup fish or chicken broth, ice cold*

¼ *cup grated carrot*
¼ *cup chopped green pepper*
½ *cup minced celery*
Lettuce leaves
¼ *cup mayonnaise (optional)*
¼ *cup sour cream (optional)*

Put gelatin and salt in a bowl, pour boiling water over them and stir until gelatin is completely dissolved. Stir in lemon juice, sherry wine and broth. Let mixture cool; stir in grated carrot, chopped green pepper, minced celery and fish. Pour into a lightly greased shallow rectangular dish (about 6 by 10 by 2 inches) and refrigerate for 4 hours or longer. Cut into 6 rectangles and remove with a cake turner and place on lettuce leaves covering individual salad plates. Combine mayonnaise and sour cream, mix well, place in a small bowl and serve with the salad to those who don't have to watch their calories.

Serves 6.

SHELLFISH AND ASPARAGUS IN SHERRY ASPIC: Substitute ¼ cup boiling sherry for ¼ cup of the boiling water. Use cooked, shelled shrimp or crayfish or pieces of king crab leg instead of fin fish or other shellfish. Pour a thin layer of gelatin mixture into bottom of any shape of attractive mold and, when almost set, arrange shellfish in it. When completely set, cover with another layer of gelatin mixture, and when that is set, proceed as in Easy Fish and Vegetable Gelatin Salad, but substitute ½ cup cooked asparagus spears cut into 1-inch lengths for green pepper and celery. When set, unmold onto lettuce leaves.

MOLDED FISH SALAD   (I)
With Fruit, Celery and Olives

1–1¼ *cups cooked fish or shellfish, flaked*
1 *15-ounce can pineapple chunks, drained*
½ *cup diced celery*
1 *unpeeled red apple, diced*
¼ *cup chopped black olives*
1 *envelope unflavored gelatin*
1 *tablespoon cold water*
¾ *cup boiling water*
¼ *cup liquid sauce from any leftover fish you may be using, or ¼*
    cup juice from pineapple chunk can
1 *tablespoon lemon juice*
1 *cup mayonnaise*
Salt to taste

Combine flaked fish, pineapple chunks, diced celery, diced apple and chopped olives in a mixing bowl. Mix gelatin with 1 tablespoon cold water, add boiling water, stir until dissolved and add liquid from leftover fish or juice from pineapple chunks and lemon juice. Combine gelatin mixture with mayonnaise and stir into flaked fish mixture. Taste and add salt if desired. Pour into lightly greased mold and refrigerate for at least 4 hours. Unmold on a bed of lettuce leaves and serve.

Serves 6–8.

SHRIMP AND RICE MOUSSE

½ pound raw shrimp
1½ cups water
½ teaspoon Shrimp Spice
2 tablespoons cold water
1 tablespoon unflavored gelatin
6 tablespoons mayonnaise
2 teaspoons lemon juice
½ cup heavy cream
¼ cup minced scallions, including some of green
½ cup cooked whole-kernel corn
1½ cups cooked rice, chilled
Lettuce leaves

Add Shrimp Spice to water, bring to a boil, add shrimp and simmer for 5 minutes or until it turns pink and is just cooked. Remove shrimp and refrigerate, strain broth, reduce by boiling to 1 cup and set aside. Put cold water in top of double boiler, add gelatin and stir until softened. Place over boiling water and stir until gelatin dissolves and is completely blended with water. Remove double boiler top from stove, stir reserved broth, mayonnaise and lemon juice into gelatin until well-blended and smooth. Refrigerate until gelatin starts to set, then place container in a bowl of ice water and beat until light and fluffy. Whip cream until stiff and mix into gelatin. Add scallions, corn and rice and all but 6 shrimps and mix well. Place 1 of reserved shrimp in each of 6 lightly greased 1-cup individual molds and divide gelatin mixture over them. Chill until firm, unmold on lettuce leaves and serve.

Serves 6.

6

Soups, Chowders, Bisques and Broths

Ah, the joy of delicious, aromatic, flavorful fish soups, no matter whether they're called bisques, broths, chowders or just plain soup. (The exact same recipe in three different cookbooks may be called by three different names, and probably none of them will adequately describe what's in it.)

Fish soups can be delicate or richly flavored fish broths based on seasoned water, with or without wine. They can be made of fin fish and/or shellfish in thickened or unthickened broth or milk, with or without cream. They can include a hearty combination of fin fish and/or shellfish with any number of vegetables.

It's no wonder the names have become mixed up and confusing, because fish soups can be just about anything you want them to be. But they can only be as good as the ingredients you put in them.

Wash fish to be used in soup by dipping into cold, lightly salted water or water that's had a little lemon juice added. Examine shellfish carefully for bits of broken shell.

Use nice, fresh, flavorful fish and don't think of the soup pot as a receptacle for worn-out, wilted, lifeless, nutritionless, tasteless vegetables. If you lack very fresh-caught fish and very fresh-cut vegetables, resort to the next best thing: good quality products that are canned or frozen *while very fresh*. If you are concerned about the cost of top grades in processed foods (which often have the nicest flavor), try buying the market's own brands, which are sometimes as much as 20 percent cheaper than the so-called name brands.

TIMING SOUPS

If it doesn't detract from the character of the finished product, it's best to cook the fish you eat in soups for the same length of time you would in any other recipe, that is *only until it's done*. Fish is not like soup meat that needs long cooking to tenderize it. An old fish doesn't grow tough, it just grows big with age.

In many fin fish soup recipes calling for fish broth, you can have perfectly cooked fish and rich broth too simply by using only the head and carcass for broth-making—cooking them as long as needed—and removing and setting aside the fillets to add back to the pot after the broth has reached the desired degree of richness and has been strained. See Fish Broth and Fumet, page 117, and Poached Big Fish with Conch Sauce, pages 333–334.

The shellfish section, page 39, tells how to make and save tasty broths during the shelling process. You can often use these broths and broths from canned or frozen shellfish. Or chicken broth or frozen fumet, page 118, or canned clam broth to flavor shellfish soups in order to avoid toughening the meat by overcooking.

TO AVOID CURDLING MILK-BASED SOUPS

To minimize the risk of having a milk soup curdle, either warm (scald) the milk or add it gradually to a pot of hot ingredients so that there isn't a sudden change of temperature. Whenever possible, add dry seasonings, lobster roe, wines or other acids, highly seasoned fumet, cream or egg yolk at the very last so they don't cook in the milk any longer than necessary. Stir constantly after adding and either turn off heat altogether or keep it very low. Never boil.

Oyster (and to a lesser degree clam) liquors, just as they come from the shell, contain a little acid and will combine much better with milk if heated first or diluted with enough water to thin them into a broth such as you obtain when steaming these shellfish open.

USING FISH SOUPS (SOMETIMES LEFT OVER: SOMETIMES NOT) AS A SAUCE

Many of the soups either with or without additional thickening make an excellent sauce to pour over rice, toast, mashed potatoes or spaghetti; whether you're using some that's left over or simply using the soup recipe when what you want is a sauced fish.

As soon as you know some of the soup will be left over, don't leave it standing around but chill it quickly. Pour it out of any heavy heat-retaining pot into another dish and set the dish in ice water. As soon as it's cool, refrigerate if you're going to use it no later than the next day.

If you can't use it that soon (and if the fish used in making your soup was very fresh—not frozen—and with the exception of the soups containing egg, roe or the lobster tomalley) pour it into a moisture-vaporproof freezer container, being sure to leave a little head space for expansion, cover tightly and freeze. If you have more than a pint, use two containers. Label, date and try to use within 10 days. Freeze at less than 0 degrees and store at no higher than 0 degrees. Defrost in refrigerator and reheat in double boiler. One cup of reheated fish or shellfish soup poured over toast can make a mighty nice lunch for one person.

Be on the safe side and reheat leftover soups, whether stored in refrigerator or freezer, to at least 140 degrees and serve at once.

Soup Quantities

Some of these soups are hearty enough to be a one-dish meal. Determine the number they will serve in this manner by checking the principal ingredients, especially the fish. The Cod Bisque, for instance, on page 191, with the addition of a large mixed salad, would make a nice meal for from 2 to 4 people, depending on how much fish and potatoes they eat. It would serve 6 if the meal included another meat or protein such as beans.

Soup Variations

We've given you many variations in the recipes that follow, demonstrating how easily one soup (of whatever name) evolves from another. Try them, then try your own innovations.

Broths, Hot and Cold

CLAM BROTH WITH MATZOH BALLS

> ½ *cup carbonated water (or substitute plain water)*
> ⅓ *cup melted butter or margarine*
> 4 *eggs, beaten*
> *Pepper to taste*
> ¼ *teaspoon finely ground tarragon (optional)*
> 1 *cup matzoh meal*
> 1½ *quarts clam broth saved when you steam open clams, see pages 39 and 45*

Stir carbonated water, melted butter or margarine into beaten eggs. Add seasonings to matzoh meal, mix, then combine with egg mixture and stir well. Cover and refrigerate for 20 minutes. Bring broth to a low boil, form matzoh-meal mixture into small balls about ¾ inch in diameter, and drop carefully and slowly into broth. Don't let the broth boil hard (or stop boiling either) or balls may fall apart. If you find it difficult to form the mixture into balls, drop instead by small teaspoonfuls into broth. When matzoh balls are cooked, pour broth into soup bowls, add 3 balls to each and serve.

Serves 6–8.

CLAM-FLAVORED MATZOH BALL APPETIZERS: Reserve one cup of clam broth in a dish. Add leftover matzoh balls and refrigerate, covered, overnight. Serve the following day as cold appetizers. If they are small and well formed, use picks; if not, salad or cocktail forks.

MATZOH BALLS IN FISH BROTH: Substitute any fish broth for the clam broth.

COLD JELLIED FISH BROTH

4–6 *cups strained fish broth made from fish including skin and bones, see page 118*
¼ *cup sour cream (optional)*

Serve chilled, jellied broth in small bowls, garnish each with about 1 tablespoon sour cream.

CALORIE COUNTERS' COLD JELLIED FISH BROTH: Serve plain or garnish each bowl with 1 tablespoon yogurt.

NOTE: The more skin and bones you include when making fish broth, the better it will jell when chilled. You can always add a little unflavored gelatin as a thickening agent. Follow the instructions on package and use about ¼ quantity required for a molded dessert.

EASY FISH BROTH SOUPS

Very easy and delicious soups can be made by combining fish broth or fish fumet with canned soups. Here are some suggestions:

EASY CREAM OF FISH AND MUSHROOM SOUP

2 *cups Fish Broth, see page 118*
1 *10½-ounce can condensed cream of mushroom soup*
1 *4-ounce can sliced mushrooms and their broth (optional)*
2–4 *tablespoons sour cream or heavy sweet cream (optional)*
Minced parsley to taste or a sprinkling of any dried herbs of your choice

Combine first 3 ingredients and heat, stirring constantly until smooth. Simmer for about 2 minutes, stirring frequently. Remove from heat, stir in cream, pour into bowls, garnish with parsley and serve at once.

Serves 2–4.

VARIATION: Add ½ to 1 cup flaked cooked fish and ¼ teaspoon Worcestershire sauce.

EASY CREAM OF FISH AND CELERY SOUP: Use cream of celery instead of cream of mushroom soup.

EASY FISH BROTH 'N' VEGETABLE SOUP

2 *cups rich-flavored Fish Broth, page 118*
1 *10½-ounce can or package of frozen mixed vegetables*

Combine, heat and simmer for 5–10 minutes, stirring often. Serve at once.
Serves 2–4.

Fish Soups with a Water or Broth Base

BOUILLABAISSE

Poems have been written about this great soup and mighty arguments engaged in about what goes into it. The Mediterranean fishermen who first made it used whatever they happened to catch, plus some good fresh vegetables. Whether you're a saltwater or freshwater fisherman, you can make it with your catch, and we're giving you recipes for both. If you're far away from ocean, pond, river or lake and must pull your fish, frozen and packaged, out of a bin at the supermarket, you, too, can make bouillabaisse. First defrost your fish and use either of the following recipes.

SALTWATER BOUILLABAISSE

Try to include at least 4 different fish. Skinned, cleaned and cut-up eel is more or less traditional as one of them. Since eel is fat, it's nice if at least 2 of the others are lean. Any assortment of shellfish is good but it's especially nice if you can include lobster and/or crab.

2 *pounds fish cut into pieces and if possible boned*
½–1 *pound of shrimp, scallop, crab and/or lobster meat (use one or more)*
1 *pound small clams, mussels, crab or lobster claws in the shell, thoroughly cleaned and ready to cook*
2 *tablespoons olive oil*
2 *tablespoons cooking oil*
1 *large onion, chopped*

1 *green pepper, chopped*
3 *cloves garlic or to taste, minced*
6 *cups fish broth, or 3 cups water, 1 cup chicken broth and 2 8-ounce*
   bottles canned clam broth
3 *tomatoes, cut in wedges*
1 *1-pound can peeled good-quality tomatoes*
¼ *teaspoon saffron shreds*
¼ *teaspoon thyme*
Salt and pepper to taste
1 *bay leaf*

Heat olive oil and cooking oil in large, heavy pot, add onion, green pepper and garlic, and lightly sauté. Add broth, tomato wedges, canned tomatoes, saffron and thyme. Stir, add salt and pepper to taste and bay leaf, bring to a boil and cook for 10 minutes, stirring occasionally. Turn down heat to a simmer, add fin fish and shellfish—according to length of time it will take each kind to cook—and cook just until shellfish opens and fin fish separate easily when gently probed with tines of a fork.

Arrange sliced French bread (plain or toasted) in soup bowls and cover with soup. Arrange fin fish and shellfish from the soup on a platter, garnished with shellfish in the shell. Serve at once.

Serves 6–8.

NOTES:

· Shellfish will open more quickly if you cover pot after adding.

· This is a very richly flavored soup. For a more delicate flavor substitute plain water for all or part of fish broth.

LEFTOVER SALTWATER BOUILLABAISSE SAUCE: Reheat Bouillabaisse and use as is to pour over rice, toast, mashed potatoes or spaghetti.

FRESHWATER BOUILLABAISSE   (O)

3 *pounds assorted freshwater fish (sweet-flavored, not muddy), half*
   filleted, half chunked with bones left in
½ *cup olive oil*
3 *onions, chopped*
3 *cloves garlic, chopped*
3 *leeks, chopped*
3 *large ripe tomatoes, chopped*
½ *cup chopped watercress*
1 *pinch nutmeg*
1 *pinch dried tarragon*
2 *pinches saffron*
1 *broken bay leaf*
3 *peppercorns*
Salt and pepper to taste

Set filleted fish aside in refrigerator. Add olive oil to bottom of a large, heavy pot and heat. Add onions, garlic and leeks, and cook 1 or 2 minutes. Stir in remaining ingredients, including the fish with bones in. Add 4 cups of boiling water or enough to cover everything well, cover and simmer for 1 hour. Remove from fire. Lift out fish, flake fish away from bones, set aside and discard bones. Strain soup and return to fire. Add flaked fish and raw fillets, and cook just until fillets break up into pieces. Serve soup in bowls, dividing the pieces of fillet into each. Serve while very hot with slabs of French bread and butter.

Serves 4–6.

LEFTOVER FRESHWATER BOUILLABAISSE SAUCE: Reheat and use as is to pour over rice, toast, mashed potatoes or spaghetti.

FISH-STUFFED CABBAGE ROLLS IN SOUP　　　　(I)

1　*cup cooked fish, flaked*
4　*nice large cabbage leaves*
1　*cup cooked rice*
1　*tablespoon lemon juice*
2　*tablespoons minced onion*
½　*teaspoon grated lemon rind*
1　*egg, beaten*
¼　*teaspoon garlic powder*
2 or 3　*drops Louisiana Hot Sauce (Tabasco Sauce)*
4　*cups fish or chicken broth*
2　*tablespoons flour*
¼　*cup water*
Salt and pepper to taste
½　*cup heavy cream or evaporated milk (optional)*
Paprika

Parboil cabbage leaves for 2 minutes and cut away enough of heavy membrane to make leaf flexible.

Combine fish, rice, lemon juice, minced onion, lemon rind, beaten egg, garlic powder and Tabasco Sauce, divide over centers of cabbage leaves, fold 2 sides of leaves over stuffing, roll up and fasten each with a wooden toothpick. Place in bottom of large, heavy pot, cover with fish or chicken broth, bring to a simmer and cook, covered, for 30 minutes. Remove cabbage rolls to a heated bowl, cover and set aside. Combine flour and water into a smooth paste, stir into broth in pot and cook until it thickens, stirring constantly. Season to taste with salt and pepper, remove from fire, stir in cream and pour into bowls. Place a stuffed cabbage leaf in each bowl, garnish with paprika and serve.

SHRIMP-STUFFED CABBAGE ROLLS IN SOUP: Substitute minced, cooked shrimp for fish in preceding recipe.

CALORIE COUNTERS' FISH-STUFFED CABBAGE ROLLS IN SOUP: To reduce calories, don't thicken soup or use optional cream.

FISH SOUP WITH LEMON SAUCE

(Psarosoupa Avgolemono)

1½ *pounds fish chunks*
1 *tablespoon lemon juice*
1 *teaspoon salt*
2 *quarts water*
2 *tablespoons olive oil*
2 *tablespoons cooking oil*
1 *large onion, chopped*
2 *carrots, chopped*
2 *stalks celery, chopped*
Pepper to taste
1 *tablespoon chopped parsley*
3 *tablespoons lemon juice*
3 *egg yolks, beaten until light and foamy*

Combine 1 tablespoon lemon juice and salt, rub into fish chunks and set aside. In large, heavy pot, bring water to a boil, first adding oils. Then add onion, carrots, celery, pepper and parsley. Cook at a brisk boil for 30 minutes or until broth is reduced by almost half, reduce heat to low simmer and add fish wrapped in cheesecloth. Cook 5–10 minutes or until fish flakes separate easily when gently probed with tines of fork. Carefully remove cheesecloth-wrapped packet of fish to a preheated bowl, cover to keep warm and set aside. Strain broth, puree vegetables and return both to pot and reheat. Slowly beat lemon juice into beaten yolks. Gradually stir 3 tablespoons of the hot soup into the lemon juice and yolk mixture. Then stir slowly into the soup but don't let soup boil. Turn off heat. Divide fish chunks into 4 bowls, pour soup over them and serve.

Serves 4–6.

GRANDPA'S CLAM CHOWDER

(According to Norman Strung, this is a by-guess-and-by-gosh recipe that you'll wind up making differently every time, but here is one version that we guarantee you'll find superb. Norman, who got the original recipe from his grandfather, a fine-hotel chef, always serves clams on the half shell at the same time and saves the liquid from them to add to what he gets from the chowder clams.)

30 *chowder clams, diced*
3 *quarts clam liquid*
1 *bunch celery, leaves included, diced*
6 *large potatoes, diced*
6 *large carrots, diced*
3 *10½-ounce cans of condensed cream of tomato soup*
3 *tomato soup cans of water*
½ *pound bacon, diced and fried, with half the resulting bacon grease*
2 *dried hot chili peppers*
6 *bay leaves*
1 *tablespoon whole thyme*
½ *teaspoon rubbed sage*
1 *large onion, diced*

Put everything in one very large, heavy pot. (Use two if necessary.) Bring to a rolling boil, turn down to a simmer and cook for from 3 to 6 hours, stirring occasionally. The longer it cooks, the better it will taste. It's best of all on the second day.

Serves 18–24.

GRANDPA'S CLAM CHOWDER LEFTOVER SAUCE: Reheat and use as is to pour over rice, toast, mashed potatoes or spaghetti.

MANHATTAN CLAM CHOWDER   (I)

1 *dozen chowder clams, chopped*
2 *slices bacon, chopped*
1 *stalk celery, chopped*
1 *large onion, chopped*
¼ *cup chopped green pepper*
1 *carrot, scraped and chopped*
3 *ripe tomatoes, chopped (peel and seed them if you like)*
5 *cups broth from clams, strained (add water if necessary to make enough)*
Salt and pepper to taste
1 *cup diced raw potato*

Steam clams open, strain broth and reserve. Chop clams. Heat bacon in large, heavy pot. Add celery and onion, and sauté with the bacon until all are lightly browned. Add green pepper and carrot, and stir-fry until well coated with bacon grease. Add tomatoes, stir for about 1 minute, then pour in clam broth. Season with salt and pepper, add chopped potato, bring to a boil, cover, turn down to a simmer and cook for 15 minutes or until vegetables are just tender but not mushy. Add clams, continue simmering just long enough for them to heat through, and serve.

Serves 4–6.

NOTE: It's worth making a double recipe of this chowder because it's much better the second day (which makes it very good for entertaining if you prepare it a day ahead). Divide the chowder before adding clams and only add them to the half you're going to eat immediately. Chill the remaining chowder quickly by setting it in ice water. Refrigerate separately from clams. Thoroughly reheat and add clams just for the last 2 or 3 minutes when serving the second time around.

FROZEN CLAM CHOWDER: If you started out with very fresh clams you dug yourself, instead of refrigerating second half of chowder after chilling, freeze it in small blocks by pouring into ½-pint freezer containers, allowing space for expansion. Freeze clams in separate containers. Pour clam broth or lightly salted water over just to cover, allowing expansion space, cover and freeze. Put separately frozen chowder and clams together in a third container so they don't get separated, label and date and store at 0 degrees. Use within 10 days, served either as a soup or as a sauce over rice, toast, mashed potatoes or spaghetti (if to be used as a sauce, you might want to leave out potatoes). A 1-cup block of chowder and a container of clams will make a nice luncheon for 1.

To heat: pour ½ cup of fish, clam, chicken broth or water into a small, heavy saucepan, add chowder, cover and heat on low. Stir often enough to prevent sticking and insure even defrosting. Bring to a boil, simmer for a few minutes, add clams and continue cooking only until they are heated through.

VARIATION: Add 1 cup of tomato juice at the same time as you add the clam broth.

MANHATTAN CLAM CHOWDER WITH CANNED CLAMS: Substitute 2 7½-ounce cans of clams for the fresh ones, 1 1-pound can of tomatoes for the fresh tomatoes and 3 8-ounce jars of clam juice and 2 cups of water for the 5 cups of broth from fresh clams.

OYSTER CHOWDER WITH VEGETABLES: Substitute oysters for clams in Manhattan Clam Chowder.

MUSSEL CHOWDER WITH VEGETABLES: Substitute mussels for clams in Manhattan Clam Chowder.

SLUMGULLION KREIDELL   .   (I)
(Fish Head Chowder)

(When Buddy Kreidell and a bunch of his fellow Harbour Knights return to the dock after an early-morning deep-sea fishing trip, they cut the fillets from a few of the large fish and refrigerate them to take home to their wives for dinner that night. Meantime, while the boys compare notes and the fish stories get bigger and bigger, Buddy whips up a great chowder from the heads, tails and bones that provides those hungry fishermen with a most satisfying lunch. Here's the chowder recipe.)

Heads, bones and tails from 3 medium cod, 2 large striped bass or whatever the catch may be
6 large onions, quartered
6 cloves garlic, halved
6 peppercorns
½ ounce salt
4 bay leaves, broken in half
1 pinch sage
1 quart dry wine
1 quart chicken broth
½ cup wine vinegar (optional)
4 quarts hot water
8 large potatoes, cubed
12 large carrots, cut in 2-inch pieces
1 16-ounce can of cream-style corn
Juice of 2 lemons

Scrape and clean heads, bones and tails of fish to remove scales and blood. Wash off and place in a large pot. Add 3 onions, garlic, peppercorns, salt, bay leaves, sage, wine, chicken broth, vinegar and hot water. Simmer about 1¼ hours or until fish meat falls off bones. Strain, pick out meat and onion. Chop cooked onions and put them with strained broth and fish back in pot. Add remaining onions and all other ingredients and simmer, covered, for about 25 minutes or until potatoes and carrots are tender. Serve with crackers, buttered toast or French bread.

Serves 15–20.

VIENNESE FISH SOUP WITH ROE

Head and tail from 4- to 6-pound fish
7 cups water
1 cup red wine
3 peppercorns
1 medium onion
1 bay leaf
Thyme to taste
Salt to taste
1 pair of fish roe
2 tablespoons bacon fat
2 tablespoons flour

Combine fish head and tail in large, heavy pot with water, wine, peppercorns, onion, bay leaf, thyme and salt. Simmer for about 1 hour or until liquid is reduced to 4 cups. Strain, remove meat from fish head and set aside. Melt bacon fat in pot, add flour and cook together, stirring constantly, 2–3 minutes; add broth and cook for 5 to 7 minutes, stirring constantly with whisk until smooth.

While fish broth is boiling, poach roe in water kept just below a simmer for 10 minutes or until thoroughly cooked through. Cut into small pieces and add to thickened soup along with meat from fish head. Stir and serve at once.

Serves 4–6.

VARIATION: Add ¼ pound sliced and lightly sautéed mushrooms or 1 4-ounce can sliced mushrooms and juice at the same time you add the roe.

MILK-BASED SOUPS

CANNED FISH AND CORN CHOWDER

3 3¾-ounce cans sardines, drained and oil reserved
or
2 7-ounce cans tuna, drained and oil reserved
or
1 1-pound can salmon
or
2 8-ounce cans sliced conch (possibly labeled "scungilli")
Cooking oil and/or reserved oil to make 2 tablespoons
½ cup chopped onion
1 cup water
2 large potatoes, diced
½ teaspoon salt or to taste
Pepper to taste
1 bay leaf
2 to 3 cups milk
1 12-ounce can whole-kernel corn
½ cup light cream or evaporated milk
Chopped parsley or chopped scallion for garnish
Paprika

Cut or break fish into small pieces. Heat oil in large, heavy pot and lightly sauté onion. Add water, potatoes, salt, pepper and bay leaf, bring to a simmer and cook, covered, for 15 minutes (add more water if necessary) or until potatoes are just tender. Remove bay leaf, add milk, corn and fish and return to a simmer. Remove from fire, stir in cream or canned milk, pour into a tureen, garnish with parsley or scallion, sprinkle with paprika and serve with crackers or buttered toast.

Serves 6–8.

LEFTOVER FISH AND CORN CHOWDER: Remove bones and skin from cooked fish, flake and substitute for canned fish in preceding recipe.

EASY CLAM, MUSSEL OR OYSTER STEW

1 quart shucked clams, mussels or oysters, strained
Liquid from clams, mussels or oysters
4 cups milk
1 cup cream or evaporated milk
2 tablespoons butter or margarine, melted
Paprika (optional)
Salt and pepper

Cook clams, mussels or oysters 1–3 minutes in their own liquid. Divide shellfish and liquid into 6 to 8 soup bowls. While shellfish is cooking, heat milk just to boiling, turn off heat and stir in cream. Divide into soup bowls containing shellfish, stir, add about 1 teaspoon melted butter or margarine to center of each, sprinkle with paprika, serve and let each diner add salt and pepper to taste.

Serves 6–8.

VARIATIONS:

· Substitute canned shellfish for fresh in above recipe.

· Crumble crackers into bowls before pouring in hot milk and cream mixture.

FIN FISH BISQUE

(A Delicately Rich, Slightly Thickened Milk Soup with Fish)

1 pound delicately flavored fillets or other boneless pieces of fish no more than 1 inch thick and no more than intermediately fat; freshwater or salt, fresh or frozen
3 tablespoons butter or margarine
2 tablespoons fresh or freeze-dried chopped shallots (optional)
2 tablespoons fresh or freeze-dried chopped chives
1 tablespoon flour
3 cups milk
1 teaspoon salt or to taste
White pepper to taste
2–4 tablespoons light sherry (optional)
½ cup heavy cream
Paprika (optional)

Defrost fish if frozen. Melt butter or margarine in large, heavy pot. If fresh shallots and chives are used, sauté lightly in melted butter or margarine, remove with slotted spoon and set aside. Stir flour into butter or margarine left in pot. Cook for 2 or 3 minutes, then pour in milk, stirring with a whisk as you add, and continue until mixture almost boils. Turn down to a low simmer, stir in fish, shallots and chives. Cook, stirring frequently. When fish falls apart, remove from fire, stir in salt, pepper, sherry and cream, pour into a tureen, garnish with paprika and serve with toast or crackers.

Serves 4–6.

VARIATIONS:

· Add 2–4 tablespoons fish fumet, page 119, for richer flavor.

· Thicken by adding 1 10½-ounce can condensed cream of mushroom soup in place of 1 cup of the milk and deleting flour and butter or margarine.

FIN FISH AND SHELLFISH BISQUE: Substitute oysters, clams or mussels for part of fish. Cook for 2 or 3 minutes only after adding shellfish.

LEFTOVER BISQUE SAUCE WITH EITHER OF ABOVE: Reheat and use leftovers from either of preceding 2 bisques as is or slightly thickened as a sauce to pour over rice, toast, mashed potatoes or spaghetti. (See "Using Fish Soups as a Sauce," page 179.)

COD (THE ECONOMY) BISQUE: The cost of fish bisque can be kept down—while still using shallots and cream—if your fish is very fresh cod, which is delicate, delicious, but often inexpensive.

FISH AND SHRIMP EGGPLANT SOUP

This is a good way to use nicely flavored but bony fish.

1 *pound mild-flavored whole (drawn and scaled) fish, fresh or frozen, salt or freshwater*
¼ *pound shrimp, fresh, canned or frozen*
4 *cups water*
1 *medium onion, chopped*
1 *clove garlic, chopped*
1 *small green pepper, chopped*
1 *teaspoon sugar*
1 *bay leaf*
1 *eggplant, peeled and diced*
2 *cups milk, heated*
Salt and pepper to taste
½ *cup chopped tomatoes (optional)*

Combine first 8 ingredients, except shrimp, in large, heavy pot and bring to a simmer. Cook for 3 minutes, then remove fish and pull meat from bones. Set fish meat aside, return carcass or carcasses to pot and continue cooking 30 minutes or until broth has a nice, rich flavor and is reduced to about 3 cups. Strain, discard vegetable pulp and bones, add eggplant to broth and simmer until eggplant is just tender. Add fish meat and shrimp, and simmer 3 minutes more or until shrimp, if raw, is cooked. Stir in hot milk and season with salt and pepper. Pour into a tureen, sprinkle chopped tomatoes over top and serve at once.

Serves 6.

LOBSTER, CRAB, SCALLOP, SHRIMP OR CRAYFISH BISQUE

½–1 pound cooked lobster, crab, scallop, shrimp or crayfish meat (or a combination of any or all of them), broken into bite-size pieces or flaked
3 *tablespoons butter or margarine*
2 *tablespoons fresh or freeze-dried shallots, chopped (optional)*
2 *tablespoons fresh or freeze-dried chives, chopped*
2 *tablespoons flour*
3 *cups milk*
½ *cup heavy cream*
1 *teaspoon salt or to taste*
White pepper to taste
2–4 *tablespoons light sherry (optional)*
Paprika (optional)

Defrost shellfish meat if frozen and carefully remove all cartilage from crab. Melt butter or margarine in large, heavy pot. If fresh shallots and chives are used, sauté lightly in melted butter or margarine, remove with slotted spoon and set aside. Stir flour into butter or margarine left in pot. Cook for 2 or 3 minutes, then pour in milk, stirring with a whisk as you add, and continue until mixture almost boils. Turn down to a low simmer, and cook for 1 minute. Add shellfish and cream, and heat for 1 or 2 minutes more, but do not boil. Stir in shallots, chives, salt, pepper and sherry, pour into a tureen, garnish with paprika and serve with toast or crackers.

Serves 4–6.

LOBSTER BISQUE WITH CORAL ROE AND GREEN LIVER: Steam 1 pound lobster (page 66), remove flesh and break into small pieces. Prepare bisque as in preceding recipe but mash liver and roe, and stir in at the same time as adding the lobster meat. Stir soup constantly after adding to prevent curdling.

CLAM, MUSSEL OR OYSTER BISQUE: Substitute 1 pint of shucked clams, mussels or oysters. Cook in their own liquid for 2 or 3 minutes—just until edges curl. Add hot shellfish to hot soup, stir, remove at once from fire and serve.

SHELLFISH AND MUSHROOM BISQUE: Sauté ½ to 1 cup sliced fresh mushrooms in 2 to 3 tablespoons butter or margarine and add to any of the preceding shellfish bisques.

LEFTOVER SHELLFISH BISQUE SAUCE: Gently reheat and use any of the 4 preceding bisques as is or slightly thickened to pour over rice, toast, mashed potatoes or spaghetti. (See "Using Fish Soups as a Sauce," page 179.)

FISH OR SHELLFISH NEWBURG: Any of the bisques in this section can be turned into a Newburg recipe by stirring a little of the hot bisque into 2 egg yolks, then stirring back into the pot. Cook for 1 minute, stirring constantly, and serve over toast, rice, noodles, etc.

NEW ENGLAND CLAM CHOWDER

1 *quart shucked soft-shelled clams*
¼ *pound salt pork or bacon*
¼ *cup chopped onion*
2 *cups strained liquid from clams (add water if necessary)*
1 *teaspoon salt or to taste*
White pepper to taste
¼ *teaspoon celery salt (optional)*
2 *cups peeled and diced potatoes*
4 *cups milk*
1–2 *tablespoons flour, depending on thickness you desire (optional; not used in traditional chowder)*
½ *cup heavy cream or canned milk (optional)*
1 *tablespoon butter or margarine (optional)*
Paprika (optional)

Cut off necks of clams and discard, coarsely chop remaining part of clam and refrigerate. In a heavy saucepan, cook salt pork or bacon and onions together until lightly browned. Add liquid from clams, salt, pepper, celery salt and diced potatoes, bring to a boil, cover and cook on medium heat until potatoes are just tender. Pour milk into a large, heavy pot, and drizzle in flour, stirring with a whisk until combined and smooth. Cook, continuing to stir, until soup thickens. Continue cooking for about 2 minutes, stirring as necessary to keep soup smooth, then add clams. As soon as clams are cooked, turn off heat, stir in hot potato mixture and cream and pour into a tureen. Add 1 tablespoon of butter or margarine, partially let it melt in center of soup, then sprinkle with paprika. Serve while nice and hot with buttered toast or crackers.

Serves 6–8.

NOTE: New England Clam Chowder can be made also from hard-shell clams.

MUSSEL OR OYSTER CHOWDER: Prepare in the same way as New England Clam Chowder, using mussels or oysters instead of clams.

CRAB, LOBSTER, SCALLOP OR SHRIMP CHOWDER: Substitute any of these shellfish for clams in New England Clam Chowder and substitute

2 cups of fish or chicken broth for strained liquid from clams. Leave small shrimp or bay scallops whole but cut other shellfish into pieces. If raw, add to hot soup just long enough to cook; if cooked, add just long enough to heat through.

SHELLFISH AND CORN CHOWDER: Prepare as in any of preceding recipes based on New England Clam Chowder method and add 1 or 2 12-ounce cans whole-kernel corn to soup pot just long enough before heat is turned off for corn to heat through.

SHELLFISH CHOWDER WITH PEAS AND/OR MUSHROOMS: Just before serving add 1 10½-ounce box of frozen peas and/or 1 cup sliced mushrooms, cooked and hot, to any of the preceding chowders made in the New England Clam Chowder method.

LEFTOVER NEW ENGLAND CLAM CHOWDER SAUCE: Reheat and use as is or slightly thickened to pour over rice, toast, mashed potatoes or spaghetti. (See "Using Fish Soups as a Sauce," page 179.)

7

Simmering, Poaching and Steaming

(Where specific instructions for simmering, poaching or steaming individual shellfish differ from those for fin fish or are a part of the basic cleaning and shelling process, they will be found in Part One, Chapter 4, in the section covering that particular shellfish.)

There are three basic ways that are best for preparing both fin fish and shellfish if you're going to eat them plain, flake them for a salad or for a loaf or whatever, cover them with a sauce, or finish them up with a quick browning in the broiler. First, of course, wash fish by dipping in lightly salted cold water. Examine shellfish and remove any bits of broken shell. Then:

1. Simmer them in a liquid. The magic word here is "simmer." Never, never boil fish. Bring the liquid just to a boil, then immediately turn the heat down so that the liquid is only bubbling around the edges; that's a simmer. The utensil may be covered or not.

2. Poach them in a liquid at a very low simmer or with the heat turned off completely as soon as the liquid boils. Put a cover on the cooking utensil to hold in the heat. A see-through cover is best. Then, if you're keeping the heat turned on, you can easily see if the rate of boiling increases. The poaching liquid usually, but not always, covers the fish. If it does not, cut a piece of waxed paper to fit, with a small hole in the center for steam to escape, and place directly on top of the fish before covering the utensil. Or, if the fish is wearing its skin, use a slotted cake turner and carefully turn it over halfway through cooking.

3. Steam the fish or shellfish on a rack or on top of vegetables or rice or some other food that holds the fish far enough above boiling liquid so that even the bubbles don't splash it and it cooks in the steam generated by the hot liquid.

The important thing to remember is that any of these three liquid-cooking methods or combinations or variations of them will result in the moistest, most flavorful fish possible.

POACHING OR STEAMING UNDEFROSTED FISH

Frozen fish no more than 1½ inches thick and individually frozen shrimp can be either poached or steamed very successfully without first defrosting; lobster tails, too, if partially defrosted. Just increase the cooking time to approximately double what the recipe calls for when cooking fresh fish. Cooked, partially defrosted king crab legs can be heated on a rack over steam.

HOW TO HANDLE

Generally, the flesh of lean fish is firmer and does not fall apart when cooked in liquid as easily as does that of most fat fish. But this doesn't mean you can't cook fat fish in liquids. Adding an acid such as lemon juice or vinegar to the liquid will add a little firmness—and a nice flavor (see "The Liquids to Use," page 197)—and wrapping it in cheesecloth will insure a safe trip from pot to platter.

Putting the fish into the cooking utensil is no problem; it's getting it out after it's cooked that's difficult. Of course, if it breaks up while you're removing it, it will still taste great. But if you want your fish to look its best and be all in one piece, whether it's lean or fat, here's what you'd better do:

· Fold it in a single layer of cheesecloth.

· Put the loose edges on top, lapping over slightly, so you can fold them back to test the fish for doneness.

· Twist the 2 ends of cheesecloth into handles and lower the fish into the liquid or onto the steamer rack.

· Fish or pieces of fish (fillets, steaks and chunks) should be in a single layer and they should not be crowded, which means the choice of the cooking utensil is important. A heavy one that holds the heat well is best. It might be a skillet, large or small, depending on the amount and size of your fish; it might be a pot or, if you're preparing for a crowd, a large roaster that extends over 2 burners of your stove.

There are very lovely fish cookers, designed in the shape of a fish, sometimes with racks that have handles, which permit you to cook with a minimum amount of broth or fish breakage. Just one thing: remember when buying fish to get one that is the right size for your cooker. If you catch your own—well, you'll have to work that out with the fish. Maybe that's why we prefer cheesecloth.

To get the fish out of the cooking utensil after it's cooked and as wonderfully tender as warm butter or a soft poached egg, lift it gently by the cheesecloth handles and transfer to a heated serving platter. Hold a broad knife against the side of the fish or insert a cake turner under it and carefully pull away the cheesecloth.

Another reason we prefer cheesecloth is purely economic: cheesecloth costs only a few pennies; a fish cooker that's any good usually will cost upwards of $20.

So now, after telling you all that about handling fish that's being cooked in a liquid, we'll tell you this: one of the simplest solutions to the problem of removing poached or simmered fish from the cooking pot to the serving platter is, don't do it. Don't even try. Instead, choose as a cooking utensil one that is fairly shallow and that you can use both to cook and to serve.

Simple, isn't it? And much cheaper even than cheesecloth!

The handling of steamed fish is fairly simple. You'll find what instructions there are at the beginning of the steamed-fish recipes on page 219.

The Liquids to Use

The liquid you use when simmering or poaching directly in it or when steaming above it can be plain water, milk, wine or beer. (See note regarding acids in improvised metal utensils, page 39.)

Most often it's water seasoned to suit the individual taste. If you feel uncertain about what you'd like in it, you can use the Fish Broth recipe on page 118. You can use canned clam broth if you're in a hurry or, for that matter, canned chicken broth. If you'd prefer something that might appear to be a bit more exciting, try the traditional Short Broth recipe that the French call court bouillon. Here it is:

SHORT BROTH
(Court Bouillon)

½ *cup dry white wine (optional)*
5 *cups water*
2 *large carrots, scraped and sliced*
4 *shallots or 1 large mild onion, chopped*
4 *green onions, chopped*
1 *sprig tarragon or ½ teaspoon dry tarragon (optional)*
1 *sprig thyme or ½ teaspoon dry thyme (optional)*
2 *sprigs parsley (add during last 5 minutes of cooking if you like a delicate flavor)*
1 *bay leaf*

1 *teaspoon salt or to taste*
4 *peppercorns or to taste*
1 *clove garlic or garlic powder to taste*

Combine all ingredients, simmer covered 40 minutes, taste and adjust seasoning. Strain through fine sieve or 3 layers of cheesecloth.

Makes 4 to 5 cups, strained, depending on how long and how fast you simmer.

If you think you'd prefer something with quite a bit more spicy zest to it, try the recipe that follows.

GULF COAST BOIL

3 *bay leaves*
1 *tablespoon whole allspice*
1½ *teaspoons crushed red peppers*
2 *teaspoons whole cloves*
2 *medium onions, sliced*
6 *cloves garlic*
2 *lemons, sliced*
¼ *cup salt*
2 *quarts water*

Tie the 4 spices in a piece of cheesecloth. Add with onions, garlic, lemons and salt to the water and simmer covered 30 minutes and strain. Quantity will be reduced to 6 to 7 cups, depending on how long and how fast you simmer.

There's also a highly spiced commercial product called either Shrimp Spice or Crab Boil that's nice to have around when you're in a big hurry and don't have time to assemble your own ingredients. (See our recipe for Poached Big Fish with Conch Sauce, pages 334–335, which gives detailed instructions for using Shrimp Spice.)

All of the poaching, simmering, steaming broths that we've just described—plus any other that we haven't—can be prepared ahead, strained, cooled and stored in the refrigerator or freezer for use as needed at a later date. The length of time they will keep depends on the ingredients you use. See page 118 for broth-freezing suggestions.

No matter what broth recipe you use, adapt the strength and the seasonings (go easy on the wine if you've never used it) to your family's taste.

You needn't concern yourself with what fish are best suited for steaming, poaching and/or simmering. They all are, be they fin fish or shellfish, freshwater or saltwater, just-caught or frozen.

Therefore, use whichever fish is available to you, simmer it, poach it or steam it, mate it with any sauce from this book, and we'll wager our favorite conch shell that whichever method you use will right then and there become your favorite method of fish cookery.

Nevertheless, don't stop there. Try all three methods. Don't stop with the fish that you happened to use the first time. Try all those available to you, whether you've ever eaten them before or not. Don't stop with just one sauce. Try all that appeal to you. The variety this will give you should stimulate and satisfy the most demanding appetites in your house for a long, long time.

Coming up now are the simmering and poaching recipes. We group them together because the cooking methodologies are exceedingly similar. Use them interchangeably with equal success. Combine them with a sauce, just about any sauce, and you can create almost limitless dishes of your own.

SIMMERING AND POACHING RECIPES

Beginning with Three Methods for Preparing Stretch Recipes such as Creamed Fish Over Rice, Toast, Mashed Potatoes, Spaghetti or Noodles

Good Economy; Good Nutrition. Fish combined with sauces and stretch foods can be the basis for some very economical yet highly nutritious meals. In most cases the amount of fish used can be tailored to the pocketbook by reducing the amount called for in a recipe and just using enough to add flavor and the needed amount of protein to the sauce.

When combining with a stretch food made of cereal grains, use only those products that have not had valuable nutrients removed (or have at least had what was removed replaced through an enriching process). Potatoes, too, contain valuable nutrients (one of them is vitamin C) that shouldn't be thrown out with the skin or in the boiling water.

METHOD ONE

Starting with Raw Fin Fish: Simmer or poach any dressed fin fish with head and tail left on in water or Short Broth to cover just until fish flakes separate easily when gently probed with a fork. Remove fish, flake meat from bones (bony fish can be easily flaked if chilled first) and refrigerate. Return bones to liquid and simmer for at least ½ hour, longer if necessary to reduce broth to about 1 cup. Strain broth. Add milk to make desired quantity of sauce and reheat. Cook 2 tablespoons flour and 2 tablespoons butter for each 1¼ cup of liquid to be used in a large, heavy skillet or pot. Add warm liquid mixture and cook on medium heat, stirring constantly with a wire whisk, until sauce thickens. Add reserved fish flakes, stir and cook for about 1 minute or until they reheat, season to taste with salt and pepper and any other seasonings you would like to add and serve over hot rice, toast, mashed potatoes, spaghetti or noodles.

NOTE: If you used a Short Broth containing wine or heavy seasonings that might curdle the milk, reduce and add to milk sauce *after* it has thickened and cooked. (See "To Avoid Curdling Milk-Based Soups," page 179.)

NOTE: This makes a medium sauce. For instructions on making thick or thin or calorie-counter sauces, see Part Two, Chapter 1.

Starting with Raw Shellfish: Follow same instructions as for creamed fin fish in preceding except that you would have no fish carcasses to return to the pot for added flavor. You can, however, return lobster and shrimp shell. Cook shucked oysters and clams for only 2 or 3 minutes or until their edges start to ruffle. Scallops only need to be heated through. See Part One, Chapter 4, for detailed cooking instructions for other shellfish.

METHOD TWO

Using Canned or Cooked (it can be leftover) Fish:
· Add fin fish or shellfish and any liquid* to a can of condensed cream of mushroom, celery, cheddar cheese or other soup of your choice. Thin with milk if necessary, heat and serve.

· Add canned or cooked fish in any combinations you would like to any of following heated sauces, making the sauce medium thick (see Part Two, Chapter 1, for suggested calorie-counter sauces) to pour over rice, toast, mashed potatoes, noodles and spaghetti. Figure on 1/3 cup or more of sauce (before adding fish or shellfish) per person:

White Sauce, Fish Broth Sauce, Cheese Sauce II, Cream Sauce or Diet Cream Sauce, Cucumber Sauce, Curry Cream Sauce, Egg Sauce, Green Grape Sauce, Herbed Wine Sauce, Lemon Sauce, Lobster Sauce I, Mushroom Sauce, Onion Sauce, Oyster Sauce (this sauce does very well as a creamed shellfish without any additional fish or shellfish), Shrimp Sauce I, Shrimp or Lobster Sauce II, Tomato Sauce, Rich Wine Sauce, Lobster Shell Sauce, Okra-Tomato Sauce, Hawaiian-Style or Polonaise, Sweet and Sour Sauce.

METHOD THREE

Using Fish Soup as a Sauce: see page 179.

CREAMED FISH AND SHELLFISH CURRY: Mix curry powder to taste with a little butter or margarine and stir into hot sauce prepared in any of the preceding methods.

---

* Don't use liquid from can if label states fish should be drained before using.

CLAMS OR MUSSELS IN OIL AND PARSLEY SAUCE

(A Spaghetti Sauce Without Tomatoes)

2 *dozen clams or mussels in the shell*
1 *tablespoon olive oil*
3 *tablespoons cooking oil*
2 *large cloves of garlic, slivered*
Liquid in which clams or mussels were cooked, strained and reduced
   if necessary to 4 cups
¼ *teaspoon oregano or to taste*
Salt and pepper to taste
6 *sprigs very fresh parsley, finely minced*
Cooked spaghetti for 4–6

Clean and simmer clams or mussels until they open (see Part One, Chapter 4), using Short Broth or plain water. Short Broth will make a more richly flavored sauce. Remove meat from shells, set aside and discard shells. Heat oils in large, heavy pot. Add garlic and cook until pale golden color. Add strained liquid, heat and stir in oregano, salt and pepper to taste. Chop clams or mussels and add with parsley, stir, heat through, pour over a bowl of drained, hot spaghetti and serve.

Serves 4–6.

SPINACH SPAGHETTI WITH CLAMS OR MUSSELS IN OIL SAUCE: Eliminate parsley from preceding recipe and substitute 2 tablespoons butter or margarine for 2 tablespoons of the cooking oil. Serve over green spaghetti that was made with spinach. Sprinkle if you like with grated Parmesan cheese.

GRANDMA LENA'S GEFILTE FISH*

4 *pounds dressed carp or any moderately fat fish*
2 *pounds any lean white fish, preferably a mixture, filleted*
4 *stalks celery*
2 *large onions*
Salt and pepper to taste
4 *eggs, beaten*
Water
2 *pounds carrots, sliced*
Grated horseradish, red or white, to taste

Carefully remove skin and bones from carp and set aside.

Cut carp into workable pieces and put through fine-blade food grinder along with white fish, celery and onions, emptying the grindings

* From *The Pennysaver Cookbook,* by Dan and Inez Morris (Funk & Wagnalls).

into a large mixing bowl. Run through a second time if necessary to assure a fine grind. Add salt, pepper, and beaten eggs. Mix well.

With your hands, roll mixture into baking potato-shaped ovals, about 3 inches long and 1½ inches in diameter. Wrap each oval in a piece of fish skin and fasten with wooden toothpicks. Place fish bones in large stewpot, cover with water and place the ovals gently on top of the bones. Add sliced carrots, bring water to a boil, turn down heat, and gently simmer about 30 minutes. Cool fish enough to handle, then carefully remove skin and discard. Remove bones from broth with slotted spoon and discard.

Return the fish to the broth and carrot mixture, place in refrigerator, and chill until liquid forms a jelly. Serve cold with grated horseradish.

Serves 16 to 20.

NOTE: Cold, as an appetizer, is the most popular way of eating gefilte fish. But if you want it as a hot main course, simply eliminate chilling, reheat to serving temperature, and serve with vegetables.

LOBSTER NEWBURG

> 1 1-*pound live lobster*
> 1 *recipe Newburg Sauce, page 148*
> *Hot buttered toast or rice for 2–4*

Simmer lobster, page 67; remove meat and cut in bite-size pieces and reserve shell for making sauce. Prepare Newburg Sauce, add pieces of cooked lobster and serve over hot toast or rice.

Serves 2–4.

OYSTERS IN OKRA-TOMATO SAUCE

(Oysters Creole)

> 1 *quart shucked oysters*
> 1 *recipe Okra-Tomato Sauce, page 149*

Use some of the oyster liquid, thinned with a little water, instead of fish or chicken broth called for in sauce recipe. Add oysters to hot sauce and simmer 2 or 3 minutes or until edges of oysters start to curl. Serve over cooked noodles.

Serves 6.

NOTE: In this as well as following Creole recipes, you can open shellfish by cooking in the shell (see Part One, Chapter 4), strain broth and use some in making Okra-Tomato Sauce. Heat cooked shellfish in the sauce (include extra broth for a thinner sauce) and serve.

CLAM CREOLE: Prepare preceding recipe, using raw shucked clams instead of oysters.

MUSSEL CREOLE: Use mussels instead of oysters in Oysters in Okra-Tomato Sauce.

SHRIMP CREOLE: Use shrimp instead of oysters in making Oysters in Okra-Tomato Sauce.

LOBSTER CREOLE: Use lobster instead of oysters in making Oysters in Okra-Tomato Sauce.

SHRIMP AND CRAB GUMBO

½ to 1 pound medium raw shrimp, cleaned and deveined
1 7½-ounce can crab meat
3 cups water or Short Broth, page 197
3 tablespoons butter or margarine
3 tablespoons flour
1 recipe Okra-Tomato Sauce, page 149
Cooked rice or noodles for 4–6

Bring water or Short Broth to a boil, turn down to a simmer, add raw shrimp and cook 2 or 3 minutes or until shrimp is done. Remove shrimp and set aside. Melt butter or margarine in large, heavy pot, add flour and cook 2 or 3 minutes, stirring constantly. Strain liquid in which shrimp cooked, add and cook, stirring constantly until sauce is thickened and smooth. Stir in shrimp, canned crab meat and Okra-Tomato Sauce. When everything is nice and hot, stir in hot cooked rice or noodles.
Serves 4–6.

SHRIMP CURRY

1 pound raw shrimp, shelled and deveined
1 small onion, sliced
1 clove garlic
¼ to ½ teaspoon ground red pepper
1 small pinch turmeric
1 slice green ginger, chopped (¼ teaspoon powdered ginger may be substituted)
1-inch piece of cinnamon
Salt to taste
⅜ cup coconut milk or water
½ tablespoon cooking oil
Juice of ¼ lime

Combine shrimp in saucepan with ½ of onion slices, garlic, red pepper, turmeric, ginger, cinnamon and salt. Mix well, add coconut milk or water and simmer for about 3 minutes or until shrimp are almost done. Set aside. Heat oil in skillet, add remaining ½ of onion slices and lightly sauté. Add to shrimp mixture, stir in lime juice and heat on slow fire for 5 minutes. Serve with rice.

Serves 4–6.

NOTES:

• A commercial curry powder can be substituted for the spices used in this recipe.

• Purchase canned coconut milk at a specialty food store, or drill holes in a fresh coconut and pour the milk out.

OYSTER CURRY: Substitute shucked, drained oysters for shrimp. Cook until edges curl.

TUNA CURRY: Substitute 2 8-ounce cans of tuna for shrimp. Add tuna after sauce has cooked.

CURRIED SHRIMP CROQUETTES: Leftover shrimp from Shrimp Curry make delicious croquettes without the addition of any more seasoning. See page 268 for croquette recipe.

SHRIMP IN TOMATO SAUCE (I)

(Shrimp Marinara)

½ *pound small cooked or canned deveined shrimp*
1 *pound medium raw shrimp, shelled and deveined*
2 *tablespoons cooking oil*
1 *tablespoon olive oil*
2 *cloves garlic, crushed*
1 *small onion, chopped*
1½ *cups peeled and chopped fresh tomatoes*
2 *8-ounce cans tomato sauce*
½ *cup white wine*
Salt to taste
1 *teaspoon brown sugar or to taste*
½ *teaspoon dried oregano*
½ *teaspoon dried basil*
Cooked spaghetti for 6
Grated Parmesan cheese

Heat oils in large, heavy pot. Add garlic and onion, and lightly sauté. Add chopped tomatoes, tomato sauce, white wine and small cooked shrimp. Bring to a boil, turn down to a low simmer and cook, stirring frequently, for 20 minutes, adding water if necessary. Add salt, brown sugar, oregano and basil. Taste and adjust seasoning. Add medium shrimp and continue simmering for 3 to 5 minutes or until shrimp is cooked. Serve with hot spaghetti and grated Parmesan cheese.

Serves 6.

CRAB IN TOMATO SAUCE: (Crab Marinara): Substitute the least expensive type of crab for small shrimp in first ingredient and nice quality chunks of crab for the larger shrimp.

CLAMS IN TOMATO SAUCE (Clam Marinara): Use from 1 pint to 1 quart of shucked clams, substituting clam liquid to taste for small shrimp and clams for the medium shrimp.

OYSTERS IN MARINARA SAUCE (Oysters Marinara): Use from 1 pint to 1 quart of shucked oysters, substituting oyster liquid to taste for small shrimp, and oysters for the medium shrimp.

DONNA BEVONA'S SQUID SAUCE NEAPOLITAN

1 *medium or 2 baby squid, cleaned, bodies cut in 1-inch pieces and tentacles in 3-inch pieces*
3 *tablespoons olive oil*
2 *cloves garlic, each cut in 3 pieces*
1 *6-ounce can tomato paste*
2½ *cans water*
½–1 *teaspoon oregano*
Salt and pepper to taste

Heat olive oil to sizzling but not smoking hot in heavy pot. Add garlic and fry until light golden. Add tomato paste and stir-fry for 1 minute. Add water, oregano, salt and pepper and raw squid. Bring to boil, reduce to simmer, cover tightly and simmer for about 30 minutes or until squid is tender and sauce is desired consistency. Serve with toasted bread rusks or spaghetti.

Serves 2–4.

SHRIMP WITH GREEN PEPPER, TOMATO, HAM AND RICE (I)

(Shrimp Jambalaya)

1 *pound raw shrimp in the shell*
2 *slices fat bacon, cut in pieces*
½ *cup chopped onion*
2 *cloves garlic, finely chopped*
1 *small green pepper, chopped*
1 *1-pound can of tomatoes*
Salt and pepper to taste
¼ *teaspoon chili powder or to taste*
⅛ *teaspoon dried basil*
½ *teaspoon Worcestershire sauce*
1 *cup uncooked rice*
½ *cup diced, cooked ham (optional)*

Simmer shrimp in water to cover for 2 or 3 minutes or until shells turn bright pink. Remove shrimp, cool, peel, devein and refrigerate. Strain broth, reduce if necessary to 2 cups and set aside. Fry bacon in heavy pot. Add onion, garlic and green pepper, and lightly sauté in the bacon fat. Add strained broth in which shrimp was cooked, can of tomatoes, seasonings and uncooked rice. Bring to a boil, turn to simmer, cover and cook, stirring frequently, until rice is tender. Most of liquid should be absorbed but watch that bottom doesn't scorch. Add water, a little at a time, if necessary. Add cooked shrimp and ham for last few minutes of cooking, just long enough to heat. Stir and serve.

Serves 4.

NOTE: Add larger proportion of rice to stretch recipe, but be sure to add more liquid (tomato juice or water) to allow for the addition.

DELICATE OVALS OF PUREED FISH   (I)

(Quenelles)

> 1 *pound skinless, boneless fish, cooked or raw*
> 1 *recipe White Sauce Croquette Base, page 151*
> 1 *pinch dried cloves*
> 2 *pinches nutmeg*
> ½ *teaspoon crushed freeze-dried shallots*
> *Salt and pepper to taste*
> ½ *teaspoon sherry or Cognac*
> 1 *egg white, beaten*
> 3 *cups clam or chicken broth*
> 5 *tablespoons butter or margarine*
> 5 *tablespoons flour*
> 1 *egg yolk*
> ¼ *cup heavy cream*

Puree fish until it is a smooth paste. This can be done by putting through a meat grinder several times or mashing with a fork (some fish fillets mash very well when about half defrosted), then worked with the back of a wooden spoon until almost as light and fluffy as whipped potatoes. Place in a bowl set in ice water (or thoroughly chill all ingredients and utensils by setting in the freezer for a few minutes), stir in White Sauce Croquette Base, seasonings and sherry or Cognac and blend well with back of wooden spoon. Fold in beaten egg white and stir just until well mixed. Heat broth to boiling in large, heavy pot and turn down to a slow simmer. Shape fish mixture into egg shapes between 2 teaspoons (dip teaspoons into hot water after forming each oval) and gently drop into simmering broth. Simmer very slowly for 10–15 minutes or until ovals are firm. While they are simmering, melt butter in heavy skillet, add flour and cook together for 2 or 3 minutes. Remove ovals to a preheated serving dish and put in a warm oven. Add butter-flour mixture to hot broth in which ovals were cooked and stir with a wire whisk until sauce is smooth and thickened. Continue cooking until sauce is the desired thickness. Add egg yolk to heavy cream, stir in a little of the hot sauce and add the mixture to the pot of sauce. Stir and either serve separately from the fish ovals or pour directly over them and serve together.

Serves 4.

NOTE: These fish ovals (or quenelles) can also be cooked in broth that is to be served as a soup with them in it.

POACHED FILLETS WITH SHELLFISH AND MUSHROOM SAUCE

(Filets Marguery)

(There are many variations of fillets cooked in the Marguery manner —Marguery in this case being the name of a famous Parisian café. Here is ours.)

> 2 *pounds delicately flavored white-fleshed fish fillets (trout or sole are most often used), freshwater or salt*
> ½ *pound small shrimp in the shell*
> 6 *oysters, shucked*
> 2 *cups Short Broth, diluted with 1 cup of water, page 197*
> ¼ *pound butter or margarine*
> 6 *tablespoons flour*
> ½ *cup sliced mushrooms, very lightly sautéed in butter or margarine*
> ½ *cup heavy cream*
> ¼ *cup grated cheddar cheese or any yellow cheese of your choice*
> *Paprika*
> *Parsley sprigs*

Heat Short Broth to simmering. Add shrimp and oysters, including oyster liquid, and cook just until done. Remove and save broth. Shell and devein shrimp and set them and the oysters aside. Melt butter or margarine in large heavy skillet or pot, add flour and cook, stirring constantly, for 2 or 3 minutes. Poach fillets in broth for 3 to 5 minutes; arrange in single layer on preheated ovenproof platter and cover to keep warm. Reduce to 3 cups and strain broth, stir into flour and butter mixture and cook on medium heat, stirring constantly, until smooth and thickened.

Add cooked shrimp, oysters and sautéed mushrooms. Continue cooking the sauce for about 30 seconds, remove from heat, stir in cream and pour over fillets. Sprinkle with grated cheese and a little paprika for color. Run under the broiler (about 3 inches from source of heat) for 3 to 5 minutes or until cheese melts and top browns slightly. Garnish with parsley and serve.

Serves 6–8.

POACHED FISH STEAKS IN OYSTER SAUCE

½ to 1 pint shucked oysters
½ cup white wine
4 mild-flavored fish steaks, fresh or frozen, freshwater or salt, about ¾ to 1 inch thick
2 tablespoons minced onion
2 tablespoons finely chopped fresh or frozen spinach (optional)
¼ cup finely chopped mushroom stems or 1 tablespoon powdered mushrooms (optional)
1 10½-ounce can cream of mushroom soup

Place oyster liquid, wine and enough water to make 2 cups in large, heavy skillet or saucepan. Bring to a boil, turn down to low simmer, add oysters, cover and poach 2–3 minutes or until edges curl. Remove oysters with slotted spoon and keep warm in covered dish. Add fish, wrapped in cheesecloth, and all remaining ingredients except mushroom soup to skillet or saucepan. Poach 4–6 minutes (in same liquid in which oysters cooked) or until fish flakes separate easily when gently probed with tines of a fork. Remove fish to heated serving platter. Boil liquids in pan to reduce to about ¾ cup, add mushroom soup and cook, stirring constantly, until smooth and reduced to desired thickness. Add oysters to sauce, pour over fish steaks and serve.

Serves 4.

WHOLE FISH POACHED IN BROTH

1 2-pound dressed fish with the head left on, freshwater or salt
About 2 quarts chicken broth or Short Broth (court bouillon)

Place fish in fish poacher or in the center of deep, heavy-duty baking pan, leaving at least 1 inch of space on all sides. Bring chicken broth or Short Broth to a fast boil, pour over fish and cover tightly with lid or aluminum foil. In 10 to 20 minutes (depending on thickness of fish) remove the foil and test fish for doneness with a fork. If it does not flake easily, re-cover and let it stand a little longer. If broth has cooled, put poacher on fire and reheat or add just enough boiling water to complete the poaching.

We have never eaten fish that tastes better than when cooked this way and it's well worth trying a few times until you get the timing just right.

Serve the fish immediately, just as it is, or with a little melted butter and lemon garnish, or with a sauce of your choice.

You can drink the broth, make it into a gravy or save it to use as the base for a soup.

Serves 2.

MEDITERRANEAN HOT POT*

(Fishermen the world over have a knack of preparing seafood in a plain yet appetizing manner. In the Latin countries of the Mediterranean they love shellfish and squid almost as much as tomatoes. When they combine all three, the results are an easy-to-prepare fisherman's "hot pot.")

> 2½ *pounds assorted shellfish (shrimp, scallops, clams, oysters, mussels)*
> 1 *pound squid*
> 3 *tablespoons fresh parsley, very finely chopped*
> 1 *garlic clove*
> 3 *tablespoons olive oil*
> 1 *cup dry white wine*
> 2¼ *cups peeled, seeded and chopped tomatoes*
> ¼ *teaspoon crushed red pepper*
> *Salt and pepper*
> 6 *slices Italian bread*
> 3 *tablespoons olive oil*

Clean the shellfish and squid. Mince the parsley and garlic. Cut squid into bite-size pieces. In large, heavy pot, sauté squid in 3 tablespoons hot oil for several minutes, turning often. Add the wine, and cook over high flame until evaporated. Add tomatoes, parsley, garlic, red pepper, salt and pepper to taste. Simmer, covered, over moderate heat for 20 minutes. Add water if necessary. While squid is cooking, simmer shellfish in salted water until shells of the clams, scallops, oysters and mussels are open and the shrimp have turned pink. Strain the liquor and reserve. Remove fish from shells and devein shrimp. A few minutes before the squid is done cooking, add shellfish and their liquor to pot.

While the mixture is cooking, fry the bread slices in hot oil. When slices are golden brown, transfer each to a shallow soup bowl. Spoon the fish and sauce over fried bread.

Serves 6.

* From *The Love Apple Cookbook,* by Don Bevona (Funk & Wagnalls).

SPICED FISH

1 *2-pound fish, dressed and cut into small chunks*
3 *tablespoons cooking oil*
1 *small minced onion*
¼ *teaspoon chili powder*
½ *teaspoon salt*
⅛ *teaspoon saffron, crumbled between the fingers*
¼ *teaspoon garlic powder*
⅛ *teaspoon ginger powder*
4 *tablespoons water*

Defrost fish if frozen. Heat oil in a heavy skillet, add minced onion and cook for 2 or 3 minutes. Combine chili powder, salt, saffron, garlic powder and ginger powder, and roll fish cubes in the mixture. Add water to skillet and stir. Add fish chunks, stir, cover and simmer for about 5 minutes, or until fish flakes easily when gently probed with the tines of a fork.
Serves 2.

SPICED FISH CROQUETTES: Leftovers from Spiced Fish make delicious croquettes without the addition of any more seasonings. See page 268 for croquette recipe.

CIOPPINO CALIFORNIA

(Cioppino is a wonderful kind of shellfish, and sometimes fin fish, stew created by Portuguese fishermen in California. It is cooked in the shell and eaten most informally with the fingers. What can't be eaten with the fingers is sopped up with slabs of hot garlic bread. The amounts given in this recipe are adjustable and you can substitute other fin fish or shellfish or add to them, according to what you like best and what's available.)

1–2 *dozen cherrystone clams, thoroughly scrubbed and washed*
1–2 *pounds striped bass or other fish, filleted*
1–2 *pounds king crab legs in the shell, defrosted and cut into 1½–2-inch lengths*
¼ *pound medium raw shrimp, shelled and deveined*
¼ *cup olive oil*
1 *clove garlic*
1 *onion, minced*
2 *1-pound cans tomatoes*
½ *cup water*
1 *15-ounce can tomato sauce*
1–2 *tablespoons finely chopped fresh basil*
1 *cup white wine*

Tabasco Sauce to taste
Salt to taste
Garlic bread and butter

Heat olive oil in a very large pot. Add garlic and onion, and lightly sauté. Add canned tomatoes, water, tomato sauce, basil and wine, and stir. Taste and add Tabasco Sauce and salt to taste. Simmer for 50 to 60 minutes or until sauce is a nice consistency. It should be thick enough to cling to fish. Add clams, cover and simmer for 9 minutes, add bass and simmer 9 minutes, then add king crab legs and shrimp. Cioppino is ready to serve when bass flakes easily, clams open, king crab legs are heated through and shrimp has turned a more or less opaque pink and white. Serve in bowls with hot garlic bread, butter, bibs and finger bowls.

Serves 6–10.

COD FILLETS POACHED IN CLAM BROTH

1½ *pounds cod fillets or any other fillets, freshwater or salt, fresh or*
     frozen
1 *tablespoon olive oil*
1 *tablespoon cooking oil*
1 *cup clam broth*
1 *shallot, minced*
⅛ *teaspoon dried basil*
Salt and pepper to taste
French or Italian bread

Defrost fillets if frozen. Heat oils in large, heavy skillet. Add fillets and slightly warm on both sides. Combine clam broth, minced shallot, dried basil and salt and pepper to taste, stir and pour over fish. Cover and poach 5–8 minutes or just until flakes separate easily when gently probed with tines of a fork.

Serves 4–6.

DRIED SALT COD CHOWDER WITH TOMATOES AND POTATOES

(Norwegian Baccalao)

1 *pound salted dried cod (or any salt-dried fish)*
3 *medium potatoes, peeled and sliced*
2 *onions, chopped*
4 *medium tomatoes, sliced*
½ *cup tomato puree*
3 *small pimentos, slivered*

½ *cup finely diced salt pork or bacon*
1 *cup fish or chicken broth*
2 *tablespoons finely chopped parsley*
2 *hard-cooked eggs, sliced*

Soak fish 2 days (in the refrigerator), changing water morning and evening. Drain, clean carefully and remove skin and bones. Cut into convenient pieces. In a greased kettle or Dutch oven, arrange a layer of potatoes, then a layer of fish, then a layer of chopped onions; repeat the layers.
Top with tomatoes, tomato puree and pimentos. Lightly sauté salt pork
or bacon and add with the melted fat. Add broth and bring to a boil. Turn
down to a low simmer, cover and cook over a very low heat for at least
2 hours. Do not stir, but shake now and again. Add a little boiling water
if necessary. When done, serve in a deep warm dish. Garnish with chopped
parsley and sliced egg.
    Serves 6.

SPANISH-STYLE CODFISH STEW AND DUMPLINGS   (I)

1 *pound codfish chunks or any other fresh or saltwater fish*
3 *tablespoons olive oil or other cooking oil*
2 *medium onions, chopped*
1 *large stalk celery, chopped*
1 *large green pepper, chopped*
1–2 *cloves garlic, minced*
1 *tablespoon brown sugar*
1 *tablespoon lemon juice*
⅛ *teaspoon oregano*
⅛ *teaspoon cumin seeds*
½ *cup tawny port wine*
2 *bay leaves*
1 *1-pound can cooked chick peas*
3½ *cups water*
1 *cup sliced fresh mushrooms lightly sautéed (optional)*
2 *large, firm tomatoes, cubed*
Salt and pepper to taste
2 *cups biscuit mix for dumplings*

Heat olive oil in bottom of large, heavy pot, add onions, celery, green
pepper and garlic, and sauté until vegetables start to soften. Add brown
sugar, lemon juice, oregano, cumin seeds, tawny port wine, bay leaves,
chick peas and water, and simmer for 10 minutes. Add sautéed mushrooms, tomatoes and salt and pepper to taste. Simmer 5 minutes more.
    Prepare dough for dumplings according to instructions on biscuit-mix

package. Add fish to stew, stir and drop dumpling dough by heaping teaspoonful on top of stew. Cover and simmer for 15 minutes.

Serves 4–6.

SMOKED COD POACHED IN MILK

(This recipe is apt to have a very hefty flavor some will like very much. We suggest you taste the poaching milk before making it into a gravy. You may prefer to substitute a plain white sauce.)

    1 *pound smoked cod fillet, or other lean smoked fish*
    2 *cups milk*
    3 *tablespoons butter or margarine*
    3 *tablespoons flour*
    Pepper to taste
    Cooked new potatoes for 2–4
    Cooked peas for 2–4

Wipe off smoked fish with a damp cloth. Heat milk just to simmering in a heavy pot. (Pot should not be too big, because you want the milk to cover the smoked fish.) Add fish, cutting it in several pieces if necessary so it will be in a single layer and almost cover bottom of pot. Return milk to a very low simmer, cover and poach 5–10 minutes or until flakes separate easily when gently probed with tines of a fork. While fish cooks, melt butter or margarine in a heavy skillet, add flour and cook together for 2 or 3 minutes, stirring constantly. Add pepper. Pour hot milk off cod (re-cover fish to keep it warm) into skillet and stir constantly with a wire whisk until gravy is smooth and thickened. Pour over smoked cod, add cooked potatoes and peas, stir gently, transfer to a preheated serving bowl and serve.

Serves 2–4.

KING CRAB MEAT OVER CAULIFLOWER

(Hai Yook Par Choy Far*)

    1 *head cauliflower (about 1½ pounds)*
    3 *tablespoons lard or shortening of your choice*
    1 *can (7½ ounces) king crab meat*
    1 *tablespoon sherry*
    1 *cup chicken broth*
    ½ *teaspoon pepper*

* From *The Hong Kong Cookbook,* by Arthur Lem and Dan Morris (Funk & Wagnalls).

½ *teaspoon monosodium glutamate (optional)*
1 *tablespoon cornstarch mixed with* ½ *cup water*
4 *Maraschino cherries*
4 *slices cucumber, peeled*
Fresh parsley sprigs
Utensil: wok or pot and frying pan

Break cauliflower into bite-size pieces and wash thoroughly in cold water. Bring to a boil enough water to cover. Add cauliflower and cook for 3 minutes. Rinse quickly in cold water, transfer to hot serving dish, and set aside.

Preheat wok or frying pan, add shortening, and when it starts to sizzle, add crab meat and stir-fry for 2 minutes. Add sherry, stir 2 or 3 times, then add broth, pepper, and monosodium glutamate. Stir until mixture reaches the boiling point. Then stir in the cornstarch mixture until the crab-meat sauce thickens. Pour over cauliflower. Fasten cherries to cucumber with toothpicks and arrange over the finished dish. Garnish with parsley.

Serves 3–4.

SMOKED HADDOCK (FINNAN HADDIE)

(Norwegian Style)

2 *pounds smoked haddock*
1 *teaspoon salt*
2 *hard-cooked eggs, finely chopped*
1 *cup melted butter or margarine*
2 *cups hot cooked diced carrots*
2 *sprigs fresh parsley, chopped*

Skin fish and cut in pieces. Bring about 6 cups of water to boil in a pot, add salt and haddock, reduce to a simmer and cook for 10 minutes. Remove fish to preheated serving dish. Add finely chopped eggs to melted butter or margarine and pour over fish and serve. Combine cooked carrots and chopped fresh parsley in another dish and serve at the same time.

Serves 4–6.

MILK-POACHED LING FILLETS IN CAVIAR CREAM

1 *3- or 4-pound ling, or any mild-flavored salt or freshwater fish*
2 *cups water*
1 *carrot, with skin left on*

1 *medium onion*
2 *stalks celery, tops left on*
1 *cup milk*
½ *cup fish broth made from ling carcass*
Salt and pepper to taste
½ *cup butter or margarine*
3 *tablespoons flour*
¼ *cup cream*
½ *tablespoon lemon juice*
1 *tablespoon caviar (whitefish roe) or to taste*
Paprika
Parsley for garnish

Scale fish and fillet (see pages 26 and 30), but don't skin. Put remaining part of carcass in pot, add water, carrot, onion and celery and bring to a boil. Turn down to a simmer and cook, uncovered, until broth is reduced to about 1 cup. Strain, freeze ½ cup of the broth for future use and set aside remaining ½ cup. Refrigerate cooked carrot for future use; discard bones and other vegetables.

Heat milk and ½ cup broth in a heavy pot or large skillet to just under a simmer. Cut fillets in half so you have 4 serving portions and lay, skinless side down, in hot milk and broth mixture and poach for 3 minutes. Very gently turn over so skin side is down and poach for an additional 4 minutes or until almost done. Using a large slotted cake turner, remove fish to 4 heated dinner plates, season with salt and pepper, and place in a heated oven to keep warm. (The fish will finish cooking in the hot oven even though the heat is turned off.) While fish is poaching, heat butter or margarine in a large skillet, add flour and cook, stirring constantly, for 3 or 4 minutes. When fish has been removed to oven, add liquid in which it was poached to butter and flour mixture, stirring with a whisk as you pour and continuing to stir until sauce has thickened. Remove from heat and stir in cream. Reheat but do not bring to a simmer. Remove from heat again, add caviar and lemon juice, stir well and divide over fillets on 4 plates, add a sprinkle of paprika to give each fillet a touch of color and add a bit of zest to the flavor, garnish with parsley and serve at once.

Serves 4.

DAMIANO'S DELIGHT*

(Damiano Bevona was a Sicilian fisherman who liked to cook what he caught. He came to America to join his cousins, Gloucester fishermen

* From *A Family Guide to Saltwater Fishing,* by Dan Morris (Crowell-Collier).

all, and they too liked to cook what they caught. This recipe was theirs, passed on to you by Damiano's grandson, Don.)

>4 *pounds mackerel, steaked*
>1 *cup olive oil*
>6 *medium onions, sliced*
>½ *cup flour*
>½ *cup red wine vinegar or 1 cup red wine*
>1 *tablespoon capers*
>*Salt and pepper to taste*

Heat ½ cup oil in frying pan at moderate temperature. Add onions and fry lightly. Remove with fork when almost cooked, leaving oil in pan. Dip steaks in flour, add remainder of oil to pan and fry mackerel until brown. Combine mackerel and onions in saucepan, add wine or vinegar, capers and seasoning, and cook for 5 minutes. Transfer to serving bowl and chill. Damiano's Delight is better eaten cold than hot.

Serves 4–6.

MUSSELS SIMMERED IN WINE OR COURT BOUILLON

(Moules à la Marinière)

>4 *pounds mussels in the shell*
>4 *cups white wine or court bouillon (Short Broth), page 197*
>*French bread*

Clean mussels, page 69. Heat white wine or court bouillon to boiling, add mussels, adjust heat to simmer, cover and cook until mussels open (3 to 6 minutes). Serve at once in the shell in bowls with cocktail forks. Quickly strain the bouillon and divide it over the mussels. Dunk French bread into the broth.

Serves 4–6 as a meal; 8–10 as an appetizer.

FILLETS OR STEAKS À LA MARINIÈRE: Steam any fillets or steaks, cover with sauce of your choice and garnish with mussels prepared as in Mussels Simmered in Wine or Court Bouillon.

STEAMER CLAMS SIMMERED IN WINE OR COURT BOUILLON: Prepare soft-shell steamer clams in the same way as mussels.

POACHED OYSTERS PIQUANTE

>1 *pint shucked oysters, drained*
>½ *cup butter or margarine*
>⅛ *teaspoon Worcestershire sauce*
>1 *pinch cayenne pepper or to taste*

Juice of ½ lemon
Salt to taste

Combine all ingredients except oysters in a small, heavy saucepan and bring to a boil. Add oysters, turn down to a very low simmer, put lid on pan and poach for 2 to 4 minutes or until edges of oysters start to curl. Serve at once, pouring sauce from pan over oysters.
Serves 2–4.

SOLE FILLETS IN HERB AND WINE BUTTER
(Filets de Sole aux Fines Herbes)

4 *skinless fillets of sole or other delicately flavored fish*
1 *recipe Herb and Wine Butter (Fines Herbes Butter), page 139*
1 *cup fish fumet, page 119, or chicken broth*

Thaw fish if frozen. Spread one side of fillets with Herb and Wine Butter. Fold each one over once so that the buttered side is on the inside and fasten with a wooden pick. Place the folded fillets in a single layer on the bottom of a cooking-serving dish, pour cup of fumet over and cover with a piece of waxed paper with small hole in the center. Cover cooking dish and poach for about 10 minutes or until flakes separate easily when gently probed with tines of a fork. Serve directly from cooking-serving dish, spooning some of the sauce over each serving.
Serves 2–4.

LOW-CALORIE SOLE FILLETS IN HERB AND WINE BUTTER: Use only the amount of butter or margarine and wine your diet permits in making the Herb and Wine Butter for the preceding recipe.

TAUTOG TEMPTATION

1 *2-pound tautog or any mild-flavored fish*
1 *cup white wine*
1 *cup water*
1 *tablespoon chopped chives*
1 *tablespoon chopped shallots*
¼ *cup minced celery*
Salt and pepper to taste
2 *tablespoons cooking oil*
2 *tablespoons butter or margarine*
3 *tablespoons flour*
¼ *cup heavy cream*
Cooked green peas and chopped fresh tomatoes

In a fish poacher or heavy pot, combine wine, water, chives, shallots and celery, bring to a low boil and cook for 3 minutes. Add tautog and when liquid returns to a boil, turn down to simmer and cook for 3 minutes. Carefully turn fish over, add salt and pepper, cover, and in about 1 minute turn off heat and let fish continue to poach in hot liquid for 5 minutes. While fish is poaching, heat cooking oil and butter or margarine in large, heavy skillet. Add flour and cook, stirring constantly, for about 3 minutes. When fish is done, remove to a heated serving platter and place in a heated oven (the heat should be turned off) to keep warm. Add liquid in which fish was poached to butter-flour mixture (do not strain) and cook, stirring constantly, until it thickens. Continue cooking 2–3 minutes, remove from fire and stir in cream. Place on dinner table in a gravy boat. To serve fish, remove boneless pieces from carcass (see page 114), place on dinner plates, cover with a generous helping of sauce and arrange green peas and chopped fresh tomatoes around the edges.

Serves 2.

POACHED RAINBOW TROUT

2 *12-ounce packages frozen rainbow trout*
1 *13¾-ounce can chicken broth*
1 *tablespoon wine vinegar*
1 *pinch pepper*
1 *pinch garlic powder*
¼ *cup melted butter*
Lemon wedges

Wash still-frozen fish and wrap in a single layer of cheesecloth. Combine all but last 2 remaining ingredients in pot or skillet and bring to a boil. Reduce to just below a simmer and add trout by gently lowering it in its cheesecloth hammock. Poach trout in the liquid, carefully turning over after first 3 minutes, covering and continuing to poach for a total of about 8 to 10 minutes or until flesh flakes easily when gently probed with tines of a fork. Serve with melted butter and lemon wedges.

Serves 2–4.

COLD TROUT IN JELLY: If you have any cooked trout left over, soften ½ teaspoon of unflavored gelatin in 1 tablespoon water, add to hot poaching liquid, stir until thoroughly dissolved, pour over fish and refrigerate. Serve cold in the jelly.

STEAMING RECIPES

Why it is he can't explain, but this is Dan's most favorite way of cooking both fin fish and shellfish. Perhaps it is because steaming is so easy. Perhaps it is because, more than any other, this is the cooking method that best preserves the delicious natural taste of fish.

Special steamer pots are made for this purpose. Buy one if you like, but it isn't necessary.

All that you need are (1) a pot with a cover (see note regarding acids in improvised metal utensils, page 39), and, if you don't have one, a pretzel can is even better; (2) a wire rack that will fit inside it; and (3) 4 wooden spring-type clothespins. That's right, clothespins. Sounds crazy, doesn't it? But it isn't. Here's how to use them:

STEAMING FIN FISH ON A RACK OVER LIQUID

· Put from 1 to no more than 2 inches of water into the pot or pretzel can, or any liquid that a particular recipe may call for, or any liquid that suits your fancy.

· Place the wire rack in the pot or can. If yours has no legs that will keep it at least ½ inch above the liquid, well—that's what the spring-type clothespins are for. Just clip them to the rack so they'll stand in place like table legs, well above the liquid when it boils and bubbles.

· Turn on the heat and bring the liquid to a boil. When the water is steaming heavily, place the fish, either fresh or frozen, atop the rack. It can be a dressed fish, but it's easier accurately to time pieces of fish such as steaks, fillets or chunks that are of a uniform thickness. They can be from ½ to 2 inches thick, but within that range the thickness should vary as little as possible.

· Now put the utensil cover in place. If you're using a pretzel can (or any other suitable can), poke 4 or 5 steam-vent holes in the cover with an ice pick or knife. If you're using a conventional kitchen utensil, excess steam should be able to lift the lid just enough to escape.

· Keep the liquid at a boil so you'll have plenty of steam, and cook 5 minutes for the first ½ inch of fish thickness and 3 additional minutes for each additional ½ inch. This is one method of fish cookery where we advise you to make the fork test as seldom as possible, and better not at all. Reason: every time you remove the lid, precious steam will escape.

NOTE: If the fish went into the pot or can while still frozen, double the steaming time.

STEAMING SHELLFISH

Steam them just as you would fin fish, by placing them atop a bed of vegetables or on the wire rack. While still in their shells, of course. You'll recall that earlier in this book, in telling you all about shellfish, we pointed out that cooking—in this case steaming—often is part of the cleaning and shucking process. So the steaming of shellfish won't take long, from about 3 minutes for a mussel to about 20 minutes for a clam-bake that's complete with lobster. Yes, you can have a clambake, which really is a steaming, indoors too. You'll find the recipe for a Kitchen Clambake on page 341.

HOW TO TIME

The timing of steamed fish that's no more than 2 inches thick begins when the steam gushes steadily, which should be almost immediately after you put the fish into the pot or can unless you are cooking lobster. For those instructions see the Kitchen Clambake.

STEAMING FISH ON TOP OF COOKING VEGETABLES

Place fish on top of cooking vegetables, well out of reach of any liquid, when the vegetables have only a few more minutes to go, just long enough to cook the fish. Use the same timing instructions as for steaming on a rack.

REHEATING COLD COOKED FISH OR
LIGHTLY SMOKED AND SALTED FISH

Steaming is the best way we know to heat cold cooked fish or lightly smoked or salted fish that needs no cooking. The juices and flavors stay in and the flesh is not dried out. Lay the fish to be heated on a rack over moderately boiling water as described above. The time required will be about one-third of that needed to cook raw fish.

FILLETS OR STEAKS STEAMED
ON TOP OF VEGETABLES
(Dieter's Delight)

1 *pound fillets or steaks, ½ to ¾ inch thick, freshwater or salt, fresh
   or frozen*
1 *large onion, sliced*
1 *small clove garlic, minced (optional)*
2 *large, firm tomatoes, sliced*
1 *green pepper, seeded, washed and cut in circles*
½ *cup fish or chicken broth*
2 *tablespoons wine*
Salt and pepper to taste

Defrost fish if frozen if you like.* Place vegetables in bottom of a large, heavy pot, pour liquids over them, season with salt and pepper to taste,

* Double steaming time if fish is not defrosted.

cover and simmer for 10 to 15 minutes or until vegetables are almost done. If liquid is almost gone, add ¼ cup of broth or water and return to a simmer. Place fish carefully on top of vegetables in a single layer, cover pot and steam gently 5–7 minutes, depending on thickness of fish, or until fish flakes separate easily when gently probed with tines of a fork. Serve fish, pouring vegetables and sauce over the top. Eat with or without bread for a satisfying meal.

Serves 2–4.

STEAMED HALIBUT STEAKS WITH MUSSELS: Add well-scrubbed mussels in the shell at the same time steaks are added to the pot. Cook as in preceding recipe. Arrange opened shellfish over top of serving platter.

NOTE: Any delicately flavored, freshwater or saltwater steak may be substituted for halibut.

ABALONE WITH OYSTER SAUCE*

(Ho Yu Bow Pan)

1 *can (1 pound) abalone*
4 *pounds celery cabbage (tin sien variety available in Chinese groceries)*
1 *can (13¾ ounces) chicken broth*
1 *teaspoon salt*
1 *teaspoon sugar*
½ *teaspoon pepper*
1 *teaspoon monosodium glutamate (optional)*
1½ *tablespoons cornstarch dissolved in 2 tablespoons water*
3 *tablespoons oyster sauce (buy in an Oriental or specialty food store)*
Parsley or watercress for garnish
Utensils: bowl; wok or pot with rack

Lay abalone flat on cutting board and slice lengthwise into thin slices. Arrange in bowl large enough to accommodate them, yet small enough to fit inside wok or pot. Set aside.

Wash celery cabbage thoroughly and cut into quarters. Bring broth to a boil, add ¾ teaspoon salt and simmer until tender, about ½ hour. Strain in colander, reserving the juice. Press celery cabbage tight and flat on abalone slices. The bowl now should be brimful but not overflowing. Place on rack in wok or pot, add small amount of water, cover and steam 15 minutes. Remove bowl, let cool enough to handle, then place warm serving platter atop it and flip to transfer contents from one dish to the other with the abalone on top. Set aside. Add reserved juice to wok or

* From *The Hong Kong Cookbook,* by Arthur Lem and Dan Morris (Funk & Wagnalls).

pot along with the remaining salt, sugar, pepper and monosodium gluta-mate, stir and bring to a boil. Stir in cornstarch mixture to thicken, then add oyster sauce and stir for about 30 seconds, pour over abalone and garnish with parsley or watercress. Serve with rice.

Serves 4.

CATFISH GUMBO   (I)

(This one-pot meal recipe came to us from the U.S. Department of the Interior.)

1 *pound skinned catfish fillets or other fillets, fresh or frozen*
½ *cup chopped celery*
½ *cup chopped green pepper*
½ *cup chopped onion*
1 *clove garlic, finely chopped*
¼ *cup melted fat or oil*
2 *beef bouillon cubes*
2 *cups boiling water*
1 *can (1 pound) tomatoes*
1 *package (10 ounces) frozen okra, sliced*
2 *teaspoons salt*
¼ *teaspoon pepper*
¼ *teaspoon thyme*
1 *whole bay leaf*
Dash liquid hot pepper sauce
1½ *cups hot cooked rice*

Thaw frozen fillets. Cut into 1-inch pieces. (If still-frozen fish is used, double steaming time.) Cook celery, green pepper, onion and garlic in fat until tender. Dissolve bouillon cubes in water. Add bouillon, tomatoes, okra and seasonings. Cover and simmer for 20 minutes. Place fish on vegetables. Cover and simmer for 15 minutes longer or until fish flakes easily when tested with a fork. Remove bay leaf. Place ¼ cup rice in each of 6 soup bowls. Fill with gumbo.

Serves 6.

STEAMED ONE-POT HADDOCK MEAL

1 *pound frozen haddock fillets (1¼ inches thick)*
2–3 *cups cold stewed tomatoes*
2 *cups cold cooked leftover rice, plain or mixed with a sauce*

Place cold stewed tomatoes in bottom of heavy pot and bring to a boil. Lay rectangle of frozen fillets on top of tomatoes, spread the rice over the fish and cover. Turn on medium heat until tomato stew starts to simmer (5–8 minutes), then turn down to low medium and cook for 20 minutes without removing lid. (Before covering, be sure there is enough liquid in pot to last for 20 minutes. If not, add hot water or tomato juice.) Eat when fish flakes separate easily when gently probed with a fork and rice is hot.

Serves 2–4.

STEAMED PARTIALLY DEFROSTED KING CRAB LEGS

1 *pound frozen Alaska king crab legs, defrosted for about 4 hours in refrigerator and still partially frozen*
1½–2 *cups melted butter*
Fish or chicken broth
Lemon wedges

Cut legs into easily manageable serving pieces, 2 or 3 inches long. Slit tops of sections lengthwise, using a very sharp knife. Insert melted butter in the opening and lay sections, slit side up, on a rack over boiling fish or chicken broth. Cover and steam for 5 minutes. Remove small pieces. Check thicker pieces for doneness and steam them 2 or 3 minutes more if necessary. Serve with nutcrackers, cocktail forks, additional melted butter and lemon wedges. Drink from cups the broth over which legs were steamed or quickly chill, refrigerate and use no later than the next day in a soup or sauce. (We sometimes serve king crab legs as an appetizer, then follow with clam chowder as the main course. The steaming broth from the crab legs is stirred into the chowder, adding to the flavor.)

Serves 2–4.

STEAMED FROZEN LOBSTER TAILS

2–4 *6-ounce frozen lobster tails, defrosted for 4 hours in refrigerator or immersed for about 5 minutes in hot (but not boiling) water, just long enough so that you can cut through shell*
4–8 *teaspoons soft butter or margarine*
2–4 *tablespoons melted butter or margarine*
Lemon wedges

Remove under shells by cutting along edges where they join thicker upper shells and discard. Remove meat from upper shells, turn meat over and slit meat lengthwise about ¼ inch deep. Saturate inside of each shell with about 1 teaspoon of soft butter or margarine. Return meat to shell, being sure to turn it upside down from the way it came out of the shell, slit side up. Spread about 1 teaspoon soft butter or margarine over each piece of meat. Place on a rack over boiling water. Cover and steam 8–10 minutes.

Remove and serve in individual dishes with melted butter and lemon wedges.

Serves 2–4.

NOTE: Quickly chill water over which tails were steamed, refrigerate and use in a soup or sauce.

STEAMED SALMON FILLETS OR STEAKS
WITH WINE AND MUSHROOM SAUCE   (O)

(Salmon Geneva)

4 *salmon fillets or steaks with some of the scraps from same fish*
1 *recipe Salmon Sauce with Wine and Mushrooms (Geneva Sauce),*
   page 131

Prepare sauce, using scraps from salmon, and keep warm. Wrap fillets or steaks in cheesecloth and steam over lightly salted water until flakes separate. Place on a serving platter, pour sauce over and serve.

Serves 4.

KITCHEN (TIN CAN) CLAMBAKE   (O)

See page 341.

STEAMED CLAMS   (O)

6 *dozen steamer (soft shell) clams**
6 *squares of cheesecloth*
6 *cups water*
Butter or margarine

Bring water to a boil, wrap a dozen clams in each cheesecloth square, fold to form a pouch, and place atop rack. Cover steamer pot or can and steam until clams open, about 5–8 minutes. Serve at once, a pouchful of clams for each diner, along with a cup of strained broth and side dishes of melted butter or margarine.

Serves 6.

HOW TO EAT: With your fingers. Grasp clam by neck, dip first in broth to remove sand, if any, then in melted butter, place between lips and tug on clam while holding back on neck so that meat will slip from inside neck's black sheath. Or bite through where neck and clam meet, if you think neck meat is too rubbery. Sand will settle to bottom of broth cup, so don't hesitate to drink from it. It's delicious.

---

* Use hard-shell clams if steamers, either fresh or canned, are unavailable.

8

Broiling

Two fish-broiling factors are unquestionable: (1) the high heat often used in the broiling process can dry out fish faster than any other cooking method; (2) broiling gives fish a very special flavor that to many people is worth the sacrifice of natural moistness.

However, there are several ways of reducing dryness to a minimum, if not eliminating the possibility altogether. We like four of those methods, and here they are, the last two being best:

1. Broil only a naturally fat fish.

2. Unless a recipe specifies otherwise, do not use the broiler rack. Remove it and place the fish directly on the bottom of the broiler pan. Then, if cooking a lean fish, baste with oil or an oily marinade. By placing the fish in the pan rather than on the rack, none of the basting liquids will run off and be lost. Brush fish with the liquid while broiling as often as you think necessary.

3. Here now is one of the methods that we prefer above all others; it's the same method that wins fine restaurant chefs praise for the delightful flavor and moist texture of fish that they broil. Their secret? They first poach, simmer, steam or bake the fish (fin or shell), then they drench it with butter and quickly run it under the broiler. Just long enough for a quick browning on top and not a moment longer.

Then there is this fourth way that we like just as well as we do the fine-chef method. Sometimes more. We call it "water-broiling." It's a method that allows fish to be both broiled and steamed at one and the same time and we think so highly of it that we've given it a section all its own. You'll find it beginning on page 240.

Take your choice of one of those four methods, then follow these basic rules and you won't go wrong:

1. Limit your broiling to fish or pieces of fish that are from ⅜ inch

to 1½ inches thick. They can be whole, split, fillets or steaks or shellfish in split shell or on the half shell.

2. Dip fish to be broiled quickly in and out of cold water that has been lightly seasoned with salt or lemon juice, then thoroughly dry on lint-free cloth or absorbent paper towels. Examine shellfish and remove any bits of broken shell.

3. Thoroughly preheat the broiler. (Or follow stove manufacturer's instructions.)

4. Remove broiler pan and rack as soon as they are warm and lightly oil only the part of the surface of the pan (or rack, if it is to be used) on which the fish will lay. Never use a wire rack, because the wires will break up the tender cooked fish. If cooking outdoors, use a lightly oiled hinged grill with wires that are close together (see Outdoor Cooking section beginning on page 343).

5. Broil raw fish from 2 to 5 inches below the source of the heat, depending on the thickness of the fish and on whether or not you are going to turn it over. If you turn it, fish can be broiled closer to the heat than if you don't.

6. It's not necessary to turn steaks and fillets unless they are more than about ¾ inch thick. Less than that, there's a good chance that they'll break if you turn; definitely so if they're less than ½ inch thick. Split fish and fillets with skin still on should generally be broiled skin side down, without turning. Turn whole fish.

7. Fish that's already been cooked by some other method can be most quickly browned no more than 2 inches from the source of heat—but watch it!

8. Fish may be dusted with flour, then basted with fat. But watch that the flour does not burn.

9. When basting, either before or while fish is in the broiler, do so only with a brush in order to cover all parts and to conserve oil or marinade.

10. Set your broiler at from 550 degrees to as high as the "broil" designation on the heat regulator, depending on how brown you want your fish to be. If set on "broil," you must watch carefully or oils may burn or even catch fire. Broilers differ, so use these recommendations and recipe directions as a guide, and adapt distances from heat and the temperature setting according to the performance of your stove.

11. The most important rule of all: **Do not overcook!**

This admonition is probably more important when broiling fish than in any other process. Check often, using your fork to probe gently, and get fish out of the hot broiler to stop the cooking process the instant flakes separate easily.

The time, according to thickness, will vary from about 3 minutes for a ⅜-inch fillet to about 15 minutes for 1½-inch, skin-on split fish.

Broiled Lobster

We give this a section all its own because lobster is the most popular of all broiled fish in the United States, and probably the world. We give it so that you will be warned: broiled lobster, or lobster tail, should never be placed under the broiler until it has been previously cooked by some other method.

If you're in what you thought was a good restaurant and your lobster comes to you with the texture of the rubber heel on your shoe, it's because the chef either didn't know any better or knew but didn't care.

With the cost of lobster being what it is, our suggestion to you is that you buy and cook your own, rather than take a chance on the whims of a strange chef in a strange restaurant.

Lobster always will be nicer if steamed or simmered, then split, drenched in butter and placed under the broiler.

Lobster tails will be better baked in the oven, then drenched in butter and placed under the broiler.

You'll find specifics in specific recipes. However, there are some cooks who swear by the right-under-the-broiler method. Who knows? You may be one of them, and so we give you, in their proper places, the two best such recipes that we're aware of.

FAT FISH IN SPICY SAUCE (O)

1–1½ pounds fat fish fillets or steaks, freshwater or salt, fresh or frozen
1 recipe of your choice from Spicy, Wine and Vinegar Sauces, page 144
Lemon wedges

Defrost fish if frozen. Cover all surfaces of fish with spicy sauce, place in a glass or nonporous ceramic dish with any excess sauce and marinate in refrigerator at least 30 minutes. Turn fish pieces at least once. Place in preheated, lightly greased broiler pan. Broil in preheated broiler, about 3 inches from source of heat, 3–8 minutes or until flakes separate easily when gently probed with tines of a fork. While broiling, brush with any sauce left in dish. It is not necessary to turn unless fillets or steaks are very thick. If a browner surface is desired, brush lightly with butter or margarine, but don't overdo it. Serve with lemon wedges.

Serves 4–6.

FAT SPLIT FISH IN SPICY SAUCE: Prepare and broil 4 pounds of fat split fish as in cooking fillets and steaks. Place skin side down, brush top only with sauce and don't turn. Leave bone in for moist fish.

FAT WHOLE FISH IN SPICY SAUCE: Fish of fairly uniform thickness will be most satisfactory. Leave head and tail on for moist fish. Prepare 4 pounds and broil same as fillets and steaks, but turn once.

LEAN FILLETS, STEAKS, SPLIT OR WHOLE FISH IN SPICY SAUCE: Prepare and broil the same as for fat fish in preceding recipes, but in addition to the spicy sauce, also baste with melted butter or margarine.

BROILED FILLETS OR STEAKS WITH
CUCUMBER-DILL BUTTER   (O)

> 1–1½ *pounds lean fillets or steaks, freshwater or salt, fresh or frozen*
> 1 *recipe heated Cucumber-Dill Butter, page 138*

Defrost fish if frozen. Place in bottom of lightly greased, warm broiler pan, about 3 inches from source of heat, and broil 3–8 minutes or until flakes separate easily when gently probed with tines of fork, brushing several times with some of the melted Cucumber-Dill Butter. Serve on preheated platter and pour remaining hot Cucumber-Dill Butter over them. Serves 4–6.

LEAN FISH IN EASY BUTTER OR
MARGARINE SAUCE   (O)

> 1–1½ *pounds lean fish fillet or steak, freshwater or salt, fresh or frozen*
> 1 *recipe of your choice from the Easy Butter or Margarine Sauces, page 136*

Defrost fish if frozen. Arrange in bottom of warm broiler pan, brush with sauce and broil about 3 inches below source of heat, brushing frequently with remaining sauce, until flakes separate easily when gently probed with tines of a fork. It is not necessary to turn unless steaks or fillets are very thick.

VARIATION: Dust fish lightly with flour, brush top and bottom with butter sauce and broil.

LEAN SPLIT FISH IN EASY BUTTER OR MARGARINE SAUCE: Prepare and broil 4 pounds of lean split fish as in foregoing. Leave bone in for moist fish. Place skin side down, brush top only with sauce and place from 3 to 5 inches from source of heat, depending on thickness, and cook 5–15 minutes.

LEAN WHOLE FISH IN EASY BUTTER OR MARGARINE SAUCE: Flat fish of fairly uniform thickness will be most satisfactory. Leave head and tail on for moist fish. Prepare 4 pounds of whole fish and broil same as split fish, but turn once. If you like, dust fish with flour before basting.

BAKED 'N' BROILED COD FILLETS

1 12-*ounce package frozen cod fillets, defrosted, but kept in solid block*
½ *egg, lightly beaten*
½ *cup toasted breadcrumbs*
Butter or margarine for dotting
Lemon wedges
Salt and pepper to taste

Dip block of fillets into beaten egg, then coat with breadcrumbs, taking care to keep fish in the solid rectangular shape in which it came from the package. Place in a shallow baking dish in which it can be both cooked and served. Dot with butter or margarine and bake in oven preheated to 375 degrees 10–15 minutes or until flakes almost separate when probed with a fork. Remove from oven and place in broiler about 2½ to 3 inches from source of heat and broil for 2 to 3 minutes or just until top of fish is lightly browned. Serve at once with lemon wedges. Add salt and pepper to suit the individual taste.
    Serves 2–3.

POACHED 'N' BROILED STEAKS WITH
AVOCADO (GUACAMOLE) TOPPING   (I)

4 *center-cut fish steaks from any fish, freshwater or salt, poached until almost, but not quite, done*
1 *small onion, finely minced*
1 *clove garlic, finely minced*
Salt and pepper to taste
1 *large ripe avocado, peeled and seed removed*
1 *firm tomato, peeled and chopped in very small pieces and drained*
¼ *cup mayonnaise*
1 *teaspoon lemon juice*
1 *teaspoon chili powder or to taste*

Arrange poached steaks on a heatproof serving platter and cover to keep warm. Mash all remaining ingredients together and spread over fish. Run under broiler, about 2 inches from source of heat, just long enough to heat avocado spread and finish cooking fish, and serve at once.
    Serves 4.
    FISH AND GUACAMOLE ENCHILADAS: Mash leftover fish meat and guacamole topping from preceding recipe. Spread on tortillas (which can be purchased in cans). Serve like an open sandwich or follow directions on can for rolling the tortillas.

FISH STEAKS WITH MIXED VEGETABLE TOPPING: Substitute Mixed Vegetable Sauce, pureed, page 149, for guacamole topping in Poached 'n' Broiled Steaks with Avocado (Guacamole) Topping. Grated cheese may be sprinkled over top before running under broiler. This is an exceptionally good recipe for calorie counters.

POACHED 'N' BROILED STEAKS WITH TOMATO SAUCE AND LEMON SLICES

  4 *lean fish steaks, freshwater or salt, fresh or frozen*
  1–2 *tablespoons butter or margarine*
  ⅓ *cup tomato paste*
  12 *lemon slices, thinly sliced*

Defrost fish if frozen. Poach in slowly simmering water for 2 minutes or until not quite done. Place on a heat-resistant platter, brush with butter or margarine, spread with tomato paste and place a row of 3 lemon slices over top of each steak. Broil in oven preheated to "broil" 2 or 3 inches from source of heat for 3 minutes or until tomato-paste topping is heated through and fish flakes easily when gently probed with tines of a fork.
   Serves 4.
   NOTE: You can prepare this recipe and broil without first poaching.

PUFFY BAKED 'N' BROILED FISH FILLETS   (I)

  1–1½ *pounds any skinless fish fillet, freshwater or salt, fresh or*
       frozen, about ½–¾ inch thick
  2 *tablespoons corn oil or other cooking oil*
  ½ *teaspoon garlic powder*
  Salt and pepper to taste
  1 *teaspoon lemon juice*
  2 *or 3 drops Louisiana Hot Sauce (Tabasco), or to taste*
  ½ *cup mayonnaise*
  1 *tablespoon finely minced parsley*
  1 *egg white, beaten until stiff but not dry*

Defrost fish if frozen. Combine corn oil, garlic powder, salt and pepper, lemon juice and Louisiana Hot Sauce, mix well and brush over both sides of fillets. Place in heatproof platter and bake 5–8 minutes in oven pre-heated to 350 degrees. Combine remaining ingredients, mix lightly and spread over tops of fillets. Broil 3–5 minutes about 3 inches from source of heat, or until sauce has puffed and is golden brown and fish flakes separate easily when gently probed with tines of a fork.
   Serves 4–6.

CLAMS IN TOMATO SAUCE ON THE HALF SHELL   (I)

12 *large clams or 18–24 smaller size, steamed open and removed*
   from shells, liquid and shells reserved
4 *tablespoons olive oil*
1 *large garlic clove, finely chopped*
1 *onion, finely minced*
1 *9-ounce can tomato paste*
1½ *cups liquid from steamed clams, strained through several layers*
   of cheesecloth (add water if necessary)
¼ *teaspoon oregano or to taste*
¼ *teaspoon crushed red pepper (optional)*
Salt to taste
½ *cup toasted breadcrumbs*
2 *tablespoons butter or margarine*

Heat olive oil in large, heavy skillet or saucepan, add garlic and onion, and cook until they are soft. Stir in tomato paste and blend well with oil. Add clam liquid, oregano, red pepper and salt to taste and bring to a boil. Reduce heat to a low simmer and cook, stirring frequently, for 15 minutes or until no longer runny. Chop clams and stir in. Divide into reserved shells, sprinkle with breadcrumbs, dot with butter and broil 4–5 inches below source of heat for 5 minutes or until nicely browned.

Serves 2–4 as main course of a meal or makes 16–24 appetizers.

OYSTERS IN TOMATO SAUCE ON THE HALF SHELL: Prepare oysters in the same way as clams.

KING CRAB ALASKA   (I)

1 *5- or 6-ounce can Alaska king crab meat, drained*
2 *tablespoons lemon juice*
2 *drops Tabasco or Louisiana Hot Sauce*
1 *cup mayonnaise*
2 *egg whites, beaten until stiff but not dry*
6 *slices white bread, toasted*
2 *medium firm tomatoes, sliced*

Chop crab meat into small pieces. Stir lemon juice and Tabasco Sauce into mayonnaise, mix well and fold into beaten egg. Arrange pieces of toast on heatproof serving platter or cookie sheet. Divide first the tomato slices, then the chopped crab over them. Spoon mayonnaise mixture over each one and broil, 4 to 5 inches from source of heat, 3–6 minutes or until lightly browned. Watch carefully to be sure topping doesn't burn.

Serves 6.

FLAKED FISH ALASKA: Substitute any flaked cooked fish or canned fish for king crab in preceding recipe.

FLOUNDER FILLETS IN CLAM SAUCE   (O)

*1½ pounds flounder or other white-fleshed fresh or saltwater fish
   fillets, fresh or frozen, at least ½ inch thick and skinless*
1 8-ounce can minced clams
3 tablespoons butter or margarine
¼ teaspoon onion powder
White pepper to taste

Defrost fillets if frozen. Drain clams, reserving liquid. Melt butter or margarine and stir in onion powder, white pepper and reserved clam liquid. Reheat, then spread half of mixture over both sides of fillets. Arrange on lightly greased preheated broiler pan about 3 inches from source of heat. Broil 5–8 minutes or until fish flakes easily when gently tested with tines of fork. While fish broils, add minced clams to second half of sauce, heat and simmer for about 1 minute or just long enough to heat clams through. Divide over fillets and serve.
   Serves 4–6.

JUICY BROILED SPLIT LOBSTER   (I)

(Lobster au Jus)

4 1- to 1¼-pound lobsters, steamed or simmered (pages 66–67)
1 cup melted butter or margarine
Salt and pepper to taste
Lemon wedges

Split and clean lobster as described on page 63. Lay in broiler pan, brush generously with melted butter and run under preheated broiler, about 2 inches from source of heat, and broil just until butter starts to brown and edges of shell start to char. Brush with additional butter or margarine once or twice while browning. Salt and pepper to taste and serve with lemon wedges and remaining melted butter (reheat if necessary so it's piping hot) in individual small bowls.
   Serves 4.

PRISCILLA STRUNG'S BROILED LOBSTER   (I)

6 1-pound live lobsters
2¼ cups melted butter or margarine
2 cups (or more) commercially seasoned toasted breadcrumbs
Lemon wedges

Kill, split and clean lobster (see page 63). Remove tomalley, mash and combine with ¾ cup melted butter or margarine and enough commercially packaged seasoned breadcrumbs to make a firm mixture. Mix well and stuff into body cavities. Place lobsters in bottom of broiler pan 4 to 5 inches from source of heat, brush with melted butter and broil 8–12 minutes or until just done. If tops seem to be browning too rapidly, reduce heat or lower broiler pan. Serve with small bowls of melted butter or margarine and lemon wedges.

Serves 6.

NOTE: 1¼-pound lobsters would be done in from 12 to 15 minutes.

LOBSTER TAIL FIORE

4 *6-ounce frozen lobster tails, preferably Brazilian, almost completely defrosted*
8 *teaspoons soft butter or margarine*
4 *tablespoons melted butter or margarine*
Lemon wedges

Remove under shells by cutting along edges where they join thicker upper shells and discard. Remove meat from upper shells, turn over and slit meat lengthwise about ¼ inch deep. Saturate inside of each shell with about 1 teaspoon of soft butter or margarine. Return meat to shell, being sure to turn it upside down from the way it came out of the shell, slit side up. Spread about 1 teaspoon soft butter or margarine over each piece of meat. Place in broiler about 4 inches from source of heat and broil until surface is light brown and meat is opaque. Brush 2 or 3 times with melted butter or margarine. Serve with additional melted butter or margarine and lemon wedges.

Serves 4.

. VARIATION: Add water or other liquid to bottom of broiler pan to add moisture.

LOBSTER TAIL KREIDELL   (I)
Baked, Then Broiled

4 *5-ounce frozen South African lobster tails**
Melted butter
Lemon juice
Lemon wedges

Place tails in hot, not boiling, water for about 5 minutes or just until thawed enough to slit with a knife completely through upper shell and

* South African lobster-tail shells are easier to cut through than are those from other areas.

almost but not quite through meat. Insert fingers under flesh and raise it up but don't loosen at tail end. Spread slit flesh over the two sides of the shell like a butterfly. Place in shallow baking pan, cover generously with melted butter and lemon juice and bake in oven preheated to 400 degrees 8–12 minutes, just until flesh puffs up. Remove at once, brush with more butter and lemon juice, and run under broiler just long enough to brown. Serve with additional melted butter and lemon wedges.

Serves 2–4.

SPLIT MACKEREL WITH BUTTER, MUSTARD AND PARSLEY (O)

4 *whole dressed and split mackerel, ½ to ¾ pound each*
1 *teaspoon butter or margarine*
Salt and pepper to taste
Garlic powder to taste
2 *tablespoons melted butter or margarine*
2 *tablespoons prepared mustard*
Juice of 2 lemons
1 *tablespoon finely chopped fresh parsley*

Rub butter or margarine over fish, inside and out, and sprinkle with salt, pepper and garlic powder to taste. Place mackerel, skin side down, in bottom of lightly greased, warm broiler pan. Broil about 3 inches from source of heat at 550 degrees for 4 minutes. Combine 2 tablespoons melted butter or margarine with prepared mustard, spread over cavities of fish and broil about 4 minutes or until flakes separate easily when gently probed with tines of a fork. Pour lemon juice over the fish, sprinkle with chopped parsley and serve.

Serves 2–4.

NOTE: If cooked outdoors, turn split mackerel over after 2 minutes of cooking skin side down.

MULLET WITH LIME (O)

(Lemon is a tradition with fish and a good one. But sometimes tradition deprives us of new and interesting taste treats, such as using lime juice in the same way as we do lemon. Try it. In the Florida Keys, they grow a small, round acid variety known as the Key lime, which they like especially well with fish and which they use in this recipe with mullet, which is also a Florida native.)

1 *pound skinless mullet fillets or other intermediate (or fat) fish, freshwater or salt, fresh or frozen*
3 *tablespoons lime juice*

1 *tablespoon melted butter or margarine*
Salt and pepper to taste
Lime wedges

Defrost fish if frozen. Rub lime juice over all surfaces of fish and marinate for 30 minutes. Place on well-greased broiler pan and broil about 3 inches from source of heat at 550 degrees in preheated broiler pan 3–8 minutes or until flakes separate easily when gently probed with tines of fork. Brush once or twice with melted butter or margarine while cooking. Place on preheated serving platter, salt and pepper to taste, garnish with lime wedges and serve.

Serves 2–4.

NOTE: Marinate fish in glass or nonporous ceramic dish.

OYSTERS BROILED ON THE HALF SHELL

36 *raw oysters*
Salt and pepper to taste
Worcestershire sauce to taste
Louisiana Hot Sauce (Tabasco) to taste
Lemon juice to taste
¾ *cup lightly toasted breadcrumbs*
½ *to* ¾ *cup butter or margarine*
Paprika to taste
Lemon wedges

Wash oysters and remove from shells (see pages 50–51). Thoroughly wash deeper half of shell and return oyster to it. Give remaining half shell to children to do with as they will. Place oysters on the half shell on rack of a preheated broiler pan; season with salt and pepper, Worcestershire sauce, Louisiana Hot Sauce and lemon juice to taste. Sprinkle lightly toasted breadcrumbs over the oysters and dot with butter or margarine. Sprinkle with paprika to taste for color and flavor and broil about 3 inches from source of heat in preheated broiler at 550 degrees for about 5 minutes or until golden brown. Serve at once in the shell.

Serves 6.

CLAMS BROILED ON THE HALF SHELL: Prepare and serve in the same way as oysters.

MUSSELS BROILED ON THE HALF SHELL: Ditto.

BROILED OYSTERS IN A BACON BLANKET

(Devils on Horseback)

24 *oysters, shucked and drained*
12 *slices bacon, cut in half*
Lemon wedges

Wrap each half-slice of bacon around an oyster, fasten if necessary with wooden picks and place on a perforated rack in broiler pan. Broil about 3 inches from source of heat for 3 minutes to a side or until bacon is crisp and edges of oyster curl. Serve with lemon wedges.

Serves 4.

NOTE: Served (2 or 3 bacon-wrapped oysters to a person) with an omelet made with some of the oyster liquid and a slice of fruit, this makes a very special breakfast dish.

BROILED CLAMS IN A BACON BLANKET: Substitute clams for oysters in preceding recipe.

BROILED OYSTERS WRAPPED IN HAM

(Angels on Horseback)

24 *oysters, shucked and drained, liquid strained and reserved*
8 *large slices of boiled ham, each cut into 3 strips*
½ *cup white wine*
½ *cup reserved oyster liquid (add water if necessary)*
¼ *teaspoon powdered garlic*
2 *or 3 drops Louisiana Hot Sauce*
3 *tablespoons butter or margarine*
2 *tablespoons flour*
½ *cup cream or canned milk*
Salt and pepper to taste

Combine wine, oyster liquid, garlic powder and Louisiana Hot Sauce in glass or nonporous ceramic dish. Add oysters, coat each well with mixture and marinate in refrigerator for at least 30 minutes. Take from marinade, wrap each oyster in strip of ham, fasten with wooden picks if necessary and arrange in bottom of broiler pan. Place pan about 3 inches from source of heat and broil, turning once, about 7 minutes or until cooked. While oysters cook, melt butter or margarine in heavy skillet or pot, add flour and cook over medium heat, stirring constantly, for 2 or 3 minutes. Add marinade liquid and bring to a boil. Reduce heat to simmer and cook 4–6 minutes or until sauce is thick and smooth, stirring as necessary. Remove from heat, stir in cream or canned milk and salt and pepper and reheat without boiling. Serve ham-wrapped oysters on toast with sauce divided over top.

Serves 4–6.

NOTE: Serve 2 or 3 ham-wrapped oysters per person with omelet instead of toast. Pour sauce over the omelet. This makes a very nice company breakfast dish. Or for any meal of the day.

POACHED 'N' BROILED SPLIT RED SNAPPER

> 1 4-*pound dressed red snapper or other lean fish, freshwater or salt,*
> *head and tail off (save them for making a supply of frozen broth,*
> *see page 118)*
> ¼ *cup melted butter or margarine*
> 1 *teaspoon prepared mustard or to taste*
> *Juice of ½ to 1 lemon*
> 1 *tablespoon crushed freeze-dried shallots (optional)*
> 1 *teaspoon tomato paste (optional)*

Combine melted butter or margarine, prepared mustard, lemon juice, crushed shallots and tomato paste; mix well and set aside. Wrap dressed fish in single layer of cheesecloth and poach for about 6 minutes in lightly salted, barely simmering water to cover. Remove to preheated heatproof serving platter, remove backbone and split so that fish lies flat, skin down, on the platter. Spread butter mixture over it and place in preheated broiler about 2 inches from source of heat. Broil just until fish is lightly browned on top and flakes easily when tested with a fork. If fish seems to be drying out, brush additional butter or margarine over the top.
Serves 4.

BROILED SCALLOPS IN WINE SAUCE
ON HALF SHELL (I)

(Coquilles St. Jacques)

> 1 *pound scallops*
> 4 *tablespoons butter or margarine*
> ½ *cup sliced mushrooms*
> 3 *tablespoons flour*
> 1 *cup dry white wine*
> ⅔ *cup water*
> 2 *sprigs parsley*
> 3 *peppercorns*
> 1 *pinch thyme*
> 1 *bay leaf*
> ½ *mild onion, chopped*
> *Salt to taste*
> 1 *egg yolk*
> ½ *cup heavy cream*
> 1 *teaspoon lemon juice*
> *Cayenne pepper to taste*
> ½ *cup breadcrumbs*
> ¼ *cup grated Parmesan cheese*
> *Butter or margarine for dotting*

Heat 1 tablespoon butter or margarine in large, heavy skillet and lightly sauté sliced mushrooms. Remove mushrooms and set aside. Add 3 tablespoons butter or margarine and 3 tablespoons flour and cook together over medium heat for 2 or 3 minutes, stirring constantly.

Combine wine, water, parsley, peppercorns, thyme, bay leaf, onion and salt in a saucepan and bring to a boil. Boil for 10 minutes, strain, return liquid to stove, add scallops, cover and simmer for 3 minutes. Remove scallops, cut them in small pieces and set aside. Reduce liquid to 1 cup, add to butter-flour mixture in skillet and stir constantly with a wire whisk until mixture thickens and becomes smooth. Stir egg yolk into cream, add a little of the hot sauce, stir into yolk mixture, then stir back into sauce and turn off heat. Stir in lemon juice, cayenne pepper to taste, sautéed mushrooms and scallops. Divide into lightly greased scallop shells or individual serving casserole dishes. Combine breadcrumbs and grated Parmesan cheese and sprinkle over the tops and dot with butter or margarine. Place on broiler rack, about 4 inches below source of heat, and broil 2–4 minutes or until top is nicely browned.

Serves 6.

NOTE: If sauce becomes too thick to handle, add 2 to 4 tablespoons of milk.

VARIATION: Sprinkle tops of filled shells with grated Swiss cheese instead of combination of crumbs and Parmesan cheese.

BAKED SCALLOPS IN WINE SAUCE: Prepare as above but put in shallow casserole and bake in oven until top is nicely browned (about 10 minutes at 400 degrees).

BROILED CRAB MEAT IN WINE SAUCE ON HALF SHELL: Substitute crab for scallop meat in preceding recipe.

SHRIMP BROILED IN OLIVE OIL WITH
LEMON JUICE AND GARLIC   (O)

(Scampi)

1 *pound raw shrimp, peeled, deveined, with tails intact, see page 76*
2 *tablespoons lemon juice*
¼ *cup olive oil (substitute 2 tablespoons olive oil and 2 tablespoons vegetable cooking oil)*
1 *clove garlic, finely minced*
½ *teaspoon salt or to taste*
⅛ *teaspoon pepper or to taste*
2 *tablespoons finely chopped fresh parsley*

Combine lemon juice, olive oil, minced garlic, salt and pepper in a bowl, and stir until thoroughly mixed. Add shrimp and stir gently until all are completely coated. Arrange shrimp in a single layer in bottom of preheated broiler pan. Pour over them any oil mixture remaining in bowl and place in preheated broiler about 4 inches from source of heat. Broil, turning once, at 550 degrees, 5–8 minutes or until shrimp are done. Transfer shrimp and oil from pan into a preheated serving bowl, stir in parsley and serve.

Serves 2–4.

SHRIMP PIZZA MUFFINS (I)

1 4½-ounce can tiny Pacific shrimp, drained
4 English muffins
8 slices cheddar cheese
8 rolled anchovy fillets
½ cup tomato paste in a decorator gun
2 slices bacon, crisp-fried, then crumbled

Break muffins in half with a fork and spread each half with 1 slice of cheese. Arrange on broiler pan rack and broil about 3 inches below source of heat for about 5 minutes or until cheese melts and starts to bubble. Don't let it brown. Remove broiler pan. Place 1 anchovy fillet in center of each cheese-topped muffin half. Then use the decorator gun to make from 5 to 8 red spokes running from anchovy out to the edge of the muffin. Press tiny shrimp into melted cheese between the red spokes and return pan to broiler and cook just long enough to heat shrimp through. Sprinkle crumbled bacon in a border around outer edge of muffin pizzas and serve.

Serves 4–8.

LEFTOVER PANCAKE PIZZAS: When you have more pancake batter than you need for breakfast, cook 1 or 2 extra large cakes and turn them into a fish pizza for lunch. Make in the same way as the preceding recipe or try something different. For example: start with a coating of melted cheese and a cooked fish: canned tuna, flaked cooked fin fish, minced canned clams. Maybe add canned or fresh fried mushrooms, some strips of green pepper. Let your imagination and available ingredients be your guide.

BROILED SHAD FILLETS WITH BUTTER, LEMON JUICE AND PARSLEY (O)

1–1½ pounds shad (or other fat fish of your choice) fillets, skin on,
    freshwater or salt
1 tablespoon lemon juice
Salt and pepper to taste
4 tablespoons melted butter or margarine

1 *tablespoon finely chopped fresh parsley*
1 *medium onion, finely chopped*

Place fillets in preheated broiler pan, skin side down. Stir lemon juice, salt and pepper to taste into melted butter or margarine and brush very lightly over fillets. Broil for 2 minutes, sprinkle with chopped parsley and onion, and continue cooking just until fish flakes easily when gently probed with tines of a fork. Reheat remaining butter or margarine mixture, spoon over fillets and serve.

Serves 4–6.

NOTE: If broiling over coals in hinged grill, brush skin side with oily sauce and turn that side down just until lightly browned; turn and finish cooking with skin side up.

SHAD ROE* BROILED IN BACON   (I)

½ *pound shad roe, ½ to ¾ inch thick*
1 *tablespoon vinegar*
2–4 *slices of bacon*

Bring 2 or 3 cups of water to boil in a pot and add vinegar. Drop in shad roe and poach for 6 minutes. Wrap in bacon slices, lay on rack of preheated broiler 3 inches from source of heat, and broil until bacon is brown and crisp on one side. Carefully turn and repeat on second side. Slice into center of roe to be sure it is cooked through and serve.

Serves 2.

WATER-BROILING

This marvelous way of cooking fish combines all the good qualities of broiling and steaming and, in the wedding, improves on both. The top surface of a fillet or steak can have all the crunchy goodness that makes broiled fish so popular, yet underneath this topping is moist, tender fish that nothing produces so nicely as hot steam. And it's all so unbelievably simple. Here's how:

1. Cut fillets ⅜ to ¾ inch thick for best results; steaks no more than 1 inch. Wash by dipping into cold, lightly salted water and dry on lintfree cloth or absorbent paper towel.

2. Preheat broiler.

3. Remove rack from broiler pan. Bring to a boil liquid to be used to produce steam and pour into the pan. The liquid can be anything you wish—plain water, milk, broths of any kind, fruit or vegetable juices, beer, water seasoned with spices, herbs, wines, anything that will permeate the fish in the form of steam.

* Or roe of any fish.

3A. The liquid must stay boiling hot while in broiler so that steam will be steady. The liquid must be at least ¼ inch deep, deeper if possible but not deep enough to touch the rack when it is returned to the pan. You can even put hot cooked vegetables in the bottom of the broiler pan, just so long as they contain enough liquid to produce steam that will cook the fish. See Recipe for Water-Broiled Cod Fillets with Spinach and Shrimp, page 242.

4. Arrange fish over rack and add any of the toppings described in the recipes in this section.

5. Return rack to broiler pan, which should be placed 3 or 4 inches below source of heat, and turn control to 550 degrees.

6. Cook 3–7 minutes, depending on the thickness of the fish and the performance of your broiler, checking often with a fork to be sure fish does not cook beyond time it takes for flakes to separate easily.

7. If topping on fillets or steaks browns before fish is cooked, lower pan, or, if a good supply of steam is still rising from liquid, turn off broiler and let fish finish cooking in heat from steam.

The Rack You Should Use When Water-Broiling: your broiler may have the type of perforated rack from which it's easy to remove tender, cooked fish. If it doesn't, we suggest you find something to use in its place. Wire racks break up the tender fish.

The best and easiest to use is a "rack" that consists of a smooth, flat piece of metal full of holes, the more holes the better. You may have an oven roasting pan with a removable perforated rack that's just right.

There are broiling pans on the market containing the sort of removable rack we describe. Before shopping for one, measure your broiler pan to be sure you get a size that will fit in it. And get one that will sit high enough so your fish doesn't touch the ¼ inch or so of liquid you will have in the pan when water-broiling.

If you're going to buy a new broiler pan anyway, you might as well try to find one that you can serve as well as cook in. There's no better way to serve your fish while it's still piping hot.

COD CANDY*   (I)

1 pound cod** fillets, about ½ inch thick, fresh or frozen
Water or other liquid
Breadcrumbs to cover
Butter or margarine for dotting (freeze a stick the day before and
    grate it over the fish for easy, even dotting)
Lemon wedges

---

* This is the basic recipe for water-broiling. All variants stem from it. It's so delicious that we serve it often to guests. With a tossed salad it's a perfect lunch, not only mighty tasty, but quick and easy, too.

** Substitute any fresh or saltwater fish that is available if cod is not.

Thaw fish if frozen. Remove broiler rack, pour water or other liquid into broiler pan and heat it to boiling point. Spread fillets over rack, cover with crumbs, dot with butter and set rack in broiler pan, making sure fish does not touch water. Return broiler pan to slot in stove that will place it about 4 inches below source of heat and broil at 550 degrees. It should be done in about 5 minutes, but check in 3. If crumbs are browning too rapidly, turn the heat down. When fish flakes easily when tested with a fork, it is ready to eat. Serve at once with lemon wedges.

Serves 3–4.

WATER-BROILED COD FILLETS WITH SPINACH AND SHRIMP (Fillets Florentine): Instead of water, place steaming-hot chopped cooked spinach in bottom of preheated cook-and-serve broiler pan and top with tiny canned shrimp that also are steaming hot. Cover with rack of fillets and proceed as above. (If spinach layer is thick enough, fish may go directly on it.) If you want, heat a can of shrimp or mushroom soup, dilute if necessary, pour over fillets, sprinkle a bit of grated cheese over the top and serve.

COCONUT COAT   (I)

> 1–1½ *pounds mild-flavored fillets, about ⅜ inch thick, fresh or*
> *frozen, freshwater or salt*
> 4–6 *tablespoons toasted breadcrumbs*
> 4–6 *tablespoons flaked coconut*

Defrost fish if frozen. Remove rack from broiler pan. Pour boiling water in pan but not deep enough to touch rack when it is replaced. Place pan in broiler and turn on heat. Arrange fillets on rack. Combine breadcrumbs and coconut, and spread over the fillets. Replace broiler rack in pan, over the steaming water. Broil 3 or 4 inches from source of heat at 550 degrees 4–7 minutes or until topping is nicely browned and fish flakes easily when tested with a fork. If topping browns before fish is quite done, turn off broiler and let steam from the hot water finish the cooking job.

Serves 4–6.

FILLETS WITH LEFTOVER WHITE
(BÉCHAMEL) SAUCE

> ½–1 *pound mild-flavored fillets, about ⅜ inch thick, fresh or frozen,*
> *freshwater or salt*
> ½–¾ *cup leftover white sauce* in any of its variations, pages 123*
> *to 132*

---

* If leftover white sauce has had no seasonings added to it, stir in 2 tablespoons grated cheese.

Defrost fish if frozen. Remove rack from broiler pan. Pour boiling water in pan but not deep enough to touch rack when it is replaced and turn on heat. Arrange fillets on top of rack. Spread leftover sauce over tops of fillets. Replace broiler rack in pan, over the steaming water. Broil 3 or 4 inches from source of heat at 550 degrees 4–7 minutes or until topping is nicely browned and fish flakes separate easily when gently probed with tines of a fork. If topping browns before fish is quite done, turn off broiler and let steam from the hot water finish the cooking job.

Serves 2–4.

VARIATION: Sprinkle with toasted breadcrumbs and dot with butter or margarine.

FILLETS WITH MUSHROOM-TOMATO TOPPING   (I)

1 *pound skinless fillets ⅜ to ½ inch thick, fresh or frozen, fresh-*
   water or salt
1 *tablespoon cooking oil*
1 *cup chopped onion*
1 *cup sliced fresh mushrooms*
1 *cup chopped fresh tomatoes*
Salt and pepper to taste
1–1½-inch square of cheese

Defrost fillets if frozen. Heat oil in heavy skillet, add onion and mushrooms, and sauté on medium heat 2–3 minutes, stirring frequently. Add tomatoes, salt and pepper to taste and continue cooking 3–5 minutes or until vegetables are almost soft. Pour boiling water into bottom of broiler pan and turn broiler on. Place fillets close together on rack. Cover with vegetable mixture and grate cheese coarsely over top. Place rack in broiler pan and broil at 550 degrees 3 or 4 inches below source of heat 4–7 minutes or until cheese is melted and fish flakes easily when gently probed with fork. If cheese melts before fish is done, turn heat off and let the hot steam finish the cooking job.

Serves 2–4.

FILLETS WITH MIXED VEGETABLE TOPPING: Substitute any combination of cooked or partially cooked vegetables you like for those used in preceding recipe.

FISH 'N' CHEESE   (I)

1–1½ pounds mild-flavored fillets, about ⅜ inch thick, fresh or
   frozen, freshwater or salt
⅓–½ pound cheese, sliced

Defrost fish if frozen. Remove rack from broiler pan. Pour boiling water in pan but not deep enough to touch rack when it is replaced. Arrange fillets on top of rack and spread sliced cheese over them. Replace rack in pan, over the steaming water. Broil 3 or 4 inches from source of heat at 550 degrees 4–7 minutes or until fish flakes easily when tested with tines. If cheese melts before fish is quite done, turn off broiler and let steam from the hot water finish the cooking job.

Serves 4–6.

NOTE: Use any cheese of your choice in this recipe. Muenster is exceptionally good.

Try hot Fish 'n' Cheese sandwiches as a change for lunch, or even for the breakfaster who rebels against eggs.

FISH 'N' GRATED CHEESE FOR CALORIE COUNTERS: Try grating just the amount of cheese your low-calorie diet allows over a fish fillet and water-broiling it. A small amount of cheese will add a great deal of flavor. For additional flavor and color you can add a bit of chopped cooked spinach, raw parsley or basil or whatever low-calorie food suits your fancy.

PEANUT BUTTER BROIL   (I)

> 1–1½ *pounds mild-flavored fillets, about ¼ inch thick, fresh or*
> *frozen, freshwater or salt*
> 3–4 *tablespoons peanut butter*

Thaw fish if frozen. Remove rack from broiler pan. Pour boiling water in pan but not deep enough to touch rack when it is replaced and turn on heat. Arrange fillets over top of rack and spread them with a thin coating of peanut butter. Replace broiler rack in pan, over the steaming water. Broil 3 or 4 inches from source of heat at 550 degrees 4–7 minutes or until fish flakes easily when gently probed with tines.

Serves 4–6.

HOT PEANUT BUTTER AND FISH SANDWICHES: Instead of just a peanut butter sandwich, try giving your children hot peanut butter and fish sandwiches for an extra nourishing and satisfying lunch.

WATER-BROILED STEAKS OR FILLETS   (I)
With Brown-Sugar Sauce and Pineapple

> 1–1½ *pounds delicately flavored white-meat fillets or steaks, fresh-*
> *water or salt, fresh or frozen*
> ½ *cup dark brown sugar*
> 3 *tablespoons lemon juice*
> 3 *tablespoons pineapple juice*
> 1 *teaspoon prepared mustard*

Salt to taste
2 *tablespoons butter or margarine*
4–6 *slices of pineapple*

Defrost fish if frozen. Combine next 6 ingredients in a small saucepan. Bring to a boil, turn down to a simmer and cook, stirring constantly, for about 1 minute, just until ingredients blend well.

Preheat broiler. Remove rack from broiler pan and arrange steaks or fillets with pineapple slices around them in a single layer. Spread brown-sugar sauce over both the fish and the pineapple. Pour boiling water into bottom of broiler pan, replace fish-covered rack and broil at 550 degrees 3 inches from source of heat 4–7 minutes or until fish flakes easily when tested with fork. Baste once with brown-sugar sauce while fish is cooking. Watch carefully that sauce doesn't burn. If it browns before fish is done, turn off heat and let fish finish cooking in steam from water in broiler pan. On the other hand, if fish is almost done before glaze browns, turn heat up to "broil."

Serves 4–6.

SALMON STEAKS IN CITRUS SAUCE

1–1½ *pounds salmon (or other fat fish) steaks, freshwater or salt, fresh or frozen, about ¾–1 inch thick*
2 *tablespoons orange juice*
2 *tablespoons lemon juice*
1 *teaspoon chili sauce*
⅛ *teaspoon onion powder*
1 *pinch garlic powder*
½ *teaspoon grated orange rind*
½ *teaspoon honey*
2 *tablespoons melted butter or margarine*

Defrost fish if frozen. Combine next 7 ingredients, mix well and pour into a glass or nonporous ceramic dish. Add salmon steaks, spread mixture over all surfaces and marinate in refrigerator for at least 1 hour. Turn 2 or 3 times. Preheat oven and pour boiling water into bottom of broiler pan. Remove warm rack from broiler pan, spread salmon steaks on it and brush lightly with melted butter or margarine. Return rack to broiler pan, place about 4 inches below source of heat and broil at 550 degrees 5–10 minutes or until flakes separate easily when gently probed with a fork. If tops of steaks start to dry out before fish is cooked, lower pan or turn off heat and let fish finish cooking in steam from pan. Brush fish lightly once more with melted butter or margarine.

Serves 4–6.

WATER 'N' FINE WINE

> 4 *steaks of any fat or intermediate fish, 3/4 to 1 inch thick, fresh or frozen, freshwater or salt*
> 1/2 *cup white wine*
> 1/4 *teaspoon fines herbes blend seasoning (or substitute your choice of dried herbs)*
> *Salt to taste*
> 1 1/2 *cups water*
> 2 1/2–3 *tablespoons butter or margarine*
> 2 *tablespoons flour*
> *Salt to taste*

Defrost steaks if frozen. Remove rack from broiler pan, grease lightly and arrange steaks over it. Combine wine, fines herbes blend seasoning, salt to taste and water in a saucepan, bring to a boil and pour into broiler pan in preheated oven. Return rack to broiler pan (be sure water in pan doesn't touch rack) and broil fish 3 or 4 inches from source of heat 5–10 minutes at 550 degrees. Brush steaks lightly once or twice with melted butter or margarine as they broil. If top of fish is cooked before bottom, turn off heat and let steam from hot liquid in bottom of broiler pan finish the cooking job.

Using a large spatula, carefully remove steaks to preheated serving platter and cover to keep warm. Measure liquids in broiler pan; reduce or increase by adding wine or water to make 1 1/4 cups. Heat 2 tablespoons of remaining margarine in heavy skillet or saucepan. Add flour and cook over medium heat, stirring constantly, for 2 or 3 minutes. (This part of the sauce making can be done while fish broils.) Add liquid from broiling pan. Taste, add salt and adjust seasoning if necessary. Cook, stirring frequently with wire whisk, 7–8 minutes or until sauce is smooth and of the desired consistency. Pour over fish steaks and serve at once.

Serves 4.

9

Frying

There are several ways of frying fish. Which one you should use depends on the size and shape of your fish and the result you want to achieve.

But whatever the method, it's essential that you cook at a hot temperature that will quickly seal in juices and turn the fish a golden brown. However, it must not be so hot that the fat smokes, because that will spoil the flavor and texture of your fish and, what is even worse, it will permeate your house (to say nothing of your cooking utensils) with an unpleasant odor. Not the sweet smell of fresh fish, which we consider just as pleasant as the smell of other fresh foods, but that horrible, strong smell that has turned so many people off from cooking fish, never realizing that it wasn't the fish but the improper method of cooking that was at fault.

PAN-FRYING

1. Completely defrost frozen fish.

2. Wash fish by dipping in and out of water that's had a little salt or lemon juice added. Examine shellfish and remove any bits of broken shell.

3. At this time you may want to refrigerate your fish for 30 minutes or more in a marinade, which is an excellent way to season it.

4. Dry thoroughly on lintfree or absorbent paper towels. All water or liquids containing water must be completely removed. If your fish is not dry, some types of batter won't adhere and even tiny drops of water, including the ice crystals in not quite defrosted fish, will cause the grease in which you are frying to spatter.

5. Now if you like is the time to season fish with salt and pepper. Or

you may prefer to mix the seasonings into the flour with which you may or may not decide to dust the fish. That, too, is strictly a matter of personal preference. Some people like fish fried that way, some do not. If you do, now is the time to so dust it.

6. Much better than flour alone, we think that a batter coating gives fish a much nicer, crunchier flavor. If you agree, now is the time to add it, either with or without a preliminary flour dusting. Like this:

· Dip in a liquid to which crumbs will adhere. The most commonly used is egg beaten with a little water, milk, wine or beer. However, after trying egg you might want to experiment with such things as evaporated milk (add a little lemon juice both to thicken and to flavor it), buttermilk, yogurt, salad dressing or other sauces without the egg.

· Thoroughly coat all surfaces with one of the following: toasted breadcrumbs (either your own made from stale bread or a commercial product), cornmeal, cracker crumbs or crushed, freshly opened breakfast cereal of the cornflakes type. Some people prefer one; some another; some like to mix two of them together. Preferences are mainly regional.

7. Spread fish coated in egg batter out on a large platter or a sheet of waxed paper to dry for at least 5 minutes. Crumbs may get soggy in a nonegg batter if allowed to stand.

Fish can be coated with egg batter, arranged on a cookie sheet or other flat dish, carefully covered with wax paper or freezer paper and refrigerated for frying anywhere from 10 minutes to 24 hours later. Or, if you have very nice fresh-caught fillets, steaks or sticks, after coating with egg batter you can put them in the freezer, uncovered, for about 1 hour (just long enough for the batter to become solidly set), then wrap in freezer paper in single-layer packages containing about 2 fillets or steaks or half a dozen sticks each and complete the freezing process. Use within a week.

8. The fat you use to fry the fish can be a vegetable cooking oil or a combination of equal amounts of butter or margarine and vegetable cooking oil. Add enough fat to a heavy skillet to cover the bottom to the depth of about 1/8 inch (1/4 inch at the very most) and heat until sizzling hot but not smoking. Add the fish but don't crowd them. It's better to use 2 pans or fry in batches than to end up with soggy, dirty brown fish, which is what will happen if you crowd too many into the pan at one time.

9. Cook until golden brown on one side, turn and repeat on second side. Test to see if fish is done. If not, turn heat down just a bit and continue frying until flakes separate easily when gently probed with tines of a fork. When turning heat down, be careful not to make it so low the fish becomes soggy with fat. If any excess fat remains on fish, drain on absorbent lintfree paper towels. Transfer to preheated platter and serve at once.

10. Do not fry a second batch of fish in the pan without cleaning it.

To Sauté

This is a way of cooking small, thin pieces of fish in a frying pan without coating them with a protective batter yet with a minimum amount of drying and toughening of the surface.

- Wash and dry the fish, season, dust with flour or not.
- Heat 2 to 4 tablespoons of oil in a heavy skillet to sizzling hot but not smoking.
- Add fish and cook without reducing heat, stirring frequently and turning, removing from pan as quickly as possible.

To Stir-Fry in Hong Kong Manner

Use a heavy skillet or a wok and heat it until it's very, very hot. Remove from heat and immediately add a small amount of cooking oil (2 to 4 tablespoons), taking great care that the hot fat does not flare up or spatter on you. Before hot oil can cool, add just a small amount of fish pieces or shellfish and stir constantly as it fries. Return skillet or wok to heat if necessary. See recipes from *The Hong Kong Cookbook,* by Dan Morris and Arthur Lem, for variations of this method of frying.

To Oven-Fry

Calorie counters and others who must limit the amount of fat they eat find that oven- rather than pan-frying of fish helps them do this.

- Prepare fish and coat with flour or batter in the same manner as for pan-frying. Use toasted breadcrumbs or crumbled cereal rather than cornmeal or cracker crumbs. Let egg-batter-coated fish stand for at least 5 minutes.
- Preheat oven to 500 degrees.
- Arrange fish in very lightly greased shallow metal baking pan, drizzle with about 2 tablespoons of oil per pound of fish or dot with same amount of butter or margarine.
- Place pan 3½ to 4½ inches from top of oven for fillets and steaks from ⅜ to ⅝ inch thick. Place a little farther away for thicker fish so crumbs won't become unpleasantly brown by the time fish is cooked. No matter what the fish thickness, watch closely, and if top browns too rapidly, lower pan and/or reduce heat.
- Cook fish 5–10 minutes, depending on thickness, or until flakes separate easily when gently probed with tines of a fork.

FISH STEAKS OR FILLETS FRIED IN BATTER (O)

1 *pound fish fillets or steaks, freshwater or salt, fresh or frozen*
Salt and pepper to taste

½ cup flour
1 egg, beaten
½ cup breadcrumbs, cracker crumbs or cornmeal
Butter or margarine
Cooking oil
Lemon wedges
Parsley for garnish

Thaw fish if frozen, season with salt and pepper, and lightly dust all sur-faces with flour. Dip in beaten egg, coat with crumbs and spread out in single layer to dry for about 5 minutes before cooking. Add equal amounts of butter or margarine and cooking oil to large heavy skillet so there is about ⅛ inch in bottom and heat until sizzling hot but not smoking. Add fish but don't crowd. Cook until golden brown on one side, turn and repeat on second side. Test to see if fish is done. If not, turn heat down just a bit and continue frying until flakes separate easily when gently probed with tines of a fork. Remove to preheated platter, garnish with lemon wedges and parsley, and serve at once. (If any excess of oil re-mains on fish, drain first on absorbent paper towels.)

Serves 2–4.

PAN FISH FRIED IN BATTER: Prepare in the same way as Fish Steaks or Fillets Fried in Batter, but you would need 2–4 pounds for 2–4 people.

FISH STICKS FRIED IN BATTER: Cut fillets that are at least ½ inch thick into sticks, prepare and fry as in Fish Steaks or Fillets Fried in Batter.

CLAMS FRIED IN BATTER: Drain shucked clams (any kind from cherrystones or steamers to chowders), thoroughly dry on lintfree or ab-sorbent paper towels, then prepare and fry in same manner as Fish Steaks or Fillets Fried in Batter. For small clams, increase quantity of batter ingredients.

MUSSELS FRIED IN BATTER: Drain shucked mussels, thoroughly dry on lintfree or absorbent paper towels, then prepare and fry in same man-ner as Fish Steaks or Fillets Fried in Batter. For small mussels, increase quantity of batter ingredients.

OYSTERS FRIED IN BATTER: Drain shucked oysters, thoroughly dry on lintfree cloth or absorbent paper towels, then prepare and fry in same manner as Fish Steaks or Fillets Fried in Batter. For small oysters, in-crease quantity of batter ingredients.

SCALLOPS FRIED IN BATTER: Prepare and fry in the same manner as Fish Steaks or Fillets Fried in Batter. Cut large sea scallops in half and double quantity of batter ingredients.

SHRIMPS FRIED IN BATTER: Peel and devein raw shrimp. Wash off and thoroughly dry, then prepare and fry in same manner as Fish Steaks or Fillets Fried in Batter. For small shrimps, increase quantity of batter ingredients.

SOFT-SHELL CRAB FRIED IN BATTER: Clean (see page 56), and prepare and fry in same manner as Fish Steaks or Fillets Fried in Batter.

BATTER-FRIED FIN FISH OR SHELLFISH IN SAUCE: Choose any sauce from sauce section and pour over fin fish or shellfish fried in batter. Make the sauce before cooking fish so fish can be eaten immediately when it is done.

OVEN-FRIED FISH STEAKS OR FILLETS IN BATTER: Prepare steaks or fillets in same manner as for Fish Steaks or Fillets Fried in Batter. Instead of frying in skillet, arrange in a well-greased shallow metal baking pan, dot lightly with butter or margarine, place pan near top of oven preheated to 500 degrees 5–10 minutes (depending on thickness of fish) or until flakes separate easily when gently probed with tines of a fork and crust is golden colored.

OVEN-FRIED PAN FISH IN BATTER: Prepare and cook flat pan fish that is not much more than 1 inch thick in same manner as steaks or fillets. For variation, remove head and remove skin from darkest side only. Lay on a bed of sliced onion and garlic (skinless side up) and coat top only with buttermilk or evaporated milk, cover with crumbs, dot lightly with butter or margarine and oven-fry.

FRIED FAT FISH FILLETS OR STEAKS   (O)

4 *large fillets or steaks from any fat (or otherwise strongly flavored)*
   fish, freshwater or salt, fresh or frozen
½ *cup white wine*
½ *cup white vinegar*
2 *pinches tarragon*
Salt and pepper to taste
2 *or 3 drops Worcestershire sauce*
¾ *cup flour*
2 *tablespoons butter or margarine*
2 *tablespoons cooking oil*

Defrost fish if frozen. Combine wine, vinegar, tarragon, salt and pepper and Worcestershire sauce in a glass or nonporous ceramic dish and mix well. Add fillets or steaks, thoroughly coat each one with the mixture and marinate for ½ hour in the refrigerator. Remove from dish, dry well on absorbent paper towels and dust with flour. Heat butter or margarine and cooking oil in large heavy skillet. When sizzling but not smoking, add fillets or steaks. Cook until golden brown on one side. Carefully turn with a large spatula and brown the second side. Serve the moment fish flakes separate easily when gently probed with tines of a fork.
Serves 2–4.

OVEN-FRIED FAT FISH FILLETS OR STEAK: Prepare steaks or fillets in same manner as for fried fish in preceding recipe. Place in a well-greased shallow metal baking pan, dot with butter or margarine and put dish near top of preheated oven. Cook at 500 degrees 5–10 minutes, depending on thickness of fish, until flakes separate easily when gently probed with tines of fork and fish is golden color.

FRIED PAN FISH WITH BUTTER, LEMON JUICE AND PARSLEY (O)

(Fried Fish à la Meunière)

4 *lean dressed pan fish, head and tail left on, ½ to ¾ pound each*
½ *cup milk*
½ *cup flour seasoned with salt and pepper to taste*
3 *tablespoons butter or margarine*
2 *tablespoons cooking oil*
1 *lemon, thinly sliced*
Juice of ½ lemon
2 *tablespoons chopped parsley*

Dip fish in milk and lightly coat with seasoned flour. Melt 1 tablespoon of the butter or margarine and all the cooking oil in large, heavy skillet. When sizzling hot but not smoking, add fish and fry for about 3 minutes or until golden brown on one side, turn and fry until second side is brown and flakes separate easily when gently probed with tines of a fork. After initial browning, turn heat down a bit if necessary to keep from getting too dark. Carefully remove fish to a preheated serving platter and arrange lemon slices over them. Add remaining 2 tablespoons butter or margarine, lemon juice and chopped parsley to skillet, heat and pour over fish.

Serves 2–4.

FRIED LEAN FISH FILLETS OR STEAKS WITH LEMON JUICE, BUTTER AND PARSLEY: Prepare in the same manner as pan fish.

FRIED SHRIMP OR OTHER SHELLFISH WITH LEMON JUICE, BUTTER AND PARSLEY: Fry peeled and deveined shrimp or shucked and drained clams, mussels and oysters in the same manner as flat fish.

FRIED FISH WITH ALMONDS (Amandine): Sprinkle roasted, slivered almonds over top of fish when serving. They can be cold or you can add them to the oils in the pan for a little heating up.

OVEN-FRIED FISH STICKS (I)

With Bacon and Spiced Peaches

(If you're tired of a routine egg breakfast, try this.)

1 *1-pound package frozen fillets, lean, freshwater or salt*
3 *slices of lean bacon, cut in half*

6 *canned peach halves*
½ *cup juice from peach can*
⅛ *teaspoon cinnamon (about)*
1 *tablespoon dark brown sugar*
1 *tablespoon lemon juice*

Defrost package of fillets overnight in refrigerator for 8 hours only. Cut fish lengthwise in three equal strips, then once across, making 6 pieces 1¼ by 1 by 4½ inches. Lay in a shallow baking pan, cover each piece of fish with a half slice of bacon and oven-fry 3½ to 4 inches from top of oven preheated to 500 degrees. The partly frozen fish and the bacon should both be done in from 12 to 15 minutes. Pour off excess bacon grease after 5 minutes of cooking.

Place peach halves, cavity side up, in small, shallow baking pan. Pour juice around the peaches and sprinkle with cinnamon, brown sugar and lemon juice. Place in the oven at the same time and on the same high shelf as the fish. Cook from 10 to 15 minutes or until they start to brown, basting them once or twice with juice in pan. Serve hot spiced peach halves with cooked fish and bacon.

Serves 6.

STICK 'EM UPS (I)

And Chips

1½ *pounds mild-flavored, white-fleshed fish fillets, freshwater or salt, fresh or frozen*
3 *drops sesame oil*
1 *tablespoon olive oil*
¼ *cup cooking oil*
1 *clove garlic, crushed*
1 *tablespoon red wine*
1 *cup grated Parmesan cheese*
1 *cup toasted breadcrumbs, thoroughly blended with 2 tablespoons melted butter or margarine*
Potato chips for 4–6

Defrost fish if frozen, cut into 1- by ½- by 2-inch sticks. Combine next 5 items, mix well and rub into all sides of each fish stick. Spread fish out in a dish, pour any remaining mixture over them, cover and marinate in refrigerator for ½ hour. Drain, coat with grated cheese, then with breadcrumbs, and arrange in a single layer in shallow, well-greased metal baking pan. Place pan near top of oven preheated to 500 degrees and oven-fry 5–8 minutes or until flesh flakes easily when gently probed with tines of a fork and fish is nicely browned. Serve to children (grown-ups too) with potato chips.

Serves 4–6.

NOTE: Marinate in glass or nonporous ceramic dish.

FISH WITH CARAWAY SEEDS   (O)

4 *fillets or fish steaks*
2 *tablespoons caraway seeds*
2 *tablespoons butter or margarine (substitute cooking oil or bacon grease if cooked outside)*
Salt and pepper to taste

Spread caraway seeds over both sides of fillets or steaks. Heat butter or margarine to sizzling but not smoking hot in large skillet and fry fish until golden brown on both sides. Fish is ready to eat if flesh flakes easily when gently prodded with tines of a fork. Season to taste with salt and pepper.

Serves 2–4.

NOTE: We must confess that this recipe was plagiarized—from *The Complete Outdoor Cookbook,* by Dan and Inez Morris (Hawthorn Books).

FRIED FILLETS TARRAGON

2 *pound flounder fillets, fresh or frozen, or any other delicately flavored salt or freshwater fillet*
1 *tablespoon sherry wine*
1 *egg*
½ *cup dry breadcrumbs, unseasoned*
1 *pinch garlic powder*
Salt and pepper to taste
½ *teaspoon dried tarragon, crumbled further between your fingers*
3 *to 4 tablespoons cooking oil*

Defrost fish if frozen. Add sherry to egg and beat lightly. Combine breadcrumbs, garlic powder, salt, pepper and tarragon, and mix well. Dip fillets in beaten egg mixture, coat with crumbs and let stand for 5 minutes. In a large, heavy skillet, heat oil to sizzling (but not smoking) hot. Add fillets, a few at a time so skillet is not cooled too much, and cook for about 3 minutes or until golden brown on one side. Turn and cook until second side is brown or until flakes separate easily when gently probed with tines of a fork. Serve immediately with lemon wedges.

Serves 4–6.

OVEN-FRIED FILLETS TARRAGON: Prepare fillets in same manner as for Fried Fillets Tarragon, arrange in well-greased, shallow metal baking pan, dot with butter or margarine and place pan near top of oven. Bake in oven preheated to 500 degrees 3–8 minutes or until fish flakes easily when tested with a fork and crust is golden-colored.

ARTHUR LEM'S FRESH CONCH WITH STRING BEANS AND SCALLIONS

(Dow Jai Chow Heung Lor)

4 *fresh live conch, prepared for cooking in the Chinese manner, see page 86*
2 *cups fresh string beans, thinly sliced on the diagonal*
1 *cup chicken broth*
½ *cup sliced mushrooms*
½ *cup sliced water chestnuts*
4 *tablespoons cooking oil*
2 *thin slices gingerroot (substitute ginger powder)*
2 *tablespoons sherry wine*
¾ *teaspoon salt*
1 *teaspoon sugar*
½ *teaspoon monosodium glutamate (optional)*
Dash of pepper
¼ *teaspoon sesame oil*
2 *tablespoons oyster sauce (buy at an Oriental grocery store or a food specialty shop)*
2 *tablespoons cornstarch*
2 *fresh scallions, chopped*

Bring 1 quart of water to a boil, add string beans and cook for approximately 2 minutes. Drain, rinse briefly with cold water and set aside.

Heat chicken broth, add mushrooms and sliced water chestnuts, and cook for 3 or 4 minutes. Drain, reserving broth for sauce.

Heat wok or large frying pan, add 2 tablespoons of cooking oil and, when hot, add ginger and sliced conch and stir-fry for no more than 2 minutes. Add sherry wine, stir and cook for another minute. Pour into colander, drain out all juice and set aside.

Thoroughly wash and dry wok or frying pan, add remaining 2 tablespoons oil, heat, add string beans, mushrooms and water chestnuts, and stir-fry for 2 minutes. Mix reserved chicken broth with salt, sugar, monosodium glutamate, pepper, sesame oil, oyster sauce and cornstarch. Stir until cornstarch is dissolved and mixture is smooth, then stir into vegetable mixture in wok or frying pan. Cook on medium heat, stirring constantly, until slightly thickened. Add conch, pour into a bowl, garnish with chopped scallions and serve.

Serves 4–6.

NOTE: This recipe and the two that follow came to us from Arthur Lem, with whom Dan wrote *The Hong Kong Cookbook* (Funk & Wagnalls). They are authentic Chinese recipes, not to be had in Chinese-American restaurants anywhere that we know of.

CRAB MEAT WHITE CLOUD WITH MUSHROOMS   (I)
(Hai Yook Par Sun Goo)

1 *cup fresh crab meat, cooked, or a 7½-ounce can*
4 *egg whites, beaten*
½ *teaspoon salt*
½ *teaspoon monosodium glutamate (optional)*
3 *tablespoons cornstarch*
½ *pint fresh milk (no substitutes)*
¾ *cup lard (no substitutes)*
2 *cups small fresh mushrooms, stems removed*
⅛ *teaspoon salt*
⅛ *teaspoon sugar*
½ *teaspoon sherry*
Utensil: wok or frying pan

Combine first 6 ingredients and set aside. Preheat utensil well, reduce heat to medium, melt 2 teaspoons lard, add mushrooms, and sauté 2 to 3 minutes. Add salt and sugar, and stir 1 minute more. Then add sherry and stir for another minute. Remove mushrooms, drain, stir into crab-meat mixture and set aside. Thoroughly clean wok or frying pan by melting small amount of lard in it and scouring with paper towels or clean cloth until not a dark speck remains. That done, reheat utensil once more, remove from heat, melt remaining lard, add crab-meat and mushroom mixture and stir until it has a lovely white color or, as they say in Hong Kong, until it looks like a summer cloud.

Serves 4.

NOTE: If lard cools hot utensil so much that crab mixture does not thicken, return to low heat and stir constantly until light and fluffy.

HARD-SHELL CRABS WITH GINGER SAUCE
(Keing Chung Kok Hai)

12 *hard-shell crabs, preferably blue claw*
2 *tablespoons cornstarch*
½ *cup soup stock*
2 *tablespoons light soya sauce*
1 *teaspoon sugar*
Dash of pepper

Dash of sesame oil
1 *teaspoon cornstarch*
5 *tablespoons lard*
2 *cloves garlic, crushed*
2 *tablespoons crushed ginger*
4 *stalks green onions (scallions), cut into 1-inch pieces*
1 *tablespoon sherry*
2 *tablespoons oyster sauce (buy at an Oriental grocery or a specialty food store)*
Utensil: wok or frying pan with cover

Remove shells from crabs, clean away the whiskers and digestive organs, and rinse in cold water. Cut each crab into 4 pieces and slightly crush the claws with side of cleaver or heavy-duty knife. Sprinkle with cornstarch, toss to assure thorough coverage and set aside.

Combine next 6 ingredients into a seasoning mixture. Set aside.

Preheat utensil, add lard, and bring to a sizzle. Add garlic, ginger, and scallions and stir-fry over high heat until brown. Add crabs and stir-fry another 5 minutes. Add sherry. Cover and leave for 3 minutes with heat on. Remove cover, add seasoning mixture and stir for another 2 or 3 minutes. Finally stir in oyster sauce and cool for a few seconds.

Serves 4–6.

FRIED EELS AND CREAMED POTATOES IN THE DANISH MANNER

(Stegt Aal med Stuvede Kartofler)

(Danish tradition has it that one must eat enough eels to form a ring of bones around one's plate.)

2–3 *pounds of eel, skinned and cleaned and cut in 3-inch pieces*
½ *teaspoon salt*
1½ *cups flour*
2 *eggs, beaten*
1½ *cups breadcrumbs*
6–8 *tablespoons butter or margarine*
Medium White Sauce, page 121, with ½ cup heavy cream added
Boiled potatoes for 4, cubed
1 *tablespoon finely chopped fresh parsley*

Stir salt into flour and coat eel pieces with the mixture. Dip in beaten egg, then in breadcrumbs and spread out to dry for a few minutes. Melt butter or margarine in a large, heavy skillet, add eels and fry, turning until browned on all sides and flakes separate easily when gently probed with tines of a fork. Make White Sauce while eel is cooking, stir hot boiled potatoes into it, garnish with chopped parsley and serve with eels.

Serves 4.

FLAMED FLOUNDER WITH GRAPES AND NUTS   (I)
(Flambé)

1 *pound flounder fillets, fresh or frozen*
Salt and pepper to taste
½ *cup flour*
2 *tablespoons butter or margarine*
2 *tablespoons cooking oil*
5 *tablespoons brandy*
1 *10½-ounce can condensed cream of mushroom soup*
½ *cup table cream or milk*
2 *tablespoons freeze-dried shallots (optional)*
1 *cup seedless grapes*
½ *cup slivered blanched and toasted almonds*

Defrost fish if frozen. Mix salt and pepper into flour and coat fillets with the mixture. Heat butter or margarine and cooking oil in large, heavy skillet until sizzling but not smoking. Add fillets, brown lightly on one side, turn, brown the second side and cook just until flakes separate easily when gently probed with tines of a fork. When fish is almost but not quite done, warm brandy by pouring into a warm dish, turn off heat under fish and pour the brandy over it carefully. Ignite vapor from brandy with a lighted taper. When flame dies, remove fish to a warmed serving platter and cover to keep warm. Stir mushroom soup into oil in skillet, add cream, shallots, grapes and slivered almonds, continue stirring until hot and serve over fish.

Serves 2–4.

NOTE: This recipe is also very good without the sauce, served either hot or cold.

OVEN-FRIED HADDOCK,
BACON AND PICKLE ROLLS   (I)

2 *pounds haddock (or fish of your choice) fillets about* ¼ *inch thick, cut in 1-inch-wide strips*
Sweet or dill pickles, cut in 1-inch-long pieces
½ *pound lean bacon, sliced and cooked in skillet until almost but not quite done*

Roll each fish strip around a piece of pickle, wrap a bacon slice around it and fasten with a wooden pick. Lay rolls in lightly greased baking pan, set it near top of oven, and oven-fry at 500 degrees 8–12 minutes or until fish flakes easily when tested with a fork and bacon is cooked.

Serves 4–6.

VARIATION: Substitute cooked asparagus or some distinctly different fish, such as canned salmon, for the pickle piece.

OVEN-FRIED OCEAN PERCH IN BUTTERMILK

1 *pound ocean perch fillets, or any ⅜- to ⅝-inch-thick lean or in-termediate fillet, freshwater or salt, fresh or frozen*
2 *tablespoons butter or margarine*
Salt and pepper to taste
¼ *cup cultured buttermilk*
⅔ *cup crushed cornflakes, made from freshly opened box*
Lemon wedges

Defrost fish if frozen. Grease bottom of shallow metal baking pan with about 1 teaspoon of the butter or margarine. Season fillets with salt and pepper to taste. Dip in cultured buttermilk and coat on both sides with crushed cornflakes. Arrange, skin side down, on greased baking pan and dot with remaining butter or margarine. Place pan about 4 inches below ceiling in oven preheated to 500 degrees and oven-fry 5–10 minutes or until fish flakes separate easily when gently probed with tines of a fork.

Serves 2–4.

FRIED ROE

(Basic Recipe for Cooking Roe)

Roe can be fried, broiled, poached or baked. Some people feel that no matter what the cooking method, it should be poached first for about 30 seconds in boiling water to firm the membrane that holds the thousands of tiny fish eggs together. We find this unnecessary when frying provided we use a medium instead of a high heat and cook it in a heavy skillet. Eat the roe plain, with eggs and/or bacon, as an appetizer or mashed or chopped in a fish stuffing. Roe should always be cooked all the way through. Slice into the center to check. If the center is the same color and consistency as the outer edges, it's cooked. The thicker the roe, the longer it will take to cook; one that's ¾ to 1 inch thick takes a total of approximately 10 minutes, uncovered over medium heat.

2 *flounder roe, ¾ to 1 inch thick, about 5 or 6 ounces*
2 *teaspoons butter or margarine*
2 *teaspoons cooking oil*
Salt and pepper to taste

Heat butter or margarine and cooking oil in small, heavy skillet on medium heat. Add roe and cook until nicely browned and crisp on one side. Turn and cook second side the same way. Total cooking time should be about 10 minutes.

Serves 2–4.

FRIED FLOUNDER ROE APPETIZER: Chill cooked roe, slice and serve as an appetizer with one of the sauces on page 144 as a dip. (It must be picked up in the fingers, as picks will make it fall apart).

NOTE: If not flounder, so what? The roe of any other fish is just as good.

SAUTÉED SCALLOPS WITH GARLIC AND PARSLEY

(Scallops à la Provençale)

1 *pound sea scallops, cut in half if very large*
Salt and pepper to taste
¼ *cup flour*
2 *tablespoons olive oil*
1 *tablespoon cooking oil*
2 *cloves garlic, finely minced*
¼ *cup chopped parsley*
Lemon wedges

Mix salt and pepper to taste into flour and lightly coat scallops with the mixture. Heat oils in large heavy skillet until sizzling hot but not smoking. Add garlic and stir-fry for about 15 seconds. Add scallops, being sure not to crowd them in the pan, and cook on fairly high heat, turning often so all sides are a pale golden brown. Turn off heat, add parsley and toss with scallops. Transfer to preheated serving platter, pour oil and garlic remaining in pan over scallops, garnish with lemon wedges and serve.

Serves 4.

PAN-FRIED SHRIMP WITH BROCCOLI

(Gai Lun Hai Kow)*

2 *quarts water*
1 *teaspoon baking soda (optional)*

* From *The Hong Kong Cookbook*, by Arthur Lem and Dan Morris (Funk & Wagnalls).

6 *cups fresh, tender broccoli spears cut into 1-inch diagonal slices*
1½ *pounds (16 to 20) fresh jumbo shrimp, shelled and deveined*
1 *teaspoon salt*
1 *dash black pepper*
1 *tablespoon sherry wine*
⅛ *teaspoon monosodium glutamate (optional)*
1½ *tablespoons Chinese light soya sauce*
3 *tablespoons corn or peanut oil*
1 *clove garlic*
4 *slices fresh ginger*
3 *scallions (white part only)*
1 *tablespoon sherry wine*
1 *teaspoon salt*
⅛ *teaspoon monosodium glutamate (optional)*
1½ *teaspoons sugar*
1 *teaspoon cornstarch mixed with ½ cup cold water*
1 *tablespoon oyster sauce (buy from Chinese grocery or specialty food shop)*
2 *or 3 drops sesame oil*
8 *scallions (green part only) cut into pieces 1 inch long for garnish*
Utensil: wok or large frying pan

Bring water to a boil. Add baking soda and broccoli, and cook for 1 minute or until broccoli is crisply tender. Remove broccoli from boiling water, rinse with cold water and set aside.

Wash shrimp with cold water and dry with lintfree towel. Combine in a bowl with next 5 ingredients. Stir well and set aside.

Now to cook: Heat oil in wok or frying pan until sizzling hot, but do not let it smoke. Add garlic, ginger and whites of scallions. Stir-fry until golden brown, remove from oil and discard.

While the oil is still hot, add shrimp and fry until they turn red. Add broccoli and stir constantly for 2 minutes, then add sherry, salt, monosodium glutamate, sugar and the cornstarch mixture, stirring constantly. When sauce has thickened, stir in oyster sauce and sesame oil. Serve with a garnish of green scallions.

Serves 4.

SHRIMP KREIDELL (I)

12 *jumbo shrimp*
1 *large onion, sliced*
4 *cups homemade onion soup or 1 10½-ounce can diluted with 2 soup cans of water*
6 *slices bacon cut in half, crosswise*

3 *eggs, lightly beaten*
¼ *cup water*
Vegetable shortening
3½ *ounces soy sauce or to taste*
3 *tablespoons cornstarch*
3 *tablespoons cold water*
4 *cups hot cooked rice*

Simmer onion slices in onion soup for 15 minutes or until tender. Shell the shrimp, leaving tail on with a bit of the shell as a handle. Cut each shrimp almost through lengthwise (butterfly style), remove vein, wash by dipping in water and pat dry on lintfree towel or absorbent paper. Wrap each shrimp in ½ slice of bacon and set aside. Combine beaten eggs and ¼ cup of water. Start vegetable shortening heating in large, heavy skillet. There should be enough to make a little under ⅛ inch in depth. Dip bacon-covered shrimp in beaten-egg mixture and, when oil is sizzling hot, arrange them in skillet. When oil returns to sizzling, turn off heat under pan and cook shrimp for about 10 minutes or until bacon is brown and shrimp has turned pink. When one side of bacon is done, turn over, turning heat on under pan whenever necessary to keep oil sizzling but not smoking hot.

Stir 3½ ounces soy sauce into onion soup, taste and add more if you like a richer flavor. Blend cornstarch and 3 tablespoons cold water and add slowly to hot onion soup, stirring constantly until it thickens. Turn down heat and let simmer for about 5 minutes or until broth turns clear. To serve divide rice into 4 ramekins,* arrange 3 shrimp attractively on side of each mound of rice and smother all in onion soup sauce. Add a touch of color with a green salad or a dish of crisply tender broccoli.

Serves 4.

FRIED SMELT

1 *pound dressed lake smelt, pan ready, or any other very small pan fish, fresh or frozen, salt or freshwater*
½ *cup tawny port or other red wine*
½ *teaspoon salt or to taste*
1 *pinch pepper or to taste*
½ *cup flour*
1 *tablespoon butter*
2 *tablespoons cooking oil*

Defrost fish if frozen. Marinate in wine for 1 to 2 hours. Mix salt and pepper with flour and coat fish in the mixture. Heat butter and cooking

* Use casserole dishes, soup bowls or plain old meat plates if you don't have ramekins.

oil together in skillet until sizzling but not smoking and fry fish on both sides until nicely browned. Total time for cooking both sides should not be more than 5 to 7 minutes.

Serves 2–4.

NOTE: Marinate in glass or nonporous ceramic dish.

FRIED SQUID

(Sciacca Fishermen's Calamari)

4 *small squid*
3 *tablespoons olive oil*
Pepper to taste
Lemon wedges

Clean and, if baby squid, leave tentacles whole; if not, cut into 3-inch lengths. Cut body into 1-inch pieces. Place in large, heavy skillet, add just enough water to cover bottom, cover and simmer over low heat until tender. This should take about 20 minutes but test with fork to make sure. Now drain water from pan, add olive oil and pepper, raise flame to high and fry until crispy. Drain on absorbent paper and serve at once with lemon.

Serves 6.

NOTE: We call for only 4 small squid in this recipe, which should be enough for a family of 4–6, but Sciacca fishermen who cook calamari this way while still at sea might easily eat 4 each. Sciacca, by the way, is a fishing village in Sicily. It's pronounced "Sock-ah."

TONGUE 'N' CHEEKS

24 *tongues and cheeks from cod or any similar-size fish*
2 *eggs*
½ *cup milk*
Salt and pepper to taste
½ *cup flour*
2 *cups seasoned dry breadcrumbs*
Cooking oil
24 *cucumber slices*

Dip tongues and cheeks in salt water to clean, and pat dry with lintfree or absorbent paper towel. Thoroughly blend eggs, milk, salt and pepper with a fork. Roll tongues and cheeks in flour, then dip in egg mixture and coat on all sides with breadcrumbs. Add just enough oil to large skillet to cover bottom, heat until sizzling hot, turn heat down, add tongues and cheeks, and fry on both sides only until a light golden brown and not a second more.

Serves 4.

TONGUE 'N' CHEEKS APPETIZERS: Prepare as in preceding recipe and serve hot on cucumber slices.

Yield: 24 appetizers.

CHEEKY TONGUES ORIENTAL

24 *tongues and cheeks from cod or any similar-size fish*
1 *tablespoon soya sauce*
1/4 *teaspoon ginger powder*
Cooking oil
1 *clove garlic*
2 *drops sesame oil (optional)*
1 *green onion (scallion), chopped into about 1/4-inch pieces*

Dip tongues and cheeks in cold salt water to clean, and pat dry with lint-free or absorbent paper towel. Combine soya sauce and ginger powder in glass or nonporous ceramic dish, add tongues and cheeks, and marinate about 1 hour, stirring gently once or twice to make sure all surfaces benefit from the marinade. Add just enough oil to large skillet to cover bottom. Peel garlic and crush under broad side of knife blade, add to oil, turn heat to high and stir-fry until garlic bits start to darken. Add sesame oil if you were able to find it in your market, stir for a few seconds, then quickly remove tongues and cheeks from marinade and sauté no more than 30 seconds. Remove at once to serving dish and garnish with scallion.

Serves 4.

CHEEKY TONGUES ORIENTAL APPETIZER: Prepare as in preceding recipe and add to appetizer table while still piping hot.

Yield: 24 morsels.

FISH AND EGGS ARE A NATURAL TEAM IN AN OMELET

For Cooking, for Economy, for Taste and for Nutrition

Eggs, like fish, need only be cooked until the protein coagulates and they turn opaque. Eggs, like fish, are an economical, top-quality protein food. And since nothing adds more to the taste of an egg than fish, it makes good sense to team them in an omelet (or in a soufflé, see page 319). Since the amount of fish used can be very small, this is a wonderful and economical way to use leftovers from most of the recipes in the book. The following omelet recipes will suggest ways to do it. For safety, reheat leftover cream-type sauces to 140 degrees before using in an omelet.

FLAKED FISH OMELET

½–1 cup cooked (it can be leftover) or canned flaked fish
1 teaspoon olive oil or bacon grease
1 teaspoon finely minced onion or shallot
2 tablespoons butter or margarine
1 tablespoon cooking oil
4–6 eggs
Salt and pepper to taste
Garlic powder to taste
1 teaspoon minced fresh basil or ⅛ teaspoon or to taste dried basil
2 tablespoons liquid (beer, water, milk, wine)

Heat olive oil or bacon grease in small, heavy skillet. Add minced onion or shallot and lightly sauté. Turn off heat, add flaked fish to skillet, stir and cover. Heat butter or margarine and cooking oil in another large, heavy skillet until sizzling hot but not smoking. Break eggs into a mixing bowl, beat lightly and stir in salt, pepper, garlic powder, basil, liquid and fish mixture from first skillet. Now pour omelet mixture into other large skillet, turn heat down to medium and gently lift edges of omelet as it jells so that uncooked portion will run underneath. If egg starts to stiffen, turn heat to low. It is done when bottom is very pale gold and top is soft but no runny egg remains. Serve on preheated plates.

Serves 4–6.

NOTE: If you're new at omelet-making, divide mixture in half and cook in two batches.

FLAKED FISH OMELET WITH SAUCE: Make any sauce of your choice from the sauce section, page 117, and pour over cooked omelet. If you have leftover fish sauce, it can be thinned with melted butter, milk, wine or water, depending on the type it is, heated in top of double boiler, beaten with a wire whisk until smooth and poured over cooked omelet. Or it can be stirred into the beaten egg before cooking.

FLAKED FISH OMELET WITH CHEESE: Add freshly grated cheese of your choice to egg mixture before cooking. Or transfer a not quite cooked omelet to preheated heat-resistant serving platter, sprinkle with grated cheese and run under the broiler (about 2 inches below source of heat) just until cheese melts and lightly browns and eggs finish cooking.

SMOKED EEL OMELET: Substitute smoked eel (or other smoked fish), flaked, for cooked or canned fish in flaked fish omelet.

LEFTOVER COOKED SHELLFISH OMELET: Break cooked shellfish into small pieces and prepare in same manner as Flaked Fish Omelet but substitute butter or margarine for the olive oil or bacon grease.

FLOUNDER, CAVIAR AND WINE OMELET

Made with Leftovers from Flounder, Caviar and Wine

4 *eggs*
2 *tablespoons milk*
Leftover sauce and fish from casserole, see page 294
2 *tablespoons cooking oil, or less, depending on size of skillet*
1 *tablespoon butter or margarine*

Beat eggs and milk together and stir in leftover sauce and bits of fish. Heat cooking oil and butter or margarine in skillet or omelet pan until sizzling hot but not smoking. Pour in egg mixture and cook at medium heat, gently lifting edges as it cooks to let uncooked portion run underneath. When lightly browned on bottom and firm on top, the omelet is ready to serve.

Serves 2–4.

CLAM OMELET

1 *pint shucked clams*
1 *10½-ounce can condensed cream of mushroom or cream of celery soup or 1 recipe thick White Sauce, page 121*
4 *tablespoons butter or margarine*
2 *tablespoons cooking oil*
Salt and pepper to taste
1 *tablespoon finely minced shallots or crumbled freeze-dried variety*
1 *pinch garlic powder*
8 *eggs, lightly beaten with 4 tablespoons water*
Minced parsley

Simmer clams in their own liquid just until edges start to curl. Drain. Strain ½ cup of liquid through several thicknesses of cheesecloth and combine with condensed soup or White Sauce in top of double boiler. Stir and heat until smooth and hot. Turn off heat, place over hot water, add clams, stir, cover and set aside.

Divide butter or margarine and cooking oil into two large, heavy skillets and heat until sizzling hot but not smoking. Stir salt and pepper to taste, shallots and garlic powder into beaten eggs and divide mixture into the 2 skillets. (If you don't have 2 skillets, cook in 2 batches.) Reduce heat immediately to medium. Gently lift edges of omelet as it cooks to let uncooked portion run underneath. If egg starts to stiffen, turn heat to low. It is done when bottom is very pale gold and top is soft but no runny egg remains. Serve on preheated plates. Divide clam sauce over top and sprinkle with chopped parsley.

Serves 4–6.

OYSTER OMELET: Prepare in same manner as clam omelet.

MUSSEL OMELET: Wash mussels and open, saving the liquid (see page 70), and prepare in same manner as Clam Omelet.

SHRIMP OMELET

¼ *pound small or medium raw shrimp, shelled and deveined*
½ *teaspoon Shrimp Spice, page 95*
4 *eggs, lightly beaten*
2 *tablespoons butter or margarine*
1 *tablespoon cooking oil*

Add Shrimp Spice to 2 cups of water in saucepan. Bring to a boil and continue boiling for about 1 minute. Add shrimp, reduce to low simmer and cook 3–5 minutes or just until shrimp are barely done. Remove shrimp and thoroughly dry on lintfree towel or absorbent paper. Strain 2 tablespoons of the cooking liquid and, when cool, mix with beaten egg. Stir in cooked shrimp (if medium size, first cut each one into 2 or 3 pieces). Heat butter or margarine and cooking oil in large, heavy skillet until sizzling hot but not smoking. Pour egg and shrimp mixture into skillet and reduce heat immediately to medium. Gently lift edges of omelet as it cooks to let uncooked portion run underneath. If egg starts to stiffen, turn heat to low. It is done when bottom is very pale gold and top is soft but no runny egg remains. Serve on preheated plates.

Serves 2–4.

VARIATION: Cook shrimp in lightly salted water instead of with Shrimp Spice.

SHRIMP FOO YUNG CANTONESE* (I)

1 *quart water*
1 *cup bok choy, white part only, shredded (substitute tender inside celery stalks)*
½ *cup bamboo shoots, shredded*
½ *cup water chestnuts, shredded*
½ *cup mushrooms, fresh or canned, sliced*
1 *cup bean sprouts, washed and drained if fresh; drained if canned*

* From *The Hong Kong Cookbook,* by Arthur Lem and Dan Morris (Funk & Wagnalls).

6 *eggs, beaten*
1 *cup diced shrimp*
1 *teaspoon salt*
1 *teaspoon sugar*
½ *teaspoon monosodium glutamate (optional)*
Dash of pepper
1½ *tablespoons oil*
Utensil: wok or pot; large frying pan

Bring water to a boil in wok or pot, add bok choy, bamboo shoots, chest-nuts, mushrooms and bean sprouts, and let boil for 2 minutes. Drain, pat dry and place in mixing bowl. Add eggs, shrimp, salt, sugar, monosodium glutamate and pepper. Stir until well mixed and set aside.

Put oil in frying pan, and when it starts to sizzle, add mixture care-fully, about a cupful at a time, as you would pancake batter. Fry until done as you like it.

Yield: 6 omelets.

CROQUETTES

Here is one more way to use leftover or canned fish in truly tooth-some ways.

1½ *cups flaked, leftover cooked (or canned) fin fish or shellfish*
½ *cup leftover rice or mashed potatoes and/or cooked and drained vegetables such as corn, mushrooms, peas, chopped spinach, broccoli, etc.*

The total of these 2 ingredients should be 2 cups but you can change the proportions to 1 cup of flaked fish and 1 cup of vegetables.

1 *tablespoon finely minced mild-flavored raw onion*
½ *cup White Sauce Croquette Base or Leftover Sauce Croquette Base, pages 151–152*
Additional seasonings as needed
½ *cup flour*
1 *large egg*
¾ *cup breadcrumbs*
Butter or margarine
Cooking oil

Combine first 5 ingredients, mix well, taste and add additional seasonings as needed for a fairly spicy flavor. What's already in the leftover ingre-dients will determine the seasonings yet to be added. Put mixture on a flat dish and gently spread it out to a thickness of no more than 1 inch. Chill for at least 30 minutes, then shape into balls or cones or cut with a cookie cutter into circles of no more than 3 inches in diameter or rectangles about 1½ by 2½ inches. Dust with flour, dip in beaten egg, coat with breadcrumbs, place on a plate, carefully cover and refrigerate for at least 1 hour.

Put equal amounts of enough butter or margarine and cooking oil in large, heavy skillet to cover bottom to depth of ⅛ inch. Heat to sizzling but not smoking hot, add croquettes (fry in 2 batches if necessary in order not to crowd them) and cook until golden brown on all sides. Turn frequently but with great care and add more oil if necessary, but heat it first in another utensil, then be very careful not to burn yourself when pouring from one utensil to the other.

Serves 4.

NOTE: A sauce of your choice may be poured over the croquettes when served. If the croquettes are spicy, a mild-flavored creamy or egg-yolk sauce will go well.

CROQUETTES WITH STUFFING: Wrap croquette mixture around lightly sautéed whole mushrooms, smoked oysters or mussels, chunks of cooked salmon, cooked bay scallops or shrimp, or any cooked food of your choice and proceed as in preceding recipe. *These croquettes make nice appetizers.*

OVEN-FRIED CROQUETTES: Prepare flat croquettes that were cut with a cookie cutter as in either of the preceding ways but cook them in the oven instead of the frying pan. Grease a shallow metal baking pan well, add the croquettes, dot lightly with butter or margarine, place so tops are about 3½ to 4 inches from ceiling of oven and bake at 500 degrees 5 minutes or until nicely browned.

FISHBURGERS: Prepare flat croquettes that were cut with a cookie cutter about 3 inches in diameter, spread with tartar or other sauce of your choice and use to fill lightly toasted hamburger or other rolls.

FISH-CAKE SANDWICHES: Fill sandwiches with croquettes cut in rectangles.

10

Deep-Frying

If you've never done any deep-frying, we suggest that, for the first time, you start with a small amount of fish, and that you serve something with it that will not require attention while you're handling the hot grease. Baked potatoes and a salad, for example, go very well with fried fish of any kind, especially if the salad is well covered with creamy sauce, which makes it unnecessary to serve a sauce with the fish.

Once you've cooked a couple of batches of deep-fried fish, you'll find it very simple. The trick is to get a nice tasty golden crust that seals out the fat and to serve the fish immediately when it is done. The batter coating can be tender or crisp, depending on the materials you use.

DEEP-FRYING BATTERS

Basically, there are 2 kinds of deep-frying batter: unmixed and mixed. The unmixed batters are the egg batters given for pan-frying. You make them and apply them in exactly the same way as described on pages 247–251. Fritters are deep-fried balls of batter into which flaked fish and/or other foods have been mixed.

There are many different recipes for mixed batters. The most common consist of roughly equal amounts of flour and liquid mixed together. You can make up easy ones of your own by following the simple, basic instructions that follow. The quantities given will generally provide a batter coating for ½ pound of cubed fin fish or shellfish or 1 pound of fillets cut into serving-size pieces. The thicker the batter, the more you will need.

· Season 1 cup of flour any way you choose, using one or more of such things as salt, pepper, tarragon, dill, garlic powder, onion powder, sugar, etc.

• Stir into one of the following and mix just until well-blended:
1. 1 cup of beer.
2. 1 beaten egg combined with lemon juice and water to make 1
   cup (1 large egg = ¼ cup; 1 lemon = 2 to 2½ tablespoons
   juice).
3. 1 beaten egg with enough milk to make 1 cup.

You can add 1 to 2 teaspoons of baking powder to (2) or (3) if you
want, mixing it into the flour. The more you add, the puffier the cooked
batter will be. One tablespoon cooking oil will make the batter more tender, but whether you add it or not also is optional. As a general rule,
batters made with water are crisper than those made with milk, while
beer results in a delightfully hard, crunchy batter.

Be sure the fish is completely dry before coating with batter.

USING THE DEEP-FRYER

1. Wash fish by dipping in cold, lightly salted water or water to
which a little lemon has been added and dry on lintfree cloth or absorbent
paper towel. Examine shellfish and remove any bits of broken shell.

2. Pour any of the cooking oils recommended on page 93 into a
deep-fryer, making sure that it is no more than half full. This will help
keep any hot spattering oil away from your hands or face. Place a thermometer made for this purpose in the oil, turn on heat and check the
position of the mercury heat indicator frequently.

3. Coat fish by dipping in the batter.

'4. Place batter-coated fish in a single layer in a deep-fryer basket.
Don't let the pieces touch each other. (You will usually need to figure on
cooking more than one batch.)

5. When the thermometer registers from 360 degrees to 375 degrees
(be sure it doesn't go much higher or the oil may smoke and the heat
may draw fish flavor out into the oil), lower the basket into the hot oil.
The temperature of the oil will immediately drop but try to maintain it at
from 355 degrees to 365 degrees.

6. Shake basket frequently to be sure pieces of fish don't stick
together.

7. The length of time it will take to cook your fish will depend on
the heat the oil maintains (the deeper it is, the easier it will be to keep
the temperature uniform), the amount of fish, its thickness and size and
the temperature of the fish when it went into the fryer. But most fish
will be done by the time your batter is nicely browned and this generally
takes from 2 to 5 minutes. Naturally, small or thin pieces of fin fish or
shellfish will cook more quickly than 1-inch-thick portions of fillet. We
don't recommend deep-frying fish that is thicker than 1 inch because it
may not be done when the crust is cooked.

Substitute for the Deep-Fryer

You don't have to have a deep-fryer in order to deep-fry fish. There are any number of utensils around most kitchens that will do very well for this purpose. A strainer, preferably one with a flat bottom and a handle, and a large, heavy pot it will fit into are perfect. Or you can use a heavy pot without the strainer simply by lowering pieces of fish in a perforated spoon or on a perforated cake turner into the hot oil. Instead of shaking them in the deep-fryer basket, turn them or separate them with a long-handled slotted spoon. The least suitable pot but one you can use—with care—is a heavy skillet. We say least suitable because a skillet is too shallow to protect you from spattering greases.

Deep-Frying Recipes

The following recipes demonstrate different batters and different methods of applying them. You can substitute any fin fish or shellfish for the ones used, but you may prefer the results you get by confining your choice to those containing no more than 6 percent fat—in other words, any fish from the "lean" or "intermediate" columns on the list of fish on page 100.

DEEP-FRIED FISH AND VEGETABLES

(Japanese Tempura)

At the same time you make any of the deep-fried fish recipes prepared with a mixed batter, make some extra batter and use it to coat and deep-fry bits of raw vegetable. Serve them with the fish. *Voilà,* you have made tempura, a popular Japanese dish. After you've prepared tempura a time or two for the family, you're almost surely going to prepare it for company (first time, serve no more than 4 people), using a good fondue cooker that will maintain oil at 360 degrees and cook Japanese style, right at the table.

The pieces of vegetable should be small so that they will be cooked in the few minutes it takes the batter to brown. They should be prepared for cooking well ahead of time and prettily arranged in a shallow bowl or on a platter. Some suitable vegetables are small cauliflower or broccoli flowerettes, small whole mushrooms (or large mushrooms, sliced), green beans, celery or green onions (scallions) sliced on the diagonal. More specifics are given in Turbot Tempura, page 279.

DEEP-FRIED FISH STEAKS OR FILLETS
IN UNMIXED BATTER

Cut each fillet or steak into pieces if necessary for easy handling. Follow recipe for Fish Steaks or Fillets Fried in Batter, page 249 in pan-frying section, and fry in deep fat according to instructions on page 271.

SHELLFISH DEEP-FRIED IN UNMIXED BATTER

Follow recipes for preparing clams, mussels, oysters, shrimp, scallops and soft-shell crab in a batter for pan-frying. Then deep-fry them according to instructions on page 271.

FRUIT FRITTERS FROM LEFTOVER BATTER

If you run out of fish before you run out of the mixed batter you've been dipping it in, don't throw the remnant of batter away. Instead, stir in a bit of chopped apple, banana, canned peach, pineapple or cooked prune (wipe off any moisture first) and drop by the spoonful into the hot oil. When golden brown, serve along with the deep fried fish. If batter is too runny to make a fritter that holds together, add a bit of flour (about 1 teaspoon to ¼ cup of batter) and mix in well. You can also add a pinch or two of baking powder if there's none in the original batter.

FISH IN BEER BATTER

1 *pound fillets from lean white fish, fresh or frozen, salt or freshwater, cut in small serving pieces*
2 *egg whites from very fresh, very clean eggs with uncracked shells*
¼ *teaspoon salt*
1¼ *cups flour*
½ *cup beer*
Vegetable oil for deep frying
Sauce of your choice

Defrost fish if frozen. Beat egg whites until stiff. Add salt to flour and sift together in a large mixing bowl; gradually stir in beer and fold in beaten egg whites. Cover bowl with lintfree towel and let stand at room temperature for 2 hours. Heat vegetable oil in deep-fryer to from 360 degrees to 370 degrees. Coat fish with the batter, a few pieces at a time, place in a frying basket, lower into the hot oil and cook 6–8 minutes or until golden brown. Serve at once with sauce of your choice, or plain if you prefer.
Serves 2–4.

CATFISH HANNIBAL

(As We Had It at the Mark Twain Hotel in Hannibal, Missouri)

(What more could two Tom Sawyer and Huck Finn fans ask for than to eat catfish in Mark Twain's hometown overlooking the Mississippi River? And no greater disappointment could they suffer than to discover that the catfish now served at the Mark Twain Hotel in Hannibal must be brought in from distant catfish farms because the waters of the mighty

Mississippi are polluted. Following is the recipe as prepared for us by Mrs. Betty Inlow, chef at the Mark Twain Hotel. The commercially bred catfish, incidentally, was much sweeter and entirely without the muddy flavor of wild catfish we had eaten elsewhere before.)

> 4 *to* 6 1-*pound catfish, dressed with tail left on*
> 1 *egg, beaten*
> 1 *cup milk*
> 1 *cup cornmeal*
> *Cooking oil for deep-frying*
> *Salt and pepper to taste*
> *Lemon wedges*

Mix beaten egg and milk together. Dip catfish in the mixture, coat with cornmeal and fry in deep fat until flakes separate easily when gently probed with tines of a fork. Serve with lemon wedges and let diners add salt and pepper to taste.

Serves 4–6.

CLAM FRITTERS   (I)

> 1 *pint clams, drained and chopped, then drained again on lintfree or absorbent paper towels*
> 2 *teaspoons baking powder*
> ⅛ *teaspoon nutmeg*
> 1 *teaspoon salt*
> 1 *teaspoon finely crumbled freeze-dried shallots (or garlic powder to taste)*
> 2 *cups flour*
> 2 *eggs, beaten*
> 1 *teaspoon grated celery*
> 1 *tablespoon melted butter or margarine*
> ½ *cup milk*
> ½ *cup clam liquid drained from clams*

Mix baking powder, nutmeg, salt and crumbled shallots into flour, then sift together. Mix beaten eggs, grated celery and melted butter or margarine with milk and clam liquid. Add to flour mixture, stir, add clams and stir again. Drop by the teaspoonful into deep oil and fry at 355 degrees to 365 degrees for about 3 minutes or until golden color. Drain on absorbent paper and serve at once while crisp and hot, plain or with a dip or sauce.

Serves 6.

OYSTER FRITTERS: Prepare in same way as Clam Fritters.

MUSSEL FRITTERS: Prepare in same way as Clam Fritters.

LOBSTER OR CRAB FRITTERS: Chop raw or cooked meat and prepare in same way as Clam Fritters. Substitute milk for ½ cup clam liquid.

SHRIMP FRITTERS: Peel, devein and chop raw shrimp or use chopped cooked or canned shrimp and prepare in same way as Clam Fritters. Substitute milk for ½ cup clam liquid.

SCALLOP FRITTERS: Chop cooked or raw scallops and prepare in same way as Clam Fritters. Substitute milk for ½ cup of clam liquid.

LEFTOVER FISH FRITTERS: Chop cooked lean or intermediate fish (remove all bones) and prepare in same way as Clam Fritters. Substitute milk or fish broth for ½ cup of clam liquid.

CRAB CAKES

1 *pound cooked crab meat, ground or chopped*
1 *tablespoon butter or margarine*
2 *tablespoons minced onion*
½ *cup soft breadcrumbs*
1 *teaspoon dry mustard powder*
1 *teaspoon Worcestershire sauce*
1 *egg, beaten*
Salt to taste
Paprika to taste
1 *egg, beaten, for batter coating*
½ *cup toasted breadcrumbs*
Oil for deep frying

Melt butter or margarine, add minced onion and lightly cook. Add to next 6 ingredients, including crab meat, mix well and form into balls 1 to 1½ inches in diameter. If mixture is too dry to hold together well, add a little milk. Dip cakes into beaten egg, coat with toasted breadcrumbs, let dry for about 5 minutes and fry in deep fat at 360 degrees to 370 degrees until nicely browned. Drain on absorbent paper and serve at once.

Serves 4–6.

FISH CAKES: Substitute cooked fish meat (such as cod) for crab and prepare and cook in the same way as Crab Cakes.

LOBSTER CAKES: Substitute lobster meat for crab.

POLLOCK PUFFS

½ *pound ¾-inch-thick pollock fillets, or fillets from any fresh or*
saltwater fish, fresh or frozen, cut into portions approximately
2 by 2 inches
Cooking oil for deep frying
Batter:
½ *of one beaten egg*
Juice of 1 lemon

¼ *cup water*
½ *cup flour*
½ *teaspoon baking powder*
¼ *teaspoon garlic salt*

Defrost fish if frozen. Combine egg, lemon juice and water. Mix flour, baking powder and garlic salt together and stir into egg mixture. Coat fish with this batter and deep-fry until golden brown. See instructions page 271. Drain on absorbent paper towels and serve at once.
Serves 2.

SCALLOPS FRIED IN LEMON BATTER

¾ *pound scallops, fresh or frozen*
½ *teaspoon salt or to taste*
Dash of white pepper or to taste
1 *teaspoon baking powder*
1 *cup flour*
1 *egg, lightly beaten*
⅝ *cup water*
2 *tablespoons lemon juice*
Oil for deep-frying

Thaw scallops if frozen, remove any shell particles, wash and dry. Season with salt and pepper. Stir baking powder into flour. Thoroughly mix together beaten egg, water and lemon juice, and gradually stir in flour mixture. Coat scallops with mixture, place in a basket in a single layer and fry in deep oil at 360 degrees to 370 degrees until golden brown. Drain on absorbent paper and serve.
Serves 4–6.

FRITTERS FROM LEFTOVER BATTER:
½ *cup leftover lemon batter*
1 *tablespoon flour*
½ *cup chopped canned pineapple, drained, or other chopped fruit*

Mix ingredients together, drop by rounded teaspoonfuls into hot oil and cook until golden brown. Serve with scallop fritters.

SWEET AND SOUR SEA BASS   (I)

(Tim Seun Sea Bass°)

1 *fresh sea bass, about 1½ to 2 pounds (or any fresh, same-sized fish)*
1 *egg, beaten*

*From *The Hong Kong Cookbook,* by Arthur Lem and Dan Morris (Funk & Wagnalls).

5 *tablespoons all-purpose flour*
1 *tablespoon melted lard*
2 *tablespoons cornstarch*
2 *tablespoons water*
½ *teaspoon salt*
1 *tablespoon baking powder*
2 *quarts peanut or corn oil*
Utensil: wok or deep-fryer

Clean fish inside and out, leaving head intact. With damp lintfree towel, pat dry and set aside. Combine egg, flour, lard, cornstarch, water, salt and baking powder, and stir into a smooth batter. Add oil to utensil and heat to 375 degrees. While it's heating, dip fish into batter mixture and coat thoroughly, then lower into preheated oil and deep-fry until golden brown. The fish should flake easily when tested with a fork. Start the fork test at about 6 minutes, probing gently with tines at thickest part of fish. Transfer to warm platter and store in warm oven while preparing sweet and sour sauce as follows.

SWEET AND SOUR SAUCE:
2 *tablespoons bamboo shoots*
1 *green pepper*
1 *carrot*
1 *red pepper*
1 *tablespoon oil*
1 *clove garlic, minced*
2 *slices gingerroot*
12 *canned pineapple chunks, including liquid*
1 *fresh tomato, diced*
½ *cup vinegar*
½ *cup sugar*
½ *cup water*
½ *cup catsup*
1 *tablespoon dark soy sauce*
½ *cup pineapple juice*
1 *small onion, diced*
1 *tablespoon cornstarch dissolved in 1 tablespoon water*
Shredded lettuce
Maraschino cherries
Chinese parsley
Utensil: wok or deep-fryer

Shred first 4 ingredients, place in utensil, add water barely to cover and boil for 2 minutes. Rinse immediately in cold water to halt cooking process. Set aside.

Wash utensil thoroughly, heat oil to a sizzle, add garlic and ginger, and sauté to a light golden brown. Add peppers, carrot and bamboo shoots and all other ingredients except cornstarch mixture, and boil for 1 minute. Now add cornstarch mixture gradually, stirring until sauce thickens. Pour immeditely over fish. Garnish with shredded lettuce, Maraschino cherries and Chinese parsley.

Serves 2–4.

NOTE: This sauce is also nice over a simmered, poached or steamed fish.

BUTTERFLY SHRIMP

1 *pound jumbo raw shrimp, shelled and deveined, with tails left on*
1 *large egg, beaten*
Juice of 1 lemon
½ *cup water*
2 *teaspoons baking powder*
Salt and pepper to taste
1 *cup flour*

Combine beaten egg, lemon juice and water. Mix baking powder and salt and pepper to taste into flour and stir into egg mixture. Continue stirring just until mixture is blended. With a sharp knife, split shrimp lengthwise down the back, stopping just before cutting through at the tail. Press out flat in shape of butterfly, dip in batter and fry (do not crowd) in deep fat between 355 degrees and 365 degrees. Fry 2–4 minutes or until batter is golden brown and shrimp is cooked. Drain on absorbent paper towels and serve at once.

Serves 4–6.

ARTHUR LEM'S CRISPY FRIED SQUID (I)
(Soo Jow Yaw Yu)

3 *cups fresh squid prepared for cooking*
2 *cups flour*
½ *cup cornstarch*
5 *teaspoons baking powder*
1½ *cups water*
2 *tablespoons cooking oil*
2 *quarts oil for deep-frying*
Lettuce

Slice squid body into ¼-inch-wide circles, tentacles into small pieces. Stir flour, cornstarch and baking powder together until well mixed.

Drizzle into water, stirring until thoroughly mixed and smooth. Stir in 2 tablespoons oil. Heat 2 quarts oil in deep-fryer to from 360 degrees to 375 degrees. Dip circles and pieces of squid tentacle into batter and drop into hot fat. As soon as they float to the top, they are done. Serve on bed of lettuce. Serves 4 as a meal, or makes appetizers for 12.

TURBOT IN BEER BATTER (I)

½ pound turbot fillets, or other lean fish, salt or freshwater, fresh or frozen, ¾ to 1 inch thick
Oil for deep-frying
Batter:
½ cup flour
⅛ teaspoon dried tarragon or other seasoning
½ cup beer

Defrost fish if frozen and cut into 1-inch squares. Combine flour and tarragon in a mixing bowl. Add beer slowly, stirring as you add, and continuing to stir until batter is well-blended. Coat fish with batter and deep-fry, following instructions on page 271. Remove fish from oil and spread on absorbent paper towels to drain.

Serves 2.

TURBOT TEMPURA: Prepare fish as in preceding recipe but double the quantity of batter. Add the following vegetables to recipe ingredients:

½ cup small raw broccoli flowerettes, no more than 1 inch across top of flower
½ cup small raw cauliflower flowerettes, no more than 1 inch across top of flower
¼ cup small raw mushrooms, or large ones, sliced
1 recipe Tempura Sauce, page 151

Prepare vegetables 1 or 2 hours before cooking. Pat dry after washing and place in colander or spread out on a towel so every last bit of moisture will evaporate. Then arrange attractively on a bright-colored platter or shallow bowl. While fish is frying, mix vegetables into remaining batter. Remove cooked fish from fryer, spread out on double layer of paper toweling, cover with a third layer and allow to drain. Place vegetables in frying basket, in a single layer and not touching, and deep-fry at 365 degrees just long enough to brown lightly. Shake frying basket or use spoon to keep pieces separated. Remove from basket, drain on absorbent toweling and serve with the fish. Divide Tempura Sauce into small individual bowls and use as a dip for fish and vegetables or substitute another sauce of your choice.

11

Baking

There are no general instructions that we can give you concerning the cooking of fish in the oven of your stove. Just look at the size of this section and you'll know why.

You can cook any kind of fin fish or shellfish in the oven. Fresh or frozen. You can cook them in any size, shape and form: dressed, split, fillets, steaks, chunks, sticks, in shell or out of shell. You can add to them any sauce that you like. You can use virtually every recipe that follows as a guide to creating a recipe of your own.

So, rather than burden you with a lot of reading here that may or may not be pertinent to the recipe you're going to prepare, we refer you to the instructions in the recipe itself or in the introduction to the section from which the recipe comes. You won't go wrong, provided you abide by the one general rulé that we've by now probably stated a thousand times: test fish for doneness with a fork, usually beginning at half the given recipe time. When the flesh flakes easily when gently probed with the tines, the fish is done. If topping isn't as brown as you'd like when fish is almost done, run dish under broiler for a minute or two. See page 225.

Don't worry about how often you open the oven door. A fish is not a cake. It will not fall.

FILLETS, STEAKS, STICKS AND WHOLE FISH
Baked in Elegant and Easy Sauces

FILLETS, STEAKS AND STICKS

Wash fish by dipping in cold water to which a little salt or lemon juice has been added and dry. Then follow the instructions given in each recipe.

FILLETS, STEAKS OR STICKS
IN EASY MELTED BUTTER SAUCE

*1½ to 2 pounds any lean or intermediate fillets, steaks or sticks,
    freshwater or salt, fresh or frozen*
*1 recipe of any of the Easy Butter (or Margarine) Sauces, beginning
    on page 136*

Defrost fish if frozen. Arrange fillets or steaks in single layer in shallow
baking pan and spread sauce evenly over the top. (If fillets are very thin—
¼ inch or so—make a double layer but spread sauce over bottom as
well as top layer.) Bake 10–15 minutes in oven preheated to 375 degrees,
basting several times with sauce in pan, or until fish flakes easily when
gently probed with fork tines. Serve at once, spooning any sauce that
may be left in pan over fish.
   Serves 6–8.

FILLETS DE LUXE

2 pounds delicately flavored fillets, freshwater or salt, fresh or frozen
1 recipe Mushroom Sauce, page 130
1 tablespoon sherry wine
½ cup slivered, roasted blanched almonds
Chopped black olives
Grated yellow cheese

Defrost fillets if frozen. Spread over bottom of well-greased baking pan.
Combine next 3 ingredients, mix well and spread over tops of fillets. Bake
in oven preheated to 375 degrees 10–20 minutes or until fish flakes easily
when gently probed with tines of a fork. Make sunburst design on top of
sauce by alternating lines of chopped olives and grated yellow cheese.
   Serves 6–8.
   VARIATION: Substitute Oyster Sauce, page 130, for Mushroom Sauce.

FILLETS WITH WINE AND GRAPES   (I)

*1 pound delicately flavored fish fillets, skinless, freshwater or salt,
    fresh or frozen*
½ pound seedless grapes
¾ cup white wine
¼ cup water
Salt and pepper to taste

Defrost fish if frozen. Wash grapes and cut each one in half. Spread the
grape halves over the bottom of a shallow baking pan and top with the

fillets. Combine wine and water and pour over the fillets. Bake in an oven preheated to 375 degrees, basting several times with the wine and water mixture, 10–20 minutes or until flakes separate easily when tested with fork. Remove to preheated serving platter and pour grape and wine sauce over the top.

Serves 2–4.

SHERRIED STEAKS

>4 *large fish steaks, fresh or frozen, freshwater or salt*
>4 *tablespoons lemon juice*
>1 *cup cocktail sherry*
>¼ *cup melted butter or margarine*
>*Salt and pepper to taste*
>¼ *teaspoon garlic powder*

Defrost fish steaks if frozen. Place in well-greased baking dish in a single layer. Combine remaining ingredients and pour over them. Bake in preheated 375-degree oven 10–20 minutes or until flakes separate easily when tested with tines of a fork.

Serves 4–6.

RED SNAPPER FILLETS IN CHAMPAGNE SAUCE

>1–1½ *pounds red snapper or any other delicately flavored fillet, skinned, freshwater or salt, fresh or frozen*
>1 *3-ounce package cream cheese*
>1 *teaspoon grated blue cheese*
>1 *tablespoon minced shallots or mild onion*
>1 *tablespoon chopped canned pimento*
>1 *cup champagne*
>1 *black olive, cut in 4 slices*
>20 *slivers of canned pimento*
>*Lemon wedges*
>*Parsley*

Defrost fish if frozen. Cut into 8 pieces. Combine cream cheese, grated blue cheese, minced shallots and chopped pimento, and mash together into a paste. Add enough of the champagne to make consistency of a spread and use to cover 4 fillet pieces. Top with remaining pieces of fillet. Place fillet sandwiches in a well-greased baking pan in single layer and pour remaining champagne over and around them. Bake in oven preheated to 375 degrees 15–20 minutes or until fish flakes separate easily when gently probed with tines of a fork. Remove to heated serving platter, place black olive slice in center of each fillet sandwich and circle with 5 pimento slices. Garnish side of dish with lemon wedges and parsley. Serve at once, passing champagne sauce separately in small bowl or gravy boat.

Serves 4.

WHOLE (DRESSED) FISH

Any size whole fish can successfully be baked, even the little smelt. Recipes, with or without a sauce, will be found on the following few pages. Recipes for stuffed fish (2 pounds and over) start on page 288.

· Whether you've caught it or bought it, now is the time to clean your fish more thoroughly. Complete the chore by dipping the fish in cold tap water to which a small amount of salt or lemon juice has been added. Then pat the fish dry inside and out with lintfree or absorbent paper towel.

· If there's room enough in your oven and if you don't need the head for making a broth or such, leave it on the fish. Its being there will seal in the juices, thereby improving the flavor.

· If you so mind, rub the fish cavity with salt.

· No matter what anyone tells you, do not slash a fish before baking it. All that will do is allow juices and flavor to escape.

· Place the fish on a well-greased baking pan.

· Brush the fish inside and out with melted butter or margarine, salad oil, sour cream, white wine or one of the butter or spicy red sauces in this book's sauce section. Or try marinating your fish in one of the marinades.

· Bake in a preheated, moderate 350- to 375-degree oven, or according to recipe.

· Very important this point: timing. Therefore you should know the thickness of the fish at its thickest part. As a rough timing guide, figure on its baking 15 minutes to every inch of thickness. If you've added a sauce, also calculate its amount; also add or subtract seconds or minutes depending on whether the sauce was hot or cold. If you've stuffed your fish, allow for that too.

What all of the preceding paragraph adds up to is this: the fork test now looms larger than ever as the best possible timing device. Probe the cooking fish as often as you like, starting at 7 minutes for each inch of thickness. When the flesh flakes easily, take the fish out of the oven.

CHUNK OF FISH

Prepare and bake a chunk or chunks of fish in the same way as whole dressed fish.

FISH MEDITERRANEAN IN FOIL PACKAGES   (O)

> 4 *dressed fish, about ¾ pound each, freshwater or salt*
> 1 *tablespoon butter or margarine*
> 1 *tablespoon lemon juice*
> 2 *tablespoons olive oil*
> 1 *tablespoon white wine*
> *Salt and pepper to taste*
> 4 *slices large red Spanish onions*
> 4 *thick slices firm ripe tomatoes*
> 4 *lemon slices*

Cut 4 pieces of foil large enough to wrap each fish separately and grease each piece in center of one side with butter or margarine. Combine lemon juice, olive oil, white wine and salt and pepper to taste, and rub over outside and inside of the cavity of each fish. Lay 1 fish in center of each greased piece of aluminum foil. Separate rings of onion slices and spread over the fish. Lay a tomato slice on each fish, top with a lemon slice and divide remaining olive-oil mixture over it all. Form the aluminum foil into 4 packages, double-folding each at the two ends and lengthwise over the top. Place in a shallow baking pan and bake in oven preheated to 375 degrees 12–18 minutes (depending on thickness of fish) before opening one of the packets to test fish for doneness with tines of fork. When flakes separate easily, serve 1 fish, in its foil package, to each person.
Serves 4.

FLAT FISH FANDANGO

> 4 *pounds small flat fish, dressed, freshwater or salt*
> ½ *cup white wine*
> ½ *cup scuppernong or muscatel wine*
> 2 *tablespoons olive oil*
> 2 *tablespoons soft butter or margarine*
> 3 *medium onions, sliced*
> 1 *clove garlic, minced*
> *Salt and pepper to taste*
> 4 *medium-size ripe tomatoes, sliced*

Combine the 2 wines in glass or nonporous ceramic dish and marinate fish in the mixture for at least 2 hours. Spread olive oil and butter or margarine over bottom of large, shallow baking pan and cover with onions and garlic. Place in oven preheated to 450 degrees and cook for 10 minutes or until onions brown slightly on bottom. Turn onions and garlic and top with fish. Sprinkle with salt and pepper. Spread tomatoes over fish, pour wine in which they marinated over all and bake in 375-degree oven 10–20 minutes or until fish flakes easily when gently probed with tines of a fork.

Serves 4–6.

PLANKED FISH (O)
A Thing of Beauty

1 *4-pound dressed fish, head and tail reserved, freshwater or salt*
1 *recipe variation of your choice of Basic Red Sauce, page 144*
1 *or 2 recipes (depending on how much gravy you like) Fish Broth Sauce, page 120, made with head and tail of the dressed fish*
3 *or 4 large carrots, cut into sticks*
1 *lemon, thinly sliced*
¼ *cup melted butter or margarine*
1 *10½-ounce package frozen peas*
Instant mashed potatoes for 6–8
Tomato wedges
Parsley sprigs

Rub fish, inside and out, with Basic Red Sauce. Place in a glass or non-porous ceramic dish, pour any remaining sauce over it and marinate fish in refrigerator for at least 1 hour. Prepare broth from head and tail so it will be ready to complete the Fish Broth Sauce just before fish has finished baking.

Put carrots on to boil. Oil a hardwood plank and place in a cold oven so it will heat thoroughly as you preheat oven to 400 degrees. Remove fish from marinade, lay at an angle across the plank, arrange lemon slices in a row on top of the fish and place in the preheated oven. Combine 2 tablespoons of the melted butter with remaining Basic Red Sauce, heat and use to baste fish as it bakes.

Put frozen peas on to cook, finish making Fish Broth Sauce and keep it warm in top of double boiler over slowly simmering water, then prepare instant mashed potatoes. Bake fish 15 minutes for each inch of thickness, or until flakes separate easily when gently probed with tines of a fork. Remove fish from oven and quickly arrange the other foods attractively around it on the hot plank. First a border of mashed potatoes around the fish, but not too close to it, because in between the fish and poatoes is where the bright green peas go. Place the carrot sticks in a splash of orange color anywhere there's space outside the potatoes and finish the decorating by arranging the parsley sprigs and tomato wedges where they look best. Drizzle remaining melted butter over the potatoes and, if everything isn't still nice and hot, run under the broiler for 2 or

3 minutes. Put your masterpiece on the table and serve hot Fish Broth Sauce in a gravy boat.

Serves 4–6.

PLANKED FISH SERVED OUTDOORS: If a camp oven is part of your outdoor equipment, a plank you can both bake and serve an entire meal on can come in mighty handy.

SMELT ITALIAN STYLE

(This recipe, which is a very pretty way to serve those very tasty little smelts, came to us from the U.S. Department of the Interior.)

    2 *pounds dressed smelt*
    2 *cups sliced onion*
    2 *cloves garlic, minced*
    ¼ *cup melted fat or oil*
    1 *1-pound 12-ounce can Italian tomatoes, undrained*
    1 *6-ounce can tomato paste*
    1½ *teaspoons oregano*
    1½ *teaspoons salt or to taste*
    1 *teaspoon sugar*
    ¼ *teaspoon pepper*
    ¼ *cup chopped parsley*
    1 *cup shredded mozzarella cheese*
    ¼ *cup shredded Parmesan cheese*

Cook onion and garlic in melted fat or oil until onion is tender. Add tomatoes, tomato paste, oregano, 1 teaspoon salt, sugar, and pepper; mix well. Cover and cook slowly, about 30 minutes, until slightly thickened and flavors blend; stir often during cooking. Stir in parsley. Spread sauce over bottom of 2- or 3-quart shallow, rectangular baking-serving dish. Arrange smelt in a single layer on sauce down the center of baking dish. Sprinkle remaining ½ teaspoon salt and cheeses across the middle only of the little fish so the upper and tail end can be seen against a background of red tomato sauce. Bake in a hot oven, 400 degrees, 15–20 minutes or until fish flakes easily when tested with a fork.

Serves 6.

BAKED WHITING WITH VEGETABLES

    1 *box frozen dressed whiting, about 1 pound 8 ounces, tails on, heads off, or any whole or chunked fish about 1½ to 2 inches thick, fresh or frozen, salt or freshwater*
    Salt and pepper to taste
    1 *1-pound can stewed tomatoes, heated*

1 *medium green pepper, parboiled about 5 minutes or until just beginning to turn soft, then sliced*
1 *large stalk celery, sliced*
1 *medium onion, sliced*
2 *tablespoons butter or margarine, melted*
1 *teaspoon lemon juice*

Defrost fish if frozen. Salt and pepper inside and out. Spread stewed tomatoes over bottom of well-greased baking dish. Cover with the green pepper slices, top them with the celery and onion. Arrange fish in a single layer over the vegetables. Bake in a preheated 350-degree oven for 25 to 35 minutes. Mix melted butter or margarine with lemon juice and brush tops of cooking fish several times with the mixture. Serve as soon as fish flakes easily when gently probed with a fork and while vegetables are delightfully crunchy. (If you don't like crunchy vegetables, sauté onions and celery lightly before adding to baking dish.)

Vegetables can be served in a ramekin over rice or mashed potatoes. Serve fish on its own plate because whiting is rather bony and therefore easier to eat if not mixed in with other foods.

Serves 4.

CHILLED WHOLE WHITING: Refrigerate leftover whole whiting and serve cold the next day for lunch. It's delicious cold and much easier to remove from the bones than when served hot.

12

Stuffings, Stuffed Whole Fish, Stuffed Fillets and Steaks

A stuffing can do two mighty important things for a fish or any part thereof, so pay heed.

1. It can transform what might sometimes be a rather drab dish into an epicurean delight.

2. It can stretch an otherwise expensive recipe for, let's say, 2 people into an inexpensive recipe for, let's say, 4 people, particularly so if you've chosen a hard-to-get and therefore costly fin fish or shellfish.

STUFFED WHOLE (DRESSED) FISH

The size of the cavity that is to be stuffed will vary greatly from fish to fish even though the overall weight might be the same. It all depends on the shape of the fish. Is it short and flat? Is it long and round? If the latter, just stuff the opening that's left after the fish is cleaned with the stuffing of your choice. If the former, there will not be much of a cavity after the cleaning, so do this:

· Using a sharp knife, make a long slit along the length of the spine, cutting on the thickest side of the fish; often this also will be the darkest side of the fish.

· Now, by cutting away from the spine and toward both outer edges of the fish, carefully separate the flesh from the rib bones. Thus you will create a pocket with two flaps that will work somewhat like a double door.

· Fill that pocket with stuffing, as much of it as you like. In fact, you can smother the fish in the stuffing. But if you don't so do, skewer the two "doors" shut and lace them together with string.

STUFFED FILLETS AND STEAKS

Very simple. Just take the stuffing of your choice and sandwich it between layers of fillets or steaks. Then, if you like, top it all with more of the stuffing.

Or, if you want a dish that looks different but tastes just about the same, spread the stuffing on a thin fillet, first slicing the fillet in half lengthwise if it's more than 2 inches wide, then roll it up as though you were going to bake a jelly-roll cake. You can keep the fillet roll intact with either a slice of bacon, wooden picks or skewers.

For the rolls that not only will look different but also will taste considerably different, instead of a bread or rice or mushroom or whatever stuffing, wrap the fillet around asparagus, pickles or another kind of fin fish or shellfish. A bit of salmon or any fish with a distinctive flavor makes a delightful stuffing for a flounder, sole or any sweet-tasting freshwater fillet. Or, instead of the salmon *et al,* stuff a clam, an oyster, a crawdad or any other shellfish inside the fillet.

WHAT MAKES A STUFFING

We give you some representative recipes in the pages that follow. But, really, that's all they are—representative—because other things that you wish to put into a stuffing for fish will be equally okay.

Flaked fin fish or chopped shellfish are excellent additions to fish stuffings. So are vegetables, nuts, fruit or cheese.

Our advice to you, then, is this: let your imagination be your guide. Slightly tempered, natch, with a bit of common sense.

BREAD STUFFING

> 6 *tablespoons butter or margarine*
> ½ *cup diced celery*
> ¼ *cup diced shallots or mild-flavored onions*
> ¼ *teaspoon dried thyme*
> ⅛ *teaspoon dried sage (optional)*
> ⅛ *teaspoon garlic powder (optional)*
> *Salt and pepper to taste*
> 4 *cups of crumbs made by crumbling or grating 1- or 2-day-old*
>   *bread (all white or part white, part whole grain)*
> 1 *to* 3 *tablespoons fish fumet or chicken broth*

Melt butter or margarine in large, heavy skillet or pot. Add celery and onion and cook for a few minutes on medium heat, stirring frequently, until vegetables start to soften. Stir in seasonings. Add breadcrumbs and continue to stir until all ingredients are well mixed. Stir in just enough of the fish fumet or chicken broth to give mixture good consistency for stuffing. Makes about 3 cups. Use to stuff 4- to 6-pound dressed fish.

OYSTER STUFFING: Follow recipe for Bread Stuffing but add ½ to 1 pint shucked raw oysters, chopped and drained. Substitute oyster liquid for fish fumet in Bread Stuffing.

SHRIMP STUFFING: Follow recipe for Bread Stuffing but add ¼ to ½ pound raw shrimp that has been shelled, deveined, washed and chopped.

ROE STUFFING: Follow recipe for bread stuffing but add ¼ to ½ pound cooked, mashed roe (see page 259).

APPLE-LEMON–SOUR CREAM STUFFING   (I)

1 *tablespoon butter or margarine*
1 *tablespoon cooking oil*
¼ *cup chopped onion*
¼ *cup chopped celery*
½ *cup chopped red apple, skin on*
2½ *cups soft breadcrumbs*
½ *teaspoon salt or to taste*
¼ *teaspoon paprika*
2 *teaspoons grated lemon rind*
¼ *cup sour cream*

In a large, heavy skillet or pot, heat butter or margarine and cooking oil to sizzling hot but not smoking. Add chopped onion and celery, and lightly sauté. Stir in chopped apple and breadcrumbs. Mix salt, paprika and grated lemon rind together, stir into sour cream and add to breadcrumb mixture. Mix well and use to stuff a 2- to 4-pound fish. Makes 2 cups.

BAKED STUFFED FISH

With or Without Stuffed Tomatoes or Bacon Rolls

4- *to 6-pound dressed fish, freshwater or salt, head and tail left on*
1 *recipe Bread, Oyster or Shrimp Stuffing, page 289*
1 *recipe of your choice from Easy Butter Sauces, starting on page 136*

Stuff fish loosely, run skewers through both sides of opening and lace with string. Any extra stuffing can be used to fill fresh tomatoes and baked along with the fish in the same dish or rolled into balls and wrapped in bacon. Use tomatoes or bacon-wrapped balls to garnish serving platter. Bake fish approximately 15 minutes per inch of thickness in an oven preheated to 375 degrees. Baste several times with Easy Butter Sauce of your choice. Fish is done when flakes separate easily when gently probed with tines of fork. Remove to preheated serving platter, garnish with lemon wedges and parsley, and pour juices from baking dish over it.

Serves 6–8.

BAKED STUFFED FISH CHUNK: Prepare and cook in same manner as preceding recipe.

FLAT FISH STUFFED WITH CRAB AND SHRIMP

1 *2–2½-pound flat fish, dressed, with head and tail left on and pocket cut for stuffing, see page 288*
1 *cup cooked or canned flaked crab meat with all cartilage carefully removed*
¼ *cup cooked shrimp, peeled, deveined and broken into pieces*
Salt and pepper to taste
2 *tablespoons melted butter or margarine*
3 *tablespoons light cocktail sherry*
1 *pinch paprika or to taste*

Rub fish inside and out with salt and pepper to taste. Mix crab meat and shrimp together, stuff into pocket cut in flat fish, skewer shut and lace with string. Place fish in a shallow, well-greased baking dish. Combine remaining ingredients, mix well and pour over the fish. Cook in oven preheated to 350 degrees, basting several times with the sauce in dish, for 15 minutes or until thickest part of fish flakes when gently probed with tines of fork.

Serves 2–4.

STRIPED BASS SMOTHERED IN WILD RICE AND MUSHROOMS

4- *to 6-pound striped bass or other fish, freshwater or salt, cleaned for stuffing, head and tail intact*
4 *tablespoons butter or margarine*
Salt to taste
1½ *cups sliced fresh mushrooms*
1 *large stalk sliced celery*
1 *large onion, sliced*
1 *pinch garlic powder*
1 *pinch sage*
1 *10½-ounce can condensed cream of mushroom soup, diluted with ¼ cup milk or cream*

¾ cup wild rice, cooked according to package instructions
¾ cup white rice, cooked according to package instructions
4 to 6 lemon wedges

Rub bass inside and out with butter or margarine and sprinkle with salt. Sauté mushrooms, celery and onion slices together in large skillet. Season with garlic powder and sage, and stir in mushroom soup, wild and white rice and heat. Place bass in a well-greased baking dish, fill cavity with some of hot rice and mushroom mixture and spread what remains around fish, leaving head and tail uncovered. Bake in preheated 375-degree oven 30–40 minutes, depending on size of fish, or until flakes separate easily when gently tested with a fork. Spread a little butter or margarine on top of rice for last 10 minutes of cooking time. Garnish with lemon wedges.

Serves 6–8.

FISH CHUNK SMOTHERED IN WILD RICE AND MUSHROOMS: Prepare in same way as preceding recipe.

BRAISED STUFFED SQUID (I)

4 small squid about ¼ pound each, cleaned without cutting open
* body, see page 81, and tentacles chopped in ½-inch pieces*
1½ cups water
½ teaspoon Shrimp Spice or to taste (optional)
½ cup Chianti wine
3 tablespoons olive oil
2 tablespoons cooking oil
2 medium onions, finely minced
2 cloves garlic, finely minced
2 large stalks celery, chopped
1 to 1½ cups crumbs made by grating good-quality stale white
* bread or rolls*
1 8-ounce can tomato sauce
2 tablespoons grated Parmesan cheese
4 generous pinches cayenne pepper or to taste
¼ teaspoon powdered rosemary

Combine water, Shrimp Spice and wine in small saucepan and boil 5–10 minutes, depending on how spicy you want the sauce to be. Strain, discard spice and reheat liquid. Add chopped squid tentacles and simmer for 10 minutes. Remove chopped tentacles with a slotted spoon and set aside. If necessary, boil further to reduce to or add water to make 1½ cups. Set aside.

Heat oils in heavy pot or skillet. Add onion, garlic and celery, and lightly sauté. Add breadcrumbs and cook, stirring frequently, for 3 or 4 minutes or until lightly browned. Add tomato sauce, reserved chopped tentacles, Parmesan cheese, cayenne pepper and rosemary, and stir well. Divide mixture into cavities of squid bodies. Lightly grease a shallow baking pan with olive oil. Lay the squid in it (there shouldn't be much bare margin left around them) and pour reserved broth over and around the squid. Cover pan and bake for 40 minutes in oven preheated to 375 degrees or until squid is tender and sauce a nice consistency.

NOTE: You can skewer squid closed with toothpicks if you like, in which case they should only be stuffed half full. Place extra stuffing around or over squid and pour broth mixture over it.

VARIATION: Cut squid bodies open when cleaning and arrange in baking pan sandwich style with stuffing between 2 layers and broth mixture poured over the top.

COLD STUFFED SQUID APPETIZER: Skewer stuffed squid closed before baking (see note above). Chill any that are left over, slice and serve as appetizers.

STUFFED FISH ROLLS

2 *pounds fish fillets, skinned and less than* ½ *inch thick, salt or freshwater, fresh or frozen*
¼ *cup melted butter or margarine*
1½ *cups Bread Stuffing, page 289*
4 *slices of bacon, lightly fried and chopped*
2–4 *tablespoons finely chopped fresh raw spinach or basil*
1 *tablespoon lemon juice*

Defrost fillets if frozen and cut in half lengthwise. Brush 1 tablespoon of melted butter or margarine over one side of fillets, divide stuffing mixture over them and spread out as you would a sandwich filling. Sprinkle with chopped bacon and chopped spinach or basil. Roll each fillet half (stuffing side in), fasten with wooden toothpicks if necessary, and place close together in a well-greased casserole. Add lemon juice to remaining melted butter and brush over rolled fillets. Bake in oven preheated to 375 degrees 25–35 minutes or until fish flakes when gently probed with tines of fork. Serves 6–8.

STUFFED FISH ROLLS WITH MUSHROOM CAPS: In butter or margarine lightly sauté the same number of large mushroom caps as you have fillets in preceding recipe. Place a sautéed mushroom cap atop each fillet roll before placing casserole in oven. You can finely chop the mushroom stems and add to bread stuffing before it is spread over the fillets.

FLOUNDER, CAVIAR AND WINE

2 pounds flounder fillets, skinned, or other delicately flavored, lean
fillets, freshwater or salt, fresh or frozen
2 tablespoons caviar
2 tablespoons anchovy paste
¾ cup sherry wine
¼ cup water
¼ cup dry breadcrumbs
2 tablespoons butter

Defrost fish if frozen. Cut in half lengthwise. Mix caviar and anchovy paste together and spread a thin layer on one side of fillet strips. Roll strips and fasten with wooden picks. Pack closely together in a well-greased casserole. Mix wine with water and pour around fillets. Top with dry breadcrumbs, dot with butter and bake in 375-degree preheated oven for 25 to 35 minutes or until fish flakes easily when tested with fork.
Serves 6–8.

FLOUNDER, CAVIAR AND WINE HORS D'OEUVRES: Remove rolls that are nicely shaped and refrigerate to serve as cold hors d'oeuvres the next day.

FLOUNDER, CAVIAR AND WINE OMELET: Refrigerate sauce and pieces of broken fish rolls in the casserole in which they were cooked and make into a delicious and unusual omelet for the next day's breakfast.

STUFFED HADDOCK FILLETS WITH CHEESE SAUCE (I)
And an Artistic Touch

2 pounds haddock fillets or fillets from any other fish, fresh or frozen,
freshwater or salt
4 scallions (green onions), chopped, including a little of the green
1 medium stalk celery, chopped
2 tablespoons butter or margarine
Salt and pepper to taste
2 cups bread cubes
2 cups Cheese Sauce, page 124, or 1 10½-ounce can cheddar cheese
soup diluted with ½ cup milk or cream
Slice of pimento (optional)

Defrost fillets if frozen. Lightly sauté onion and celery in butter or margarine. Add salt and pepper and bread cubes. Stir well, then spread mixture over a well-greased baking dish and top with fillets. Pour cheese sauce over the fish and bake in oven preheated to 375 degrees 15–25 minutes or until fish flakes separate easily when gently probed with the tines of a fork. Using a cookie cutter or a small sharp knife, cut a fish shape from slice of pimento and place in center of top of casserole. If you want to go a little further, give your fish a sliced-olive eye and cut some thin scallop shapes from green pepper to serve as waves for him to swim over. If you don't trust your own talents, turn the art work over to your less inhibited children—then don't be surprised if their enthusiasm for eating fish suddenly increases.

Serves 6–8.

NOTE: Decorating suggestions will be successful only if dish is large enough for sauce to spread out and not be thick, about 2 x 7½ x 11½.

SHRIMP-STUFFED HALIBUT STEAKS

4 *center-cut halibut steaks, cut as thin as possible, or any mild-flavored steaks, fresh or frozen, freshwater or salt*
1 *recipe Shrimp Stuffing, page 290*
¼ *cup melted butter or margarine*
1 *10-ounce can frozen shrimp soup, defrosted*
¼ *cup cream (optional)*
Salt and pepper to taste
Parsley

Defrost steaks if frozen. Place 2 of them in a well-greased, shallow baking pan, divide Shrimp Stuffing over them and spread out as you would a sandwich filling. Top with remaining 2 fish steaks, brush with some of the melted butter and place in 375-degree preheated oven. Bake 25–35 minutes, basting several times, or until fish flakes easily when gently probed with tines of a fork. Just before fish finishes cooking, heat can of defrosted shrimp soup just to simmering, remove from heat and stir in cream. Season fish sandwiches with salt and pepper, pour hot shrimp soup over them, garnish with parsley and serve.

Serves 2–4.

OYSTER-STUFFED FISH STEAKS: Prepare as above, using oyster instead of Shrimp Stuffing and frozen oyster instead of frozen shrimp soup.

LOBSTER-STUFFED FISH STEAKS: Prepare as above, using lobster instead of Shrimp Stuffing and frozen or canned lobster instead of frozen shrimp soup.

FISH-STUFFED VEGETABLES

For a meal that's deliciously different, colorful and highly decorative on any table, try vegetables baked with a fin fish or shellfish stuffing. Such creations make an interesting side dish, too. If that is not enough, they also are exceedingly simple to make.

They're a great second-day meal or snack, too. Eat them cold, steam them whole, or slice and fry them; you'll like them. (Avocados are the only exception to this second-day bit. They should be eaten at once.)

The stuffings in the recipes that follow can be interchanged; just cook longer if you're using a wide, deep (vegetable) dish; cook less if the stuffing is in something narrow and shallow.

A word of caution in any such fish-stuffed vegetables that you create: fish cooks much more quickly than do most vegetables. Therefore, some vegetables should be precooked in varying degrees, depending upon the recipe, before the fish is added to the dish.

CAULIFLOWER DELUXE

Made with Leftovers from Any Fish Cooked in or with a Sauce

    1 6-ounce box cooked and frozen Alaska king crab, defrosted
    1 to 2 cups leftover fish and sauce
    1 small, very fresh cauliflower
    ½ teaspoon salt or to taste
    1 10½-ounce can condensed cream of mushroom soup
    ½ cup toasted breadcrumbs
    ½ cup grated cheese of your choice

Wash cauliflower; cut out heart but leave head intact. Put in heavy pot, add salt and 1 cup of water. Cover, bring to a boil and cook 15–20 minutes or until not quite tender and most of water has disappeared. Place cauliflower head, the cavity facing up, in lightly greased casserole 2 to 2½ inches deep. Combine leftover fish and sauce, crab meat and cream of mushroom soup, stir well and pour over cauliflower so that cavity is filled and top and sides are coated with the mixture. Combine crumbs and grated cheese and sprinkle over the sauce. Bake in oven preheated to 400 degrees for 20 minutes or until crumbs are nicely browned and cauliflower is tender but not soft. Serve in casserole.

Serves 4.

EGGPLANT-SHRIMP BOATS   (I)

    ½ pound frozen cleaned and deveined shrimp
    1½ cups water
    1 large eggplant or 2 small ones
    1 cup canned tomato puree
    ⅛ teaspoon tarragon powder
    Salt and pepper to taste
    2 scallions (green onions), chopped, including a little of the green
      tops
    ½ clove garlic, finely minced
    ⅓ cup butter or margarine
    1 cup dry breadcrumbs

Dip frozen shrimp in cold salt water for about 1 minute to defrost partially. Remove any bits of black vein that may remain. Simmer gently in 1½ cups water for about 3 minutes or until shrimp are done. Drain and retain liquid. Cut eggplant in half lengthwise. Scoop out pulp, leaving a ¼-inch-thick shell, chop and reserve. Turn shells upside down in a pan of cold water. Reduce water in which shrimp was cooked to ¾ cup, add chopped eggplant pulp, tomato puree, tarragon and salt and pepper. Simmer for about 10 minutes or until pulp is tender. Lightly sauté onion and garlic in butter or margarine and stir into breadcrumbs. Add shrimp to pulp and tomato puree mixture. Fill eggplant shells with alternate layers of pulp and tomato mixture and buttered crumb mixture, stacking it high and topping with the crumbs. Fill a small, well-greased ramekin with any leftover mixture. Bake in preheated 400-degree oven 20–25 minutes or until crumbs are brown.

Serves 4.

SCALLOP-STUFFED MUSHROOM CAPS (I)

20 *raw bay scallops or quartered sea scallops*
20 *fresh mushrooms, about 2 inches in diameter*
1 *tablespoon butter or margarine*
1 *tablespoon cooking oil*
2 *tablespoons fresh minced shallots (or freeze-dried) or mild onions*
1½ *cups fine soft breadcrumbs made from stale bread*
1 *egg, lightly beaten*
¼ *cup grated cheese*
Paprika

Thoroughly wash mushrooms; remove stems and trim off tough ends and discard. Set mushroom caps aside to drain and mince stems. In a heavy skillet, heat butter or margarine and cooking oil to sizzling hot but not smoking, add minced mushroom stems and shallots, and lightly sauté. Combine with soft breadcrumbs and beaten egg. Place 1 bay scallop in each mushroom cap and pack it in by piling breadcrumb mixture over and around it. Sprinkle with grated cheese, then lightly dust with paprika. Place in well-greased heat-resistant serving platter and bake in oven preheated to 350 degrees for 20 minutes or until mushroom caps are tender and scallops are cooked. Serve while hot.

Serves 4–6 or makes 20 appetizers.

PEPPERS STUFFED WITH BABY SQUID AND MUSSELS

(Calamari e Peoci al Basilico)

1 *pound mussels in shell, cleaned and removed from the shell, liquor saved*
4 *baby squid, cleaned*

¼ *cup olive oil*
2 *slices white bread, cubed*
3 *tablespoons minced broad-leaved parsley*
4 *tablespoons chopped fresh basil or 2 tablespoons of a dried variety*
2 *cloves garlic*
1 *4-ounce can black olives, pitted and quartered*
2 *ripe firm tomatoes, peeled, seeded and chopped*
Salt and pepper to taste
4 *large bell peppers, tops sliced off and seeds and pulp removed*

Heat 2 tablespoons olive oil in large, heavy skillet. Add bread cubes and fry until light golden color. Chop parsley, basil and garlic together finely. Add to skillet. Add olives, tomatoes, mussels and salt and pepper, and stir together. Parboil peppers for 5 minutes, drain and stand in a baking dish. Coat baby squid with remaining olive oil. Place 1 in each of the 4 pepper cavities and stuff vegetable-mussel mixture around the squid. Pour mussel liquid around the peppers, cover dish and bake at 350 degrees for 35 minutes or until peppers are cooked.

Serves 4.

PEPPERS STUFFED WITH MUSSELS: Prepare in the same way as preceding recipe but eliminate squid. Mussels can be steamed open in 1 cup of water (see page 70), the steaming liquid strained, poured around cooking peppers, then over them when serving.

TOMATOES STUFFED WITH POACHED BONY FISH   (I)

1 *to 1½ pounds alewives, shad, whiting or other bony fish, fresh or saltwater, poached in Short Broth, page 197, and flaked*
8 *large tomatoes*
2 *cups soft breadcrumbs*
1 *egg, lightly beaten*
½ *cup reduced Short Broth (court bouillon) used in cooking fish*
Salt and pepper to taste (you won't need any if reduced court bouillon tastes highly seasoned)
1 *small onion, minced*
8 *slices cheese of your choice*

Slice tops from tomatoes, scoop out pulp and invert shells to drain. Chop tomato pulp and stir in breadcrumbs, beaten egg, Short Broth, salt and pepper to taste, onion and flaked fish. Stuff tomatoes with mixture and place in well-greased baking dish containing about ⅛ inch of water. Bake excess stuffing in well-greased ramekins. Bake 10 minutes in preheated 350-degree oven. Remove from oven and place slice of cheese on top of each stuffed tomato. Return to oven and bake another 10–15 minutes longer or until cheese melts and tomatoes are cooked but not mushy. Add a little more water to pan if necessary to keep bottoms of tomatoes from browning.

Serves 6–8.

VARIATION: Use canned or leftover cooked fish for stuffing, substituting undiluted condensed canned beef or chicken broth for reduced court bouillon.

STUFFED PEPPERS: Prepare as in foregoing recipe, substituting peppers for tomatoes, and whole chopped tomatoes for tomato pulp. Parboil peppers for 5 minutes and drain well before stuffing.

TOMATOES STUFFED WITH FISH
AND VEGETABLES (I)

> 2 *pounds bony fish, lightly poached, chilled, and flaked from bones, or 1-pound can salmon or mackerel*
> 8 *firm medium tomatoes*
> ¼ *cup olive oil*
> ½ *pound very fresh green beans, broken into pieces*
> 2 *cloves garlic, minced*
> 2 *large onions, chopped*
> ¼ *cup canned green chili peppers, chopped, or cayenne pepper to taste*
> ½ *cup water or poaching liquid from fish*
> *Salt to taste*
> 1 *1-pound can chick peas (garbanzos)*

Cut tops from tomatoes, scoop out insides and set aside. Heat olive oil in large, heavy pot so it is very hot but not smoking. Add green beans, garlic and onions and stir-fry until thoroughly coated with oil. Chop the scooped-out insides of tomatoes and add with green chilies and water to pot. Stir in salt to taste and simmer, covered, until green beans are crisp tender. Stir in chick peas and flaked fish. Arrange tomato shells in shallow, lightly greased baking dish and spoon vegetable-fish mixture into cavities, pouring leftover mixture around the tomatoes. Bake for 20 minutes in 350-degree oven or until everything is hot and tomatoes are cooked but not falling apart.

Serves 4–6.

VARIATION: Use green peppers.

STUFFED ZUCCHINI (I)

> 1 *to 2 cups cooked or canned fish, flaked*
> 4 *zucchini, medium size*
> 1 *medium onion, chopped*

¾ *teaspoon salt*
¾ *teaspoon pepper or to taste*
¼ *teaspoon oregano*
½ *cup breadcrumbs*
½ *cup cottage cheese*
3 *tablespoons chopped parsley*
4 *slices lean bacon, lightly fried and chopped*
2 *cups tomato sauce*
1 *cup tomato paste*
½ *cup grated cheese of your choice*

Wash zucchini and place in salted boiling water to cover. Boil 5–8 minutes. It should still be firm but slightly softened. Drain, cool and cut in half lengthwise. Scoop out pulp to form pockets in each half. Refrigerate pulp for future use. Combine all remaining ingredients except tomato sauce, cheese and tomato paste. Blend well and pile into zucchini cavities.

Place in well-greased baking dish. Combine tomato sauce and tomato paste, spread over zucchini and sprinkle with cheese. Bake in 350-degree oven 25–30 minutes or until well heated and zucchini is fork-tender. Serve. Serves 4–6.

FISH-STUFFED BAKED POTATOES   (I)

2 *cups flaked cooked or canned fish*
2 *large baking potatoes*
2 *tablespoons butter or margarine*
1 *pinch garlic powder*
⅛ *teaspoon onion powder*
Salt and pepper to taste
½ *to 1 cup heated milk*
1 *cup grated sharp cheddar cheese*

Bake potatoes in their skins 45–60 minutes in oven preheated to 450 degrees to 500 degrees. Remove from oven, slice in half lengthwise, scoop out insides (reserve skins) and combine in bowl with butter or margarine, garlic powder, onion powder and salt and pepper to taste. Add heated milk as you mash with a potato masher or beat with an electric beater. Use only enough milk to make a nice, fluffy consistency. Stir in fish flakes and pile into reserved potato skins. Divide grated cheese over the tops, return to oven, reduce heat to 400 degrees and bake 20–25 minutes or until potatoes are nicely browned on top and heated through.
Serves 2–4.

13

Baked Shellfish in the Shell

SOME WITH A STUFFING, SOME WITHOUT

CLAMS ON THE HALF SHELL
WITH GREEN PEPPER AND BACON   (I)
(Clams Casino)

24 *cherrystone clams*
Rock salt
1 *tablespoon blue cheese*
1 *teaspoon Worcestershire sauce*
2 *tablespoons butter or margarine*
¼ *cup minced onion*
¼ *cup minced green pepper*
4 *slices bacon, diced*

Open clams, see page 43; remove clams and set aside. Reserve liquid for another time and reserve one half of each shell. Fill 4 small pie tins about ¾ full of rock salt and imbed 6 of reserved half shells in each. Blend blue cheese and Worcestershire sauce into butter or margarine and spread over insides of half shells. Place a clam in each and divide minced onion, green pepper and bacon over them. Put in oven preheated to 400 degrees and bake 10–15 minutes or until edges of clams curl and bacon is cooked. (If you like very crisp bacon, partially cook it before dicing.) Serve in pans of rock salt.
   Serves 4.

301

BAKED KING CRAB LEGS

1 *pound frozen Alaska king crab legs, defrosted in refrigerator*
Melted butter or margarine
Lemon wedges

Cut legs into easily manageable serving pieces, 2 or 3 inches long. Slit tops of sections lengthwise, using a very sharp knife. Lay on sheet of aluminum foil, insert melted butter in slits and fold foil over to make sealed packages. Bake in preheated 400-degree oven 5–10 minutes or until crab meat is heated. Serve with additional melted butter in individual dishes and lemon wedges.

Serves 2–4.

BAKED PARTIALLY FROZEN KING CRAB LEGS: Defrost legs for 4 hours in refrigerator or until shells can be slit with very sharp knife. Proceed as above, but cook a little longer.

DEVILED CRAB IN SHELLS

1 *pound cooked or canned crab meat in small chunks*
4 *tablespoons butter or margarine*
2 *tablespoons minced onion*
2 *tablespoons chopped green pepper*
2 *tablespoons flour*
½ *cup milk*
1 *teaspoon powdered mustard or to taste*
1 *teaspoon Worcestershire sauce*
3 *drops Louisiana Hot Sauce (Tabasco)*
¼ *cup breadcrumbs made from day-old white bread*

Melt 2½ tablespoons of the butter or margarine in large, heavy skillet or pot. Add minced onion and chopped green pepper, and cook on medium heat just until they are beginning to brown. Add flour and stir for about 2 minutes. Stir in milk, beating with wire whisk as you slowly add, and continue stirring until sauce is smooth and thick. Blend powdered mustard into ½ tablespoon of remaining butter or margarine and stir into the sauce along with Worcestershire and Hot Sauce. Add crab meat, stir well and divide into 6 well-greased crab or scallop shells or individual 5-ounce custard cups. Melt remaining tablespoon butter or margarine in heavy skillet, add breadcrumbs and stir-fry until lightly toasted and all fat is evenly distributed in the crumbs. Sprinkle over crab mixture and place shells or individual custard cups in a preheated 375-degree oven and bake 15–20 minutes or until lightly browned.

Serves 6.

DEVILED CRAB APPETIZERS: Stuff mixture in preceding recipe into small scallop shells or clam shells, bake and serve as hot appetizers.

LOBSTER TAILS BAKED IN A HOT SAUCE
(Lobster Tails à la Diable)

4 *frozen lobster tails*
¼ *cup olive oil*
2 *cloves garlic, finely minced*
1 *tablespoon minced shallots or mild onion*
1 *9-ounce jar tomato paste*
1 *cup white wine*
½ *cup tomato juice*
¼ *teaspoon oregano*
Salt to taste
⅛ *teaspoon cayenne pepper or to taste*

Defrost lobster tails overnight in refrigerator. Heat olive oil in heavy skillet or saucepan. Add garlic and cook for about 1 minute. Add remaining ingredients except lobster tails. Stir well, bring to a boil, turn down to a simmer and cook for 5 minutes, stirring frequently.

Remove and discard under shells from lobster tails by cutting along edges where they join thicker upper shells. Remove meat from upper shells, turn over and slit meat lengthwise about ¼ inch deep. Place upper shells in shallow casserole that can also be used as a serving dish and pour half of the steaming-hot tomato sauce into the shells. Return meat to shell, but turn it upside down from the way it came out of the shell, slit side up. Cover tails with remaining sauce and bake in oven preheated to 400 degrees 10–15 minutes or until lobster meat is cooked. Baste several times with the sauce. Serve with heated French bread and a salad.

Serves 4.

BAKED LOBSTER WITH BREAD STUFFING

2 *1-pound lobsters, killed and prepared for cooking, see page 64*
Tomalley (green liver and coral roe) from lobsters
2 *cups soft breadcrumbs*
1 *pinch garlic powder or to taste*
Salt and pepper to taste
2 *tablespoons minced shallots or mild onion*
½ *cup melted butter or margarine*
Lemon wedges

Combine tomalley soft breadcrumbs, garlic powder, salt and pepper, minced shallots or onion and 2 tablespoons of the melted butter or margarine, mix well and stuff lightly into body cavities of lobster. Bake in 400-degree preheated oven 15–25 minutes or until meat loses its translucency and is lightly browned. Serve at once with lemon wedges and remaining melted butter.

Serves 2.

RICHLY SAUCED LOBSTER MEAT
BAKED IN THE SHELL   (I)

(Lobster Thermidor)

2 *2-pound live lobsters*
½ *recipe Short Broth, page 197*
9 *tablespoons butter or margarine*
1 *teaspoon lemon juice*
1 *pinch salt*
⅓ *pound mushrooms, sliced*
4 *tablespoons flour*
½ *cup heavy cream*
1 *egg yolk*
1 *pinch cayenne pepper*
2 *reserved lobster tomalleys (coral and green liver), mashed*
2 *or 3 teaspoons prepared mustard (optional)*
⅓ *cup grated Parmesan cheese*

Steam live lobsters over plain water. Strain steaming liquid, combine with Short Broth, reduce to 1¾ cups and set aside. Cut lobsters in half, removing intestinal vein and stomach. Remove meat from tail and body, chop into small pieces and set aside. Heat 1 tablespoon of the butter or margarine in small heavy saucepan. Add lemon juice, salt and sliced mushrooms. Cook over medium heat for about 1 minute, stirring constantly. Remove mushrooms and set aside. Pour lemon-butter mixture into reduced Short Broth. Melt 6 tablespoons of the remaining butter or margarine in a large, heavy skillet or pot, stir in flour and cook for 2 or 3 minutes, stirring constantly, over medium heat.

Add lemon-butter and broth mixture and continue cooking over medium heat, stirring constantly with wire whisk, until it comes to a boil. Turn down to a simmer and cook, stirring frequently, for 3 or 4 minutes or until smooth and thick, then turn off heat. Combine heavy cream, egg yolk, pinch of cayenne and lobster tomalley, and mix well in a bowl. Stir in ½ cup of the sauce from the stove, 1 tablespoon at a time. Then stir it all into the sauce remaining on the stove. Add chopped lobster meat and mushrooms, and stir. Rub a very thin coating of prepared mustard over lobster-shell cavities, then fill each one with sauced lobster and mushroom mixture. Sprinkle each with grated Parmesan cheese and dot with remaining 2 tablespoons of butter or margarine. Bake in oven preheated to 400 degrees 10–15 minutes or until thoroughly heated and cheese starts to brown. Serve 1 half shell of lobster to each person.

Serves 4.

NOTE: If you have difficulty fitting all the sauce and lobster mixture into shell cavities, pour any excess into a ramekin, cover with grated cheese, dot with butter and bake.

MUSSELS NEAPOLITAN STYLE* (I)
On the Half Shell

(This is Don Bevona's recipe, which we told you about on page 68.)

2 *pounds mussels*
3 *tablespoons olive oil*
1 *large garlic clove*
1 *6-ounce can tomato paste*
2½ *cups liquid (mussel liquor plus sufficient water)*
½ *teaspoon oregano*
½ *teaspoon capers*
Salt and pepper
Crushed red pepper (optional)

Clean mussels as described on page 69. Reserve and strain liquid. Place mussels in a small bowl, and reserve 1 half shell for each person. Lay each mussel on a half shell in a shallow baking dish and set aside. Add enough water to liquor to equal 2½ cups.

SAUCE: Heat the oil in a saucepan. Sliver the garlic lengthwise into quarters and brown in the oil. Add the tomato paste and fry for 2 minutes with garlic. Then add mussel liquor and water mixture, oregano and capers (which should be rinsed and drained well). Simmer, covered, for about 30 minutes. Salt and pepper to taste. Add red crushed pepper if desired, but do not use more than ¼ to ½ teaspoon. Pour sauce over mussels and bake in oven preheated to 425 degrees for 15 minutes. Serve over flat Italian whole-wheat biscuits or sliced, toasted Italian bread.

Serves 4.

OYSTERS WITH A MONEY-COLORED COAT
(Oysters Rockefeller)

(There are few famous recipes shrouded in so much mystery or with so many different versions as Oysters Rockefeller. It is said by some that the genuine article, first prepared at Antoine's in New Orleans around

* From *The Love Apple Cookbook*, by Don Bevona (Funk & Wagnalls).

the turn of the century, did not even contain spinach, the principal ingredient (next to oysters, or sometimes clams) in shellfish recipes now bearing the famous financier's name. The green color of spinach, so some of the stories go, represents the green of old John D.'s money.)

> 24 *shell oysters, opened, liquid and deep halves of shell reserved, see page 51*
> ¾ *cup oyster liquid, strained through several layers of cheesecloth*
> 1 *cup butter or margarine*
> ¼ *cup minced celery*
> ¼ *cup minced fresh parsley*
> ¼ *cup minced shallots or mild onion*
> ½ *cup minced fresh spinach leaves from which coarse stem has been removed (substitute a combination of minced fresh tarragon, basil and chervil leaves)*
> ¼–½ *teaspoon Louisiana Hot (Tabasco) Sauce*
> *Salt to taste*
> ½ *teaspoon Tia Maria or some other coffee-flavored liqueur*
> 6 *tablespoons lightly toasted breadcrumbs made from stale white bread*
> *Lemon wedges*

Melt ½ cup of butter or margarine in heavy skillet. Add all remaining ingredients except oysters, oyster liquid and ½ cup of the butter or margarine and lemon wedges. Cook on medium heat, stirring constantly, for 5 minutes. Set aside.

Fill 4 small pie tins about ¾ full of rock salt and imbed 6 of the reserved oyster shells in each pan. Heat oyster liquid and remaining ½ cup of butter or margarine together until steaming hot, stir well and divide into oyster shells. Carefully place an oyster in each half shell so it's swimming in the buttery liquid. Divide the green-leaf mixture over tops of the 24 oysters, spreading it out to cover each as evenly as possible. Place pans in a 400-degree oven and bake 10–15 minutes or until topping just starts to brown and edges of oysters curl. Garnish with lemon wedges and serve 1 pan of 6 oysters, still imbedded in rock salt, to each person.

Serves 4.

SNAILS BAKED IN THE SHELL

In a Special Butter Sauce

> 48 *snails*
> ½ *to 1 recipe Short Broth (Court Bouillon), page 197*
> 2 *recipes Snail Butter, page 143*

Prepare snails as described on page 84, using Short Broth or plain water to simmer them in. Thoroughly wash shells and divide half the snail butter into them. Press 1 snail into each shell, cover with remaining butter, and place in special snail pans or close together in a shallow baking pan. Bake in oven preheated to 425 degrees for about 10 minutes or until snails are thoroughly heated through. Serve at once.

Serves 4–6 as a meal; makes 48 hot appetizers.

ABOUT SNAIL PANS: You can buy snail pans, which are made with indentations for holding snails in place so they don't roll around and spill their butter sauce while baking. Snail pans also are available in kits that contain reusable snail shells. With such kits, you can buy canned snails that have been removed from the shell and simplify the preparation. (Use pans for serving.)

14

Flaked and Baked

MOSTLY FLAKED FISH (FRESH COOKED OR
CANNED), BUT INCLUDING SOME SMALL
CHUNKS AND SMALL WHOLE SHELLFISH

CASSEROLES

A fish casserole consists of almost any combination of flaked or chunked
fin fish or small whole shellfish combined with a sauce and baked at a
moderate temperature until all ingredients are heated and flavors are
pleasantly blended.

The casserole may or may not include other foods such as vegetables,
rice, cheese or noodles. It can be topped with breadcrumbs and/or grated
cheese or sliced cheese and baked uncovered until it has a crisp, golden-
brown crust. Then it is sometimes but not always called "au gratin."

A scalloped casserole is one containing milk and sometimes cooked
in layers of different foods or with layers of cracker crumbs or breadcrumbs providing the thickening for the milk sauce.

As with most fish dishes, the designations overlap and interchange,
so don't be confused by their names; just look over the ingredients in
each, see which suits your fancy and try it. Then try your own combinations of food depending on what you have on hand.

Casseroles can be one of the most delicious of dishes because of the
combination of different flavors. This makes them especially suitable for
those people who must delete salt or other seasonings because of dietary
problems. Equally important, the very combination that makes a casserole so delicious can result in a very inexpensive dish, because it serves
as a wonderful way to use up fish, vegetable, rice, pasta and sauce leftovers. You can easily, too, include everything you need for a 1-dish meal.

PIES

Fish pies are nothing more than fish casseroles with a crust. The crust can be the same crust you'd use on any pie: your favorite self-made one, a quick and easy mix or a biscuit mix.

The size of the pie is strictly up to you, too. Make them normal-sized in 8- or 9-inch tins; make them individual-sized in 4- to 6-inch tins. Or, if it's a deep-dish pie that you've a hankering for, then just bake a fish casserole and top it with any kind of crust you like.

As for the filling, you can use any proportions that you like. But if you've never made a fish pie before, we suggest that you try mixing 2 cups of flaked fish and other foods you may be including with 1 cup of medium-thick White Sauce or Fish Broth Sauce or one of their variations. Or use a can of condensed soup such as cream of mushroom and dilute it with from ¼ to ½ cup of milk or whatever amount is needed to produce a medium-sauce consistency.

If you add potatoes, rice or bread cubes to your filling, they will absorb liquid to varying degrees, so you should cover them with a sauce that's a little thinner than medium.

SHEPHERD'S PIES

If you'd like to make shepherd's pies, pour your filling into individual casseroles, prepare whatever amount of whipped potatoes you will be serving for dinner and, instead of piling them into a bowl to set on the table, make a potato border around each casserole, top with a little melted butter and bake at 375 degrees to 400 degrees just until nicely browned.

CASSEROLES MADE FROM ANY FLAKED FISH IN WHITE SAUCES OR FISH BROTH SAUCES

2 *to 2½ cups flaked fish, cooked or canned*
1 *recipe of White Sauce or Fish Broth Sauce, page 121, made medium thick, or a sauce of your choice using one of these sauces as a base (recipes start on page 124)*
2 *tablespoons butter or margarine*
1 *cup soft breadcrumbs*

Mix flaked fish and sauce together and pour into a well-greased casserole or loaf pan in which the mixture will be at least 1 inch deep. Melt butter or margarine in large, heavy skillet, add soft breadcrumbs and stir-fry until lightly toasted. Spread over top of fish mixture, put in oven preheated to 375 degrees and cook 15–20 minutes or until mixture is very hot and crumbs are nicely browned.

Serves 4–6.

MRS. SPORTS'S SHRIMP PARMESAN

(Abe Weinberg is his right name. He owns and operates Mister Sports, an athletic-goods store in Long Beach, Long Island, where we live, and he makes one of the finest fishing rods that you ever did see. Not only does he make them, but he uses them in fine manner, too. Many is the fighting fish that Abe has taken from the Long Beach surf, fish that taste as well as they fight.

Yet, Mister Sports's favorite eating fish does not come from Long Island waters. Nor is it even a fish that he's caught himself. His preference is for shrimp imported from faraway waters, when cooked in this, his favorite recipe, created by Mrs. Sports, his lovely wife, Grace.)

1 *pound raw peeled and deveined medium shrimp*
½ *cup flour*
1 *large egg, beaten*
1 *cup toasted breadcrumbs*
Butter or margarine
Cooking oil
1 *4-ounce package mozzarella cheese (the semisoft variety that comes unsliced), thinly sliced*
1 *1-pound jar or can marinara sauce*

Lightly dust all surfaces of shrimp with flour. Dip in beaten egg, coat with crumbs and spread out in single layer to dry for about 5 minutes before cooking. Add equal amounts of butter or margarine and cooking oil to large, heavy skillet so there is about ⅛ inch in bottom, and heat until sizzling hot but not smoking. Add shrimp but don't crowd. Cook until pale golden brown on one side, turn and repeat on second side. Arrange in 2 layers in a well-greased, shallow casserole, spread half of cheese slices between the layers and half over the top. Cover with marinara sauce and bake in oven preheated to 375 degrees 20–25 minutes or until cheese melts and sauce is very hot.

Serves 4–6.

SCALLOPED FISH WITH APPLE

1 *pound any boneless raw fish fresh or frozen, salt or freshwater*
1 *red apple, skin on, sliced*
1 *cup milk*
1 *egg, beaten*
1½ *tablespoons melted butter or margarine*
1 *teaspoon prepared mustard*
2 *teaspoons lemon juice*
1 *teaspoon brown sugar*

Salt and pepper to taste
1½ cups breadcrumbs made from stale bread
1 tablespoon butter or margarine for dotting

Defrost fish if frozen and cut into small pieces. Mix fish pieces, apple, milk and beaten egg. Combine melted butter or margarine, mustard, lemon juice, brown sugar and salt and pepper, and stir into fish mixture. Place ½ cup of the breadcrumbs in bottom of well-greased casserole. Spread fish mixture over them and top with remaining crumbs. Dot with butter or margarine and bake in oven preheated to 350 degrees for 30 minutes or until mixture is firm and nicely browned on top.

COLD SLICED FISH AND APPLE LOAF: This dish is very nice chilled and sliced for lunch or buffet.

SCALLOPED TUNA: Substitute canned tuna for raw fish in above.

SCALLOPED OYSTERS

(A Fine Christmas Eve Dish)

1 pint oysters, shucked and drained
½ cup butter or margarine
2 cups cracker crumbs
Salt and pepper to taste
¾ cup milk
¼ cup cream (or evaporated milk)
⅛ teaspoon Worcestershire sauce

Melt butter or margarine in a skillet. Remove from fire, add cracker crumbs and stir well. Season with salt and pepper to taste and spread ⅓ over bottom of a well-greased casserole. Top with ½ of oysters. Add another layer of cracker-crumb mixture, then the remaining oysters. Combine milk and cream, stir in Worcestershire sauce, mix well and pour over contents of dish. Top with remaining crumbs and bake in oven preheated to 350 degrees for 30 minutes or until nicely browned on top.

Serves 4–6.

SCALLOPED CLAMS: Prepare in same way as Scalloped Oysters.

SCALLOPED MUSSELS: Steam mussels open, see page 70, and prepare in same way as Scalloped Oysters.

CLAM PIE

2 cups minced clams, cooked or canned, drained and liquid reserved
¼ cup butter or margarine
¼ cup flour
1 cup milk

½ *cup liquid from clams, strained*
¼ *cup cream or canned milk*
1 *tablespoon chopped green onions*
½ *cup finely minced celery*
¼ *teaspoon white pepper or to taste*
1 *tablespoon chopped fresh parsley or chives*
Salt to taste
Pastry for 2-crust 9-inch pie

Melt butter or margarine in large, heavy skillet or pot. Add flour, stir together and cook for 1 or 2 minutes on medium heat. Add milk and liquid from clams and stir with whisk until thick and smooth. Turn off heat and stir in cream or canned milk. Add onions, celery, white pepper, chopped parsley or chives, clams and salt to taste.

Line 9-inch pie pan with pastry; prick with a fork. Roll out top crust. Pour filling into bottom crust, cover with top crust, seal edges and slash a design on the top through which steam can escape. Bake in 450-degree oven for 10 minutes; reduce heat to 350 degrees and bake for 40 minutes or until crust is nicely browned.

Serves 6–8.

VARIATION: Add 1 cup cubed potatoes and reduce quantity of clams.

OYSTER, MUSSEL, SHRIMP OR FLAKED FISH PIE: Make in the same way as Clam Pie.

FISH AND FLAT NOODLES   (I)

(Lasagna)

1 *pound any cooked or canned fish, flaked*
1 *tablespoon olive oil*
1 *onion*
1 *clove garlic, minced*
1 *1-pound can peeled tomatoes*
1 *8-ounce can tomato sauce*
Salt and pepper to taste
½ *teaspoon dried rosemary*
½–¾ *pound lasagna or any flat noodles, freshly cooked*
½ *pound mozzarella cheese (do not use the presliced kind)*
½ *pound ricotta cheese*
¼ *to ½ cup grated Parmesan cheese*

Heat olive oil in large, heavy skillet and lightly sauté onion and garlic. Add canned tomatoes, tomato sauce and seasonings, stir well, cover, and simmer slowly for 20 minutes or until ingredients are blended and sauce is no longer runny. Add fish, stir and pour ¼ over bottom of a baking dish (12 by 8 inches or a little smaller). Arrange ⅓ of lasagna over the sauce, spread ⅓ of mozzarella and ricotta cheese over the lasagna. Then repeat these layers 2 more times and top with remaining fish-tomato sauce. Sprinkle with grated Parmesan and bake, uncovered, for 30 minutes in oven preheated to 350 degrees. Remove from oven and let stand for 5 minutes or a little longer before cutting.

Serves 6.

15

Loaves, Puddings, Soufflés and Crepes

LOAVES

Take any fresh-cooked or leftover or canned flaked or ground fish or shellfish and, using these recipes as a guide, create other loaves. You can make them very elegant and tasty, yet keep the cost to a minimum by combining inexpensive frozen or in-season fresh delicately flavored white-meat fish with a more expensive delicacy such as king crab. The recipe on page 315 for King Crab and Fish Loaf is a good example of this principle, besides also showing how to create eye appeal by combining white fish meat with the colorful king crab.

To bake a fish loaf do this:

1. Remove any bones from fish. Examine shellfish and remove any bits of shell or cartilage.

2. Use a Pyrex baking dish if you have one, because you can see through the transparent sides and regulate the heat so that the sides don't overbrown and become dry by the time the center of the loaf is firm and set. Test with a sharp, thin-bladed knife as you would a cake. Insert in center of loaf; if it comes out clean, your loaf is done.

3. Allow 45 to 60 minutes in an average 2¾-inch-deep baking dish. The shallower the loaf, the more quickly it will bake. If too shallow, say less than 1½ inches, the loaf may dry out before the sides brown.

4. If you like a loaf that is crusty on the outside, turn oven temperature up to 450 degrees for the last 10 minutes of baking. If you like a very moist loaf, with only the top browned, set baking dish in a pan of hot water while it is baking in the oven. If top browns before loaf is cooked, cover with foil.

KING CRAB AND FISH LOAF

> 1 *cup canned Alaska king crab meat or leftover lobster meat, finely chopped*
> 1 *cup delicately flavored white-meat fish, fresh or saltwater, cooked and finely flaked*
> 1 *tablespoon minced shallots or mild onion*
> 1 *cup soft breadcrumbs*
> 1 *egg, lightly beaten*
> ½ *cup light cream*
> *Salt and white pepper to taste*
> ¼ *cup dry breadcrumbs*
> 2 *tablespoons grated Parmesan cheese*
> 2 *tablespoons butter or margarine*

Combine shellfish and fish flakes and mix together very well. Add next 5 ingredients, mix and lightly press into a well-greased loaf pan. Mix breadcrumbs and grated cheese together, sprinkle over top of loaf and dot with butter or margarine. Set in a pan of hot water and bake in oven preheated to 350 degrees for 45 minutes or until loaf is firm in the center and brown on top. Serve plain or with a delicately flavored sauce of your choice.

Serves 6.

CHILLED FISH AND CHEESE LOAF (I) : Substitute delicate white cooked fish flakes for the cup of canned crab meat in foregoing. Place half of loaf mixture in baking dish, top with ¼ pound sliced cheese, add remaining half of mixture and bake for 25 minutes. Top with an additional ¼ pound of sliced cheese and continue baking for an additional 20 minutes or until loaf is firm in the center and top is lightly browned. Decorate top with sliced olives, chill and serve on a buffet.

FRUSTRATED FISHERMAN'S CONSOLATION LOAF

(You won't be disappointed in a day's fishing that yields just one small fish if you use it to make this fish loaf.)

Loaf ingredients:
> 1 *small fish that will yield ½ to 1 cup flaked meat after poaching*
> ½ *to 1 cup canned salmon, bone and skin removed and flaked*
> ½ *cup dry breadcrumbs*
> ½ *cup broth in which fish was poached*
> ¼ *cup juice from salmon can*
> 1 *small cooked carrot from poaching broth, finely chopped*
> 1½ *cups soft bread cubes*

2 *eggs, beaten*
½ *cup cream*
Salt and pepper to taste
Poaching liquid:
    1½ *cups water*
    ½ *cup white wine*
    1 *small carrot, scraped*
    1 *small stalk celery, chopped*
    1 *small onion, chopped*
    ¼ *teaspoon salt*
    ⅛ *teaspoon pepper*

Combine ingredients for poaching liquid in a small, heavy pot and bring to a boil. Turn down to just under a simmer, add fish and cook for 2 minutes. Carefully turn the fish over and continue to cook for 4 minutes or until flakes separate easily when gently probed with the tines of a fork. Remove fish from pot and set aside to cool. Turn liquid up to a low boil, cover and continue cooking until it is reduced to approximately ½ cup. Strain.

Flake fish meat away from the bones and combine with enough flaked salmon to make 2 cups.

Grease a loaf pan and sprinkle bottom and sides with dry breadcrumbs. Combine all loaf ingredients except the dry breadcrumbs, mix well and press into loaf pan. Bake in oven preheated to 350 degrees for 50 minutes or until center of loaf is firm and outside is a golden brown. If outside browns before center is done, set baking dish in pan of hot water to finish cooking.

Serves 6.

OYSTER LOAVES (I)
(Poor Boy Sandwich)

1 *pint shucked oysters, drained and thoroughly dried*
4 *French (or submarine) rolls*
¼ *cup melted butter or margarine*
2 *eggs, lightly beaten*
1 *cup seasoned toasted breadcrumbs*
2 *tablespoons cooking oil*
½ *cup mayonnaise*
1 *tablespoon catsup*
2 *tablespoons chopped sweet pickles*

Cut tops from rolls by slicing lengthwise, leaving a ¾-inch-thick slice to act as a lid. Hollow out centers of rolls and brush cavities and inner surfaces of lids with melted butter or margarine. Place in oven preheated to 350 degrees for 10 minutes or until very lightly toasted. Set aside.

Dip oysters in beaten eggs, coat with seasoned breadcrumbs and set aside to dry. Put 2 tablespoons of the remaining melted butter and the cooking oil in large, heavy skillet and heat until sizzling but not smoking. Add batter-coated oysters and fry. When nicely browned on one side, turn and brown second side. This should take only a minute or so. Don't crowd into pan. Remove as soon as browned and divide into French roll cavities. Combine mayonnaise, catsup and chopped pickles and spread over oysters. Replace roll top "lids," return to oven and bake at 400 degrees for 5 minutes or until thoroughly heated through.

Serves 4.

CLAM LOAVES: Prepare in same way as Oyster Loaves.

SHRIMP LOAVES: Prepare in same way as Oyster Loaves.

FLAKED FISH LOAVES: Prepare in same way as Oyster Loaves but do not fry the flaked fish.

PUDDING

Fish pudding is a routine, everyday dish in Scandinavian homes and for very good reason: it's, oh, so deliciously different and delicious.

Making one does involve a little work and know-how, though, and you may have to try your hand at it two or three times before you really get the feel of doing it properly. But once you, your family, your friends and, most of all, your children taste a fish pudding, we think you'll join the Scandinavians and make it often.

Make it and serve it in just about any way: hot as a main course or a side dish, cold in a sandwich, as an appetizer or as an unusual addition to a hors d'oeuvre table, even sweet as a dessert or an after-school snack.

A pudding, too, is just about the most perfect dish there is for introducing children—and stubborn grown-ups—to the goodness of fish.

As we said, making one may be a trifle difficult, but there are shortcuts. In the Scandinavian countries, housewives use wooden spoons and such for mixing, but by incorporating the use of both our electric blender and our electric beater into our recipe procedure, we've managed to cut down the work quite a bit. You may have equipment that will simplify the procedure even further.

Any delicately flavored lean fish is suitable for a pudding, but we suggest that you use inexpensive fish so that you can feel free to experiment as much as you think you will need to. And then—wonderful surprise!—you'll discover that using more costly fish would be just a waste of money.

To give you an idea: all of the ingredients called for in the pilot recipe that follows (using frozen fish), including those for the Herbed Wine or Lemon Sauce or Apricot Relish which are optional, cost no more than $1.60 at the retail store. Yet out of that recipe you can easily get 4 main-course servings, about 24 appetizers and we don't know how many sandwiches. Which means that the price per main course is about 40 cents.

You can't possibly feed your family so nutritionally well for less.

MOLDED FISH PUDDING   (I)

¾ to 1 pound lean, delicately flavored white-meat fish, skin and bones removed (use fillets and save skin and remainder of carcass for making a sauce if you plan to serve one)
Salt to taste
¹⁄₁₆ teaspoon nutmeg
⅛ teaspoon white pepper
¼ cup butter or margarine
1 tablespoon flour
½ cup light cream
½ cup heavy cream
1 recipe Apricot Relish or Herbed Wine Sauce, page 127, or Lemon Sauce, page 128 (optional)

Purée fish by mashing with a fork (if fish is partially frozen, this works very well) or putting through a meat grinder several times, using a fine blade and then working the fish with the back of a wooden spoon until it becomes a gelatinous pureed mass.

Work seasonings into the puree, and cream the butter or margarine, working the flour into it as you do. Now work the fish mixture into the flour and butter mixture with the back of a wooden spoon, or, better yet, use the electric blender and mix about ⅓ of it at a time. The blade of the blender will finish the job of chopping any chunks that got overlooked in previous operations. Put mixture in the freezer to get very cold.

Mix light and heavy creams together and put them in the freezer, too, and leave both mixes there for about 30 minutes. Remove from freezer and use a wooden spoon or your electric beater to beat the cold cream mixture slowly, a little at a time, into the cold fish mixture in such a way that the cream is completely incorporated and you have a pudding mixture almost as light and fluffy as whipped cream. Pour mixture into a buttered mold and cover with lid. Set in a pan of hot water in an oven preheated to 325 degrees and bake 50–60 minutes or until a thin knife blade inserted into center of pudding comes out clean.

Serve hot as a main course or side dish, cold as an appetizer, snack or sandwich, sweet as a dessert (directions follow); if hot, serve it either plain or with Apricot Relish (recipe follows), Herbed Wine or Lemon Sauce; if cold, plain or with cold Apricot Relish.

Yield: 4 hot main-course servings or, when chilled and cubed, about 24 appetizers.

MOLDED FISH PUDDING MADE WITH CONDENSED MILK: Substitute ½ cup evaporated milk and ½ cup Eagle Brand sweetened condensed milk for the cream in preceding recipe. The result is a sweet-flavored pudding that is especially pleasing to children.

APRICOT RELISH:
1 *1-pound can apricot halves, drained*
½ *teaspoon curry powder or to taste (optional)*
2 *tablespoons butter or margarine*
1 *tablespoon lemon juice*
1 *tablespoon apricot juice from canned halves*
¼ *cup dark brown sugar*
¼ *teaspoon salt*

Place apricot halves in a small, shallow casserole from which they can be served at table. Blend curry powder into butter or margarine in a saucepan. Add remaining ingredients, heat to simmering point and continue cooking on medium heat for about 1 minute, stirring constantly. Pour over apricot halves and bake at 350 degrees 15–20 minutes, basting several times. Serve hot with hot Fish Pudding or cold with cold Fish Pudding. Serves 4–6.

SOUFFLÉS AND CREPES

We said it in the fried fish section, but it bears briefly repeating here: fish and eggs are a natural team. And that's just as true for baked dishes such as the two idea-triggering soufflé and crepe recipes we give you next as it is for the fish omelets that you fry. Eggs, like fish, provide our bodies with top-quality protein that's also economical; doubly so if you use leftover fish.

LEFTOVER FISH SOUFFLÉ (I)

¾ *to 1 cup fin fish or shellfish from leftover casserole, including any leftover vegetables*
½ *cup toasted breadcrumbs*
¾ *cup leftover sauce from casserole*
3 *egg yolks, slightly beaten*
Salt to taste
4 *egg whites, room temperature*

Grease a soufflé dish or straight-sided casserole, add breadcrumbs and shake and rotate dish until completely covered with crumbs, then shake out any excess. Preheat oven to 375 degrees. While doing so, stir leftover sauce gradually into beaten yolks and beat with a wire whisk until smooth.

Remove and discard bones, if any; chop fish and any leftover vegetables very finely or put through fine blade of meat grinder. Add to the egg-yolk mixture with salt to taste and stir until well mixed. Pour into top of a double boiler over simmering water and cook for 2 minutes, stirring constantly, or until heated through and just beginning to show signs of cooking.

Remove at once from over the hot water and let cool to barely lukewarm. While mixture cools, beat egg whites, using a balloon wire whisk if you have one or electric beater (whichever will incorporate the most air into the egg white), until they are stiff and hold a good peak. Fold ⅓ of egg whites into lukewarm yolk and fish mixture and mix very well. Fold in remaining beaten white, mix lightly (it doesn't matter if some small blobs of egg white remain unincorporated) and pour into crumb-coated soufflé dish or casserole. Place in pan of hot water and bake in center of bottom shelf 30–40 minutes (do not open door during first 20 minutes) or until sharp knife gently inserted into center (in the hollow of a crack if there is one) comes out dry. Serve at once.

Serves 4–6.

NOTES:

· If there is no sauce left over from your casserole, or if you are using canned instead of leftover fish, prepare ¾ cup of White Sauce Croquette Base, page 151, and use instead.

· To use leftover fish loaf, slice it and lay pieces on bottom of soufflé dish or casserole. Unless you have leftover sauce, make White Sauce Croquette Base and proceed in same way as in Leftover Fish Casserole Soufflé.

CRAB CREPES WITH SHRIMP SAUCE (I)

(This recipe came to us from the United States Department of the Interior.)

Crepes:
> ½ *cup milk*
> 1 *egg*
> ½ *cup sifted flour*
> ¼ *teaspoon salt*

Filling:
> 1 *cup (6 ounces) frozen snow or queen crab meat, flaked (or any flaked leftover or canned fish)*
> ½ *cup thinly sliced celery*
> 2 *tablespoons thinly sliced green onions*
> ¼ *cup salad dressing*
> 2 *tablespoons diced pimento*

1 *teaspoon curry powder*
1 *teaspoon lemon juice*
¼ *teaspoon Worcestershire sauce*
Sauce:
1 *10-ounce can frozen, condensed shrimp soup, defrosted*
½ *cup milk*
½ *cup tiny, cooked Pacific pink shrimp (optional)*
1 *teaspoon lemon juice*

To make crepes: Combine milk, egg, flour and salt; beat until smooth. Fry crepes, one at a time, in lightly greased 6- or 7-inch skillet, using 3 tablespoons batter for each crepe. Pour batter into skillet; tilt pan quickly so that batter will cover bottom of pan. Cook until lightly browned on both sides, turning once. Stack and keep warm while preparing filling.

To make filling: Thaw crab meat; combine crab meat, celery, onion, salad dressing, pimento, curry powder, lemon juice and Worcestershire sauce; mix carefully. Spread an equal amount of filling over each crepe, and roll up. Arrange filled crepes on heatproof platter. Cover with aluminum foil, crimping foil to edges of platter. Bake in a moderate oven, 350 degrees, about 15 minutes or until well heated. Prepare sauce while crepes are heating.

To make sauce: Combine soup, milk, shrimp and lemon juice; warm to serving temperature over low heat, stirring constantly.

To serve: Uncover platter and pour sauce over crepes.

Makes 6 crepes or 6 servings.

16

How to Bake Frozen Fish
Without First Defrosting

Heed these few basic instructions and you'll find that the baking of still-frozen fish fillets and steaks will provide you with a meal that (1) is in-expensive as all get-out; (2) is at least as quick to cook as many of the so-called convenience foods; (3) is not much more difficult to prepare; and (4) is ten times more tasty. The fillets particularly, which come in solid blocks weighing from 12 to 16 ounces, are ideal for oven creations that are decidedly different.

WASHING

Dunk the fish 2 or 3 times in a pot of cold tap water the moment you remove the wrapping and pat dry with a lintfree towel or absorbent paper.

THE BAKING UTENSIL TO USE

Odd-shaped oven baking dishes, such as pie plates, are strictly taboo for frozen fillets because they (the fillets) can't be twisted, molded or cut into oddball shapes. However, some steaks might fit into some pie plates.

The utensil that we've found to best fit the dimensions of a frozen fillet block is a 10- by 6- by 1¾-inch oven baking dish. This size makes a snug receptacle for the rectangle of fillets, and usually steak, because it (1) leaves enough open space on all four sides to hold a cup or less of sauce at a depth that won't evaporate and yet (2) is still deep enough to hold almost 3 cups of liquid as is sometimes necessary.

Therefore, if you don't already have such a dish, we urgently recommend that you buy one. At this writing they cost only $1.19. Plus, of course, tax.

OVEN TEMPERATURE

It should be quite high: 450 degrees to 500 degrees in a preheated oven, and the baking pan should be placed on center shelf.

TIMING

If you've just purchased your frozen fish, you can figure that it will have defrosted to some degree by the time you reach home and make it ready for the oven. If that is the case, figure on 20 to 24 minutes for each inch of thickness.

However, if you've just taken the frozen fish from a 0-degree home freezer and wasted no time in preparing it for the oven, then you'll have to figure on its baking somewhat longer than 24 minutes per inch of thickness. If the fish is surrounded by a sauce that's cold and deep, the time it takes to cook will be increased even more.

Which all adds up to this: the fork test is still the best test for doneness. Start testing at 15 minutes, no matter whose freezer the fish came from, for blocks that are 1-inch thick; at 20 minutes for blocks that are 1¼ inches thick. When the flesh flakes easily, the fish is done.

Evenly cut fish steaks can be timed this way, too.

GRAY SOLE FILLETS

> 1 12- to 16-*ounce package frozen gray sole or any mild-flavored salt or freshwater fillet*
> 1 *tablespoon margarine, melted*
> 1 *tablespoon butter, melted*
> 1 *tablespoon lemon juice*
> ¼ *teaspoon salt or to taste*
> *Pinch of pepper*
> ¼ *teaspoon paprika or to taste*
> 1 *teaspoon grated onion*

Place still-frozen rectangle of fillets in a well-greased, shallow baking dish. Combine remaining ingredients, mix well and pour over and around fillets. Bake in 450-degree preheated oven 20–30 minutes or until fish flakes apart when gently probed with a fork.

Serves 2–4.

FISH CAKE (I)

(Fillets in a Yummy Sauce Topped with Soft Breadcrumbs Crisped in Butter)

> 1 12- to 16-*ounce package any mild-flavored fresh or saltwater fish fillets, skinned, frozen*

2 *tablespoons Dijon mustard*
3 *tablespoons butter or margarine*
1 *cup soft breadcrumbs*
¼ *cup toasted almond slivers*
½ *cup dairy sour cream*

Blend mustard and 1 tablespoon of the butter or margarine together and spread over surface of still-frozen fish block. Place in shallow baking pan and bake in preheated 450-degree oven 15–25 minutes or until fork test shows fish to be almost done. Meantime, melt 2 tablespoons butter or margarine in large, heavy skillet, add soft breadcrumbs and stir-fry until lightly toasted. Combine almond slivers and sour cream, and spread over top of fish. Pile toasted crumbs on top of cream mixture, return to oven and continue cooking for 5 minutes or until fish is done.
    Serves 4.

FROZEN FILLETS IN EASY MELTED BUTTER SAUCES

1 12- *to 16-ounce package any lean or intermediate still-frozen fish fillet*
½ *recipe of any of the Easy Butter (or Margarine) Sauces, beginning on page 136*

Place block of fish in a shallow baking pan of a size that will not leave much margin around the fish. Make sauce, using the melted butter or margarine version of the recipe, and pour over the fish. Bake in oven preheated to 450 degrees 20–30 minutes, basting several times with the sauce, or until fish flakes easily when gently probed with tines of a fork. Separate fillets or cut the block into serving portions and serve with sauce.
    Serves 2–4.

NUTTY FILLETS   (I)

1 12- *to 16-ounce package frozen flounder fillets or other delicately flavored fresh or saltwater fish fillets*
¼ *teaspoon curry powder*
¼ *teaspoon garlic powder*
½ *cup peanut butter, regular grind*
Juice of 1 lemon
½ *cup mayonnaise*
½ *cup chicken broth*
½ *cup milk*
¼ *cup flaked coconut*
¼ *cup toasted breadcrumbs*

Place still-frozen block of flounder fillets in baking pan. Blend curry and garlic powders into 1 tablespoon of the peanut butter. Add lemon juice to the curry-garlic powder blend, mix and add to remaining peanut butter and the mayonnaise. Stir well, add chicken broth and milk, and stir again until all ingredients are well blended. Pour over and around frozen fillets and bake in oven preheated to 450 degrees 20–30 minutes or until fish flakes easily when gently probed with a fork. About 10 minutes before you expect fish to be done, combine flaked coconut and breadcrumbs and sprinkle over top of fillets and sauce.

Serves 2–4.

NOTE: This is good with canned or spiced fruit.

CRUNCHY FILLETS IN LEMON SAUCE

1 12-*ounce package frozen skinless fillets of any delicately flavored fish, freshwater or salt*
2 *tablespoons lemon juice*
¼ *teaspoon salt or to taste*
1 6-*ounce can evaporated milk*
1 1-*ounce box freshly opened cornflakes, crushed*
Butter or margarine

Add lemon juice and salt to evaporated milk and stir well. Dip block of still-frozen fillets into milk mixture, reserving the excess. Coat chunk of fillets on all sides with crushed cornflakes and place in a well-greased baking dish that leaves very little margin around the block of fish. Dot with butter or margarine and bake in an oven preheated to 450 degrees 20–24 minutes or until fish flakes easily when gently probed with tines of a fork. When fish is almost done and will need no more than 5 minutes longer to cook, pour reserved milk and lemon mixture around but not over it and continue cooking until sauce is heated. If top is turning too brown before fish is done, turn heat down to 400 degrees. Serve at once when done, spooning a little of the sauce over each serving.

Serves 2–3.

FANCY FROZEN FILLETS

With Clam and Crab

1 1-*pound box delicately flavored frozen fillets, skinless*
1 6-*ounce package frozen Alaska king crab*
1 8-*ounce can minced clams*
Salt and pepper to taste (optional)

Place blocks of still-frozen fillet and still-frozen crab in a well-greased baking dish. Open can of clams and drain liquid into a measuring cup, adding water to make ¾ cup. Heat liquid and pour over the 2 frozen blocks and add minced clams around them. Bake at 450 degrees in preheated oven for about 25 minutes or until almost done. Remove dish from oven, cut block of fillets crosswise into 1-inch-wide strips and spread them and the crab meat around in the liquid. Add salt and pepper to taste. Return to oven, turn off heat and let stand while fish and shellfish flavors blend and until the pieces of fillet finish cooking in the hot broth, about 10 minutes or until flakes separate easily when gently probed with the tines of a fork.

Serves 4–6.

NOTES:

· Dieters, divide fillet portions in bottom of soup plates, spoon chopped clams and colorful crab meat on top and surround with broth from pan.

· Nondieters serve fish, shellfish and broth over mashed potatoes, rice or spaghetti.

· Dieters who cheat may thicken broth by adding 1 10½-ounce can of condensed cream of mushroom soup, heating and pouring over rice. Top with fish and shellfish.

FILLETS OR STEAKS IN ORANGE SAUCE

1 12- *to 16-ounce package delicately flavored frozen white-fleshed
    fillets or steaks, salt or freshwater*
Salt and pepper to taste
1½ *tablespoons orange juice*
1 *teaspoon grated orange rind*
2 *tablespoons butter or margarine, melted*
½ *teaspoon lemon juice*
1 *small pinch nutmeg*

Place fish in well-greased baking pan. Combine remaining ingredients, mix well and pour over the fish. Bake 20–30 minutes in oven preheated to 450 degrees or until fish flakes easily when gently probed with tines of a fork. Serve at once, dividing sauce from pan over fish portions.

Serves 2–4.

FROZEN FISH STEAKS MARINARA   (I)

2 *12-ounce packages frozen fish steaks*
1 *1-pound jar marinara sauce*
1 *4-ounce package mozzarella cheese (use semisoft, solid pack, not
    the presliced)*

Spread pieces of steaks over bottom of well-greased baking pan. Pour about ¾ of the marinara sauce over fish. Slice cheese in about ⅛-inch-thick pieces and spread over sauce-covered fish. Cover with remaining sauce and bake in preheated 450-degree oven 20–24 minutes or until fish flakes easily when gently probed with the tines of a fork.
Serves 4.

FLOUNDER SHARPS (I)

8 *small flounder fillets or those from other delicately flavored fresh-water or saltwater fish you have frozen yourself, in a single layer, see page 248, item 7 under Pan-Frying*
½ *cup mayonnaise or salad dressing*
½ *cup shredded sharp cheddar cheese*
1 *teaspoon grated blue cheese*
1 *cup crushed very fresh and crisp potato chips*

Place still-frozen fillets in single layer in a very shallow baking pan and spread mayonnaise or salad dressing over them. Combine remaining 3 in-gredients, sprinkle over the top and bake in oven preheated to 400 degrees 8–15 minutes or until fish flakes separate easily when gently probed with the tines of a fork.
Serves 4.

HOT CHILI MACKEREL WITH CHICK PEAS (I)

1 *14-ounce package frozen mackerel fillets or any other salt or freshwater fish fillets with a distinctive flavor*
1 *1-pound can Puerto Rican style chick peas*
2 *peppers, finely chopped, from 10-ounce can very hot Chilies Jala-penos, or cayenne pepper to taste*
1 *teaspoon liquid from canned chilies*
½ *cup chicken broth*
½ *cup tomato paste*
¼ *pound sharp cheddar cheese, sliced*
¼ *to ½ medium head lettuce, shredded*
1 *large onion, finely chopped*

Place still-frozen fillets in a baking pan. Combine next 5 items in a sauce-pan. Heat and pour over and around the fish. Arrange sliced cheese over top of fish and bake in oven preheated to 450 degrees 23–28 minutes or until flakes separate easily when gently probed with tines of a fork. Serve at once and pass the shredded lettuce and chopped onion.
Serves 4–6.

NOTE: Taste the green chilies before you add. Grown in Mexico and our Southwest, they are very hot. Southwesterners who know how good they are and are accustomed to their nip may want to increase the quantity of chilies and liquid from can.

DIETERS: Substitute lean fish for the mackerel, eliminate sliced cheese and sprinkle just a little grated cheese over fish when serving.

OCEAN PERCH WITH A SHRIMP TOUCH

2 12- *to 16-ounce packages frozen ocean perch or other mild-flavored*
  fresh or saltwater fish fillets, skin on
1 *10-ounce can frozen shrimp soup*
1 *cup clear chicken soup*

Place blocks of still-frozen fillets side by side in bottom of a baking pan. Cut frozen shrimp soup into ½-inch slices and spread over fillets. Pour chicken broth around them. Bake in oven preheated to 500 degrees 20–30 minutes or until fish flakes easily when tested with a fork. Cut fish into chunks, stir until sauce is well blended. Serve at once over rice, spaghetti or noodles or as a soup.

Serves 6–8.

SALMON STEAKS IN MUSTARD SAUCE

2 *12-ounce packages frozen salmon steaks*
2 *tablespoons Dijon mustard*
1 *tablespoon lemon juice*
1 *tablespoon melted butter or margarine*
Salt and pepper to taste
1 *tablespoon chopped shallots (optional)*

Place still-frozen steaks on sheet of aluminum foil in bottom of baking pan. Sheet of foil should be more than twice the size of the steaks. Combine remaining ingredients, mix well and spread over the steaks. Fold excess foil over the steaks and double-fold all edges to seal them securely. Bake 20–40 minutes in oven preheated to 450 degrees, or until fish flakes easily when gently probed with tines of a fork. (Don't test it before it has cooked for 15 minutes or steam will escape too soon from package.)

Serves 4.

NOTE: Substitute any frozen fish steak that's available if salmon is not.

EASY WHITING DE LUXE

1 *1-pound package frozen whiting or other delicately flavored fillets,*
  salt or freshwater

1 *10½-ounce can condensed cream of mushroom soup*
½ *cup sherry wine*
½ *tablespoon freeze-dried minced shallots or chopped onion*
¼ *teaspoon paprika*

Place still-frozen block of fillets in baking pan, combine all remaining ingredients except paprika and pour over the top and around sides of fish block. Bake in oven preheated to 450 degrees 20–35 minutes or until fish flakes easily when gently probed with tines of a fork. Sprinkle with paprika and serve.

Serves 2–4.

NOTE: To speed cooking, heat sauce before pouring over fish.

17

Company Menus

When company comes, these are our favorite fish feasts. Indoors or out.

Many-Fish Fondue Menu

MANY-FISH FONDUE

FONDUE BROTH

FRUITS IN SEASON

CHEESES

TEA, WHITE WINE

MANY-FISH FONDUE (I) (O)

(Yeu Dar Bin Loo)

The original of this wonderfully festive recipe came from Arthur Lem, who taught it to Dan when they were writing *The Hong Kong Cookbook*. Arthur brought it with him from China, where it has been a wintry way of eating for thousands of years and precedes the famed Swiss fondue for we don't know how long. The Dar Bin Loo came into being through womanly originality, desperation, necessity, frustration—call it what you will. The menfolk would come in from the fields for their noontime or nighttime meals, then would crowd around the cooking fire to warm themselves, thus preventing the lady of the house from going on with the cooking. And, of course, they almost immediately began clamoring for food. So Mama created the Dar Bin Loo, simply by cutting everything she had intended to cook into raw, bite-size pieces and placing them around the fire in small dishes. She filled the cooking pot ("wok" is the Chinese word for it) with water, and each man would dip his own food and hold it there with chopsticks until it was eating ready. We created the Fish Dar Bin Loo mainly by eliminating the meat and poultry that might otherwise be included. As for the meaning of the

Chinese words "Dar Bin Loo"? Arthur's literal translation is this: "Everyone Gather Around the Fire for a Happy Family Feast." "Yeu"? That's Cantonese for "fish." It's pronounced *ye-ooh.*

It's especially appropriate for entertaining (any number from 2 to 20), because it can be cooked and served in the kitchen, the dining room or the living room, on the porch or in the yard. Depending on how many people are involved, you'll need 1 or 2 large cooking dishes and 1 or 2 electric plates or fondue units or other heating utensils powerful enough to maintain liquid at a simmer. If your equipment is electric, check to be sure it's been inspected for safety and reliability, and you'll need a heavy-duty line. Otherwise, a fuse may blow and what started out to be your most successful dinner of the year will come to an abrupt and disappointing end.

> 2 1-*pound bags frozen shrimp (individually frozen)*
> 1 1-*pound package frozen bay scallops*
> 2 *pounds fresh fish fillets; flounder, sole or halibut type of fish (or substitute frozen)*
> 1 *small bunch celery (if you have access to a Chinese grocery store, substitute 1 bunch bok choy)*
> 2 10-*ounce packages raw spinach*
> ½ *to* 1 *pound raw mushrooms*
> 1 5-*ounce càn water chestnuts*
> 1 5-*ounce can bamboo shoots*
> *Rice to make a minimum of 1 cup (cooked) for each diner*
> 4 *quarts chicken broth*
> 1 *cup soy sauce or teriyaki sauce*
> 1 *cup mustard*

Defrost frozen shellfish (and fish, too, if it's frozen) by placing in the refrigerator the night before.

Wash celery, spinach and raw mushrooms, and place in colander or spread out to dry. Wash shrimp, scallops and fish by dipping in cold salted water, then spread out on absorbent towels (lintfree cloth or paper) to dry.

The next procedure is to slice or tear most of the food into bite-size pieces and place them in small serving bowls (4- to 6-ounce cereal or soup dishes or individual casseroles are perfect). We serve this meal often and Inez clears off the kitchen tables, seats the ladies around it, gives each one a suitable knife and puts them to work slicing. If your entertaining isn't so informal, you'd better prepare your food an hour ahead of serving time in order to have everything ready on time. Slice the following into bite-size pieces: the scallops if you couldn't find bay and bought the larger sea scallops instead, the fish fillets, the celery (slice it about

¼ inch thick, on the diagonal), the raw mushrooms and the water chestnuts. Tear spinach into pieces roughly 2 by 2 inches.

Cook the rice on the kitchen stove while you slice the other foods. Divide broth into 2 large bowls, set on heating units and bring to a boil. Divide soy sauce and mustard each into 12–15 individual small serving dishes. Put everything on the serving-cooking table buffet style. (Perishable fish should be placed over ice, and for this purpose you can freeze an inch or so of water in the bottom of a 2½-inch-deep pan, cover with a platter set across the sides of the pan, and set your small serving dishes on the platter.) Put both chopsticks and fondue forks on your table if you have them. If not, dinner forks are fine. You'll also need several large perforated spoons for dipping cooked morsels out of the broth.

Now you're ready for your guests to start cooking, fondue fashion, whatever morsels appeal to them. Call them to the table and explain that they should cook the spinach in one bowl and the rest of the food in the other. Not a bit should take more than 2 or 3 minutes. The mustard and soy sauce can be used as dips or not, according to each person's individual taste. After all the food has been cooked, ladle the delicious broth into cups for those who appreciate great flavors to sip and enjoy.

Serves 12–15.

NOTE: *When serving, hold whatever amount of perishables you think may not be eaten in reserve in refrigerator. Use to refill emptied serving dishes as needed or for second-day eating. Throw out any fish or broth that has stood around on the serving table.*

LEFTOVERS: For delicious second-day eating, combine all the leftover fish and vegetables with leftover rice, stir in a can or two of mushroom, celery or cheese soup (dilute it with any leftover broth), pour into a well-greased casserole and bake 30–40 minutes in a 350-degree oven.

TEMPURA: Another version of the fish fondue is the Japanese tempura, the recipe for which will be found in the deep-fat frying section of this book, page 279. While this is very nice for a few adults, it makes for a much less versatile meal than the Dar Bin Loo because hot fat and batter are involved.

POACHED BIG FISH WITH CONCH SAUCE MENU

POACHED BIG FISH WITH CONCH SAUCE

CARROTS USED IN SAUCE MAKING

INSTANT MASHED POTATOES

TOSSED SALAD

FRUITS IN SEASON

COOKIES

COFFEE, BEER, TEA, WHITE WINE

If your husband is a sports fisherman, there will come a time when he proudly presents you with a 6- to 10-pound fish at 5 o'clock in the afternoon and says, "Could you please cook it tonight because on the way home I bumped into Bill and Alice and showed it to them and invited them over to share it with us at dinner. They'll be here about 7, 7:30. With their three kids." Don't faint. Instead, have a feast. Like this one that Inez literally whipped up on the cold winter evening that Dan brought home an 8-pound cod and 6 fishing friends to share it. We were all mighty glad she did (even Inez), because we discovered that there is absolutely nothing so good or so easy to cook perfectly as a very big fish.

The first thing Inez did was check her shelves to see what she had on hand and built the menu around that. The next thing she did was rush Dan out to the local hardware store before it closed to buy a large, reusable aluminum-foil roasting pan (20½ by 13 by 4 inches), which he got for only 99 cents. The third thing she did was send a couple of Dan's buddies down into the basement to complete the cleaning that Dan had given the fish while still aboard the boat. She also had them remove the head, an important operation because she needed it to get the sauce started so that it would be ready to pour over the rest of the fish as soon as it was cooked.

CONCH SAUCE

1 *large fish head*
1 *small onion*
4 *carrots*
4 *stalks celery*
1 *tablespoon wine vinegar*
Liquid from can of conch (don't use if you freeze extra broth)
½ *cup white wine*
2 *to 3 cups water*
2 *10½-ounce cans cream of mushroom soup*
Meat from 8-ounce can of conch, chopped
½–1 *cup heavy cream*

One hour before poaching fish, put fish head in pot and add next 7 ingredients, using enough of the water nearly to cover. Cook for about ½ hour at a low boil or until liquid is reduced to about half and has become rich in flavor. Strain broth, combine about 1 cup with mushroom soup in a heavy saucepan, beat with a whisk until smooth and heat, stirring frequently. Just before serving, stir in conch meat and enough cream to add richness and give desired consistency to sauce. Do not boil after adding cream. Pour into serving bowl and ladle over individual servings of fish.

NOTE: Serve the carrots from sauce with dinner. Pour remaining broth into freezer jars and freeze for future use (see page 118). If you have a cat, before discarding head, remove and save the meat, which will provide your feline with several much-appreciated meals, even though greatly overcooked.

POACHED BIG FISH   (O)

6- to 10-pound dressed fish, tail on, head off
Water to cover (or nearly so)
3 tablespoons Shrimp Spice (also called Crab Boil) (optional)
2 tablespoons vinegar
1 tablespoon salt

Set a roasting pan over 2 burners on the stove and fill it a little more than half full of hot water. Stir in Shrimp Spice, vinegar and salt, and bring to a boil. Add fish and adjust 2 burners so water will return to a low simmer and stay there. Cover tightly with aluminum foil and continue simmering for 20 minutes. Remove cover and test for doneness. When all but the thick, head end of the fish is done, ladle out and discard most of the poaching liquid, leaving an inch or two in bottom of pan, turn off the heat and start serving at once. Use the spatula and large perforated spoon to lift cooked flesh off the fish directly onto preheated dinner plates. (Informality is the name of the game at this dinner party.) Ladle a generous serving of Conch Sauce over the fish and let the diners (who should be eating a tossed salad prepared by one of the guests during this procedure) help themselves to mashed potatoes (the instant variety) and carrots. After serving the upper side of the fish from tail up to the part that's not quite done, carefully turn the fish over and serve from the other side. By the time you get to the thickest part it will have finished cooking in the hot water and your guests will be coming back for seconds. If there's any meat left, arrange it on a small platter and place the platter over a dish of ice cubes to chill. When fish is cool, pour about a cup of poaching liquid (including the spices) over it just to cover, and refrigerate. You have the most important part of a beautiful Scandinavian-style jellied-fish appetizer to serve the following day. You might even decide to make it the beginning of a second feast.

NOTE: This is a great dish to cook outdoors, over a keyhole lay fire (page 349) or a bed of charcoal (pages 344–345).

COLD FISH IN JELLY

Platter of leftover jellied fish (about 1 pound)
½ cup mayonnaise

¼ *cup heavy cream, whipped*
2 *eggs, hard-cooked, peeled and sliced*
2 *small tomatoes, thinly sliced*
Sprigs of watercress or parsley

Combine mayonnaise and whipped cream, and pipe a border around jellied fish. Make a border of alternating egg and tomato slices, either outside or inside the piped border. Garnish with watercress or parsley and serve.

Serves 8–10 as an appetizer.

ALL FISH BUFFET MENU (I) (O)

SMOKED MOLLUSKS IN ONION BOATS

FISH DIP

STEAMED CLAMS (see page 224)

STEAMED SALMON STEAKS IN ASPIC

CAESAR SALAD

SMOKED FISH POTATO SALAD

SCALLOP, SHRIMP, NUT AND FRUIT MOLD

POTATO CHIPS, SHRIMP CHIPS, CRACKERS

BREAD AND BUTTER

BEER, SODA, LEMONADE, WHITE WINE

AND FOR DESSERT MUCH LATER:

BAKERY CHEESECAKE

COFFEE, TEA, MILK, COCOA

Nothing is more fun, nothing is more informal, than an all-fish buffet party that includes every member of every family, no matter how young. Indoors or outdoors, preferably the latter, and something for everyone to do. Even the toddlers. The more the merrier, and with only the slightest bit of direction, because the objective is not perfection and magazine-cover good looks. Fun and flavor are the passwords for the day and if a child has fun piping a picture across the middle of the salmon aspic instead of around it, so be it, because it will not detract from the flavor. Nor does it make any difference if an expedition sets out for soft-shell steamer clams, and a youngster proudly digs a hard-shell chowder clam instead.

SMOKED MOLLUSKS IN ONION BOATS (O)

(This is our favorite appetizer, not just because it's so easy to prepare, but because it's also very, very good. We've been eating it at least twice a week, in one form or another, for years, whether we have company or not.)

> 1 *medium sliced onion*
> 1 *3½-ounce can of smoked or barbecued mussels or smoked clams or oysters*

Quarter each onion and separate layers into several boat-shaped pieces, arrange on a small serving platter, place mussels, clams or oysters in each boat and serve.

Makes about 24 appetizers.

NOTE: These appetizers can be prepared an hour or so before needed, covered with airtight cover and refrigerated. To waft away onion odor, take from refrigerator, remove cover and let stand in kitchen for a few minutes before serving.

FISH* DIP   (O)

> 1 *cup cooked fish, minced*
> *½-pint container commercial sour cream*
> 1–2 *tablespoons crumbled freeze-dried shallots or mild onion*
> 1–2 *tablespoons finely minced raw spinach, scallion tops or parsley*
> *½ teaspoon garlic powder*
> 1 *teaspoon lemon juice*
> 1 *teaspoon Worcestershire sauce*
> *Paprika*

Combine all ingredients except paprika, mix well, sprinkle with paprika for color and serve with crackers, chips or cross-cut slices of cucumber, carrot, heart of cabbage, young broccoli stem or 2- or 3-inch slices of celery stalk.

Makes 2 cups.

NOTE: Dip can be prepared 2 or 3 hours ahead of time, covered tightly and refrigerated.

STEAMED CLAMS

See page 224.

STEAMED SALMON STEAKS IN ASPIC   (I)
Decorated to Look Like a Fish

(This dish can be partially prepared the day before and finished up just before serving.)

* Any fish will do, fin fish or shellfish, home-cooked or canned.

3 *salmon steaks, ¾ to 1 inch thick*
1 *stuffed olive, sliced*
1 *piece of canned pimento*
1 *green pepper, washed and seeds removed*
1 *envelope unflavored gelatin*
¼ *cup cold water*
½ *cup chicken broth (your own if possible), strained*
½ *cup white wine*
1 *teaspoon lemon juice*
½ *cup mayonnaise*
½ *cup sour cream*
3 *hard-cooked eggs, sliced (optional)*
1–2 *cucumbers, sliced (optional)*

Step One of Preparation the Day Before: Put about 1 inch of lightly salted water in bottom of steamer or heavy pot, bring to a boil and turn down to a low boil. Place rack above it. Wrap each salmon steak in a piece of cheesecloth, place on the rack and cover. Steam for 5 to 7 minutes, depending on thickness of fish or until flakes separate easily when gently probed with a fork. When making this dish it's much better that the salmon be a little underdone than the slightest bit overcooked, so lift fish immediately out of the hot pot and onto a cool platter. When cool enough to handle, carefully remove the skin and bones, keeping steaks as nearly intact as possible. Using a spatula, remove steaks to a serving platter and arrange them in the shape of a fish. (Don't worry about the authenticity of its appearance. A mere suggestion of fish shape will do nicely.) Decorate salmon (or let your uninhibited children do it), using sliced stuffed olive for an eye, pimento strips for a mouth, green pepper strips for fins and to outline tail. Cover carefully, so as not to disturb decorations, and refrigerate.

Sprinkle unflavored gelatin in cold water, stir, combine chicken broth and wine and bring to a boil, add to gelatin and stir until gelatin is dissolved. Stir in lemon juice and let gelatin stand until it is consistency of egg white. Remove salmon from refrigerator, uncover and spoon a layer of the aspic over it. Re-cover and return to refrigerator. When layer of aspic is firm, repeat the process and keep repeating it until salmon is covered with a nice glaze. If aspic gets too firm to spread, heat it, then let it stand until it is the right consistency again.

Step Two of Preparation Just Before Serving: Combine mayonnaise and sour cream in decorating gun and pipe a border around outline of fish (another job for the children). Arrange a row of alternating egg and cucumber slices around edge of platter. Put platter over a foil-covered pan of ice and place on the buffet table.

Serves 6–8.

CAESAR SALAD*   (I) (O)

(A 2-step salad perfect for entertaining since most of the work is planned for doing ahead.)

2 *small heads romaine lettuce*
1 *clove garlic, cut in half*
10 *tablespoons salad oil*
1¼ *teaspoons salt*
¼ *teaspoon pepper*
¼ *teaspoon Worcestershire sauce*
½ *teaspoon anchovy paste*
½ *teaspoon creamy mild mustard*
6 *slices stale white bread*
1 *egg, very fresh*
½ *lemon in tightly closed small plastic bag*
1 *tablespoon crumbled blue cheese in tightly closed small plastic bag*
2 *tablespoons freshly grated Parmesan cheese in tightly closed small plastic bag*

Step 1: Cut stem end from romaine lettuce, discard any spoiled or unsightly leaves, and wash under running water, being sure to get rid of all the sand. Shake off moisture, then place leaves in a large, clean linen towel, hold ends securely and shake to remove the remaining moisture. Cut and discard heavy rib from each of the larger leaves. Place leaves in a plastic bag and close tightly.

Combine ½ the garlic clove in a jar with ½ the salad oil, salt, pepper, Worcestershire sauce, anchovy paste and mustard, and shake. Cover tightly and set aside.

Lay slices of stale bread in a flat pile, cut away crusts (save them for another recipe), and cut bread into ½-inch cubes. Put bread cubes into a plastic bag and fasten shut.

Combine second ½ of garlic clove with remaining salad oil in a small jar, cover tightly, place in a paper bag together with the plastic bag of bread cubes, and set aside.

Assemble the bag of romaine lettuce, the jar of salad oil mixture, the paper bag containing bread cubes, the oil, egg, ½ lemon, and the plastic bags of cheese and put them all together in a bag and refrigerate. If you're afraid of breaking the egg, wrap it in tissue and put it in a jar. Now everything's ready for the second step. Step 1 can be prepared the night before a buffet dinner in your outdoor dining room or just before packing your cooler to take on a picnic or aboard your boat.

* From *The Complete Outdoor Cookbook*, by Dan and Inez Morris (Hawthorn Books).

Step 2: Take bowl of salad ingredients from refrigerator or cooler. Remove the small bottle of oil and bread cubes. Discard clove of garlic and pour the oil from the bottle into a large shallow pan. Spread over the bottom of the pan and scatter the bread cubes over the coating of oil. Put pan in 400-degree oven and toast cubes for about 15 minutes, stirring often or until they are crisp and have a light golden color. Transfer to a covered bowl or jar.

While bread cubes are browning, tear romaine lettuce into bite-size pieces and put them in a large salad bowl.

Carry bowl of lettuce and other salad ingredients (including toasted bread cubes) on a tray to the serving table and mix and serve. Caesar salad is one of those dishes that is rather special and should be served with a proud flourish!

Shake bottle of oil dressing, pour it over salad, and toss with salad fork and spoon. Add both packages of cheese and toss again. Break the raw egg into the salad bowl, squeeze juice of the lemon directly over egg and then immediately mix the egg into the greens. Keep at it, tossing thoroughly until not a trace of yolk or white remains to be seen. Dump warm, toasty bread cubes into the bowl, mix lightly, and serve at once on individual salad plates.

Serves 12 to 16.

NOTE: If you prefer egg to be slightly cooked, put it in a small pan, cover with cold water, bring the water just to boil, turn off and immediately remove the egg. If you put the egg in the water just after putting the bread cubes in the oven, it should be ready at the right moment.

SMOKED FISH POTATO SALAD (I)

1 *pound smoked fish, boned, skinned and flaked (smoked eel, tuna, salmon, sablefish, etc.)*
3 *cups freshly cooked diced potatoes*
½ *to 1 recipe Tartar Sauce, page 132, or Mayonnaise and Cream Sauce, page 134, the amount depending on how moist you like your salad to be*
⅓ *cup chopped onion*
¼ *teaspoon celery seed*
½ *teaspoon salt or to taste*
Pepper to taste
1 *cup chopped celery*
½ *cup tiny raw, well-cleaned mushroom caps, whole (optional)*
½ *cup pitted sliced ripe olives*
Lettuce leaves
½ *cup sliced radishes*

1 *hard-boiled egg, peeled and sliced*
1 *tomato, cut in wedges*

Combine cooked potatoes (if possible while they are still warm), sauce, chopped onion, celery seed, salt and pepper, mix well and refrigerate for at least 3 hours. Add celery, mushrooms, olives and fish, mix and pile into a bowl lined with lettuce leaves. Garnish with radishes, sliced egg and tomato wedges and serve.

Serves 6–8.

SHELLFISH POTATO SALAD: Substitute ½ pound shellfish, flaked or chopped, for smoked fish in preceding recipe. Substitute Shrimp Sauce, page 131, for tartar sauce.

Serves 6–8.

TOMATOES STUFFED WITH FISH OR SHELLFISH POTATO SALAD: Drain 8–10 tomato shells and stuff with smoked fish or shellfish potato salad.

SCALLOP, SHRIMP, NUT AND FRUIT MOLD   (I)

¼ *pound raw, individually frozen cocktail shrimp*
¼ *pound fresh raw sea scallops*
2 *cups of water*
Juice of *½ lemon*
⅛ *teaspoon garlic powder*
1 *stalk celery, cut into pieces*
1 *tablespoon grapefruit juice*
2 *tablespoons orange juice*
1 *3-ounce package lime gelatin*
¾ *cup boiling water*
½ *cup ripe seedless (or seeded) grapes, chilled*
½ *cup peeled grapefruit sections, chilled*
½ *cup peeled orange sections, chilled*
½ *cup roasted blanched slivered almonds*
¼ *cup mayonnaise*
1 *3-ounce package cream cheese*
Shredded lettuce

Combine water, lemon juice, garlic powder and celery in small saucepan. Cover frozen shrimp with cold water. Let stand 1 minute. Lift shrimp out of water one at a time. Pick off any bits of sand vein, place shrimp in saucepan and bring to a simmer. Cook for 3 minutes at a simmer, turn off heat and test for doneness. Let stand in hot broth if necessary to finish cooking. Remove from broth and refrigerate as soon as almost cool. Cook sea scallops for 1 to 3 minutes or until just done in same broth. Remove scallops, cool, cut into pieces approximately ½ inch square and refrigerate.

Discard celery and all but ¾ cup broth. Strain, add grapefruit and orange juice, cool and set in freezer to get ice cold. Dissolve gelatin in boiling water, add ice-cold broth and juice mixture, stir well and let stand until it's beginning to set. Mix shellfish, fruit and nuts together, stir into gelatin and pour into 5-cup mold. Use an electric mixer to blend mayonnaise and cream cheese together until smooth. Stir lightly into upper half of mold. Chill from 2 to 24 hours, unmold on a bed of shredded lettuce and serve.

Serves 6–8 as a salad; 10–12 as an appetizer.

SHELLFISH, FRUIT AND NUT MOUSSE: Beat slightly thickened gelatin into cream cheese–mayonnaise mixture, then stir in fruit and nuts and pour into lightly greased mold.

KITCHEN CLAMBAKE MENU

(O)

KITCHEN CLAMBAKE

TOSSED SALAD

GARLIC BREAD

FRUITS IN SEASON

CHEESES

COFFEE, COCOA, BEER

KITCHEN (TIN CAN) CLAMBAKE (O)

Elsewhere, we give you detailed instructions for preparing and serving a traditional New England Clambake at beach or picnic ground. Here, now, is the way you can very easily get almost the same results in your own kitchen or backyard. All you do is load a 5-gallon pretzel can or store-bought steamer with the same goodies you'd expect to pile into a clambake pit, add some salt water, poke a few vent holes in the lid if you're using a pretzel can, bring to a boil and let it steam for 20 minutes. Here's a list of ingredients you'll need to serve 6 people and the details of how to do it:

Water, salted to taste
6 *1-pound live lobsters*
6 *ears of corn, husked*
6 *dozen steamer clams*
6 *baking potatoes*
1 *pound melted butter*
6 *lemon wedges*

Pour water into steamer or pretzel can until it's about 2 inches deep. Pick up lobsters by the back of the neck (see page 64 if you want to kill them first) and add to the pot. Pile the husked corn on top of them. Divide the steamer clams into 6 disposable aluminum dishes or tie in cheesecloth bags and put them on top of the corn. Put your potatoes into the kitchen oven to bake, then cover the pretzel can (remember to poke at least 3 holes in the lid) or steamer and turn the heat on under it. When a good, steady stream of steam pours from the holes, start timing. In 20 minutes your clambake will be ready to serve. Start with the clams, serving 1 dish or bag to each person, along with an individual dish of melted butter and a wedge of lemon. Strain broth from bottom of can or steamer, serve a cupful steaming hot to each person, who should use it, first, to dip each clam in to remove any sand, then, after sand settles to the bottom, to drink. While your guests sip the delicious broth, you can clear away the clam shells (pop any untouched clams into refrigerator) and bring on the lobster, corn and potatoes, with a fresh supply of hot melted butter. Page 65 shows you just how to go about getting the lobster meat out of its shell.

Serves 6.

18

Things You Should Know About Outdoor Fish Cookery

Certainly you must be sure of it by now. Fish is our favorite food. Any kind of fish. Cooked any kind of way. And sometimes, some fish, cooked not at all.

But what you don't know is this: the place we like to cook and eat fish most of all is outdoors: beside a mountain stream, a meadow lake, the seaside surf, an isolated strip of sand reachable only by boat, our own backyard. That's where we like fish best. Outdoors. Once you've tried it, we think you will, too.

As for the fish that you'll like better than any other, it will be the one you've just landed and cooked over a wood fire, the clam you've just dug, opened and eaten raw, the inland crawdad you've just caught and steamed over rocks as if it were a New England clambake.

Or, if you're a can't-get-away city dweller, it will be the frozen fillet that you've bought at market and cooked over a hibachi, perched high on an apartment-house balcony, or a lobster tail steamed on a back-yard charcoal grill.

There is only one meaningful difference between outdoor and indoor cooking: the fire. It is, really, only a little difference. But as Spencer Tracy said to Katharine Hepburn (if any of you can remember back that far) in the film *Adam's Rib: "Vive la différence!"*

Indoors, the fire is in or on your kitchen stove. Outdoors, it depends pretty much upon where you are—in the yard, in camp, on the beach, aboard your boat, on an apartment-house terrace.

Living on a barrier-reef island off the south shore of Long Island as we do, we have them all practically right at our doorstep and we love it. Catch a saltwater fish a block from home and cook it minutes

later over charcoal in our yard, quick inland jaunts for freshwater trout
and then a camp cooking fire, clambakes on the beach, golden-flame
sunrise breakfast aboard our boat or on an isolated sandspit that no
man can reach either by foot or by car, visits to friends in New York
and a hibachi cookout on their righ-rise balcony.

Try any one of them, or all of them, where you live and you'll love
them, too.

Here's how:

THE YARD FIRE

You don't need much of a yard in order to cook outdoors. If you have
the space for a small charcoal grill (the trade now calls them "charcoal
stoves") and room to move around it, that's enough. Build a small fire,
keep water handy and an eye open for flying sparks and you're in business. Just cook your fish and carry it inside to eat.

However, most people have more yard space than that and so
we'll talk mainly about that.

Flooding the outdoor marketplace today are all sizes and sorts of
charcoal cookers. Some have ersatz-charcoal stones that achieve a
charcoal glow and a charcoal taste and tap into the household gas line
for fuel, others roll around like a cart and are fed by a small outboard-
motor type gas tank, still others operate on electricity.

You pays your money and you takes your choice.

They all burn well. But none of them burns better than a charcoal
grill that you can pick up for about $3.00. True, they'll do more things—
such as roast a turkey or baste a hefty hunk of beef. But we're talking
about cooking fish, remember. For that, you don't need all that kind of
gadgetry.

In fact, you don't even have to spend that $3.00 for the dime-store
grill. We have the greatest possible, for our purposes, charcoal stove in
our yard. We put it where we want it, we raise or lower it in a jiffy, we
make it as big or as little as necessary for what we're going to cook.
And it didn't cost us a dime.

All we did was make do with what was already lying around our
house and, we're sure, around your house, too—two concrete blocks, a
half-dozen red bricks, an oven grate from a long-gone kitchen stove, a
sheet of aluminum foil.

We lay the foil on the ground, place the blocks parallel to each
other, turning the holes in them in accordance with the direction of the
wind in order to provide a perfectly controlled draft and moving the
blocks in or out in accordance with the size of the fire we'll need; then
we spread the oven rack atop them and we're in business. Oh yes, the
red bricks. We use them for raising and lowering the grate. To raise it,

onto the concrete blocks go some bricks, onto the bricks goes the rack. To lower it, vice versa. Also they're sometimes a help in reducing or enlarging the size of the fire hole.

It's the most versatile outdoor cooker you'll ever see, whether it cost $3.00 or $300.00. We haven't patented the idea. Not yet. So the Super-Special Morris Outdoor Grill will cost you nothing.

The important thing about backyard cooking is not the stove, it is the fire—what you burn, how you burn it, how you use it. There is nothing better than charcoal for fish cookery. And never will you need much of it. For beef yes, for fish no.

Just lay in your fire bed as many chunks of charcoal as you'll need for your particular size and cut of fish, more for a whole dressed fish, less for a fillet. Light your fire, let the coals burn until they're a red-flecked gray, set your grate about 4 inches above them, set your fish atop the grate and test it with a fork just as you would indoors. When it flakes easily, it's done.

That's all there is to cooking fish outdoors in your own backyard.

HOW TO START A CHARCOAL FIRE

We give this special attention because we think it's important that you know how to start a charcoal fire properly. By "properly" we mean swiftly, surely, easily, and most of all—safely. There are three methods that we know of which may or may not meet the first criteria, but only one that also meets the all-important fourth criterion—safety.

Here's what's wrong with the first three methods:

• *Electric starters.* You've seen them, maybe you've used them; either straight or oval-shaped metal rods attached to an electric cord that you just plug in. Poke the rod into the cold coals, the rod gets hot and the coals catch fire. Fine. Except that, for some reason unknown to us, sometimes the rods blow up.

But what's much worse and even more probable: if a youngster accidentally or otherwise touches the rod, you'd better call a doctor quick; if a woman brushes a dress against it, you'd better roll her in a blanket quick; if you forget to pull the plug, maybe you'd better call the fire department quick.

• *Fluids and jellies.* We don't have to say anything about these horrors other than to tell you to read the label on any can of the stuff you see in the store. You'll be shocked out of your mind at all the cautions, the warnings, the poison symbols that you'll find there, including the warnings against the possibility of death!

Besides, they make the fish taste bad.

• *Quick-start briquettes.* Virtually all the food we eat in these days of profit-before-people has been chemically treated, either by accident or by design. But we don't have also to cook our food over chemicals. It is chemicals that make it possible for briquettes to catch fire quickly and so we urge you not to use them. Not only will they taint the taste of fish, they also are expensive.

So now we'll tell you about the perfect way of starting a charcoal fire. You do it with a gadget that looks like a short length of stove pipe and is called an "Auto Fire," the "Auto" being short for "automatic."

Dan discovered it a few years ago while prowling among the booths at an alleged sportsmen's show in the New York Coliseum. There, stuck away in a corner amid the potato peelers and cherry pitters and onion slicers, was this exhibit with not a single spectator within 15 yards of it. The words "charcoal fire" caught Dan's eye; he walked over and the man there explained how it worked. We were writing *The Complete Outdoor Cookbook* then and for months we had been trying everything under the sun in the hope of finding something that we could honestly recommend to our readers—bits of candles set amid tepee-pile kindling, waxed milk cartons, fuzz sticks. You name it, we tried it.

So Dan took an Auto Fire home with him, we tried it, we raved about it in *The Outdoor Cookbook* (which, incidentally, was an Outdoor Life Book Club best seller) and now we rave about it again in this cookbook.

The Auto Fire is about 15 inches high, and about one-third the way up from the bottom is a trapdoor. Around the perimeter of the lower part of the Auto Fire and in the trapdoor are a series of holes about 1 inch in diameter. You set the Auto Fire in your charcoal stove, put a wad of newspaper under the trapdoor, pour the cheapest kind of charcoal you can buy into the top part of the Auto Fire, poke a lighted match through one of the holes to ignite the paper, wait 6 to 10 minutes, depending upon how much charcoal you're using, then pick up the Auto Fire by the handle.

Lo, the trap door opens up, hot coals drop into your fire bed and you're ready to start cooking.

Eureka, our search had ended!

Well, the man Dan had spoken to in the Coliseum turned out to be the one who had invented the Auto Fire—Garner B. Byars is his name—and we wrote to him and asked where our *Complete Outdoor Cooking* readers could buy it. Byars replied that since stores weren't exactly flooding him with orders, they'd better write to him.

So we printed his address and, we're happy to say, he was flooded with orders and stores are now beginning to stock the Auto Fire. We think Sears, Roebuck is one of them but we're not sure, so we'll repeat the address:

G. B. Byars, President, The Auto Fire Corporation, P. O. Box 487,

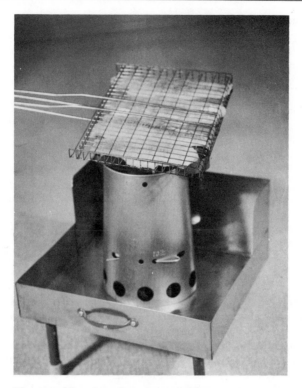

The Auto Fire: the safest, surest, quickest way to start a charcoal fire we know. And a fine fish-cooker too.

Corinth, Mississippi 38834. The price is $4.95 for an aluminized one, $8.95 for the stainless-steel version, and you won't be sorry you spent the money on either. Besides, the Auto Fire has 2 added dividends: you can take it ice fishing with you to keep warm, and you can set a small rack atop it and broil a small fish right then and there. Like a recipe we created and call Byars' Bass Barbecue. It's on page 366.

Camping and the Campfire

If you've never camped out, if you've never cooked a just-caught fish over a wood fire, you haven't yet really begun to live. If you are physically and mentally up to it, you could backpack, horseback or canoepack deep into the wilderness. But if you are like so many millions of Americans who have discovered, and are increasingly discovering, that 4-wheel vehicles of every conceivable size, shape and form can pack them to at least the edge of the wilderness, why, someday soon you'll be off on a camping jaunt, too.

You'll love it. Especially when you get that first smell of a campfire, that first nighttime sound of a fish plopping back into the water after leaping for a nocturnal morsel, that early-morning aroma of coffee perking.

A camping trip is more rugged, true, than living at home. Still, though, in this day and age it doesn't have to be primitive. Why, on an auto-camping trip that took us from Long Island to Colorado and New Mexico we ate meals that might have come straight from an epicurean kitchen, all because Inez had the foresight to pack along condiments, seasonings, ingredients that most campers for some reason think can be used only at home. Not only that, but a couple of good cooking utensils that we use constantly in our kitchen.

Our car was only a compact one, a Plymouth Valiant, we had no trailer, and we had to take along gear enough for a 6,000-mile, 7-week safari. And yet Inez managed, by careful planning and storage, to take all this along, too: onion powder, garlic powder, fresh lemons, dry mustard, soy sauce, canned pineapple cubes, honey, wine vinegar, sherry wine, tawny port wine, brown sugar, arrowroot, raisins, nuts, olive oil, instant broth, dry salad dressing, sauce mixes, thyme, tarragon, marjoram, Worcestershire sauce, dill, sage, toasted breadcrumbs, red chili powder, Louisiana Hot Sauce and paprika. Plus such utensils as a 5-quart heavy aluminum pot with cover, 2 large iron skillets, a long-handled hinged wire grill and an Auto Fire for charcoal cooking when we couldn't find wood.

All of that (!) but not necessarily in their market-size containers. Of whatever was bulky—wine, sugar, vinegar, for instance—Inez poured only what she thought we'd need into small screw-top jars and such. Whatever could go into smaller packages did, even such items as spices and raisins.

Result: we ate like royalty. Especially when Dan caught fish.

You'll find recipes for all the fish dishes we created on that memorable camping trip, recipes that made use of those ingredients, recipes prepared outdoors, cooked outdoors (at least one in a driving rainstorm) and eaten outdoors. Cooked mostly on wood fires, sometimes on charcoal, and sometimes on a propane-gas camp stove.

We urge you, we beg you: go camping sometime soon. First a weekend. Then a week. Then longer. And cook over wood as much as you can.

THE CAMPFIRE

There are at least a dozen ways that we can think of for building a campfire, all of them good, but the one that we think is best for all-around camp use is what outdoorsmen call the "keyhole lay."

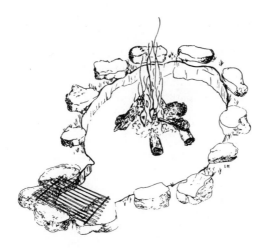

The keyhole lay camp fireplace.

The fireplace looks just as you'd expect, like a keyhole. And very simple to shape. Collect stones 4 or 5 inches in diameter, and arrange them to form 2 connecting circles, one large, one small. Dig out inside the circles to about a 4-inch depth. Build a wood fire in the large pit for warmth, for cozy camaraderie, for sitting around and telling tall tales by. Rake hot coals from the big circle into the small circle for cooking over. Spread a wire grate over the small-circle rocks and that's the top of your stove. Before you get that far, though, you have to collect wood to burn and know how to burn it.

COLLECTING CAMPFIRE WOOD

First of all, the most visible source of supply is absolutely out. A growing tree, we mean, and for a variety of reasons: it's tough to cut; it will take too long to burn; when it does, if it does, it will give off too much smoke; and we have to start conserving our green-growing things if mankind is to survive, because they make oxygen, the very air we breathe.

Still there are plenty of sources of supply:

· Dead trees that are still standing, preferably saplings.

· Hangers, meaning a dead sapling that started to fall but got hung up on some foliage.

· Tree stumps.

· Tree stubs, meaning a standing dead tree whose top long ago fell away.

· Logs, meaning heavy limbs, trunks and tops of dead trees that lie on the ground.

That gives you a lot to choose from. So, please, leave that growing bush or tree alone.

You'll need 3 sizes of wood, in this order: tinder, kindling, firewood.

The tinder can be only a handful of anything that will catch fire swiftly and then will burn quick and hot—dry leaves, pine needles, pine cones, grass, small twigs, bark (birch is best), bits of wood splinters from stubs or stumps, even a loose wad of paper.

A bit larger than tinder is the kindling, which next goes on a campfire. It can be small dry branches, or shavings whittled with a small knife from any dry piece of wood. Woodsmen swear by "fuzz sticks," which are nothing more than shavings that never quite make it to the ground. To make one all you need is a 12- to 18-inch-long core of about 1-inch dry wood. Notch shavings into it from end to end but don't quite sever them; they'll roughly resemble a porcupine's quills. That's a fuzz stick.

Finally comes firewood, the stuff that you warm yourself with, the stuff that makes fine cooking coals. Which means logs, or lengths of wood no more than 2 or 3 inches in diameter. A good rule for determining the right size is this: a piece of dry wood that you can cut through with 2 swipes of a sharp hatchet.

It can be softwood or hardwood, the only difference being that you'd use more soft than hard because it burns more quickly. You should, however, try to avoid resinous woods, because they give off sparks. However, a grill with crisscross wiring laid across the fire will help dissipate the sparks before they can do damage. The best rule to go by though is the Boy Scout standby: be prepared. Or another way of saying it: be ready to combat effectively, affirmatively, any emergency situation that may arise. In the woods that goes for everything, not only fires.

As for folks who do not camp in forested areas, there is plenty of dead wood lying around for the taking just about anywhere you happen to be. On a beach or cn a riverbank it is driftwood. Just about every town has a sawmill or a lumberyard and they have lots of scrap wood to get rid of.

YOUR COOKING FIRE

Lay a long, fat length of firewood in the large end of the keyhole. Against it, about amidships, loosely pile your tinder. Lean your kindling, including the fuzz stick with its porcupine ends pointing down, in a crisscross pattern around the tinder and against the base log. The result should look like the frame for half a tepee. Stand with your back to the wind, strike a match and set the flame to the tinder.

As the flames take hold and the wood burns down, add more to the

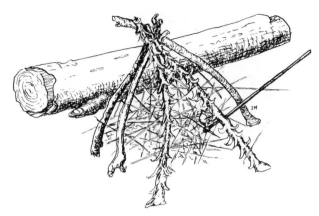

Lay a cooking fire to look like this.

fire and rake the coals into the smaller end of the keyhole. Fill the pit to ground level and the coals will be 4 inches deep, ideal for cooking a full camp meal. Bury potatoes in the coals at the outset, because they'll take longest to cook, then spread the grill atop the circle of stones. It will be your cooking surface. On it place the coffee pot almost immediately, because it will take a while to perk, then the soup, then the vegetables.

Last, but by no means least, add the fish to the grill (in a long-handled hinged grill), because they'll cook most quickly. Test them with a fork for doneness—the potatoes, too—and don't be surprised when it turns out to be a tie. If perchance the coffee, soup and vegetables were done before the potatoes and fish, set them on the side to keep warm.

TIMING

Timing is a tricky business when cooking outdoors, so we'd suggest that you pay little attention to the clock and a lot to feel and taste. Don't hesitate to poke that fork into fish and potato, to pinch or nibble a bit of vegetable or sip a spot of soup. All of that is especially important if you're in high country, because the greater the altitude, the longer the cooking time. For example, at 6,000 feet it will take 5 minutes to boil a 3-minute egg.

The Clambake and Other Beach-Cooking Fires

We'll save the best for last—the clambake. Specifically, the New England clambake, the one the Indians introduced to the Pilgrims. We'll tell you how you, too, can enjoy one, although you may live in Minnesota or Montana or Manitoba, which are a few miles removed from Maine and Massachusetts. Because, you see, you do not need the sea in order to have a clambake. First, though, let's talk about more mundane cooking methods.

You cook on the beach, any sand beach, just as you would cook anywhere else, except that your fireplace will be easier to construct, because all you need do is scoop out a hole with your hands and build up the sides with sand instead of stones. Or, if you have kids, give them each a clam shell and let them do it. Watch them, though. Otherwise your fireplace may turn out to be their sand castle.

The durability of your fire hole will be determined by the length of your stay. If you intend to make camp for a week or more, you ought to shape it like a keyhole lay (page 349). But line the bottom with aluminum foil so that you'll scrape down coals, not sand, when it comes time to cook.

If you plan only a weekend outing, a trench fireplace will do fine. Dig it about 12 inches deep, 12 inches wide and 30 inches long. Slope the sides. Build the fire in the center of the trench and straddle it with a wire rack about 18 to 24 inches long. Thus you'll be able to feed it fresh wood from either end without disturbing any pots or pans sitting on the grate.

A slit-trench fireplace.   This shaped hole makes a good fireplace too.

If you plan only a 1-day outing, or if you want to cook only the fish you've just caught, you can have a perfect cooking fire by doing nothing more than digging a hole about 10 inches deep in the sand. If you're planning a full-scale beach picnic for the family and perhaps some friends, make the hole about 16 inches wide. If there is only to be you and a fish, an 8- or 10-inch-diameter hole will be fine. In either case, however, slope the sides.

This firehole in the sand is ideal for cooking in foil. Just wrap a chunk of fish, or a whole fish if it's small enough, in a piece of heavy foil, bury the package in the coals and relax. The fish will be done in a matter of minutes. You can tell by looking and feeling or, if you have a fork with you, by applying the fork test. You know, when the flesh flakes easily the fish is done. Don't worry about opening the foil package. You won't harm the fish and you can always rewrap it if need be.

As for the wood that you'll need for a beach cooking fire—the same as in camp, tinder, kindling, firewood. Only you'll have less trouble gathering it, because the water will most likely have washed it ashore for you. So, too, for the wood that you'll need for what comes next.

THE NEW ENGLAND CLAMBAKE

There are two kinds, the Maine Clambake, and the Rest of New England Clambake. The difference, though, is not in the end results: the fun, the sport, the gaiety, the wonderful taste. The key variant is the pit that serves as the fireplace. In Maine it is shallow, elsewhere it is not. We'll tell you about both, and after that you're on your own.

But before we do, let's tell you that the word "clambake" is a misnomer, because it is not a "bake" at all. Rather, it's a "steam." And why, when the Pilgrim Fathers gave name to it, they did not call it a "clam-steam" we'll never know.

What's more, it isn't only clams that go into a clambake. It's clams, plus lobster, plus fin fish, plus potatoes, plus corn, plus chicken, plus whatever else suits your fancy. Or you can leave out any of them. Including the clams.

That's because a clambake, you see, is more than just something different to eat. It's also a state of mind, a mood, a party, a delightful daylong adventure by the sea. That is, if you live near the sea. If you don't, no matter. You can still have clambake, complete with all the sea-grown ingredients. Just have your fishmonger order the clams and lobster for you. Or buy canned clams and frozen lobster tails.

Or leave one or both of them out. Substitute crawfish instead. As we said, a clambake is a state of mind, and the more people, the merrier the state. In fact, it might be something of a waste if you planned a clambake for only the immediate members of your family, unless, that is, you have a very large family. Not only will you have more fun, but there will be less work for each of you to do. A clambake, a true Indian-style clambake, that is, involves a lot of work. But don't call it work. Rather, call it play, because that's what it will be if there are plenty of people to divvy up the various chores. Twelve, we'd say, would be a perfect number. So here now a clambake, not recipe, but menu for 12.

CLAMBAKE MENU FOR 12

RADISHES, OLIVES, PICKLES, GREEN ONIONS, CELERY, CUCUMBERS,
   CARROT STICKS

STEAMED CLAMS WITH MELTED BUTTER

STEAMED FISH WITH MELTED BUTTER

STEAMED LOBSTER WITH MELTED BUTTER

STEAMED CHICKEN WITH MELTED BUTTER

STEAMED CORN WITH MELTED BUTTER

STEAMED POTATOES WITH MELTED BUTTER

LETTUCE AND ONION SALAD WITH FRENCH DRESSING (page 147)

SALT AND PEPPER

LEMON

APPLE PIE

CHEDDAR CHEESE

WATERMELON

COFFEE, TEA, MILK, FRUIT ADES AND BEER

That's the menu. Quite a feast. Quite a contemplation. Quite a bit of advance planning and preparation. Mind you, that's a menu for 12 people,
which means that, not counting fixings such as bread and butter and radishes and desserts and such, you'll need this:

   144 *clams, preferably steamers, tied* 12 *to a bundle in cheesecloth*
   12 *fish steaks or fillets or* 12 *small pan fish*
   12 *lobsters, each weighing about* 1¼ *pounds*
   12 *serving-size pieces of chicken. Be sure the·chicken is the young
      quick-cooking kind. Keep the pieces small; cut breasts in half and
      separate legs from thighs*
   12 *ears of corn, husks pulled back, silk removed, washed and husks
      restored*
   12 *medium potatoes, scrubbed and still in their jackets*

That, mind you, is only the stuff that actually is going to be cooked.
Okay. How much of it can you be certain of acquiring while at the
beach? Meaning, are you definitely going somewhere where you can surely
dig clams? Are there fishermen in your party expert enough to guarantee
that they'll catch fish? Is there a gung-ho skin diver among you who can
guarantee that he will spear those 12 lobsters? Or will you have to buy, or
otherwise acquire, all those things before you ever leave home? That's
what we meant when we mentioned advance planning and preparation a
few paragraphs back.

Then, to all the edibles that you'll have to tote along, add all the things that you'd need at any cookout: napkins, dishes, knives and forks and spoons, tablecloth, glasses, beer-bottle opener (we don't say "beer can" because we hope you'll buy returnable bottles and return them to the store when done with them), and a dozen other things that you'll surely think of. And something that you won't: pillow slips. Yes, pillow slips. They're perfect receptacles when, at the beach, one of you heads up a children's expedition for seaweed and kelp among the rocks and in the surf. Or, if yours is going to be an inland clambake, for collecting grass and leaves and dunking them well in lake, river, stream, pond or wherever you're going to be. (Be sure inland foliage is nonpoisonous.)

That, you see, is because you can't have a clambake without steam, and it is the wet seaweed or foliage that makes the steam. So you'll need lots of it.

Plus a couple of bushel baskets and tire tubes to set them in for the clam diggers in your midst, plus a coffee pot and a saucepan for melting butter, plus a couple of coolers for perishables and such, plus boxes for stowing everything else in, plus 2 or 3 motor vehicles for getting all of it and all of you to where you're going.

For the pit and the fire, you'll also need a square-blade shovel, an old broom, 10 or 12 large burlap bags and/or a 5- or 6-foot square of canvas.

At the beach, after you've all had your initial romp in the water, there is work to be done, plenty of it for everyone. Kids to collect seaweed and dig clams, accompanied by adults, of course, to watch over them. Sure-shot Izaak Waltons to catch fish (don't let them tell you that they won't have time to do anything else). Skin divers to spear or otherwise seize lobsters without killing them. Men and boys (and girls if they so mind) to collect rocks and lots of driftwood. Football-sized rocks that also are hard, nonporous and heat-holding. And someone to dig the clambake pit.

Here's the step-by-step on what to do with that all-important pit, first the traditional Indian-style one that is so popular still in all of New England, except Maine:

This is a clambake pit, New England style.

· Dig it about 4 feet long, 2 feet wide and 2 feet deep. Or make it circular if you like.

· Line it on the bottom and all four sides with the rocks. Fit them as closely together as possible and level the tops as best you can.

· Sweep the pit clean of all dirt or sand.

· Build a fire as described on page 350. Once it catches hold, be certain it is distributed to cover all the bottom rocks evenly. Keep it burning well, its flames licking up the sides, because its purpose is to heat all the rocks; they must be intensely hot in order for the clambake to work. Keep the fire going for at least 2 hours, longer if necessary, but never less, because it will take at least that long for the rocks to reach the necessary clambake temperature.

· When the rocks are hissing hot, swiftly remove every speck of still-burning wood, coal, ember and cinder with the broom and shovel. If the broom catches fire, so be it. That's why we told you to take along an old one. But whatever you do, don't wet it. It's expendable and water will cool the rocks.

From this step on, time is all-important. Don't waste a second, because every one of them will mean loss of precious heat.

· Immediately place a 4-inch layer of sopping-wet seaweed atop the rocks, spreading it carefully to cover every bit of the pit.

· Place the potatoes and lobster, side by side, on the seaweed.

· Cover them with a ¼-inch layer of wet seaweed.

· Place the chicken and corn atop that. Wrap the chicken in foil if you don't mind losing a bit of flavor in order to eliminate sand.

· Now another ¼-inch layer of wet seaweed.

· Atop that go the clams and fish.

· And over that goes a 2-inch layer of wet seaweed. Make sure it also covers the tops of the circle of rocks.

· Over everything now goes the burlap bags, soaking wet, and the sheet of canvas, also soaking wet.

· Anchor them down by placing rocks around the entire canvas perimeter, making sure the canvas is taut and the rocks are close enough together to eliminate any possibility of steam escaping.

· Let it steam for an hour, then carefully lift up one small leeward edge of canvas and peek. Everything should be done and ready to eat. If not, batten down and steam some more. Make sure you do your looking at the side that's away from the wind, otherwise it will get under the canvas and blow precious steam away while letting in an excess of cool air.

That's the way the Indians did it, every step of the way, except that they used rawhide instead of gunnysacks and canvas. That's the way most New Englanders do it today, except those rugged Down Easters, the people who live in Maine, where being different and doing things differently is a way of life.

Maine folk dig their clambake pit only 8 or 10 inches deep and line only the bottom with the same football-sized rocks. Then, instead of a 4-inch bottom layer of wet seaweed, theirs is 6 inches deep. That is all the seaweed they use—none between foodstuffs, none on the top. Everything in the way of edibles goes into the bake as before, except that clams go in with the lobster. And they top it all off with the same sopping-wet piece of canvas, wrapped tightly around the sides as well as across the top, and held down by a ring of rocks.

The eating and the enjoying are the same.

Try either one of them. You'll love it. Or, if you'd prefer a much more simplified clambake, read on.

THE TIN CAN CLAMBAKE

Elsewhere in this book you'll find a section that we call "Company Menus." Among them, you'll find the play-by-play for a Kitchen Clambake.

Well, if you don't want to go to the trouble (trouble?) of a New England Clambake, or if it's impossible to gather all the rocks you'll need, you can have a Kitchen Clambake. But, since you're on the beach, call it instead a Tin Can Clambake. Just straddle the can across a trench fireplace such as we described a page or so back and you're in business. There is no limit to the size of the can you use. In the Kitchen Clambake we suggest a 5-gallon one, because that's about the limit that a stove burner will accommodate. But on the beach, straddling a trench, you can use even a 30-gallon can. The determining factor need only be the number of people you'll be clambaking for. The more mouths you have to feed, the bigger the can will have to be.

The Balcony Cooking Fire

There is something good to be said about living in a big-city apartment house, and that is this: folks who live there can cook outdoors more easily than anybody. All they need is a balcony, which real-estate types have come to call "terraces," and a hibachi. If the balcony is small, too small for also eating outdoors, so be it. Cook outdoors, eat inside. Summer or winter makes no difference. All you need is warm clothes while cooking if the weather is cold.

As for the hibachi, make sure it's the old-fashioned Japanese type, preferably one that comes from there, and not one of the new-fangled ones that are being ground out like popcorn lately by American manufacturers. A good hibachi should be made of good metal, it should have short legs, it should have a solid chopping-block type base. A bad hibachi is made of pot metal and it has long, table-height legs, the latter allegedly to save you the effort of bending over. However, they are not sturdy: they can be too easily knocked over by adults, children and maybe even the cat or the wind. That's why we urge the low wooden-base hibachi. Just set it atop a table, an outdoor table, and start your charcoal fire with an Auto Fire as we described on page 346.

A word of warning about balcony charcoal cookery, or charcoal cookery anywhere, for that matter. Never burn charcoal indoors unless every window is open wide, because charcoal uses up oxygen like mad. So, too, if your balcony is enclosed. If it's impossible for you to ventilate it properly, don't burn charcoal on your balcony.

Cooking Aboard a Boat

There is so much to be said about boat cookery, so many dangers to guard against, that we hesitate to bring up the subject. Space just does not permit us to go into them all. But this is a fish cookbook and boats are used for catching fish and fish taste best if cooked the moment they come from the water. So, obviously, we must talk about cooking aboard a boat, capsulizing in as few paragraphs as possible what we took many pages to say when we wrote *The Complete Outdoor Cookbook*.

The danger of boat cooking is fire, any kind of fire, no matter how minute. The slightest spark, the slightest ash or spilled drop of hot grease can cause an explosion. If you want to know all of the whys and where- fores, either get a copy of our outdoor cookbook or write to either the National Fire Protection Association, 60 Batterymarch Street, Boston, Massachusetts, or the Yacht Safety Bureau, 21 West Street, New York, New York, for literature on fire prevention aboard boats.

Meantime, take our word for it that the dangers are there, and abide by these few simple rules:

· If your boat does not have a stove already built into it, don't at- tempt to install one.

· Never use a portable stove aboard a boat. This means that char- coal burners and camp stoves are out.

· The safest boat-cooking fuels are, in order, these: electricity, coal, coke, or wood, canned heat, alcohol, kerosene, and liquid petroleum gas (LPG). So dangerous that it is not even on the list of alternates is gaso- line. If your boat has a gasoline stove on it, don't use it. Convert it or get rid of it.

· No fuel is safe if the stove has not been installed properly, if the galley is not properly ventilated, or if flammable objects (such as curtains) can brush against it.

· Never light a stove, or strike a match, or flip an electric switch, or create a flame of any kind until you are sure that the boat and all its nooks and crannies have been adequately ventilated.

· Never deep-fry aboard a boat. When pan-frying, use as little grease as possible. Preferably none.

· Never refuel a stove's fuel container while the stove is hot.

· Don't overfill boat tanks or stove tanks.

· Don't store fuel in unmarked containers.

Well, that will give you an idea. We could go on and on. As for cooking aboard a boat, if you've observed all the safety rules, you have a boat galley that is not much different than your kitchen at home. So cook there the same as you would at home.

If you don't measure up to all the safety standards, no loss. In fact, we think you're ahead of the game, because much better than cooking on a boat is to nose your craft up to an isolated beach, go ashore and have yourself a cookout, either by campfire or charcoal fire.

Camp Stove

If you have the room, it is always wise to take a camp stove along with you. On an extended camping trip, definitely yes. On a weekend outing, ditto. On a clambake or a 1-day outing, maybe yes, maybe no. Stoves come in mighty handy for that quick pot of morning coffee, for example. And where on a clambake would you set a pot of coffee? Nor does wood or charcoal do a thing for soup. So why not make it on a camp stove and save your open-fire cooking space for things whose flavor and aroma will be enhanced by live embers?

There are many makes of camp stoves on the American market, most of them good, one or two of them very good, but the make that we have found to be best of all is a fairly recent import from Sweden. "Primus" is the name and we recommend that you look them over when camp-stove shopping you go. Some of the Primus stove assets: they're light to carry, compact with no waste space, well styled, they burn only liquid petroleum (propane) gas, which is a safe, odorless fuel, and they're sturdy, foolproof, tip-proof.

We have three Primus stoves in our outdoor-cooking storage bin. The one we use most often is called the "Sportsman." It has 2 sure-fire burners, each operating on its own disposable fuel tank, and a removable windshield, yet weighs less than 14 pounds. Open and ready for use, it is 19 inches long, 9½ inches wide and 8¼ inches high. It folds down to less than 5 inches for easy carrying. The Sportsman is ideal for weekend and 1-day outings.

For longer camping trips we have what Primus calls a "Deluxe camp kitchen." It consists of a sturdy yet compact 2-burner stove, fold-

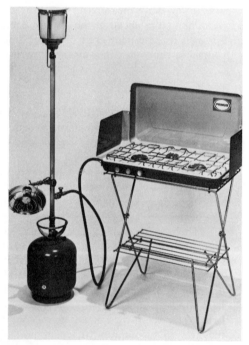

Above—The Primus Sportsman: ideal for light-travel camping trips.

Center—The Primus Deluxe complete with lamp, heater, table: perfect for all-the-comforts-of-home camping trips.

Below—The Primus Grasshopper: great for backpacking and quickie cookouts.

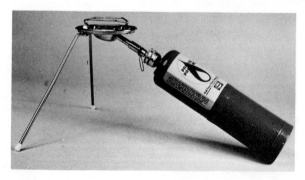

ing table, lamp post and lantern and 10-pound-capacity refillable LPG tank.

As an extra burner standby, we sometimes tote along a Primus Grasshopper, which looks like nothing more than a small tripod but which quickly heats up a pot of anything and easily stows away in a backpack or picnic hamper.

How to Extinguish Wood and Charcoal Fires

Please don't pass this section by. It's too important. Too many forest fires have been caused by fires that campers thought were out. Too many people have been burned by cooking fires that supposedly had been extinguished.

Slowly pour at least 2 full buckets of water on it while a companion stirs the fire with a stick. If you're alone, figure out for yourself how to perform both chores at once. But do them and make sure that every spark, every ember is completely saturated, is completely out. If you need more water, go get it. When you're sure that the fire will never come to life again, fill your fire pit with dirt, level it and pat the surface firm.

CHARCOAL FIRES

Extinguish a charcoal fire the moment you're through cooking. If your stove has a hood, shut the dampers and close the cover, and the fire will swiftly smother from lack of oxygen. If your firebox has no hood, perhaps you can smother it with some fireproof gadget or other. If not, resort to water. Fill the firebed with it, lots of it, and wait until every coal, every spark is dead. Then dump them on a screen, and leave them in the sun to dry. Sift and you'll have reusable coals that can easily be relighted, a great money saver.

NEVER FORGET THESE TWO PERILS

In many forest areas the subsurface is virtually all humus, rotting leaves and foliage, which act like punk. A spark overlooked today can spring to life in a roaring blaze a month from today and perhaps a mile away. In fact, in most states campfires are permissible only in certain areas. Therefore, check with local authorities or forest rangers to make sure you'll be building your fire in a safe place.

· Even after cooking in a sand pit on an ocean beach, you must never make the mistake of thinking that you can put out a fire merely by covering the coals, the embers, with sand. The reason: sand is a conductor of heat. The result: days later, someone (probably a child) might poke a hand into that spot of sand and be seriously burned. Therefore, use water, lots of water, to douse a beach fire; stir with a stick to make sure that every ember is thoroughly saturated. Only then should you fill and level the pit with sand.

19

Outdoor Recipes

In this portion of the outdoor section of this book, you'll find 20 recipes that we consider highly indicative of how versatile, how simple, how good outdoor cooking and eating can be. Most of them were created especially for this book; the four at the end of this section appeared originally in *The Complete Outdoor Cookbook,* which we happily researched and wrote, which Hawthorn Books happily published, which the Outdoor Life Book Club happily chose as its July 1970 selection and which happily sold more than 100,000 copies.

But there are lots more than only 20 outdoor recipes in this book. In fact, we'd say that at least half the other recipes between these covers can be cooked as easily outside the house as in. We've indicated some of them with the letter "O" in the upper right-hand corner. We're sure, though, that in going through the book you'll find many others.

So, too, with the marinades and sauces. We may suggest that a certain such recipe ought to be combined with a certain fish recipe. But that isn't meant to mean, or even imply, that therefore all other marinade and sauce recipes are out.

Don't hesitate to combine just about anything in this book with something else in this book. That's what makes for originality in cooking, especially fish cooking. That's one of the reasons that fish cooking is a pleasure.

SALT POACH IN A POUCH

> 4 *just-caught saltwater fish, about* 1 *pound each*
> Large pot of seawater
> 4 *oblong pieces of cheesecloth*
> ¼ *pound melted butter or margarine*
> Pepper to taste
> Lemon, quartered

Dress fish, leaving heads on, within minutes of the time they're caught and wrap each in a hammock-shaped cheesecloth pouch. Bring seawater to a boil and lower each pouch, using the ends as a handle, into the pot. Poach about 10 minutes or until flesh flakes easily at thickest part of fish when tested with a fork. Lift pouches gently from water by the ends, remove cheesecloth and serve fish with melted butter or margarine, pepper and lemon wedges.

Serves 4.

NOTE: If straight seawater makes the fish too salty for your taste, dilute with fresh water.

STUFFED TROUT IN FOIL PACKAGES

> 4 *trout, 8–10 inches long, or any salt or freshwater fish of similar size and shape that is not excessively bony*
> 1 *teaspoon garlic powder*
> 1 *teaspoon red chili powder*
> *Salt (optional)*
> ½ *cup toasted breadcrumbs*
> ¼ *cup finely chopped fresh, very young dandelion leaves or spinach or parsley*
> *Pinch of thyme*
> *Small pinch of sage (optional)*
> *Small pinch of tarragon (optional)*
> ½ *cup piñon nuts (optional)*
> *Salt to taste for stuffing*
> 1 *egg, lightly beaten*
> 4 *slices bacon*
> 4 *pieces aluminum foil*
> ¼ *cup wine, red or white, or* 1 *tablespoon wine vinegar diluted with 3 tablespoons water*

Combine garlic powder, chili powder and salt to taste and rub into skin and cavity of fish. Combine breadcrumbs, chopped dandelion leaves or spinach or parsley, thyme, sage, tarragon, piñon nuts, salt and egg, and mix well. Stuff cavities with the mixture and wrap a piece of bacon securely around each fish to help hold stuffing inside. Place each fish in center of a piece of aluminum foil, sprinkle 1 tablespoon of wine over each fish and securely wrap the foil in leakproof packages, see page 284. Lay packages on grill, about 4 inches above burned-down coals, and cook for about 10 minutes. Turn and cook the other side for same length of time. Or bury the packages completely in coals and cook 20 minutes. Open one package carefully and fork-test the trout for doneness before opening the others. The temperature of cooking coals is apt to vary widely as the result of many factors, so testing should begin in about half the cooking time.

FISHERMAN'S SHORESIDE SANDWICHES

> 1 *pound fillets cut from fresh-caught perch or pickerel (or whatever fish you catch)*
> *Salt and pepper to taste*
> *Garlic powder to taste*
> 2 *tablespoons catsup*
> *Sliced cheese*
> *Sliced onion*
> *Butter or margarine*

Season fillets with salt and pepper and garlic powder. Spread catsup over one side of each fillet, fold the plain side of fillet over a slice of cheese and a slice of onion (if fillet is too stiff to remain folded, cut it in half), place in long-handled grill and cook the sandwiches over hot coals. As the fish cooks, baste with butter or margarine. When each fish sandwich is brown on one side, turn it over. Cook for a total of about 4 minutes or until fish flakes easily when gently probed with a fork. Eat as is, or between slices of bread.

BONELESS SMELT KEBABS   (I)

(The little smelt is one of the most delicious fish obtainable and well worth the trouble of deboning in order to introduce it to young children. Add the extra flavor of charcoal broiling, and the fun of kebabs—and this should be a winner.)

> 1 1-*pound package frozen smelt*
> 8 *cherry tomatoes*
> 8 *chunks canned pineapple*
> 8 *pieces very mild onion*
> 8 *slices green pepper*
> 1 *recipe Paprika-Butter (Coral) Sauce, page 142, or butter or margarine*

Defrost smelt in refrigerator 4–6 hours. They should still be firm and icy. Working with one fish at a time, cut off tail (head, too, if it's still there) and fins, and slit from belly to tail end. Flatten out fish—which will release one line of bones—then, holding both sides of fish from underneath with left hand, use the right hand gently to lift out the backbone and attached bones, starting at head end. (With a little practice, it will go quickly.)

Divide smelts, tomatoes, pineapple chunks, onion and green pepper into groups of 4. Roll the boned smelts and arrange with the other ingredients on 4 skewers. Brush with barbecue sauce or butter or margarine and broil about 4 inches above burned-down coals 6–10 minutes or until fish flakes are beginning to separate when gently probed with the tines of a fork. Turn frequently, brushing on more sauce as you do so.

Serves 4.

BYARS' BASS BARBECUE

(We created this recipe in honor of Garner B. Byars, the man who not only invented the Auto Fire Charcoal Starter but who also happens to be one of the best fly fishermen in America's Southland, and his wife, Kay, who also is expert with a fly rod. Their favorite game fish is the largemouth bass, their favorite fishing ground is the Tennessee Valley Authority's Pickwick Lake, where Mississippi, Alabama and Tennessee meet.)

> 2 *largemouth bass fillets or steaks*
> 1 *cup dry white wine*
> *Juice of* 1 *lemon*
> 1 *tablespoon Worcestershire sauce*
> 1 *clove garlic, crushed*
> *Melted butter or margarine*
> *Salt and pepper to taste*

Combine wine, lemon juice, Worcestershire sauce and crushed garlic in glass or nonporous ceramic baking dish, add fish and marinate 1 or 2 hours, turning 4 times. Place fish in long-handled wire grill and cook atop Auto Fire (or over any charcoal or wood fire bed) about 4 inches above the coals for only 2 or 3 minutes to each side. You'll know when fish is done by applying the fork test: when the flesh flakes easily it's time to eat. Serve with melted butter or margarine, salt and pepper.

Serves 2.

NOTE: There's nothing to stop you from cooking this dish indoors, in the broiler section of your kitchen stove.

CHARCOAL-BROILED CAMP TROUT

> 6 7- *to* 9-*inch fresh-caught rainbow trout, dressed, or other fresh-*
> *water or salt game fish*
> *Salt and pepper to taste*
> *Garlic powder to taste*
> 2 *tablespoons butter or margarine*
> *Lemon wedges*

Arrange trout in long-handled hinged grill and broil about 4 inches above burned-down charcoal coals. Cook about 3 or 4 minutes to a side or until flesh flakes easily when gently probed with the tines of a fork. Serve at once and let each fisherman spread butter over his own hot fish and sprinkle to suit his own taste with salt, pepper, garlic powder and fresh-squeezed lemon juice.

Serves 2–4.

PAN FISH FRIED IN BATTER

2 *to* 4 *medium pan fish, fresh or saltwater*
1 *egg, lightly beaten*
¼ *cup milk or canned milk diluted with water*
½ *cup toasted breadcrumbs, cracker crumbs or cornmeal*
2 *to* 4 *tablespoons olive oil or other cooking oil*
Salt and pepper to taste
Lemon wedges

Combine egg and milk or canned milk, dip pan fish in the mixture, then coat with crumbs or cornmeal and lay on a clean, flat surface to dry 3–5 minutes. Heat oil in large skillet to sizzling (but not smoking) hot. Add fish, fry until golden brown on one side, turn and repeat on second side or until flesh flakes easily when gently probed with tines of fork. Serve at once. Pass the salt, pepper and lemon wedges and let individuals season to their own taste.

Serves 2–4.

BROOK TROUT POACHED IN WINE

2 *medium-sized brook trout or any other pan fish, freshwater or salt, fresh or frozen*
1 *good-sized pinch of dry mustard*
2 *tablespoons butter, margarine or hydrogenated vegetable oil*
1 *tablespoon soy sauce*
1 *teaspoon honey*
¼ *cup sherry wine*
1 *cup water*
¾ *teaspoon arrowroot*

Defrost fish if frozen. In a large, heavy skillet, stir mustard into 1 table-spoon butter or margarine or vegetable oil until well blended. Add soy sauce, honey, sherry and water, stir well and heat to boiling. Turn down to simmer and cook for 5 minutes. Add fish, cover and continue cooking for another 5 minutes or until flesh separates easily into flakes when gently probed with the tines of a fork. Remove fish to a warm dish and cover to keep warm. Blend arrowroot with remaining tablespoon butter, margarine or vegetable oil and add to sauce. Cook, stirring constantly, until thickened. Pour over trout and serve.

Serves 2.

BONED TROUT WITH NUTS AND RAISINS   (I)

Make Brook Trout Poached in Wine, page 367, bone the trout after cooking (this will be easier to do if you chill it first), reheat in sauce, add 2 handsful each of store-bought nuts and raisins and serve over toast, potatoes or rice. This is a good recipe for making fish eaters (and avid fishermen) out of children. To turn this recipe into real gourmet fare, substitute very ripe wild berries (be sure you know they're edible before picking) for the raisins, and pine nuts, especially those gathered from the piñon tree, for the commercial kernels.

EASY BEACH CLAM CHOWDER

(A Hearty 1-Dish Noontime Meal for Four People)

*About 12 fresh-dug clams**
2 10½-ounce cans condensed vegetable soup

Scrub clams thoroughly in seawater, thus rinsing them in the process, and place in large pot. Add 2 cups of fresh water and heat just until shells open. Remove clams from pot, shuck meat from shells, pour liquid from shells back into pot, chop meat and set aside. (If you don't like a bit of sand in your soup, you'll have brought several layers of cheesecloth and an extra pot with you from home and you'll at this point strain the broth from one pot to the other in order to rid it of the sand that all clams ingest. And maybe a bit of mud, too.) Bring the broth to a boil, add the condensed soup and simmer for a few minutes. Add the chopped clam meat, return to a simmer, and let the flavors blend for about a minute, stirring once or twice.

CHARCOAL-BROILED ALASKA KING CRAB LEGS

1 pound frozen Alaska king crab legs, defrosted overnight in refrigerator
Melted butter or margarine
Lemon wedges

---

* How many clams you add to this tasty waterside chowder is dependent upon several factors: (1) how many clams you've dug, (2) how large they are, and (3) how clammy-rich you want your chowder to be.

Cut crab legs in serving-size portions, 2 or 3 inches long. Slit shells length-wise with a sharp knife and insert melted butter. Place 3 or 4 inches above burned-down coals and heat through. Serve with cocktail forks and nut-crackers, additional melted butter and lemon wedges.
Serves 2–4.

BARBECUED CATFISH FILLETS

2 *pounds skinned catfish fillets or other freshwater or saltwater fillets*
1 *recipe Basic Red Sauce or any of its variations, page 144*

Marinate fillets in sauce in refrigerator for at least 30 minutes (use glass or nonporous ceramic dish), turning once or twice and brushing both sides with sauce. Remove fillets, arrange in well-greased hinged wire grill and cook 3 or 4 inches above burned-down coals for about 4 minutes to a side or until flakes separate easily when gently probed with tines of a fork. Brush any sauce remaining in dish over fillets as they cook.
Serves 4–6.

BARBECUED JUMBO SHRIMP

1½ *pounds raw jumbo shrimp, peeled and deveined*
1 *recipe Curry-Mushroom Butter, or Herb and Wine Butter, page 139,*
   or any marinade of your choice in sauce section
Lemon wedges

Use a cooking oil when preparing either of the butter recipes, thoroughly coat shrimp with it and marinate in refrigerator for 30 minutes. (Use a glass or a nonporous ceramic dish.) Remove shrimp from marinade (reserving any marinade left in dish) and carefully place in a hinged wire grill, fastening securely so they can't fall out. Cook 3 or 4 inches above burned-down coals, brushing with remaining marinade several times, for 3 or 4 minutes to a side or until done. Do not overcook or shrimp will be tough. Serve with lemon wedges.
Serves 6.

BARBECUED OYSTERS: Prepare large shucked oysters in the same way.

OYSTER KEBABS

1 *quart large shucked oysters*
1 *or 2 recipes Southwest Barbecue Sauce, page 146, French Dressing,*
   page 147, or any marinade of your choice in sauce section
6 *slices bacon, lightly cooked, then each slice cut in 4 pieces*
12 *mushroom caps (optional)*

12 *chunks canned pineapple (optional)*
6 *wedges onion*
3 *medium, firm tomatoes, cut in 6 wedges each*
1 *to 2 green peppers, seeded, washed and cut in chunks*

Put shucked oysters in a glass or nonporous ceramic dish, cover with sauce of your choice, stir well and marinate in refrigerator for at least 30 minutes. Remove from bowl, reserving any leftover marinade, and string on skewers, alternating with other ingredients. Brush everything with marinade and lay skewers across barbecue grill which is placed about 4 inches above coals. Cook just until edges of oysters start to curl, brushing with any of the marinade that may be left.

Serves 6.

NOTE: Parboil green peppers if you like them well cooked.

SHRIMP KEBABS: Prepare large shelled and deveined shrimp in same manner as Oyster Kebabs.

LOBSTER KEBABS: Prepare chunks of raw lobster meat in same way as Oyster Kebabs.

SCALLOP KEBABS: Prepare sea scallops in same way as Oyster Kebabs.

FISH CHUNK KEBABS: Prepare chunks of raw fish in the same way as Oyster Kebabs. Lean fish will hold together better than will fat fish and you should use an oilier marinade for lean than for fat fish.

ROASTED OYSTERS IN THE SHELL

36 *oysters in the shell*
1 *cup melted butter or margarine, divided into 6 small dishes*
6 *lemon wedges*
Salt and pepper
Paprika

Wash oysters well, arrange in hinged grill and place about 4 inches above burned-down but very hot coals. Roast 10–15 minutes, or until shells open. Serve in shells, giving each person a dish of melted butter and a lemon wedge and passing the salt, pepper and paprika.

Serves 6.

BARBECUED STEAKS OR FILLETS

4–6 *good-sized fish steaks or fillets that contain no more than 6 percent of fat, freshwater or salt, fresh or frozen*
1 *recipe any of the Easy Butter or Margarine Sauces, p. 136, or Spicy, Wine and Vinegar Sauces, p. 144*
Lemon wedges

Prepare sauce of your choice. Fasten steaks or fillets in well-greased hinged wire grill and brush with sauce. Cook about 4 inches above burned-down but hot coals 4–6 minutes to a side or just until flakes separate easily when gently probed with tines of a fork. Serve with lemon wedges.

Serves 4–6.

NOTE: Baste fat fish only once or twice with the butter sauce.

DANDELION FISH SOUP

1 *pound fish or head and other trimmings from filleted fish*
1 *medium onion, chopped (substitute dried onion flakes)*
½ *teaspoon salt*
½ *clove garlic, finely minced*
6 *cups water*
¼ *teaspoon ground black pepper*
1 *pinch of saffron (optional)*
1 *pinch of sage*
¼ *teaspoon dried dillweed*
3 *or 4 young, tender dandelion leaves, torn into bits*

Combine all ingredients except dandelion in saucepan and simmer for about 40 minutes. Strain through strainer (reserve fish to flake for use in other dishes such as fish cakes or omelet or, if you prefer, add it to the soup). Return broth to saucepan, add dandelion leaves and enough water to make 4 to 6 servings, cook for an additional 5 minutes, and serve.

Serves 4–6.

BARBECUED SALMON STEAKS

2 *pounds salmon steak*
¼ *cup brandy or dry vermouth (optional, substitute 2 tablespoons*
    vinegar)
¼ *cup melted butter or margarine or cooking oil*
⅓ *cup lemon juice*
3 *tablespoons chopped chives*
1 *teaspoon soy sauce or salt to taste*
⅛ *teaspoon garlic salt*
Pepper to taste
½ *teaspoon marjoram*

Mix together all ingredients except salmon steak and marinate the fish in the mixture for at least 1 hour before cooking. (Use a glass or non-porous ceramic dish.) Turn fish occasionally and be sure all surfaces are covered by the sauce. Place fish in well-greased hinged grill and barbecue

4 to 6 inches above cooking coals until both sides are nicely browned (3 to 6 minutes to a side) and fish flakes easily when tested with a fork. While cooking, baste with any sauce left in the marinating dish.

Serves 4–6.

FISH LUAUS

4 *fillets (approximately 1 pound) of sole, flounder, or ocean perch, each about 6 inches long*
½ *pound fresh spinach leaves*
Salt and pepper to taste
Onion or garlic salt to taste
Juice of 1 lemon
1 *tablespoon soy sauce*
1 *10-ounce package frozen fried rice, thawed, or 1 13½-ounce can fried rice*
4 *squares of heavy-duty aluminum foil, 12 by 12 inches*

Wash spinach leaves well, cutting off tough stems and singling out the largest leaves. Drain.

One at a time, place fish fillets between two pieces of waxed paper. With a mallet or the side of a heavy knife, pound each fillet lightly until it is flattened to approximately 4 inches across the widest part. Sprinkle fish with seasonings, lemon juice and soy sauce. Divide fried rice over 4 fillets and wrap fish around rice to make a fat roll.

Place 4 or 5 good-sized spinach leaves in the center of each square of foil. Set each fish roll on spinach leaves and wrap leaves around fish. Wrap foil around spinach in tight bundles, sealing ends tightly to prevent juices from leaking out during cooking. Place bundles on barbecue grill about 6 inches above gray cooking coals and cook for 20 to 35 minutes, turning frequently. Or place in baking pan and cook in 350-degree preheated oven for 20–30 minutes. Test one bundle to see if done before opening them all. They're ready to eat if the fish separates easily into flakes when gently probed with a fork.

Serves 4.

NOTE: These fish bundles can be part of the menu at a luau.

DR. KENNETH KRAEMER'S FOIL-BAKED FISH

1 *2-pound fresh-caught fish, dressed and cut into 2 chunks*
2 *tablespoons butter or margarine*
Garlic salt and pepper to taste
1 *large onion, sliced*
1 *teaspoon chopped parsley (substitute dried flakes to taste)*
Lemon juice

Place each fish chunk on a double square of heavy-duty aluminum foil. Divide butter or margarine, seasonings, sliced onion and chopped parsley over the two chunks. Fold foil into two packages and seal so butter or margarine won't leak out when it melts. Lay packages 4 to 6 inches above burned-down cooking coals on grill and cook 15–20 minutes, turning frequently, or until fish flakes easily away from the bone when gently tested with a fork. Serve at once with lemon juice.

Serves 2.

NOTE: You can bury foil packages in coals instead of placing them on the grill, but test to see if they are done after about 20 minutes. Thin fish, such as flounder, will be done about 5 minutes sooner than timings given above.

Index

377